I0124937

A Sense of Belonging

Bloomsbury Advances in Religious Studies

Series Editors: Bettina E. Schmidt, Steven Sutcliffe and Will Sweetman

Founding Editors: James Cox and Peggy Morgan

Bloomsbury Advances in Religious Studies publishes cutting-edge research in the Study of Religion/s. The series draws on anthropological, ethnographical, historical, sociological and textual methods among others. Topics are diverse, but each publication integrates theoretical analysis with empirical data. The series aims to refresh the interdisciplinary agenda in new evidence-based studies of 'religion'.

A Phenomenology of Indigenous Religions
James L. Cox

American Evangelicals
Ashlee Quosigk

Appropriation of Native American Spirituality
Suzanne Owen

Becoming Buddhist
Glenys Eddy

Community and Worldview among Paraiyars of South India
Anderson H. M. Jeremiah

Conceptions of the Afterlife in Early Civilizations
Gregory Shushan

Contemporary Western Ethnography and the Definition of Religion
Martin D. Stringer

Cultural Blending in Korean Death Rites
Chang-Won Park

Free Zone Scientology
Aled Thomas

Globalization of Hesychasm and the Jesus Prayer
Christopher D. L. Johnson

Individualized Religion
Claire Wanless

Innateness of Myth
Ritske Rensma

Levinas, Messianism and Parody
Terence Holden

New Paradigm of Spirituality and Religion
Mary Catherine Burgess

Orthodox Christianity, New Age Spirituality and Vernacular Religion
Eugenia Roussou

Post-Materialist Religion
Mika T. Lassander

Redefining Shamanisms
David Gordon Wilson

Reform, Identity and Narratives of Belonging
Arkotong Longkumer

Religion and the Discourse on Modernity
Paul-François Tremlett

Religion and the Inculturation of Human Rights in Ghana

Religion as a Conversation Starter
Ina Merdjanova and Patrice Brodeur

Religion, Material Culture and Archaeology
Julian Droogan
Abamfo Ofori Atiemo

Rethinking 'Classical Yoga' and Buddhism
Karen O'Brien Kop

Secular Assemblages
Marek Sullivan

Spirits and Trance in Brazil
Bettina E. Schmidt

Spirit Possession and Trance
Edited by Bettina E. Schmidt and Lucy Huskinson

Spiritual Tourism
Alex Norman

Theology and Religious Studies in Higher Education
Edited by D. L. Bird and Simon G. Smith

The Critical Study of Non-Religion
Christopher R. Cotter

The Problem with Interreligious Dialogue,
Muthuraj Swamy

UFOs, Conspiracy Theories and the New Age
David G. Robertson

A Sense of Belonging

*Religion and Identity in British
Fishing Communities*

Stephen Friend

BLOOMSBURY ACADEMIC
LONDON • NEW YORK • OXFORD • NEW DELHI • SYDNEY

BLOOMSBURY ACADEMIC
Bloomsbury Publishing Plc
50 Bedford Square, London, WC1B 3DP, UK
1385 Broadway, New York, NY 10018, USA
29 Earlsfort Terrace, Dublin 2, Ireland

BLOOMSBURY, BLOOMSBURY ACADEMIC and the Diana logo are trademarks
of Bloomsbury Publishing Plc

First published in Great Britain 2022

This paperback edition published 2023

Copyright © Stephen Friend, 2022, 2023

Stephen Friend has asserted his right under the Copyright, Designs and
Patents Act, 1988, to be identified as Author of this work.

For legal purposes the Acknowledgements on pp. ix–x constitute an extension
of this copyright page.

All rights reserved. No part of this publication may be reproduced or transmitted
in any form or by any means, electronic or mechanical, including photocopying,
recording, or any information storage or retrieval system, without prior
permission in writing from the publishers.

Bloomsbury Publishing Plc does not have any control over, or responsibility for, any third-
party websites referred to or in this book. All internet addresses given in this book were
correct at the time of going to press. The author and publisher regret any inconvenience
caused if addresses have changed or sites have ceased to exist, but can accept no
responsibility for any such changes.

A catalogue record for this book is available from the British Library.

Library of Congress Control Number: 2021950363

ISBN: HB: 978-1-3502-7820-2
       PB: 978-1-3502-7824-0
       ePDF: 978-1-3502-7821-9
       eBook: 978-1-3502-7822-6

Series: Bloomsbury Advances in Religious Studies

Typeset by Deanta Global Publishing Services, Chennai, India

To find out more about our authors and books visit www.bloomsbury.com and
sign up for our newsletters

Dedicated to my hardworking research assistants:
Angela Bryan, Sue Parkes and Dr Julie Hirst.

Contents

Illustrations

Figures

Tables

Acknowledgements

I am grateful for the help provided by the staff of the libraries at the University of Hull, York St John University, the University of York, Leeds University Library and to the staff of a range of public libraries, especially at York, Hull, Grimsby, Filey, Scarborough, the British Library in London and at Boston Spa, Dr Williams Library in London; public libraries at Penzance, Brixham, Barking, Great Yarmouth, Gorleston, Lowestoft, Scarborough, Norwich and the Colindale Newspaper Library; the National Library of Scotland at Edinburgh; and a wide range of archives. The staff at all these institutions have been very helpful with their advice and patience, especially in obtaining out-of-print books and a number of theses. Staff in a number of archives have also been helpful, especially at Lincoln, Northallerton, Beverley, Hull, North-East Lincolnshire, the National Archives at Kew, Norwich, Lincolnshire, Lowestoft, the GLC Archives; the Salvation Army Archives, the Family Welfare Association files (now in the GLC Archives, London), and the Borthwick Institute (University of York).

The staff (past and present) of the various Seafarers' Missions have been enormously helpful and patient with my constant requests for help with locating relevant materials and have kindly allowed me to reproduce material from their various publications, minutes and other documents. These societies include the Royal National Mission to Deep Sea Fishermen (RNMDSF), the Missions to Seamen, the Seafarers' Society, the Apostleship of the Sea and the Sailors' Families' Society in Hull. I am especially grateful to past secretaries of the various fishermen's missions who have given of their precious time, including David Macmillan, MBE, Bernard Clampton, MBE, and Paul Jarrett and all past secretaries of the RNMDSF.

A range of organizations have also been helpful, including the Winston Churchill Memorial Trust which kindly provided support and funding for me to visit maritime missions in the United States and Canada, including Newfoundland and Nova Scotia. York St John University provided funding for me to carry out research trips around the British coast and visits to New England and Southern Australia, as well as supporting the oral history research project along the Yorkshire coast. The National Heritage provided funding for this project.

I am grateful, too, for the openness of churches around the country in allowing me to visit and record details. These include St Andrew's Church, Grimsby; St Andrew's Church, Gravesend; Staff at London Road Baptist Church, Lowestoft; St Nicholas Church, Great Yarmouth; staff at St Andrew's Church, Gorleston; and Fr Tony Cotman at St John the Baptist Church, Newington, Hull, who allowed me to take photos of the inside of his church.

I would also like to thank staff and colleagues at York St John University and Hull University who listened to my seminar presentations and provided helpful and insightful feedback. I am especially grateful to Professor Sebastian Kim and Professor

Pauline Kollontai, both of whom read through my notes and offered helpful comments. Thanks to my students at York St John University, especially those who showed an interest in my research and offered constructive suggestions. Thanks, too, to my research assistants on the Women's Voices Project: Angela Bryan, Suzanne Parkes and Dr Julie Hirst. Thank you for your support, patience and kindness over the life of the project.

There have been innumerable individuals who have responded to my enquiries in person and by letter and email, and while these are too numerous to mention I do hope they will accept my thanks. My special thanks must also go to my son, Christopher, and my daughter, Ruth, whose patience during the long period of research was inspiring. Deb Gillanders for advice with ganseys and 'maiden's garlands', and for her innovation in religious services with her 'Propagansey' event; Lindy Rowley, Margaret Taylor – who were enormously helpful with the Women's Voices Project – and to all those women who were willing to be interviewed. Dr Alec Gill, MBE, whose wealth of knowledge about the Yorkshire fishing industry has also been an inspiration.

And, finally, I am very grateful for the support and encouragement of a number of people, especially Dr Sarah Williams, Dr Jane Nadel-Klein and Dr Robb Robinson. Also, to my tutors at the University of Hull, especially Dr Rodney Ambler, Dr David J Starkey and Dr David Bagchi, for their support and encouragement. Thanks, too, to my PhD examiners: Professor Hugh McLeod of Birmingham University and Dr Douglas Reid of Hull University for their suggestions and recommendations. Thanks also to Lalle Pursglove at Bloomsbury for her patience and to the three anonymous reviewers, who provided welcome suggestions and helpful feedback. Any remaining errors in this study are of course my own responsibility.

Abbreviations

BFBS:	British and Foreign Bible Society
BPP:	British Parliamentary Papers
CELAM:	Consejo Episcopal Latinoamericano (Latin American Episcopal Conference, that is the conference of Latin American Roman Catholic Bishops). CELAM organized the 1968 Conference at Medellin, Columbia, that officially supported the concept of 'base ecclesiastical communities'.
CTS:	Catholic Truth Society
FVOA:	Fishing Vessel Owners' Association
GFWA:	Gloucester Fishermen's Wives' Association
MS & LR:	Manchester and Sheffield & Lincolnshire Railway
MtS:	Mission to Seafarers (the Missions to Seamen has had several name changes: it began as the Missions to Seamen Afloat at Home and Abroad in 1856. In 1858 the name was changed to the Missions to Seamen and in 2000 the Mission to Seafarers).
PM:	Primitive Methodist
PMM:	Primitive Methodist Magazine
RNMDSF:	Royal National Mission to Deep Sea Fishermen (for name changes see note 38 on page 217)
SS:	Sailors' Society (The society has had several name changes over the years. It began as the British and Foreign Sailors' Society, then the British Sailors' Society in 1925, then to the British and International Sailors' Society in 1995 and to the Sailors' Society in 2007).
SAWM:	St Andrew's Waterside Mission (renamed the SAWCM in 1892)
SAWCM:	St Andrew's Waterside Church Mission (for name changes, see p. xx)
SPCK:	The Society for the Promotion of Christian Knowledge
TCM:	Thames Church Mission
WM:	Wesleyan Methodist

1

Introduction

Overview

This study is concerned with the relationship between identity and religion in British fishing communities, with special attention being given to the three Yorkshire and North Lincolnshire communities of Filey, Scarborough and Grimsby through the nineteenth and early twentieth centuries. The nineteenth century was a significant era that saw the rise, development and eventual indications of decline of the North Sea fishing industry, and while the twentieth century saw a period of rapid but short-term improvement during the 1950s and 1960s, restrictions on fishing during the two preceding periods of world war had helped to preserve and increase fish-stocks in the North Sea.

Scholars have long argued for the close relationship between identity and religion, including Émile Durkheim for whom the deity and society were effectively one and the same, and who believed that a major function of religion was to reinforce social solidarity and community spirit.[1] A consequence of this view was that religious practice helped individuals and groups as they progressed through life's difficulties and shaped major life events such as 'rites of passage' and important 'festivals'.[2] Religious practices may therefore have had a profound effect on the way people organize and interpret their everyday experiences. This close link has not gone unnoticed by modern scholars, including John Wolffe who pointed out in the UK context that between 1800 and 1940 the link between religion and national identity was particularly strong. Callum Brown also implied a strong historical link when he controversially argued for a sharp break from Christian culture and society in Britain during the early 1960s.[3] He argued that the period saw a sexual revolution, increasing feminism, the abandoning of religious values by women, and a dramatic increase of secularization, an abrupt cultural revolution during which Christianity in Britain entered a period of terminal decline. While account has been taken here of the nature of the distinction between official and popular religion in the three fishing communities of Grimsby, Scarborough and Filey, the major part of the investigation concerns the nature of popular religion, which is examined more fully in Chapter 6, including a summary of the present state of knowledge about the research in this area. One of the earliest attempts to explore the nature and impact of 'official and popular religion' appears to have been the work of Vrijhof and Waardenburg, who in 1979 edited a collection of international essays on the subject.[4] Nancy Tapper's review of the work in 1982 pointed out Vrijhof's claim in the introduction that the term 'official and popular religion' was not well known in religious studies. She also pointed out that there is now an extensive literature on the Great and Little Traditions, which appear to have been ignored (see Chapter 6.2 for further comments on Vrijhof and Waardenburg's work). Yoder also quotes the work of Ichi Hori (1968) on the Great and Little Traditions in Japanese religion.[5]

The scope of religious practice in the UK has been explored by a wide range of authors, from the 1851 census of religion by Mann, via Thomas Wright's questioning of Mann's emphasis on official religion, and the later work of historians such as E. R. Wickham and K. S. Inglis, who argued that with the move from rural to urban settings the working classes became alienated from the Christian churches – a situation responded to by church-building programmes and aggressive missions.[6] Wickham's argument drew heavily on the increase in church and chapel building when Sheffield experienced a religious boom during the second half of the nineteenth century (a situation reflected in the extensive church-building activity in Scarborough and Grimsby following 1860). The evidence here suggests support for Wickham's view on the alienation of working-class participation over and against Alan D. Gilbert's argument for a decline, especially in Nonconformity following 1840.[7] The approach of Wickham and Inglis was challenged by revisionists such as Cox and Mark Smith during the later years of the twentieth century, who argued that the working classes attended the churches on a wider scale than had previously been recognized, and by Brown's questioning of some traditional approaches to the nature of secularization.[8]

Scholars have shown an increasing interest in the nature of popular religion although many, including James Obelkevich and David Clark, have continued to maintain a dualistic distinction between official and popular religion. Sarah Williams is an important exception in that her research in the London Borough of Southwark helped to provide a radical reinterpretation of the influence of popular religion on the local population, pointing out that there is not a sharp distinction between official and popular religion, but that the two spheres are part of a complex matrix of meaning where there is a good deal of overlap. Hence the discussion in Chapter 6 includes an examination of her findings and influence.[9]

During the 1970s and into the twenty-first century, a number of studies explored the nature and impact of the official religion in the UK. For example, Gilbert examined the relationship between religion and social change; Currie, Gilbert and Horsley analysed the patterns of church growth; Snell and Ell explored the geography of Victorian religion and Hugh McLeod discussed the nature of working-class religion in Britain.[10] These studies have helped to move the discussion on and taking note of the broader picture, the present study adds an extra element by focussing on three specific fishing communities. It is therefore important for us to take both accounts (the impact of both official and popular religion) into the mix, and the discussion in Chapter 4 offers the balance to the discussion in Chapter 6.

In contrast to the work on urban communities by such scholars as Wickham in Sheffield, Cox in Lambeth and Smith in Oldham and Saddleworth, there has been relatively little discussion on the rural situation. However, the work of Obelkevich and Ambler has provided helpful material on religion in rural Lincolnshire, and John Rule explored the impact of Methodism, popular belief and village culture in Cornwall.

Fishing towns and villages present us with an overlap between urban and rural communities but while there has been a fair amount of research here, especially in Scotland, very little has dealt in any depth with the relevance of the concept of 'popular religion' – with the significant exception of Clark's work in Staithes in Yorkshire, England (although Clark preferred the term 'folk religion').[11] Other researchers have noted the role of religion in specific rural British contexts, including Paul Thompson and Trevor Lummis in East Anglia and Scotland, Tony Wailey in Lancashire, Diedre E. M. Chalmers and Jane H. Nadel in Scotland, and Anthony P. Cohen on the Shetland island of Whalsay.[12] These scholars have also noted the importance of the role of women in fishing communities, an aspect of life that is important for our understanding of the relationship between religion and identity, given that it was the women who were the main attenders at local churches. The women also had close relationships with other members of the community and were the main carriers of tradition. Peter Frank published his book *Yorkshire Fisherfolk* in 2002, including an important chapter on the roles of women.[13] Lynn Abrams has also explored the roles of women in Shetland, including material on religion, superstitious belief and folklore.[14] An in-depth study on the 'centrality of women's work to the success of the fishing industry' in Nova Scotia and Newfoundland was conducted by Marian Binkley in the 1990s. Her findings, although more detailed, were not dissimilar to those of researchers in England and Scotland.[15]

While the scholars mentioned earlier referred to the role of religious beliefs and practices in British fishing communities, some wider studies on religion and society have had an important role to play in helping us understand the nature of this aspect of such community life.[16] This is especially the case with the role of Primitive Methodism in Christian revivalism, for example in Grimsby, Scarborough and Filey.[17] Anglo-Catholicism also had an important presence in Grimsby,[18] although there were significant differences between the three fishing communities. Chapter 2 also offers a brief overview of the work and development of maritime missions, an important nineteenth-century innovation that embraced both official and popular religion, but which few historians have explored until recently.[19]

In order to demonstrate the importance of the role of religion in the formation and development of identity in British fishing communities we will, in Chapter 4, examine the nature of official religion in the three fishing communities. Chapters 5 and 6 investigate the roles of popular religion in Christian revivalism, and Chapter 7 draws upon the foregoing to examine the nature of popular religious Christian identity and its links with religious and secular change. We are also concerned with a number of other objectives.

First, it is argued that 'popular religion' represents an important narrative in a complex matrix of cultural meanings that has had a significant influence on the construction and development of identity in UK fishing communities (and by extension more widely). Chapters 4–7 explore religion as a range of discourses or narratives that provide an insight into the nature of identity. Chapters 5 and 6 add strength to the criticisms of Mann's view that the nineteenth-century working classes tended to be 'unconscious secularists'.[20]

Second, 'religion' (in both its official and popular forms) is seen to be an important factor in social change. The nature of this change is embedded in the *third* objective, demonstrated in Chapters 5 and 7, which further explore how change takes place. Those communities characterized by Durkheim as 'mechanical solidarities' (such as Filey and to some extent Scarborough) are generally small communities that initially resist change but eventually experience a dramatic paradigm shift; conversely, change in 'organic solidarities' (such as Grimsby and Hull) tends to be a more gradual process taking place over several generations.

Fourth, in Chapters 4, 6 and 7 the roles of ritual and performance are shown to play a part in the process of change, thereby providing an important link between official and popular religion, and they help to provide an enduring sense of security and stability. Thus, religion remains an important factor in popular practices of religion, as can be seen especially in the Filey Revival of 1823 and during the 1870s in Scarborough and Grimsby, where rapid church growth occurred during a period of difficult social transition. Deborah Valenze has provided a thoughtful and helpful analysis of religion in Filey, exploring the relevance of various theories here and rejecting E. P. Thompson's thesis of Methodism's role in avoiding revolution. She has also explored the experience of women in the town while sidestepping the male bias and examining the effects of popular religion.[21] David Bebbington follows Valenze's view by pointing out that women must have been largely responsible for the cottage prayer meetings, which helped in the generation of the spirit of revival.[22]

Members of fishing communities have been influenced by both forms of religion (official and popular), although there was a tendency for nineteenth-century working people to make use of the institutions as and when it suited them, such as for rites of passage and special events as festivals. It should also be remembered that the churches often provided a service in terms of clothes and food for those people in need. Even so, allegiance to some of the churches raises questions as to the reasons for their popularity, and some common denominators may be noted here. For example, those Anglican churches that did well in terms of membership tended to have clergy and lay-workers who took a special interest in the fishing community, visiting the fishermen's families at home and the fishermen at sea, providing counselling, welfare and medical support, offering a range of local facilities (reading rooms, clothes and food stores), taking the beliefs and practices of the fisherfolk seriously and offering sermons that did not overtly criticize local community members. For more details on this point, see Friend, *Fishing for Souls*.[23] There were also adaptions, especially during the later years of the nineteenth century, of many practices that gave the fisherfolk a special status, such as Blessings of the Sea/Boats/Nets, Harvest of the Sea services and services offered at sea. Some of these issues will be discussed briefly in Chapter 4.

Identity and religion

Identity is not a static quality but rather a dynamic process involving the two foundational criteria of similarity and difference.[24] Identity also involves a synthesis that is the outcome of internal and external perceptions of self-hood – the image we have of ourselves and the image others have of us. An *essentialist*, as opposed to a *constructed*, view of identity is appealing, especially with reference to nineteenth-century fishing communities. Such community members saw themselves as distinct from other communities, with identities that identified them as unique. This image was reinforced by their shared history, with stories of tragedy being told and retold in verbal form, written and illustrated stories, songs and artwork – such that some major events gradually took on mythic proportions. Nevertheless, an essentialist perspective is difficult to maintain. When we take a longitudinal view of the development of fishing communities we see that identity is constantly being challenged and changing, often in subtle ways as, for example, with the desire for personal and social status, which is not merely selfish but may represent an important struggle for the survival of the group or community.[25]

The wide range of movement between fishing communities, and the relocation of fisherfolk, during the nineteenth century caused much disruption to traditional beliefs and practices. Hence, Grace Davie has pointed to the importance of religion in maintaining identity in an unfamiliar place. Minority groups (Irish Roman Catholics, Greek Orthodox, Jewish, Muslim and more recently West Indian and groups from various European, Middle Eastern, Asian and African countries) have relocated to Britain for various reasons over the past 200 years and have each tended to associate closely with their particular cultures and religious beliefs and practices. Davie has commented on this situation, saying that 'membership of a particular religious group is perhaps of more importance than the associated beliefs'. She has further argued that this attachment to their religious institutions is one aspect of the minority group's need to maintain its identity.[26] This factor was clearly present among Yorkshire and Lincolnshire fishing communities, especially in the development of Grimsby, Scarborough and Hull, where people gradually achieved positions of authority and power in the towns – such as the number of Primitive Methodists who became prominent in the fishing industry and members of the Jewish community who became mayors of Grimsby. But such a situation is not a simple relationship as numerous factors connect religion, identity and community. A variety of arguments have been put forward to explain the apparently strong religious commitment in communities where change takes place rapidly. Thompson, Gilbert and others, for example, have made the point in different ways, often referring to revivalism acting as a short-term buffer providing security in difficult times.[27] At the same time we cannot explore the nature of local communities without recognizing that reality tends to be culturally constructed and that the many ways in which individuals experience life are determined by a range of discourses or narratives that help provide a sense of meaning and purpose.

The sources of identity are numerous, including family, peer group, education, social, employment and religious influences. Identity is also rooted in a shared kinship and a shared history, especially in the small fishing communities found along the Yorkshire coast, such as Filey, Staithes, Runswick Bay and Robin Hood's Bay. Symbols, both ostensibly religious and otherwise, also play a significant role here as do differences between the communities. When we look at the longer-term picture we discover that the norm tends to be with *constructed* identities. In the light of this we also need to explore the nature of change in fishing communities (see Durkheim's model of mechanical and organic solidarities discussed in Chapter 7).

Identity in nineteenth-century fishing communities, especially along England's North-East coast, was linked closely to migration. An important aspect of this was noted by Gerrish, who began her study of migration to Grimsby by discussing the work of E. Ravenstein, one of whose foundational points was that migration for most people tends to be over short distances. Gerrish has demonstrated that this was not necessarily the case in fishing communities. For example, many fisherfolk moved to Grimsby via periods spent in other ports such as Great Yarmouth and Scarborough although others travelled a longer distance from, for example, Ramsgate and Brixham, and many of the families gave birth to some of their children at these various ports. The evidence from nineteenth-century census data clearly shows that the majority of people moved to Grimsby from practically every fishing port in Britain, as well as numerous places around the world (Appendix 5).

The relationship between religion and identity is therefore not merely to be linked with the religious institutions. Indeed, the present study argues for the importance (possibly the *primary* importance) of the influence of popular religion. That popular religion had a significant impact on the lives of people in the Victorian era has been shown via the research of a number of scholars, such as Obelkevich, Cox, Smith, Clark and Williams, and if we step back and take the broader view we can observe that even for many conventionally religious people their beliefs and practices are often far from orthodox. Even rites of passage and prayers are frequently overlaid with superstitious belief, folklore and magic. The churches, however, have tended to offer Christian interpretations of persistent non-orthodox beliefs and practices while rejecting as 'mere superstitious belief' others that cannot be so easily accommodated. By exploring such beliefs and practices with an emphasis on, for example, ritual we can acknowledge the fundamentally spiritual nature that links these to our concept of personal and social identity.

Popular religion

As with a number of the major concepts discussed in this study (especially community and identity), there is a good deal of ambiguity and difference among scholars over the terminology about religion and spirituality. In recent times scholars have tried to distinguish between these two terms by relating the former to official religion and the latter (although there is a good deal of overlap) to a sense of transcendence experienced via rites of passage, pilgrimage, times of sadness and joy, celebrations, festivals and in a wide variety of activities such as the production of material arts, storytelling, drama, painting, singing and so on.[28] Frances Wilkins's recent book, *Singing the Gospel*, for example, provides an excellent overview of the role of singing, song and music in fishing communities.[29] As the term 'popular religion' can also be misleading, some scholars have chosen to make use of the term 'spirituality' when discussing the non-official aspects of religion.[30] There are, however, numerous other terms that have been developed to identify a range of religious experiences, including 'common religion', 'confessional religion', 'folk religion', 'implicit religion', 'civil religion', 'lived religion' and 'everyday religion'.[31] While none are perfect, Davie, who provided a longer list, has pointed out that 'taken together they are probably getting somewhere close to the truth'.[32] McGuire defined popular religion (she calls it 'non-official religion') as 'a set of religious and quasi-religious beliefs and practices that are not accepted, recognized or controlled by official religious groups'.[33] This is a little misleading as the established churches have long adapted and adopted a number of popular beliefs and practices while giving them a Christian interpretation, a point made by numerous scholars, including Vrijhof in 1979, and Williams in her study of popular religion in Southwark in 1999.[34] This is an important point given that the present study argues for models that reflect areas of discourse or narratives as indicators of religious meaning.

For the purpose of this study we will make use of the distinction between the two concepts of *official religion* and *popular religion*. *Official religion* refers to the formal religious perspectives such as churches, dogma and a wide range of associated symbols, beliefs and practices; *popular religion* refers to the range of experiences that are not seen as the main, or an officially adequate, focus of formal religious beliefs and practices. The division, however, is by no means simple as many beliefs and practices originally seen to be outside the Christian religious institutions have been embraced by official religion and reinterpreted in Christian terms. Nevertheless, some practices, which have long been accepted by the religious institutions, such as 'Churching', still embrace elements of superstitious belief. In the light of this we will also include some discussion of superstitious belief, magic and folklore in Chapter 6, inasmuch as they may be perceived as aspects of popular religious experience.

Part of the confusion over the terminology here relates to the common usage of the term 'popular religion' that often refers to the various practices that are believed to possess a clear religious reference, such as religious festivals and ceremonies, special services, visits to shrines and special places such as holy wells, and the religious symbolism evident in a wide range of material culture often associated with personal belief and practice. It will, however, be argued that by 'popular religion' we mean those cultural actions, activities, symbols, beliefs and practices that provide an opportunity for individuals and groups to give meaning and purpose to their lives. Day in her recent book argues for a sense of meaning and purpose in the lives of people.[35] But there are limitations here, especially with regard to those negative activities that cause harm or are associated with a range of immoral behaviours. On the positive side, festivals, civil ceremonies, storytelling, material culture, dress, language, naming and a range of rites and rituals all have something to add to our perspective on making sense of the world we share. In the later twentieth and early twenty-first centuries there has been a range of literature, drama, art and film aimed at exploring the issues here, including Harvey Cox's *Feast of Fools*, Timothy Jenkins's *Religion and Everyday Life* and Andrew Greeley's *God in Popular Culture*.[36] The relationship between theology and literature, theology and film, and theology and art, is being explored widely today.[37]

If we are to adequately understand the role of popular religion within specific communities, we need to begin with an overview of the official religious perspectives. The present study therefore offers an overview of the official religion in the three towns of Filey, Scarborough and Grimsby, and as relatively little published material has offered an objective analysis of the religious institutions in these three communities, Chapter 4 is a brief response to this need by providing an outline of the official religious developments.

Revival

The concept of 'revival' (as a form of religious awakening) refers to a movement within the Christian tradition that places a particular emphasis on emotional and subjective experience. The phenomenon has a long history, although its modern expression is embedded within the Puritan and Pietistic reaction to Enlightenment rationalism and tends to be associated with American evangelical religion. Nineteenth-century influences were particularly associated with Theodore J. Frelinghuysen (New Jersey, 1725), Jonathan Edwards (New England, late 1730s), George Whitefield (American colonies and Britain, 1738) and John Wesley (Britain). Other influential revivalists included Charles Grandison Finney (especially during the 1820s and 1830s) and Dwight L. Moody and Ira Sankey, who had an important influence on British evangelical and revivalist religion during the 1870s and 1880s. There were also numerous influential female preachers working with the various revival movements in Britain and America.[38] Janice Holmes provides an extensive chapter on female preachers in her book *Religious Revivals in Britain and Ireland*, 1859–1905. Holmes mentions a number of important women including Ellen Ranyard; and Deborah M. Valenze in her book *Prophetic Sons and Daughters* has a chapter on female revivalists, with special attention given to the charismatic Ann Carr (see Chapter 5 for more information).[39]

The numerous religious revivals during the eighteenth and nineteenth centuries had a major influence on religion internationally, although revivals in Britain never achieved the respectability they had in America and tended to be seen as a peripheral aspect of British religious life at the heart of evangelical spirituality. At the same time concern was expressed about the physical effects encountered during the highly emotional services, including charismatic phenomena such as glossolalia, healing, prophecy, visions and a strong emphasis on millenarianism. Old superstitious and folk beliefs and practices also tended to be incorporated into the faith world of the revivalist adherents. Members of some religious traditions, however, were not happy with this situation nor with the emotional excess that often characterized the meetings. Hobsbawm has commented on revivalism that it was

> Totally untheological, unintellectual and emotional. It is characteristic of working-class sects that they were designed for the uneducated, so that passion and morality, in which the most ignorant can compete on equal terms, were the exclusive criteria of faith and salvation.[40]

Popular religion was therefore an integral aspect of revivalism, and many such aspects of belief and practice were important to Primitive Methodism when it developed in the early nineteenth century. We will explore this further in Chapter 5. Revivalism, then, while involving much that we might identify as 'popular religion', also included a good deal of ritual and performance, a topic that will be discussed further in Chapter 6.

Revivalism is an area that embraces both formal and popular religion and has seen a significant amount of research from scholars such as Halévy, Hobsbawm, Thompson,

Gilbert, Valenze, Luker and Bebbington.[41] Revivals are not isolated events in that they link closely with the life of local churches. Indeed, Currie, Gilbert and Horsley (1977) have argued the case for a five-phase life cycle that offers an explanation for the rise and fall in membership of churches: *depression–activation–revival–deactivation–declension*.[42] In this model revival clearly follows a period of activation that may be a response to a period of social and economic depression. Whether or not such a cyclical process is evident in Yorkshire and North Lincolnshire fishing communities, similar to that observed in Cornwall by Luker (1986), remains to be seen (see the discussion in Chapter 5). It is also quite possible that periods of revival, like periods of Methodist growth, were especially active during times of Anglican parochial weakness.[43] In his study of transatlantic revivalism, Richard Carwardine reinforced this point, based on the American situation. He also argued for a regular cycle of growth and decline that occurs in 'an inverse conformity with the business cycle, rising with the hard times and falling with the good' (quoting Whitney Cross). But he goes on to point out that the relationship between economic depression/prosperity and church growth/decline is not a 'mechanical or wholly predictable relationship'.[44] Luker is clearly right in pointing to a range of factors that may lead to revival, a point supported by Thompson and Carwardine.[45] Nevertheless, Thompson's 'oscillation' theory has been criticized by Hatcher who argued that the evidence from his own research, as well as that cited by Thompson, does not fully support Thompson's 'narrow' thesis, and it is far from being substantiated. At the same time it must be borne in mind that Thompson himself put a boundary up to 1832 on the relevance of his theory after which he would not allow for the application of the thesis: 'My thesis was never offered for universal, instant application I proposed only that taking this period as a whole, the emotional evangelism, and the "inflamed state of mind" accompanying it, can be seen as the chiliasm of despair.'[46] Hatcher preferred Hobsbawm's broader 'theory of affinity' as a better explanation of events. Quoting L. Pope, Hobsbawm (1959) pointed out that a lack of social security is compensated for by the fervour of congregational response. He argued that Methodism and radicalism often advanced together and that revivals did not normally occur when trade depressions were at their lowest.[47] Gilbert (1976) modified Thompson's thesis by arguing that revival is a short-term response to social and economic deprivation; and Luker saw revivalism as in part a response to rapid change rather than to economic uncertainty alone. While not wishing to minimize the complexities it is useful to note that Hobsbawm's thesis subsequently gained support from others. Nadel (1986), for example, argued that revivalism in Ferryden was a means of achieving respectability for the fisherfolk who found themselves at the bottom of the social pile:

> Effectively disenfranchised from participation in decision-making and deprived of economic alternatives, Ferrydeners turned in large numbers – when given the opportunity in the middle of the nineteenth century – to a powerful patron who they believed represented their interests: Jesus.[48]

Valenze argued a similar point saying, 'Through Methodism, servants sustained a rigorous piety that gave them autonomy – even a certain superiority – under the constraints of their employment.'[49]

There therefore appears to be fairly general agreement on the link between social conditions and the appearance of religious revivals, although the actual mechanisms are hotly debated. Luker, for example, wisely pointed out (like Thompson) that we should not assume one overriding theory here but acknowledge the possibility that revival may well be a response to a range of conditions in different situations. And it should not be forgotten that much nineteenth-century comment on revivalism was made by those with a strong sympathy for the movement. Thus George Shaw (1897) commented, somewhat optimistically, that in the early nineteenth century the Filey Revival brought religion to the village.[50] Even so, Hatcher has warned that in accounts of missions and revivals there is always the danger of bias and distortion. In particular, Shaw's history of Filey has presented us with an image of a pagan community prior to the advent of Primitive Methodism, although Valenze and Hatcher pointed to much earlier local religious activity, and there was the psychological impact that an emotionally charged revival had on other groups in the area. Once the movement was established, it tended to perpetuate itself with the psychological expectation of revival. Donald Meek has, for example, provided a helpful analysis of the cause, context and transmission of the 1921 revival during which the herring fishermen and their families, when they returned home to the North-East and Western islands of Scotland, took with them their experience of revival. Luker's study of revivalism in theory and practice among Cornish Methodists also offers an insightful analysis of the nature of revivalism.[51]

While the Primitive Methodists had a good deal of success in missioning fishing communities along the Yorkshire and Cornish coasts we must be wary of assuming too much here. Several other groups and individuals worked along the Yorkshire and North Lincolnshire coasts, including the missionaries of the Port of Hull Society and the Wesleyan Methodists, who established work in practically all the fishing ports well before the Primitive Methodists arrived on the scene. Indeed, the Wesleyan Methodist Yorkshire Revival occurred during the years 1792–6, a period before the development of Primitive Methodism.[52] This of course begs the question as to why the Primitive Methodists made such claims for Paganism prior to their missioning of the area – and based on what evidence? There is perhaps a psychological explanation here in that the point was not so much to focus on the negative aspects of the earlier state of the local community but to emphasize the quality of the new situation. The hagiographical nature of the stories about the preachers, such as John Oxtoby, also served to heighten the status of the 'saint' as opposed to the low status of other religious leaders.[53] Other traditions also support this understanding, such as the oft-cited claim that by the early nineteenth century Wesleyan Methodism had lost contact with the working classes and thereby precipitated the advent of Primitive Methodism, the Bible Christians and other similar groups. This, however, is an oversimplification. Robin Hood's Bay, for example, has never had a Primitive Methodist chapel, although the Wesleyans have had a very strong continuing presence there. And without the Wesleyan Methodist presence in many of the villages visited by the Primitive Methodists, it is likely that the latter would have found it even harder to obtain a hearing. While Hatcher's study of Primitive Methodism in Hull provides us with a good overview and analysis of developments, the work now needs extending to further explore the role of the Primitive Methodists in other coastal communities. At the same time, it is helpful to look at other groups that also appealed to working-class people.

Ritual and performance

In her study 'Believing and Belonging' Day undertook a range of interviews including a number that identified the telling and retelling of stories of loss and bereavement. The storyteller engaged in a performative ritual (following Gennep's structure), thereby creating a situation in which the interviewee was the performer and the interviewer was the audience. Perhaps significantly the repetitive stories often relate to the loss of loved ones.[54] On reading Day's accounts I was struck by the similarity of the stories told about the loss of life in fishing communities by interviewees of our *Women's Voices* oral history project.[55]

Performance is very much part of the life of fishing communities. Music especially plays an important part, as Frances Wilkins has demonstrated in her recent book *Singing the Gospel along Scotland's North-East Coast, 1859–2009*.[56] Among the many aspects of song and singing Wilkins provides examples of fishermen singing over the ship-to-shore radio for their families and friends, especially Jim Mair of Peterhead who became well known for his singing during the 1950s and early 1960s. Alec Gill has also provided examples of Hull fishermen singing at sea. Gill tells of one Hull skipper who called for his crew to play their musical instruments when they had a good catch. Gill also pointed out to me that the music played over the ship's loudspeaker tended to be 'Country and Western'. And here again Wilkins says that the Scottish fishermen also enjoyed the 'Country and Western' music.

Williams discusses the evidence of ritual in the lives of the residents of Southwark and offers numerous examples carried out during trivial and elaborate practices. She offers an *analysis* of the relevance of ritual involved in 'Churching', folk beliefs, charms and the use of mascots, amulets, and 'strategies for controlling, allaying, or transferring illness'.[57] Clearly there is a good deal of performance going on here. Studies by Catherine Bell, Roy A. Rappaport and Tom F. S. Driver, as well as earlier material by Victor Turner, also point to the relationship between ritual and performance, although not all agree with the emphasis on performance here.[58] Performance was, and is, evident in many of the activities engaged in fishing communities, such as parades, processions, festivals and religious services on shore as well as on board the fishing vessels, involving singing, customs and superstitious practices. The ritual and performance engaged in on a daily basis has much in common with the rituals and performance in religious services and other events, and it is the transformative element in both cases that underpins the sense of meaning identified with the activities. Nevertheless, it is important that the formal aspects of religion are clearly identified before the discussion can develop; hence Chapter 6 outlines the situation here in relation to the fishing communities of Filey, Scarborough and Grimsby.

Personal research

In 1999 I was awarded a Winston Churchill Travelling Fellowship to visit fishing communities in the United States and Canada, including Newfoundland and Nova Scotia. What I found there was a similar situation to home, with the fishing industry in decline and families decimated by the situation with many of the children leaving home to settle in the cities where there were better employment opportunities. However, a number of communities, especially in Newfoundland, seemed to be doing quite well. When I enquired why this was, I was told that the local women had seen an opportunity to develop their communities into tourist attractions preserving the traditional buildings and workplaces and employing people to do their traditional jobs, hence Trinity and Bonavista are now very popular among tourists. In St Anthony I found that the women had been prominent in turning Sir Wilfred Grenfell's house into a museum, and local people were employed in developing crafts for sale. Grenfell Handicrafts produce a range of 'hooked mats' (known in the UK as rag rugs, clip-rugs and so on). The 'hooked mats' at St Anthony display scenes from daily life in Newfoundland and Labrador and are not as symbolic as those made in British fishing communities (see Chapter 6 for a discussion on this).

I later discovered a similar approach to the dire situation in Newfoundland faced by fishing communities in Gloucester, Massachusetts. In 1969 the wives of local fishermen were faced with the dramatic decline of the fishing industry and a sharp decrease in fisherman's jobs. The leader of the group, Angela Sanfilipo, herself a fisherman's wife, together with her friends established the Gloucester Fishermen's Wives Association. When I visited their offices in 1999 it was a very well-established organization and employed a number of people in different aspects of the work. On the walls were three large panels displaying cut out fish with names on them. Angela explained that the first panel listed the number of people who have been re-educated, the second panel listed those who had been retrained and the third panel those who had been employed in various new occupations. Angela then asked me what the fishermen's wives in England were doing. I was embarrassed to say that I knew of nothing comparable to the work she and her friends were employed in – but I would explore the situation when I returned home. Sadly, despite contacting friends around the country I could find no similar groups although there had been some short-term responses to difficult problems, such as the loss of three Hull trawlers and their fifty-eight crew members, during three weeks in the winter of 1967/8. The fishermen's wives, led by Lilian Bilocca, confronted the trawler owners, politicians and the media, under the auspices of the Hull Trawler Women's Association. This campaigning contributed much to the formal hearing later that year, making a number of important recommendations for improving conditions. A mother ship, the *ORSINO*, was also established and sent out with the fleet. Facilities included a small hospital ward, extra accommodation for sick and injured fishermen and a weather advisory officer was stationed on board – many of these facilities reflecting the early work of the RNMDSF.[59] Although Lillian and her team achieved changes to the shipping laws that greatly improved the safety of the fishermen, there was no long-term development for the group.

On my return home I received support from my university to travel around the British coast visiting fishing communities. I spoke to many people about the situation I found in the United States and Canada, but I was saddened to see very few fishing communities still active. However, I became more intrigued that the lives of women in fishing communities were rarely mentioned in books about the deep-sea fishing industry. This gave rise to my desire to explore the situation further, and I set about establishing a research project covering the topic. After researching the subject matter and talking with colleagues and friends I applied for grants and was rewarded with a substantial grant from the Heritage Trust, which was supplemented by grants from other bodies, including York St John University, and we began the work. All this allowed for the employment of a research assistant and appropriate equipment to carry out interviews. The project also saw the development of a travelling exhibition and the production of a DVD about the interviews, all of which attracted much interest. Responses from many of these interviewees form an important part of Chapter 6.

Sources

The sources used in this study make use of a wide range of material, including official secular and religious census data, newspaper censuses of religion, archbishops' visitation records, membership figures and baptismal data where these were available, and a wide range of academic and other sources including some of the results of the local oral history project carried out by the author and his research assistants.[60] The detailed official census returns are currently available up to 1911, although determining the criteria for 'fisherman' here is not straightforward. Workers in a maritime environment have been listed variously as seafarer, seaman, sailor and mariner, some of whom were fishermen. With the development of steam fishing vessels in the later years of the nineteenth century 'engineers' and 'trimmers' became more evident. 'Smack owners' and 'fishing vessel owners' also appear regularly, as do 'fishing apprentices', and there are some 'retired fishermen'. Determining which categories should be included under the term 'fisherman' causes problems in terms of making contrasts and comparisons with other studies – although it should be noted that there are few studies that have analysed the details of fishing families in the census data to any great extent. One important exception is Margaret Gerrish, and I have adopted her criteria here in that she listed fishermen, when the census was taken, as:

Smack-owners
Smack-master
Master fisherman
Fisherman
Apprentice fisherman
Fisherman absent at sea.[61]

The census data, however, provide only a partial picture of fishing communities in that the fishermen at sea are not always listed. But by using various sources that occasionally list numbers of fishermen registered in any one port it is possible to compare these figures with those taken from the censuses. It is not, however, possible to show complete figures for the nineteenth century. Few records of the number of fishermen working from each port were kept prior to 1881, a point emphasized by His Excellency Spencer Walpole writing in the 'Fisheries Exhibition Literature' of

1883, who stated that 'There is now no means of ascertaining with precision such simple facts as the number of persons engaged in the sea-fisheries of England and Wales'.[62]

The census data alongside the baptismal records provide helpful information in terms of residence and enable us to identity the localities in which the fishermen and their families lived at regular intervals throughout the century. This is especially important with regard to Grimsby as there was only a very small fishing community there during the first half of the nineteenth century, and while new houses were erected for fisherfolk after 1850, the rapid influx of fishermen and their families put a significant strain on the local resources. While there is a wide range of data within the censuses still to be explored I have made use of the data most relevant to the present study that could be effectively accessed during the research. The census data are also a good source for a range of information about the lives of the fisherfolk. We can, for example, discover the average age of fishermen, follow the families as they travel and migrate from port to port and see when they established themselves in ports for an extended period of time – as Gerrish has done in her University of Hull thesis of 1992.

Baptismal and membership records of the churches have also proved useful. Hence, the baptismal records for Anglicans and Methodists (Appendices 7a–7d), and membership records for the Methodists and Baptists (Appendices 6a3–6a6) have been tabulated, and details of Anglican membership have been provided in Tables five, six and seven. At the same time there is a very wide range of qualitative data available in the newspaper reports, articles, novels, official reports, magazine articles and a range of scholarly productions. The oral history of people living in fishing communities today also allows us to add a comparative dimension to the study, and the data here relies on the memories of people, especially the women. The views expressed also often draw upon the memories of parents and grandparents, thereby reaching back into the nineteenth century. Nevertheless, account has been taken of the methodological problems inherent in relying on personal memories, and the views expressed have been checked against other sources such as nineteenth-century written accounts and paintings from the period. Approximately fifty women were interviewed by my research assistants, using a grounded theory approach. Each interview lasted approximately one hour (although in some cases a second interview was carried out). These interviews were video-recorded and typescripts made – which was important as the author is deafened and relied on the written accounts. The project, however, also included the development of a travelling exhibition that was well received wherever it went. The author and his assistants also gave radio and newspaper interviews and spoke to various groups, including the children at a school in Filey.

In her 1992 study, Gerrish pointed out that 'with very few exceptions, the majority of nineteenth century populations that have undergone study have done so in isolation from each other'.[63] Hence, there is great difficulty in making comparisons between the various studies. Margaret Stacey, too, in 1969, pointed out that we need to be more consistent in our approach to such methodological issues.[64] With all this in mind I have used three very different fishing communities as the basis of this study and, especially with the collection of empirical data, have hopefully thereby allowed for future studies to make useful comparisons with this work.

It should also be noted that the study is interdisciplinary, drawing on the work and methodologies of historians, anthropologists, sociologists and theologians. Some aspects of the study work well within a historical framework (such as the development of the churches), while other aspects (such as superstitious belief and folklore) are more difficult to view as history given that there were very few major changes here either in the content or in the pervasiveness of such beliefs and practices. One change, however, may be the general reticence in recent years to admit to being superstitious (which is odd given that sportspeople and those in entertainment today seem to thrive on their superstitious beliefs and practices!)

Conclusion

This study, then, offers a contribution to the debate about the nature of religion in the construction and maintenance of identity, especially with regard to the influence of popular religion. Popular religion should be seen as important in its own right as well as a perspective of official religion, and, more especially, that aspects of popular religion are seen as contributing to the range of discourses and narratives that make up our religious sensibilities. Popular religion is also an important aspect of popular culture in that many aspects of the latter may be seen to fulfil some of the functions that are normally attributed to the official religion. The discourses here include the need for security, the maintenance of hope, a feeling that the individual has some sense of control over the environment and the ups and downs of everyday life, a sense of meaning and purpose and the means to cope with the tragedies that have been so much a part of life in fishing communities. These discourses often include a good deal of ritual practice where this is in the form of superstitious beliefs and practices, customs, traditions, festivals and rites of passage. The link with ritual and performance tends to provide a strong desire to engage in transformative activities that include many aspects of official and popular religion.

2

The culture, community and identity
of fishing communities

Introduction

Religion in fishing communities cannot be studied merely in terms of church attendance in the manner of Mann.[1] No matter how useful the statistics on church allegiance, they provide only a partial understanding of the nature of religion, especially Christianity, and only a glimpse of the relationship between religion and identity. However, as Gilbert has demonstrated, modern quantitative analysis can provide some helpful insights into our understanding of religious practice, and recent developments in the use of qualitative analysis have added to our understanding of this complex phenomenon.[2] Numerous scholars, such as Gilbert, Moore, Obelkevich, Williams and Jenkins, have pointed out that there are different ways of belonging to a religious institution, and regular attendance at Sunday services is only a part of this.[3] By assuming that the practice of faith is dominated by church and chapel attendance, we are almost immediately drawn into a dualistic view of religion that sees the world in sacred/secular terms – with implications for the way the church sees its social, ecumenical and missionary roles. In an early response to Mann, Thomas Wright (1868) drew upon his own personal knowledge and experience of working-class life and argued that if we are to understand the nature of religious belief and practice, especially in working-class communities, we must shift our perspective in order to view it from the standpoint of the members of the community and not from that of the religious institution.[4] This approach involves us in acknowledging the value of *popular religion* as an important aspect of religious belief and behaviour.

Both official and popular religion are important aspects of the life of the community, providing narratives and discourses that offer meaning and purpose for its members. At the same time official religion can also provide a means by which the community's leaders can support (and perhaps manipulate) the wider community in terms of norms of belief and behaviour that support the status quo. These norms have been so pervasive that it is only in recent years that serious research has been undertaken into the wider aspects of belief and behaviour from the perspective of the community's members. Much of this work, however, has tended to centre on larger urban communities, important examples being the work of Williams in Southwark (1999), Jenkins in Bristol (1999) and Robson in Birmingham and the

Black Country (2002).[5] But there have also been some significant studies in rural communities by such scholars as Obelkevich (1976) and Ambler (1984 and 2000) in Lincolnshire, and Rule (1982) and Luker (1986) in Cornwall.[6] The research in English fishing communities, however, has been somewhat limited, with Clark's study of Staithes (1982) still holding its own as the most relevant study here. Other important studies have been undertaken by Thompson, Wailey and Lummis (1983), and Lummis's own work in East Anglia (1985).

More recent work has been opening new doors by concentrating on important perspectives, which have only cursorily been referred to in earlier studies – especially the role of women in fishing communities. This is significant for the study of religion because it is often the women who are the main links with the religious and other institutions, and they are also often the main carriers of tradition. The anthropologist Jane Nadel-Klein has discussed the nature of women as matriarchs within a patriarchal society, and she has pointed to several earlier scholars, such as Peter Anson, who argued that 'it was the women who ruled over most fisher families'.[7] There have been a number of women's support networks and occasional politically active women's groups in British fishing ports, although these groups tended to have a short lifespan.

Nor have the occasional attempts by British fishermen to establish fishermen's unions met with the success they deserve, mainly because of the difficulty of marshalling support for meetings and the opposition of the local Fishing Vessel Owners' Associations. An example is pertinent here: during the early 1970s, an East Anglian fisherman told the present author that he had tried to establish a union, but a member of the local Fishing Vessel Owners' Association advised him that if he carried on with the proposal he would not be able to obtain work on any of the local vessels. With a family to support, the fisherman naturally desisted from his activities.

In reality it is the women who have the major responsibilities in the fishing communities, especially responsibility for the home, children and finance. The women tend to have good networks in the community and deal with any day-to-day problems that arise. Nevertheless, when the women banded together to seek changes for the benefit of the local fishermen, they found themselves criticized by some other members of the community.[8]

The present contextual overview will concentrate on three main areas: *first*, we will explore the nature and focus of the research in fishing communities and the important developing area of gender studies; *second*, we will look briefly at the literature dealing with the nature of religion in fishing communities, including official and popular religion, revivalism and maritime missions; and *third*, we will briefly examine the literature dealing with the relationship between culture, community and identity.

Research in fishing communities

During the 1950s community studies suffered from a lack of consensus on the nature of the concept 'community', borne witness to by innumerable definitions. Most studies based their ideas around Ferdinand Tönnies's concepts, which emphasized the relationship between social change and social bonds within the life of a community.[9] By the 1970s the proliferation of definitions of community gave rise to a lack of coherence and an urgent need to redefine terms and to tackle methodological anomalies. The emergence during the 1980s of concepts of community as an invention that relies predominantly on symbolic construction reflected a growing concern with a range of interpretations, and this in turn led to a resurgence of community studies in the 1990s that tended to explore communities by taking into account new spatial categories and vocabularies.[10]

Although there is no clear dividing line between these different research interests, two major trends are discernible in the research conducted in fishing communities over the last seventy years. The first trend, especially apparent during the period 1950–80, was concerned with the *traditional community study* approach, with an emphasis on fieldwork and extensive use of social statistics, participant observation and oral history. The second trend, evident from the 1980s, was an *environmental approach*, where the emphasis was on the relationship between the community and its maritime environment. In more recent studies both approaches have been utilized, and the faults of the earlier methodologies have been acknowledged. For example, Chalmers (1988) and Nadel-Klein (1988), both of whom did their research in Scotland, noted that studies concerned with the *traditional community approach* tended to concentrate on the role of the men – women generally being perceived as having passive and domestic functions, with their roles in both the productive and expressive spheres being largely ignored.[11] Chalmers further argued that this research emphasized the relationship between fishing and the economy, with a tendency to politicize the ethnographic data (i.e. reinforcing notions of gender differences and downplaying the economic roles of the women). There has, however, more recently been some attempts to establish a balance here. The work of Gillian Munro, for example, uses an ethnographic approach in her study of the lives of young married women in North-East Scotland fishing communities.[12]

The spate of research in fishing communities during this early period was precipitated by Horobin who, in 1957, led the way with his study *Community and Occupation in the Hull Fishing Industry*.[13] He was followed by Tunstall (1962) who concentrated on the Hull trawling industry.[14] Clark (1982) explored the relationship between 'official' and 'folk' (popular) religion in the life of the North Yorkshire fishing village of Staithes, and Peter Frank (1976) published his research on Yorkshire fisherfolk in 2002, including an important chapter on the roles of women, which he originally researched in the 1970s.[15]

By far the main bulk of studies about fishing communities have been undertaken outside England, especially in Newfoundland and Scandinavia. Some of these important studies include Johansen et al., in Denmark (1993), Moring in Finland (1993), Dyrvik in Norway (1993), Davis in Newfoundland (1986 and 2000), Grønbech (2000) and Skaptadóttir in Iceland (2000), Hapke in South India (2001), Marshall in Canada (2001), Hagmark in the Åland Islands (2003) and Fabio Rambelli's study *The Sea and the Sacred in Japan* in 2020.[16] Marian Binkley conducted her study of fishwives in Nova Scotia (2002), and the research in Britain has tended to focus on Scottish fishing ports with studies by Thompson (1983), Chalmers (1988), Nadel-Klein (1984–2000), King (1992–3), Munro (1993) and Webster (2013), among others.[17] Even so, as Donna Lee Davis pointed out, such studies have explored 'the material aspects of the division of labour in the fishery' with the male–female roles being portrayed as quite separate, if complementary. Davis' research in a Newfoundland fishing village thereafter offers a useful and balanced analysis of the domain where gender roles overlap.[18]

Despite these developments, much of the research prior to the 1980s suffered from a lack of coherence over the nature of concepts such as 'community'. Subsequent discussion sought to clarify the issues, and the debate led to important changes in perspective. By the 1980s researchers adopted an *environmental approach* that focussed on concerns about cultural values and physical resources. This approach also took the issue of women's roles more seriously, hence a spate of theses, articles and books took up the challenge.

Thompson in *Living the Fishing* (1983) expanded on Frank's work and included a chapter entitled 'Women in the Fishing', in which he pointed out that while fishing is usually thought of as a man's trade, 'it is an occupation peculiarly dependent on the work of women'; and he went on to discuss the roles of women in a range of fishing communities.[19] The studies during the 1980s included work by Lummis in East Anglia (1985), Wailey in Lancashire (1983), Thompson in Scotland (1983), Cohen on the Shetland islands of Whalsay (1985) and Gilligan in Padstow, Cornwall (1990).[20] With a few exceptions, however, studies of the fishing communities in Yorkshire appear to have come to a halt by the end of the 1980s, although earlier researchers have continued to publish articles and books, such as Frank's *Yorkshire Fisherfolk* (2002). While there are therefore problems with the *traditional community studies* approach, anticipated by Stacey in her 1969 study, much useful material was published from sociological, anthropological and ethnographical perspectives, as Stacey herself acknowledged. Nevertheless, the material on religion in communities is even more sparse and where it is present it tends to have been viewed from the perspective of the religious institutions – an approach also common to wider community studies until recently, although this perspective had been challenged as early as 1967 by Brian Harrison.[21]

The second trend, evident among those researchers who have responded to concerns about methodological weaknesses in the 'community study approach', involved the adoption of an *environmental approach*. The main emphasis here is on the wider environment of fishing communities and on exploring a particular ecosystem relating to a marine environment, where the concern is with the relationship between 'cultural values and a community's physical resources' (a move away from the function and tradition of the male-centred study).[22] The focus is on the 'expressive roles' (the ideational, emotional and expressive aspects of male–female relationship), which complements the 'instrumental roles' (the tangible and functional – the active roles of women, responsibilities for running a household and raising children). Studies here have tended to concentrate on the roles of women, a growing trend clearly evident during the 1980s and 1990s that was generated partly by the significant impact of the women's movement of the 1960s and 1970s. The environmental approach was anticipated by comments on the scarcity of research about women in fishing communities by Anderson and Wadel (1972) and later explored by others, notably Smith (1977), Nadel (1984), Chalmers (1988) and Munro (1997).[23]

Some of the earlier traditional community studies in Britain did take gender roles into account, but few researchers invested much time here. This is surprising given that even as early as 1868, the Revd Arthur Pettit had pointed out that 'the men only have to catch the fish, their labour as a rule, being over as soon as the boat touches the sand'.[24] Chalmers has rightly drawn attention to the oddness of the focus on the men, given that women tend to take responsibility for most roles on shore within the community (with some notable exceptions such as the clergy and council leadership). Peter Frank's work during the relatively early period of the mid-1970s has already been noted, but while his observations were reflected in later work, such as that of Thompson (1983) and King (1992–3), few others referred to this aspect of his study. Lummis did offer a chapter on female waged labour in Chapter 9 of his 1985 book *Occupation and Society*, although he had earlier in the book alluded to a more extensive female influence. Nadel-Klein picked up this theme in her review of Lummis's book and argued that a major weakness was his failure to follow up on his intriguing comments about the relationship between gender, community and class.[25]

While Scottish fishergirls are not the main focus of the present study, there are important similarities in the roles of women along the Scottish, Yorkshire and North Lincolnshire coasts. Thompson, in his study *Women in Fishing: The Roots of Power between the Sexes* (1985), generalized his findings to present a model intended to help explain the women's roles.[26] Because of the regular absence of the fishermen, the women often had more power in the economic and spatial spheres (territorial autonomy) than is the case in many other types of communities. Even so, this power suffered to some extent in that the fishing industry tended to rely on the power and control of others. J. M. Acheson has commented that 'since fishermen are absent so much of the time, they are often unrepresented in the political arena and are usually dependent on middlemen and ship owners who are often in a position to exploit them'.[27]

Nadel-Klein and Davis (1988), however, point out two weaknesses in Thompson's model: first, that he does not subject ideological factors (e.g. religion) to a similar rigorous analysis; and second, his study has a European bias – thereby not sufficiently acknowledging the range of attitudes and practices relevant to the division of labour in a variety of cultures. While it is not unusual for women to be involved in the processing of fish, it is not so common to find women working on fishing vessels, at least in Britain. In North American fishing communities the practice is more common as Nadel-Klein and Davis have observed: 'in some places, both men and women fish; in others, only men fish. In some places, women weave nets; in others, that is a man's job.'[28] When women do fish, they do not necessarily see their role in the same terms as the men. Yodanis (2000), for example, has argued that the women in fishing communities generally define their work as 'not fishing' – even when they work on fishing vessels alongside the men.[29] Hart and Davis (1982) provide a similar example from the North Carolina coast where one woman maintained: 'I am a fisherman and I mean fisherman. I'm not a fish person or a fisherette or any of those strange words. The word says what I do, I fish. The word has been around a long time and it deserves respect.'[30] This attitude, says Yodanis, means that gender in fishing communities is socially constructed and not defined by the work an individual does. But this is not the only view. Nadel-Klein, on visiting the Fisheries Museum at Lunenberg, Nova Scotia, asked why women were absent from the displays. She was shocked by the reply: 'Why should they be there? They never had anything to do with the fishery. They had to stay at home with their family.'[31] The respondent here is assuming that the kind of work engaged in *is* determined by gender. In some cases, although these appear to be rare, women do work as independent entrepreneurial fishers.[32] An important person here is Linda Greenlaw, who is the only female skipper working on the North American East Coast.[33] She became well known following the publication of her book *The Hungry Ocean*, in 1998, and featured in the film of Sebastian Junger's book, *The Perfect Storm*. There are, nevertheless, significant differences within different types of community, the sociocultural dynamics being related to ecological and evolutionary paradigms.[34] But relatively little research has been done in this area.[35]

Given that men in fishing communities are usually associated with the sea, and that women take responsibility for most day-to-day activities on shore in the community, the main focus of recent research is perhaps not surprising, whether this be from a historical perspective (Marshall, Johansen et al., Dryvik and Moring) or within a contemporary context (Nadel-Klein and Davis, Hapke, Skaptadóttir, Grønbech and Yodanis).[36] Even so, these developments have not yet made the impact they should have done on historians. The publication of *England's Sea Fisheries*, for example, presents essays by a range of scholars on a variety of topics – but no study is included of the wider role of women in fishing communities.[37] The few relevant references tend to concentrate mainly on the role of women in processing fish (an interesting example of Chalmers's concern that such studies tend to concentrate on women only in so far as they have an economic role).[38]

Other scholars follow a similar pattern. Horobin (1957), for example, acknowledged that fishing tended towards matrilocality, the result of sustained male absence; and Tunstall discussed the roles of women as girlfriends, wives and prostitutes, but provided very little insight into the daily lives of women in fishing communities. Tunstall also, significantly, argued that fishing tends to attract males who feel awkward and uncomfortable with women – perhaps one reason for their eagerness to return to the familiar security of the all-male environment at sea after a short amount of time ashore. Sally Festing (1977), on the other hand, is an interesting exception in that she has a chapter about the fishermen's wives in Norfolk with a range of views expressed by the women themselves.[39]

The fishermen, in contrast to the women, do not have community links in the sense of close regular contact with friends and neighbours (other than those male neighbours who perhaps work on the same fishing vessel), nor, given the nature of their work, are they able to establish strong community networks. In their study of the trawling towns of Hull and Grimsby, Edwards and Marshall (1977) demonstrated that during the 1970s the nature of deep-sea trawling meant that the men not only rarely saw friends and family, they had little effective control over their lives and jobs.[40] There was no real opportunity to buy their own fishing vessels, as did their early nineteenth-century forebears, and with so little control over their lives it was extremely difficult for them to form effective pressure groups for change through organizations such as trade unions.

This variety of approaches to studying fishing communities is encouraging, although there is a need to undertake longitudinal studies that embrace a more comprehensive perspective. Nadel-Klein's work points to aspects of life in fishing communities that provide cultural meaning: 'locally distinct modes of speech, secret nick-names, maritime religious services and, perhaps, most of all, their memories'.[41] But by saying that in the early nineteenth century fisherfolk 'had begun to seek comfort in evangelical religion' she implicitly gives support to the theories of Hobsbawm (1957), Thompson (1963), Gilbert (1976) and other historians who have argued that religion, and especially revivalist religion, is a response to social, political and economic crises.[42] (It should, however, be noted that while there is agreement about Thompson's questions, there is no real consensus about his answers.)[43]

Religion in fishing communities

Among the few English-language studies published on the nature of religion in fishing communities, Clark's work in Staithes (1982) is of particular note. Luker (1987), in his doctoral study of revivalism and Cornish Methodism, also provided some relevant material, although fishing communities were not the main focus. Duthie (1983) offered an insight into the revivals along the North-East coast of Scotland and East Anglia during the 1920s – a significant event that has received very little attention from historians; and Valenze (1985) and Hatcher (1993) provided some important information on religion along the Yorkshire coast during the nineteenth century.[44]

Many of the researchers into the life of fishing communities have included religious beliefs and practices as part of a much broader social investigation. At the same time religion is barely mentioned in many significant studies, such as P. H. Fricke's *Seafarer and Community* (1973).[45] Papers are, however, occasionally published in academic journals, which highlight the subject. In approaching the study of religion in the fishing communities along the Yorkshire and North Lincolnshire coasts there is very little specific research into the religious life of the communities to build upon, with the notable exception of Clark's research.

In examining the relationship between fishing communities and religion during the nineteenth century there are a number of perspectives that need exploring – the relationship between fisherfolk and religious institutions, and the nature of popular religion and the extent and manner in which this was embraced by some religious groups, especially Primitive Methodists and maritime missions. The relationship between fisherfolk and the religious institutions has often been gauged by 'religious practices' such as attendance at services. But even here there is a range of factors that need to be taken into account, including the time fishermen spent at sea (allowing for nineteenth-century attitudes to work on the Sabbath) and the class gap between churches and the working classes. This situation begs a number of questions – What was the nature of the variety of religious experience and practice? Which official religious groups were successful and why? What was the nature of the relationship between official religion and popular religion? What was the impact of religion on the community?

Maritime missions

Some major religious groups, which have received very little academic attention, are the maritime missions, even though they had a significant influence on fishing communities. The vast majority of literature on this subject is that produced by the many maritime mission societies themselves and, as such, tends to focus on promoting their own religious and charitable work. There was no shortage of such societies in English fishing communities, with many traditions within the Christian churches being represented.[46] However, during the last thirty years a considerable body of research has been compiled in the exploration of the work and role of maritime missions among seafaring communities, although there has been relatively little specifically on the roles of such organizations in fishing communities. The research by Roald Kverndal (1986), Alston Kennerley (1988), Robert Miller (1989 and 2003), Paul Mooney (2005) and Stephen Friend (2018) has been helpful in identifying the historical outlines of the many and varied maritime missions and the parameters of the work of these organizations. But much work remains to be done.[47] The maritime missions, like the Primitive Methodists, built upon a working-class base during the nineteenth century (although the many initiators of these missions, like the Primitive Methodists, were at least middle class), and many fishermen were employed in various aspects of the work in fishing ports.

The relationship between maritime missions and other groups remains to be more fully explored, although we would expect to see some close links with Methodism, and Kverndal has argued this very point – although these links are mainly with Wesleyan Methodism.[48] In the North-East coast fishing ports maritime missions avoided establishing themselves as a religious institution to rival others, and they tended to rely on the support of a range of Nonconformist denominations. In Whitby, for example, the Whitby Seamen's Friend and Bethel Union (founded in 1822) held its meetings in a range of Nonconformist chapels in rotation. And although the various maritime missions gradually provided Seafarers' homes, canteens, medical and social support, as well as religious services at sea and on shore, there was never any intention of taking fishermen away from the local churches, quite the contrary. When the new Grimsby hostel was built in 1964, the superintendent, Donald Tucker, suggested that an evening service should be held and called it the 'Nightcap'. As this was held at 8.00 pm there was no fear it would clash with the evening services of local churches.

Some of the literature on this subject still remains to be identified and indexed, although the Hull History Centre has recently provided a home for much of the extant British material. Other museums and archives have also had materials deposited with them, thereby making it easier for researchers to identify and access relevant documents. Sadly, however, much material has been lost or destroyed over the years when owners found themselves with less space to accommodate it, and staff failed to recognize its historical value.

Maritime missions offer an interesting insight into how missions have adapted to the specific needs of the maritime communities, and the growing amount of academic literature in this area bears witness to an increasing interest here.

Culture, community and identity

Culture and community

The relationship between revivalism and economic conditions points to a wider relationship between religion and culture. Religion is ubiquitous in human society, providing meaning and purpose via stories, ritual, art and morality – all of which are often moulded within a religious and cultural framework. In exploring fishing communities within the cultures of the nineteenth and early twentieth centuries we need to draw upon this matrix of meaning, in order to reconstruct, as far as is possible, the community life. The extent to which culture is influenced by religion or vice versa is not necessarily an issue, as the purpose of the present study is to explore the reciprocal relationship. The two approaches are not mutually exclusive, although there is a good deal of evidence that popular religion has a far more influential impact on the construction and development of identity than has usually been attributed.

The term 'culture' implies a consistency that is homogenous. Yet it is clearly difficult to identify a specific nineteenth-century culture without modern preconceptions. We tend, for example, to assume the existence and influence of long-held traditions, yet Hobsbawm has quite clearly demonstrated that many of our traditions are relatively new inventions.[49] At the same time, cultures long thought to be homogenous have been shown to be far more diverse than previously believed – a point brought forcibly home when we see the diverse array of artwork and myths embedded under the generic term 'Celtic' (for a brief discussion of the issues here, see Trubshaw, 2002).[50] The development of the heritage industry has clouded the waters even more as Nadel-Klein pointed out in her book *Fishing for Heritage*. Talk of fishing communities conjures up a stereotypical, romanticized image that may well attract tourists but often bears only a vague relation to the communities as they existed half a century earlier.

While many communities are not tied to a particular place the activity of place-making 'and the resultant sense of place are an essential part of how people experience community'.[51] The importance of place is at the heart of the sense of community (and the phenomenal growth of family history in recent years bears testimony to this claim). Nadel-Klein is significant among those anthropologists who have been rethinking the relationship between people and place, and has explored the way in which the loss of place often precipitates a renewed search for cultural and community identity.[52] This sometimes takes the form of compromise in order to meet the requirements of the tourist industry. While this process was predominantly a late twentieth-century one, there are clear links with changes in the nineteenth century. The folklorist Trubshaw, in discussing eighteenth-century perceptions of 'customs' and 'culture', pointed out that 'By the later nineteenth century folklorists saw themselves restoring or regenerating a traditional rural culture that, they believed, had been all but obliterated by the advance of industrialisation'. The point that much in the way of tradition has been lost has also been well made by a number of other scholars, including Bob Bushaway, Robert D. Storch and Ronald Hutton.[53] The regenerated 'rural culture', however, was highly influenced by puritan ideologies:

> Many 'traditional customs' simply did not reappear. Those that were 'restored' were much more organised by the gentry for the populace than before the Commonwealth when the customs had been sustained by the populace with little reliance on the gentry.[54]

Taking up a slightly different but related point by Michelle Zimbalist Rosaldo, Valenze argued that the status of women is often determined by the status of the home, and that the women's status is at its lowest when the public and domestic spheres are separated and the roles of women become more distinct – usually as the result of various forms of industrial development that employ waged labour. But as Sally Cole has shown, the improvement in quality of life for the fishing family, as a result of the women taking paid employment in local factories, can often lead to a sharper segregation of male and female roles.[55] An important implication here, as Elizabeth Bott observed, is that

> The degree of segregation in the role relationship of husband and wife varies directly with the connectedness of the family's social network. The more connected the network, the greater the degree of segregation between the roles of husband and wife.[56]

The wife of the fisherman, therefore, comes into her own when her husband is away at sea, in that she has the greater role to play in family life, and the women in the community are reliant on each other for help and support.

In small traditional fishing communities such as Filey, Robin Hood's Bay and Staithes, in Yorkshire, where inshore fishing was the norm, we might expect there to have been a stable environment as the public and domestic spheres were well integrated. Within the larger community, where the men were engaged in deep-sea fishing (such as Scarborough, Hull and Grimsby), the distinction between the private and public spheres was likely to be more evident, and when the husband came home from sea the wife's status was quite low – the husband's needs tended to be paramount. At this point there is no time for the wife to pursue activities in the public sphere other than those that are absolutely necessary for the comfort of the husband and the well-being of the children. The roles and identity of the men and women therefore vary depending on the nature of the local fishing industry.

Identity

The religious impulse (John Kent has referred to this as the 'primary religious impulse') is often manifested in the transformation of personal identity.[57] Such a transformation, however, is not necessarily always positive, as Leo Walmsley demonstrated in his novel

Master Mariner (based in Robin Hood's Bay, renamed 'Bramblewick') where the main character, Tom Bransby, transforms from the selfish character of a local drunkard into the selfish character of a local religious enthusiast.[58] No doubt there were many such transformations along the Yorkshire coast, as well as many people who became self-less, during the various religious revivals predominantly associated with Methodism and Evangelicalism. Such transformations of personality would embrace both official and popular aspects of religious belief and behaviour. Primitive Methodism in particular helped its members find 'a sense of identity and a degree of emotional security' in difficult periods of social change.[59] They were willing, too, to accept the more informal range of religious expression that falls under the general heading of spirituality. It should also be noted here that it is usually the women who are to be found attending services in churches and chapels. In his study of gender in the English constituency of Oxford, Clive Field noted that over the period of 1651–1950 Nonconformist membership for each quarter of a century there was a two-thirds majority of female membership. While Field advises caution in generalizing from these figures the statistics available for Malton in Yorkshire do seem to support a significant number of females present over the males. Field is also hesitant in drawing conclusions from his evidence, although he does say that

> The Proportion of women in a lay religious community seems to be in direct proportion to the level of commitment – spiritual, intellectual, social, financial – demanded of that community; the less that is required by way of active involvement or personal sacrifice, the greater the number of men.[60]

This raises a number of questions for fishing communities in that the men could not always be present at services, and because of the nature of their work they were not able to be involved with the range of week-day activities of the churches – let alone with the family. Yet we cannot generalize too much here. In Filey, for example, the fishermen were Sabbatarian in the later years of the nineteenth century and this allowed for a higher proportion of men to be present at Sunday services. Fishermen also had strong links with the various 'Friendly Societies' and managed to gain much support for each other as the result of meetings and rituals. In the trawler ports during the same period the religious institutions provided an opportunity for the women to meet socially on Sundays and during the week. Clearly, therefore, the religious institutions played an important part in identity formation. The religious institutions also provided strong links with the past and were often the focus of family rites and rituals, such as rites of passage.

Nadel-Klein has pointed to a number of ways in which identity is formed and has argued that identity formation is very much part of a process rather than a given. Hence, it is 'learned, lived, transmuted, and always contextualized'.[61] This involves being part of a group that involves both seeing themselves as others see them and considering possibilities as to what the future might hold. And while the individual is part of a common heritage their identity also involves them in being creative in the ways that help them to construct their future. A similar point was made by Cohen when he stated that 'the perception of identity is relational: the sense of self is founded, at least in part, on a sense of the other'.[62]

The earlier discussion, under the section 'Culture and community', suggests that while men and women have regularly sought ways in which they can express their identity, there are, nevertheless, important and creative means, especially via rituals, festivals and superstitious beliefs. When, for example, women are seen as polluters and jinxers this perception may be implicitly perceived in functional terms as an attempt by the men to preserve *their own* autonomy and identity. At the same time, the women are often regarded as being intermediaries between the natural and supernatural, and innumerable superstitious beliefs embraced by the community serve as a function of enabling the women to preserve their autonomy and identity.[63] This general view has been reinforced by the Church of England in its legitimizing of folk practice regarding the need for purification, by formalizing the process in the ceremony of 'Churching'.

Identity can also be manifested in the expressions of art found in fishing communities. This is especially important in that it is an area where official and popular religion and culture meet. Alfred Gell has taken this point to heart, arguing: The nature of the art object is a function of the social-relational matrix in which it is embodied. It has no intrinsic 'nature, independent of the relational context'.[64] Perhaps the concept of 'art for art's sake' ultimately provides us with a paradox in that the concept itself was a reflection of a cultural context. Marshall Sahlins has made a similar point in arguing that customs and physical objects are a dynamic aspect of cultural meaning and historical change.[65] Artistic expression can take many forms, and the reinvention of fishing communities under the umbrella term 'heritage' embraces a broad range: the folk art of the community members in terms of dress, ritual pageants, festivals, stories and tapestries; and the material arts, embracing rope work, shell pictures, boats, knitting and so on (although the appellation 'folk art' does tend to perpetuate a false dichotomy between 'high' and 'low' art). There is also a wide range of art *about* fishing communities, especially paintings, pottery and photographs, which provide some insights into the daily lives of fisherfolk, although the idealized images can often mislead. Henry Pickering's *The Gospel Ship* with biblical texts on the sails has been especially popular in fishing communities.

The rapid decline of the fishing industry in Britain during the late twentieth century, as with many other European and American fishing communities, has left fisherfolk feeling socially dislocated. A common response has been to *reinvent* fishing communities in the romantic image often created by novelists, photographers and artists. Twentieth-century authors such as Leo Walmsley in Yorkshire, Stephen Reynolds in Devon, Neil M. Gunn in Caithness and George McKay Brown in the Orkney Islands offer some interesting and helpful insights into the daily lives of the men, women and children who depend largely on the fishing industry for a living.[66] But while they wrote from a more realistic perspective than their nineteenth-century forebears, they still often present a romanticized image – a view reinforced by early films such as *Turn of the Tide* (based on Walmsley's *Three Fevers*).

Victorian writers, on the other hand, had no such concerns and often took advantage of the fact that few ordinary people had visited the seaside. They drew idyllic portraits of life in fishing communities and added a little bit of melodrama to keep interest. R. M. Ballantyne and James Runciman were among the more popular writers of this genre – although, significantly, both were writing partly to publicize the work of the

Mission to Deep Sea Fishermen, and both drew attention to problems such as the liquor traffic in the North Sea during the 1880s.[67]

Victorian photographers also created romantic images and published their prints as postcards and books for visitors to the seaside – with nostalgia playing an important role. Many of these publications draw especially on the work of photographic pioneers such as James W. Herald in Arbroath, Hill and Adamson in Edinburgh, Lewis Harding in Cornwall, Ford Jenkins in Lowestoft, George Wood in Hastings, Francis Frith in Grimsby and Frank Meadow Sutcliffe in Yorkshire. Even allowing for the need to contrive scenes (the result of heavy equipment and early photographic processes) Victorian photographers tended to capitalize on comfortable images, which people were happy to display in their homes. As such, they (like the early film-makers) built upon the techniques and styles used by painters who also travelled to the fishing communities in droves, in many cases forming colonies and schools, such as those in Staithes, Newlyn and St Ives. But given all this work, very little research has been undertaken into the extent to which these portrayals reflected the life of the communities in which they operated and the effect on the communities of the images they produced.[68]

The result since the mid-nineteenth century, and especially today, is a rapid growth in the tourist industry in fishing ports, where members of the public have been offered sanitized displays and exhibitions coupled with festivals, pageants, ceremonies and publications that, more often than not, have reinforced the idyllic image.[69] This was clearly evident in Newfoundland fishing villages when the author visited the area in 1999.[70] And visits to Scottish and Irish fishing communities during August 2002 have confirmed this observation. Of twenty-five fishing ports visited in North-East Scotland only four remain significantly involved in fishing, although museums and heritage centres are developing rapidly along the coast.

In Buckie, where the fishing industry is still active, the tourists are offered a brief history of the industry in a pristine museum called the 'Buckie Drifter'. Sadly, at the time of my visit, the local view was that this museum was imposed on the community rather than being developed in harmony with the local fisherfolk. Despite some early support by the fisherfolk they later tended to avoid involvement and have been critical of the development, preferring to put their energies into their own museum located in a few rooms behind the local library. My own experience in talking with community members followed the experience of Jane Nadel-Klein in her book *Fishing for Heritage*. In her examination of this and other developments in fishing ports Nadel-Klein offered an analysis of the demands and effects of tourism: 'Fishing villages are marketed for tourist consumption, where culture has become a commodity'. Drawing upon fieldwork, novels, folk music and travel literature, she has explored how these influences have affected the local sense of identity within a modern European nation.[71]

The significant roles of women in fishing communities are an important aspect of the community's identity – and it is often the women who publicly stand up to make the case for improved conditions, and within the fishing communities the women generally have a high status. In her article Nadel-Klein concluded that the contemporary focus on women as symbols of fishing communities (she talks here about the emphasis given *within* fishing communities) helps to remind the fishermen of their masculinity in earlier days. In the light of this it is noteworthy that with the decline of the European and American fishing industries, it is the women who have been proactive in responding to the crisis. Examples of such groups are the Gloucester Fishermen's Wives' Association set up in 1969, the Coastal Women's Action Group in Norway and the Norwegian Fishermen's Wives Association.

There have also been a few notable women who were prominent in political protests against the conditions imposed on fishing vessels – especially the work of Lillian Bilocca, who led a group of Hull women during 1968, following the loss of three trawlers, demanding changes in the trawling industry. They were very successful here as changes took effect quickly. The painting in Hull bears witness to Lilian's leadership (Figure 1).[72]

Figure 1 Lillian Bilocca led a group of Hull women in 1968, following the loss of three trawlers, demanding changes. They were very successful here as changes in the trawling industry took effect quickly. This painting in Hull bears witness to Lillian's leadership. Photo: S. Friend, May 2016.

Conclusion

The constant change of fortunes in fishing communities during the nineteenth century meant a relentless need to adapt to new situations, and the fishing families did so in a range of ways. Sadly, the role of religion here has often been ignored by historians and social scientists, and much work remains to be done before many fishing villages' and towns' links with the fishing industry disappear forever. The relationship between religion and community is a complex phenomenon, with the nature of the community often being substantially determined by the religious influences within it. This is no less true of fishing communities than of others. Clifford Geertz has made the perceptive observation that

> sacred symbols function to synthesize a people's ethos – the tone, character and quality of their life, its moral and aesthetic style and mood – and their world view – the picture they have of the way things in sheer actuality are, their most comprehensive ideas of order.[73]

Coming from a different direction, Donna Lee Davis has called for more analysis of the 'ideational emotional or expressive aspects of the fisher/husband/wife relationship' and the 'relationship of the fishing enterprise to the overall community ethos'.[74] The direction of recent studies of fishing communities has been, first, to offer a balance to the earlier male-focussed research and, second, to explore the wider material and non-material perspectives of culture and community. It is surely no accident that the role of religion in helping people to cope with change is also a significant area for research. But in the process, questions are being posed about the various traditional theories put forward about the relationship between religion and social change.[75]

The nature of fishing communities

The nature of communities

The traditional meaning of the term 'community', which centres along with the human need for social interaction, generally involves the three areas of community of *place*, *interest* and *attachment* (the territory, social relationships and the shared identity of the group). More recently the goalposts have shifted with an emphasis being placed on the *imagined* and *symbolic* concepts of community, as developed by Benedict Anderson and Anthony P. Cohen.[1] Cohen argued the case for the symbolic construction of community: 'Whether or not its structural boundaries remain intact, the reality of community lies in its members' perception of the vitality of its culture. People construct community symbolically, making it a resource and repository of meaning, and a reference of their identity.'[2] The earlier concepts nevertheless remain important, and present-day researchers embrace a range of perspectives while applying a rigorous methodology. This chapter begins with an overview of these developments and looks at the nature of fishing communities before going on to examine, briefly, the nature of the three communities under consideration here: Filey, Scarborough and Grimsby.

The concept 'community' remains conceptually useful despite problems of clarity. Suggestions for alternative terms have been put forward by scholars, including Cook who proposed the use of the term 'localities' and A. Gibbins who preferred the concept 'locales'.[3] Indeed, studies in a range of disciplines have led to new and creative insights over the last forty years. In particular, Cohen has argued that a 'community' is predominantly a symbolic concept that exists in the mind of its members and is therefore essentially subjective by nature – a view anticipated by Margaret Stacey in 1969 when she pointed out that 'physical proximity does not always lead to the establishment of social relations'.[4] Boundaries such as 'place', 'interest' and 'attachment' have therefore been identified for the sake of convenience. Perhaps a two-tier approach here is helpful in that when the *symbolic* community is superimposed over the other boundaries we can begin to make use of a three-dimensional model to understand the nature of particular communities. But Cohen's approach has often been misunderstood and the criticism that he abandoned the social aspect of community is misleading. At the same time Cohen expressed dissatisfaction with his most popular work, *The Symbolic Construction of Community*, and claimed that many authors have misrepresented his views. He said that the term 'community', of its nature, lacks precision, and he went further by stating that there is no real point in spending time trying to define the word 'community' in terms of an analytical category, and that the most helpful approach is to make use of its ordinary popular usage. Clearly in the light of the debate Cohen has made an important point. Amit, for example, has argued: 'It is difficult to discern much in the way of coherence among the multitude of definitions, descriptors and claims of community which occur in quotidian conversation as well as within a variety of scholarly work.'[5] Such problems, however, have not been restricted to the concept of 'community' alone but are evident in numerous terms that have been applied to complex concepts such as 'religion' and 'identity'. The problem here is that all-embracing, analytical and descriptive definitions have often been sought. One method of dealing with this lack of clarity is to restrict the definition to the particular study being undertaken, although we may run into methodological difficulties with respect to comparative analysis. An alternative approach might be to formulate a definition for a particular *aspect* of the study. For example, in studying attitudes to death we need to define clearly what it is we are studying (fear of death, death phobia, death anxiety, latent death anxiety, etc.).[6] We also need to remember that the nature of complex concepts change over time. Peter Fricke has drawn attention to this and has argued that while change is an integral aspect of community development we should not abandon earlier models. In the light of this he offered a definition that embraces this perspective, 'We conceive of community as changing over time, of becoming differentiated with the advent of new skills but also integrating itself through a common tradition and social life.'[7] More recent research in community studies has highlighted the need to take into account the individual and communal sense of the past.[8] Such change relates closely to social and emotional interaction. It must also be remembered that a social and emotional sense of community helps to create and maintain a sense of personal and communal identity, with shared meaning found within social codes, special local interest groups and local conventions and values and the 'transmission and interpretation of customs, languages and beliefs'.[9] Conversely, a loss of personal identity often follows on from a loss of a sense of community (an issue explored in many contemporary novels and films). The past, therefore, impacts upon the present in important ways, and there can be an invisible boundary between those who claim several generations' descent in the community and those who are relative newcomers – a theme explored not only by research such as that conducted by Clark in Staithes and Tunstall in Hull but also in novels such as Walmsley's trilogy about life in Robin Hood's Bay.

Perhaps, not surprisingly, modern research in communities has embraced the need to explore both the social and emotional attachments. E. Day and J. Murdock, for example, have argued for exploring and analysing the importance of the ways in which people see their relation to society as well as their location (place).[10] The emphasis here is particularly on an emotional link between the community and its members. Such points clearly take on board the need to be more rigorous in our methodology. During the 1950s and 1960s, there was little by way of an agreed methodological approach that allowed for comparative analysis, and this led to a dearth of research in community studies during the 1970s while scholars argued over the criteria. The work of Stacey is of crucial importance here in that she tackled this lack of methodological rigour and emphasized the need for a more solid methodological foundation that allowed for comparative analysis between different research projects in a variety of communities. Today, researchers are more inclined to place their sphere of research within a wider social context in order that comparative analyses may be carried out. Modern researchers are again approaching the subject matter with the vitality evident in earlier community studies. A major problem, however, may be how we integrate the earlier studies into this more rigorous approach.

The nature of fishing communities

A concept such as the 'British fishing community' conjures up an idealized, romanticized image in the public mind that is not unlike the idealized image portrayed by Victorian and Edwardian painters, novelists, photographers and later by films. These constructed views of fishing communities tend to idealize the situation and thereby distort the reality of community life. Such conscious identity within a community context is usually the perception of the elderly, who tend to compare and contrast an *Idealized* past with the present. Nevertheless, there may also be some form of conscious perception of a constructed community by those fishermen who may have a tendency to idealize their home community while spending a considerable time away.

The problems inherent in defining a community are generally no less an issue when we try to define a particular fishing community – let alone the concept of a national fishing community. Definitions that take account of the fishing environment and the significance of the life of the local population are helpful but restricted. Such definitions will need to emphasize a number of factors, such as local economic dependence on a range of employment-related maritime activities, and other ways in which the sea is important to the people, such as social structures, cultural perceptions and local traditions. In some small fishing villages and towns, such as the Yorkshire towns of Staithes, Robin Hood's Bay, Runswick Bay, Flamborough and Filey, a relatively large percentage of the population was directly involved in the fishing-related trade during the nineteenth century, although the proportion changed dramatically over time; while with the larger fishing communities, such as Scarborough, Whitby, Bridlington, Hull and Grimsby, the community was part of a much wider and more complex social and economic local structure.[11] During the eighteenth century Scarborough, Whitby, Bridlington and Hull were the only harbour ports along the Yorkshire coast and of these only Scarborough was concerned primarily with fishing. Other smaller Yorkshire ports, however, had more important fishing communities, such as Staithes, Robin Hood's Bay and Flamborough.

Within and between such communities there were also a variety of social divisions that often took the form of symbolic boundaries distinguishing 'insiders' from 'outsiders' – individuals and groups often being identified according to how long they had been resident in the locality. 'Insiders' were often referred to more colloquially in such terms as 'Filey, born and bred'. Even among those who had a long association with the community there were geographical divisions that occurred over time: for example, in Grimsby and Hull the trawler skippers tended to move away from those areas of the town dominated by the crews, thereby making a physical statement about their rise in status. They also tended to patronize what became known as their own pubs and clubs where they socialized with each other.[12] Fishing vessel owners, too, tended to live in the more exclusive areas of the towns where they became part of the nouveau riche. Hence, within the fishing communities there were a variety of communities, each with their own concept of place, history and identity – a point noted by Robin Pearson in a different context when he argued that community 'was perceived by the Victorian lower middle class standpoint, and defined with a keen eye on the barometer of local social relations'.[13]

There is also another kind of social division – that between the home and the workplace, and for fishermen this division was often more thoroughgoing than that between the factory labourer and his or her family. The nineteenth-century fishing community's relationship with the sea was a very precarious and ambivalent one. For the women the vessel on which the fishermen sailed was a rival mistress who could appear to be jealous and demanding, hence the prevalence of superstitious beliefs such as those that forbade women on board fishing vessels. In some fishing communities, especially where inshore fishing dominated during the nineteenth century such as Staithes, Runswick Bay, Robin Hood's Bay, Scarborough and Filey, the women collected and prepared bait for the fishing lines, mended nets and helped to launch and beach the fishing boats.

The unique setting of the North Sea means that it has had a significant impact on those countries that border it, and there has been a good deal of social movement that has impacted on the nature of the communities in the various European countries.[14] Many Danish fishermen, for example, settled in Grimsby during the 1950s and 1960s when the fishing industry there reached its modern peak. Local fishing owners provided vessels for them to pursue seine-net fishing, and several men gradually managed to purchase their own vessels. The Danish Seamen's Mission acted as a social centre keeping the memory of home alive with language and traditions. The men also met regularly in a local public house. By the 1970s many of these fishermen had married local girls and built up local links that in turn led to them settling permanently in the town. Some of the visiting herring girls also met and married local fishermen, and I was surprised to meet some Yorkshire women in Scottish ports who had gone through this process and settled in their husband's hometown.

While the old generations still retain a sense of a local Danish community the number is rapidly diminishing. The second generation retained some Danish links, most notably in terms of familiarity with the Danish language, customs and festivals (e.g. Christmas is celebrated on Christmas Eve). But the third generation has tended to lose this link (something rather odd given that we would normally expect the third generation to identify closely with the ideals of the first). The Danish Seamen's Mission effectively closed in the 1990s, and to all intents and purposes the Danish community has been absorbed into the wider community.

Research in fishing communities

Rural life may sometimes be thought of as the ideal of community life, possessing consensus, cohesion and stability, and fishing communities are often thought to follow the rural pattern. Yet such a model is inherently misleading, despite the fact that many members of early British fishing communities both farmed and fished according to the season. With technological innovations, nineteenth- and twentieth-century fishing communities were moulded more by the nature of the work rather than being constructed by their members, although there was some overlap here. The isolation of some fishing communities, such as Filey, Runswick Bay, Robin Hood's Bay, Staithes and Flamborough Head, clearly had an effect on their nature, but others such as Whitby, Scarborough, Bridlington, Hull and Grimsby were part of a more complex social and economic structure. During some periods (especially Hull and Grimsby during the late nineteenth and mid-twentieth centuries) the fishing community was more influential on the local economy than at other times. While fishing communities are unique in that there is a significant separation between the workplace and the home for the men, even to the extent of a fishing vessel sometimes being viewed as a 'total institution', there are significant ways in which the two dimensions of life at sea and on shore overlap and are integrated especially in small villages where the emphasis is on inshore fishing. The nature of such communities has drawn many to view and write about them. But intriguingly there have been relatively few sociological studies of fishing communities generally.

There is of course a great danger in romanticizing and idealizing late-nineteenth-century fishing communities, and there are plenty of examples of just this approach. Cohen's model would appear to be of particular benefit in analysing the nature of seafaring, especially fishing, communities. His concept embraced a number of elements, including symbols (such as dress, speech and art) and rituals – some more fixed and universally acknowledged, others more mundane and idiosyncratic.

The lack of consensus in the definition of 'community', and the lack of methodological rigour in early 'community studies', has made comparative analysis with earlier studies difficult. Stacey offered some criteria that simplified the approach when she argued that a community study should be undertaken within a context where propositions can be tested. The context should allow us to explore a hypothesis that in turn sets the scene for comparative studies with aspects of the wider society. Her research was extended by a spate of studies that further developed the use of oral history and participant observation. Among the most important research here was Clark's study of Staithes, Lummis' research in East Anglia, Thompson's work in Scotland, Frank's study in Yorkshire and Wailey's research in Lancashire.

Despite the fallow period during the 1970s for community studies generally, there was in contrast a significant number of researchers working in British fishing communities during the second half of the 1970s. Nevertheless, with a few notable exceptions, such as Cohen's work on Whalsay, Shetland, in 1987 and Gilligan's study of Padstow, Cornwall, in 1990, this research had greatly diminished by the early 1980s – although it was during this period that several of the above authors published their work.[15] Why this research should have been curtailed is something of a puzzle – even allowing for the problems of methodological rigour that were undergoing intense scrutiny and discussion. The rapid decline and in some cases the demise of British fishing communities that may well have been a major factor giving rise to these studies should have provided raw material for a wealth of research similar to that which took place in mining communities during the 1980s and 1990s. But it may be that despite their apparent simplicity, the very complex and rapidly changing nature of fishing communities has been part of the problem.

A major influence on the shore-based fishing community was usually the domain of the women. This was often the case where the men were engaged in an offshore fishery with long days and erratic times of fishing preventing them from being involved with any major engagement in the wider day-to-day social activities.[16] This is especially applicable to fishing communities in that women are in many ways the essence of the community: it is the women who keep the rites alive, who dominate the membership of local institutions and who continue the community's customs and traditions. In contrast, fishermen have tended to form their own social world onshore, which is often exclusively male, such as Friendly Societies (e.g. the 'Shepherds' and 'Oddfellows' in Robin Hood's Bay), the Filey Fisherman's Choir and music groups such as the Scarborough Primitive Methodist Band (Leo Walmsley described the development of a local band in Robin Hood's Bay in his novel, *Phantom Lobster*). But there are some activities in which both males and females play a joint role, such as at festivals, concerts and social activities in times of great trauma.

There are of course particular problems in studying fishing communities that existed during the early and mid-nineteenth century where oral history is of little use. There seems to be a dearth of source materials, although it has to be said that this may only be apparent. Indeed, a wide range of source materials may be found, including newspapers, parish magazines, government reports and the reports published by local charities. Even so, this is not to diminish the problems of accessibility and the regular destruction of such materials, often because the various archives and museums do not have the space, resources or the interest to accommodate them.

The present study will concentrate on three fishing communities, two on the Yorkshire coast (Filey and Scarborough) and one on the North Lincolnshire coast (Grimsby, although Cleethorpes is included here). Filey is a small town that retains only a small number of fishing vessels and has no harbour. Scarborough is an ancient town with a harbour but currently has only a small number of fishing vessels. Grimsby is a large town that grew from a market town in the mid-1800s, and while it no longer has a fishing fleet a few vessels do continue to catch fish.

Filey

The growth of the town

Filey is an ancient and small town on the North Yorkshire coast situated in a sandy bay, 8 miles south of Scarborough and 11 miles north of Flamborough. There is evidence that the area was populated during the Bronze Age, and the Romans later built a signal station and perhaps a small settlement there. Following the Roman exit from Britain the sheltered area around Filey saw the arrival of numerous invaders before the village settled down to a sustained period of occupation during the medieval period, when Filey, like many other villages, established itself and saw the building in the twelfth century of the substantial parish church of St Oswald. There was very little change in Filey's population from *c.* 500 people in the sixteenth century to *c.* 505 in 1801.[17] But by 1841 the census shows the number had increased to 1,231 and by 1901 had risen to over 3,000.

A proposed harbour was never built and Filey remained isolated with a local culture that changed little in 1,000 years, although a railway introduced in 1846, when the town's isolation became part of the attraction as the leisure industry developed, made it a popular Edwardian resort with regular visitors travelling to the town from Scarborough. The second half of the nineteenth century saw an increase in the growth of the leisure industry, local societies and public services. Writing in his *Guide for Visitors* in 1853, Edward William Pritchard said of these developments:

> The new town, the chief resort of visitors, has been entirely built within the last fifteen years. It is principally made up of three ranges of buildings or terraces; one facing the sea, called the Crescent; the second facing inland, called Clarence Place; and the third, forming a side of a yet unfinished square, called Rutland Terrace; add to these Taylor's Hotel, several detached and well suited villas for lodgings, and the large new Hotel, now nearly finished, which adjoins the Crescent.[18]

For many years Filey had just one main thoroughfare, Queen Street, which housed fishermen, farmers and a number of local tradesmen. The development of 'new Filey' in the 1830s saw the rapid expansion of the town, especially with tourists during the summer months.

The Filey fishery

Legend claims that the Yorkshire cobles originated with the Viking longships, and this suggests the existence of a local fishery reaching back to at least the ninth century. Written evidence also exists of the Filey fishing community in the early twelfth century (and incidentally of the Grimsby fishing community) as indicated from details about local disputes, such as a disagreement between the monks at Whitby and the Abbot of Bridlington about paying tithes of fish and later, before 1196, between the Prior of Bridlington and the Prior of Grimsby, 'about the tithe of fish taken at Filey'.[19] While such records are rare the occasional references suggest an ongoing local fishery.

By the late eighteenth century, the fishing vessels had developed into two-masted luggers with crews of six, and in 1833 the first of the Yorkshire yawls was built in Scarborough. The Filey fishing fleet appears to have reached its zenith in the 1860s with thirty-four yawls, seventeen cobles and sixty-four inshore cobles. The vessels had crews of six for the yawls, four for the herring cobles and three for the inshore cobles. Hence, there were approximately 400 men and boys fishing during this period, although by the end of the century the number of vessels and fishermen were declining (Table 1) – but Filey's prosperity increased. At the parish tea of 1897, the priest, Canon Cooper, pointed out that the nature of Filey as a fishing village had changed and it

Table 1 Fishermen and Fishing Apprentices in Filey

Year	Filey population	Fishing apprentices	Fishermen
1881	505		
1811	579		
1821	773		
1831	902		
1841	1,231	1	132
1851	1,511	2	146
1861	1,881	4	150 (1886: 392)*
1871	2,267		202
1881	2,337		175
1891	2,481	3	188 (1896: 252)*
1901	3,003	1	200
1911	3,228		
1921	4,549		

Sources: Census figures; other sources, such as *The English Coble, Maritime Monographs and Reports, No. 30*, National Maritime Museum, London (1978) 34, provide higher figures. This document shows the figures reaching a peak in 1912, after which there was a sharp decline. *G. Waller (March 1958) *Filey Advertiser*.

was now a fashionable tourist attraction, with local people being able to rent out their houses to visitors.[20]

John Cole, writing in 1828, had identified four distinct periods in the Filey fishery during the year. These were the *spring fishing* (February to Easter) involving large vessels (yawls: two-masted vessels of 50–60 tons burthen) with a crew of six men and two boys who conducted line-fishing for cod, ling, skate and haddock, and sailed southwards to take advantage of the markets at Hull, Boston and Kings Lynn. During the *summer fishery* (Easter to August) the fishermen worked at sea from Monday to Friday returning home at the end of the week to sell their fish (turbot, halibut and haddock) on the Filey sands, and to deliver the rest of their catch (mainly ling and cod) to the fish salters for curing. During the *autumn fishery* (mid-September to November) the ten or twelve Filey yawls engaged in the *Yarmouth herring fishery* and took their families with them to live in the town until the end of November, where the women looked after the children and mended nets on shore. But by the 1840s and 1850s trade declined and the annual visits to Yarmouth were gradually abandoned.[21] The *winter fishery* (December and January) was a period when the local fishermen sailed their cobles 10–15 miles off the coast.

With no harbour to assist the daily launch of vessels at Filey the fishermen relied on manpower and a team of horses until the 1950s when tractors took over the role with the men joining in rhythmic chanting in order to synchronize their activities. With the growing market for fish as the nineteenth century progressed, and the clear advantages of working from a port with a harbour, many of the Filey fishermen travelled by train to Scarborough on Monday to sail their yawls, returning to Filey for the weekend. It should perhaps be pointed out that the Filey fishermen were Sabbatarians, and although this has been generally attributed to the religious revival of 1823, Sabbatarianism did not take hold until ten years later.

Table 1 shows a gradual increase in the number of fishermen throughout the nineteenth century, although there was a small decrease during the 1880s. There is, however, a discrepancy here as some sources provide different figures. There could be several reasons for this: some fishermen away at sea were not recorded on every census, and some fishermen may have been working from other ports such as Scarborough on the day of the census. Apprentices are not very much in evidence, with only one recorded as such in the 1841 census; later censuses simply recorded the younger fishermen as 'fisherboys'. Filey, therefore, does not appear to have had many boys registered as apprentices. Given the nature of the fishing community it would seem that the young fisherboys would on the whole be those sons of fishermen who had reached an age when their fathers were willing to take them to sea.

The women were involved in collecting bait (limpets, called 'flithers') along the Yorkshire coast and spent many hours each day during the winter fishing season baiting the lines. The 1861 census shows twenty females recorded as 'bait gatherers', all of whom were unmarried except one recorded as a widow (Appendix 3c). The ages ranged from fifteen to twenty-eight years, and one, the widow, who was aged forty-two years. The origins of this bait gathering activity by the women have been lost, although Arthur J. Munby recorded his contact with the flither girls of the Yorkshire coast in his diaries during the 1860s. While the main focus of flither-picking centred on the Filey women, there were others from Staithes, Whitby, Scarborough and Flamborough.

Peter Frank has argued that the development of flither-picking was the result of the decline in mussels during the nineteenth century. Later, during the mid-twentieth century, mussels were transported from East Anglia and the need for flither-pickers declined. But the women still needed to work at 'skeining' (the process of removing the mussels and limpets from the shells and attaching them to the long lines ready for the fishermen to take to sea the next morning). Skeining was usually done in the home, although a shed was provided for the Scarborough women who worked together. The work was laborious and hard as it was done in cold water during the winter months, and the women had to complete the work of skeining several thousand limpets before getting on with their various household duties. The work of the women was therefore very hard, and one of Frank's interviewees during the 1970s (James Cole, a fisherman in his nineties) stated, 'Well to tell you the truth. A woman in Staithes did more work than a man that went off to sea.'[22]

Fishing in the nineteenth century was of course a very hazardous occupation, conducted mainly in the open sailing boats, and many lives were lost at sea especially from the small open Filey fishing vessels. The Revd C. Kendall's book *God's Hand in the Storm* provides some detail about the great storm of October 1869.[23] That no Filey fishermen were lost on that occasion was regarded as miraculous by the local population, although many fishermen were lost over the years in other winter storms, not only at Filey but all along the Yorkshire coast. For example, the storm of 10 February 1871 saw the loss of almost 150 seafarers at the port of Bridlington. Given the many injuries suffered by fishermen, and the great loss of life, various societies were gradually developed in the fishing communities to provide financial support for the fishermen's families. Cole gives a few details about one such society that developed in

Filey in the 1820s, although as there was no major loss of life among the fishermen for some years the society eventually lapsed.[24]

Scarborough

The growth of the town

The earliest record of inhabitants living on the Scarborough headland (where the present castle was eventually built) is *c.* 500 BC.[25] In 1745 the town's population was about 5,000 and by 1801 this had risen to 6,688.[26] The latter half of the eighteenth century saw a significant increase in immigrants, especially of apprentices who were attracted to the growing importance of the maritime trades – although Whitby's shipbuilding industry had surpassed that of Scarborough by 1801. By the mid-nineteenth century there was just one shipyard left in Scarborough, which was owned by the Tindall family whose last ship was launched in 1863. Nevertheless, Scarborough's population continued to grow throughout the nineteenth century reaching over 38,000 by the beginning of the twentieth century. But the impetus in the fishing industry was gradually lost to Hull and Grimsby, both of which were located more strategically on the banks of the River Humber.

The Scarborough fishery

Scarborough is the second-largest town after Hull on the Yorkshire coast. Unlike Grimsby it has consistently been engaged in seafaring, notably trading and fishing, although boat building remained significant during the period 1691–1801.[27] The fishing industry was established early here and there was a significant international herring trade by the fourteenth century.[28] By the early 1800s there were only three fishing communities of any note along the Yorkshire coast: the three harbour ports of Scarborough, Whitby and Bridlington, but only Scarborough could rank as of any importance as a fishing station, although during the nineteenth century Scarborough also became a fashionable seaside resort and attracted many to the spa waters and bathing. The harbour and fishing vessels acted as a picturesque backdrop for the visitors and was no doubt one of the attractions (Table 2).

While seasonal visits to Scarborough had been of long standing by, for example, the Brighton fishermen who had fished the North Sea for cod since the late sixteenth century, it was not until the mid-nineteenth century that the Devon and Kent fishermen relocated there after several years of seasonal visits.[29] By the 1830s visiting fishermen were using trawling methods and this caused a good deal of friction with their hosts. The local Scarborough fishermen relied mainly on line-fishing throughout the year and drift-net fishing during the late summer and autumn herring season. Yet with the visiting fishermen sweeping through the fishing grounds with their trawlers there was soon antagonism between the two groups that sometimes led to violent conflict such as the stabbing of a southern fisherman by a Scarborough fisherman. Even so, by the 1840s trawling became an established method of fishing in the port, leaving Staithes

Table 2 Fishermen and Fishing Apprentices in Scarborough

Year	Scarborough population (Census)	Fishing apprentices	Fishermen
1801	6,699		
1811	7,067		
1821	8,533		
1831	8,760		
1841	10,048		99
1851	12,915	2	148 (Gerrish says 164)
1861	18,377	10	234
1871	24,259	4	359 (Gerrish says 355)
1881	30,504	16	497
1891	33,776	14	347
1901	38,161	0	227

Sources: Census; George Alward, *The Sea Fisheries of Great Britain and Ireland*; Binns, *The History of Scarborough* (2003); BPP (1887) Vol. XXVIII, *c.* 5412.

and Filey to retain their dominant role of line-fishing. While this situation eventually calmed down, and the Scarborough fishermen adopted trawling, many of the visiting fishermen relocated to Grimsby and Hull where the facilities were tailor-made to meet the needs of the trawler fishermen.

Grimsby

The growth of the town

The North Lincolnshire town of Grimsby developed from a market town of just over 1500 residents in 1801 to the country's leading fishing port by 1900, with a population of over 36,000. Grimsby was significantly different to most fishing towns in its nature, development and impact. It was not a case of merely expanding an already existing infrastructure, which had gradually built up around a fishing town, but of starting from scratch even to the extent of building the fishing docks on reclaimed land from the River Humber.

Lying on the east coast of England on the south bank at the mouth of the River Humber, Grimsby had been a busy port in the Middle Ages, but by the late eighteenth century trade had declined and the harbour had silted up, thereby allowing Hull to claim a monopoly of the seagoing trade. Anderson Bates wrote in 1893 that the town 'may be described as so obscure that it probably owed its place in maps and topographical dictionaries to its privileges as a Parliamentary and municipal Borough'.[30] In the 1790s Grimsby was a market town with a small population. Very little fishing activity took place there during the early 1800s, although a small number of fishermen worked from Cleethorpes.[31] An attempt to reverse the decline in the town's fortunes was made in 1800 with the formation of the Grimsby Haven Company, initially by building a lock at the point where the Haven met the Humber and by dredging the river up to the River Head. The short-term situation improved but the lack of an infrastructure linking Grimsby to the wider population, and the failure of the Ropery in 1832, one of the major local employers, led to another population decline. Perhaps not surprisingly people sought jobs and business opportunities elsewhere.[32]

With the commencement of work on the Royal Dock in 1841 the situation changed dramatically and during the next ten years the town experienced an influx of over 5,000 people, the population more than doubling from 3,700 to 8,860 (Table 3). Even so, *The Times* correspondent, who covered the laying of the Royal Dock's foundation stone by Prince Albert in 1849, wrote that Grimsby was 'one of those places that few of our readers have ever heard of, and less number have seen, but which a London contractor would cart away in three weeks'.[33] With the extension of the railway line to Cleethorpes in 1863 there was a significant increase in the Cleethorpes population, from 325 in 1861 to 2,059 in 1871 and 11,620 in 1881. Hence, Grimsby benefitted not merely as a centre for trade and industry associated with its docks but as an adjunct to the rapidly growing excursion traffic to the coast.[34]

Grimsby's expanding population came from four significant sources – first, navvies who built the docks (600 of them, the majority of whom were Irish); second, migrating fishermen and their families from ports such as Brixham, Ramsgate and Barking; third, fishing apprentices who were brought to Grimsby from orphanages, prisons, reformatories, workhouses and training ships around the country, many of whom were as young as twelve years old, by 1872 the apprentices outnumbered fishermen by 1,350 to 1,150 (Tables 3 and 4);[35] and fourth, migrating people from Britain and Europe

Table 3 Comparative Chart of the Grimsby Fishing Community

Year	Grimsby population (Census)	Clee with Weelsby population (Census)	Fishermen (Census)	Fishing vessels registered at Grimsby	Fish landed (excluding foreign landings) in tons
1801	1,524	103			
1811	2,747	115			
1821	3,064	154			
1831	4,048	177		29	
1841	3,700	199	13	30	
1851	8,860	195	17	64	188 (1855)
1861	11,067	325	209	179	5,300
1871	20,244	2,058	646	302	30,000
1881	28,503	11,620	1,402	607	49,000
1891	33,283	18,775	3,588*	636	64,000
1901	36,857	26,400		478	99,000
1911	74,659			575	190.000
1921	82,355			622	138,000

Sources: Population excludes Scartho, Cleethorpes and Humberston. In 1911 the figures for Clee and Weelsby were included with Grimsby. The figures for fishermen and vessels differ according to the source used. I have relied here on Margaret Gerrish for the 1861 census figures. Details of fish landed are from Gillett (1970) 301. Other details are taken from the *Victoria County History, Lincolnshire (1901)*. *Figures from B. Lincoln, *The Rise of Grimsby, Vol. I, From the 9th century to 1865; and Vol. II, 1865-1913* (1913) Grimsby, Farnol, Eades, Irvine & Co.

Table 4 Grimsby Fishing Apprentices

Year	Grimsby apprentices indentured	Grimsby number of apprentices employed	Grimsby total by decades
1861	38		
1868	231		
1869	534		
1871		200	
1872	424	1,350	
1877	534	1,794	
1878			1868–78: 4,277
1881	277	320	
1886	343	1,026	
1891	215	805	
1899	111	378	1890–1: 1,574
1901	61		
1909			1900–9: 590
1911	28		

Sources: Boswell, op cit, (1974), 32–40; *Annual Reports of the Inspectors of Sea Fisheries (England and Wales)*.

(Jewish, Mennonites, Mormons and so on, many of whom left for Liverpool and the United States, but some of whom stayed in Grimsby seeking to take advantage of the growing business opportunities). The 1851 census shows that the town had already absorbed a number of European migrants from Poland, Germany, Sweden and some from further afield, such as the East Indies and Australia. Many others came from all across Britain (Appendix 5).[36]

The Grimsby fishery

The rise of the North Sea Fishing Industry during the mid-Victorian era, especially with the discovery of the Silver Pitts on the Dogger Bank, gave impetus to the development of Grimsby and numerous other fishing ports along the North-East coast. This development was facilitated in Grimsby by a new infrastructure that included the construction of a railway network during the years 1846–9, the Royal Dock during 1841–52 and a fish dock in the 1850s. Both docks were constructed by the Manchester, Sheffield and Lincolnshire Railway (MS&LR).[37] The town now had two important railway branch lines – west to Manchester and Liverpool, and south to London. Further increases in the local population took place quickly between 1840 and 1870, then doubling from over 20,000 in 1870 to over 40,000 by the early 1900s and reaching over 82,000 by 1921 (the figures being significantly higher if Cleethorpes, Scartho and Humberston are included, see Appendix 2a). The local fishing industry, too, developed quickly from having only nineteen fishermen in 1861 to over 900 vessels and over 3,000 fishermen in the late 1880s.

In the late 1850s the MS&LR also acknowledged the need to provide houses for incoming fishermen in order to develop a permanent fishing population in Grimsby, and twenty-five houses (the Worsley Buildings) were built in 1858. The 1861 census shows that seventeen of the twenty-five occupants were smack owners. All this was in addition to the Cleethorpes oyster fishermen who, according to George Alward, provided the nucleus of crews for the Grimsby fishing vessels.[38] The rapidly increasing population created a number of social problems such as poor sanitation, inadequate housing, a lack of healthy water supplies and poor roads. At the same time there were, in the early 1850s, two distinct populations: the old town centred on the Old Market Place in the Bull Ring, overlooked by the parish church; and the new town rapidly developing around the docks. By 1855 the population of the new town exceeded that of the old, and within a few decades the old medieval market town was practically obliterated.[39] Gerrish has argued that the Thames fishermen appear to have moved directly to Grimsby from their home ports during the period 1857–60. This view led to the important observation that the fishermen moved almost directly from communities with a high degree of social and residential stability to a town that was little better than a noisy, bustling frontier situation.

Unlike smaller fishing towns along the Yorkshire coast, Grimsby was not picturesque. In 1873 a Hull journalist described the scene:

> There is no centre to the town. There is certainly a small market place, but it is quite at one end of the town; there is another market place, styled new, which does not seem to be patronised at all except on Saturday nights and then chiefly by cheap-jacks, paltry shows and punching machines. The town is straggling, without order, method or construction. Freeman Street is by far the most compact and uniform and should properly be the main artery of the town, but Victoria Street which takes precedence by inheritance is a long, winding, rambling place with dirty hovels, good houses, gaunt timber yards and modern cottages all jumbled together in a manner offensive to the eye. The road to Cleethorpes is spoilt by ugly gaps and small rows of shops falling to pieces, and the causeway in front rotting into gaping holes.[40]

The growth of the town continued unabated, and, as if to announce the new town's emergence, a 300-foot-high hydraulic tower modelled on the tower of the Palazzo Publico in Sienna was completed in 1852 and was used to open and close the lock gates. With the growth of the fishing industry the Royal Dock quickly reached saturation point. The Dock Tower has, nevertheless, remained a potent symbol of Grimsby.

While the fishing vessels used the Royal Dock initially, they moved to the newly built fish dock in 1857. Another fish dock was added in 1877 and there were further enlargements to both docks over the next ten years. With the improvements to dock facilities and the rapid increase in the fishing workforce, the industry quickly experienced a shortage of labourers and tried to attract men to the industry. One aspect of this was the recruitment of fisherlads (apprentices) brought to Grimsby from workhouses and orphanages across the country. This was an adaption of an existing system already in use in some other fishing ports and presumably advocated by the immigrant fishermen from Barking who were already familiar with the apprenticeship system.[41] While local employers argued that the system of apprenticeship controlled entry to the industry and ensured a good standard of training, others saw the system as one of exploitation by which the employers obtained cheap labour, and the poor-law unions disposed of their young paupers. Pamela Horn has argued that there was an element of both in the Grimsby industry, and at least one publication referred to the apprenticeship system as little more than slavery.[42]

The number of indentured apprentices between 1870 and 1937 is provided by Boswell and the *British Parliamentary Papers*. Other sources providing actual numbers in Grimsby are somewhat diverse, including the census figures and a number of reports. Martin Wilcox has argued that apprentices from respectable labouring families generally made up the greater proportion of the apprentices in the smaller, more traditional fishing communities. The newer ports, such as Grimsby and Hull, tended to recruit a much higher number of pauper apprentices – resulting in a range of social problems.[43]

Boswell says that 4,277 boys signed indentures during the period 1868–78; and Fleming's report estimated there to be 200 apprentices engaged in fishing in 1871.[44] The various estimates, along with the *Annual Reports of the Inspectors of Sea Fisheries (England and Wales)*, give the numbers of apprentices in Grimsby (Table 4).

The work did not appeal to all the apprentices, many of whom had never seen the sea before their arrival in the town, let alone having had experience of working on fishing boats. Some absconded and, when caught, were sent to prison (over 1,000 fisherlads between 1870 and 1880).[45] The problem became the subject of outrage and was gradually addressed, the working conditions improved and the threat of imprisonment abandoned. Fatalities were also high: one in eighty-four for fishermen, one in twelve for apprentices. Approximately one-quarter of the apprentices ran away and a significant number of others lost their lives during the course of their apprenticeship. Horn also pointed out that during the 1880s only about 35 per cent of the Grimsby fishing apprentices completed their term.[46] But it was the newspaper attention that reported abuses suffered by the apprentices, and a number of deaths at sea, that gave rise to a national outcry against the conditions in which boys were expected to work. The number of apprentices in Grimsby dropped dramatically after the First World War, and the system was finally abolished in the 1930s, partly due to economic problems. Horn also pointed out that the rapid growth of the local population increased the number of local young people looking for work and this tended to negate the need for apprentices from outside agencies, a need that had become evident as the local fishing industry rapidly developed following the mid-nineteenth century.

There is equally great difficulty in recording accurate numbers of fishermen. His Excellency Spencer Walpole, writing in 1883, pointed out that there was 'no means of ascertaining with precision such simple facts as the number of persons engaged in the sea-fisheries of England and Wales'.[47] More recently Pat Midgley, writing of the King's Lynn fishing community, observed: 'We know the figures of fishermen are inaccurate (for King's Lynn) because during a hotly contested General Election in 1911 ... the candidate, Holcombe Ingleby, took over 400 fishermen on a picnic to his estate at Ringstead'.[48] The census for that year apparently recorded a considerably smaller number of fishermen.

Following 1880 the sailing vessels were gradually replaced with steam trawlers, and, as costs rose, few fishermen could by that date look forward to the day when they would own their own vessel. Other changes affected the nature of the industry, such as the demise of the 'fleeting system', but Grimsby nevertheless continued to prosper well into the twentieth century.

Changes in Grimsby's social structure

With the discovery of new fishing grounds, and the development of an efficient infrastructure for the town, there was a significant migration of fishermen into the port during the late 1850s. By 1858 twenty fishing smacks had left other ports to register in Grimsby.[49] This influx of labour had a reciprocal effect upon the port's facilities in that the fishermen petitioned for improvements, and the improvements once made attracted more fishermen. In 1851 48 per cent (109 fishermen) of all males in Cleethorpes were employed in fishing.[50] By 1872 there were 1,150 fishermen in Grimsby (see Table 3).

Most fishing smacks in the nineteenth century were owned by working skippers, some of whom gradually moved on to owning several vessels and then becoming fish curers and managers. In due course members of this new group became leaders in the town as councillors, magistrates and respected businessmen. By the 1880s owners and skippers were living in large houses in the town's suburbs to the south, and Cleethorpes to the east, while fishermen lived in the cramped housing around the docks. Inevitably, this situation gave rise to the proliferation of pubs, clubs, boarding houses, brothels and the social paraphernalia associated with a large vibrant port, all of which tended to be located within a fairly defined area, bounded by Alexandra Dock, Eleanor Street and Park Street. Initially the fishing community lived close to the docks on the west side of the railway line (along the main thoroughfares: Burgess Street, King Edward Street and Victoria Street), but as the town expanded, the fishing community moved eastwards, with a few finding accommodation in the West Marsh (Appendix 1b). Within this community there were small groups that maintained their own identity, such as the Jewish immigrants who had now settled in the town. The local Jewish community had eighty-seven members in 1871. This figure rose to 113 in 1881, 149 in 1896 and reached a peak of 450 in 1899 – a number that remained constant for twenty years before declining slowly throughout the twentieth century.[51]

During the 1840s through the 1860s there was little sense of 'belonging' in Grimsby, and even in 1871 that year's census showed that only one smack owner out of forty-one had been born in the town.[52] The many diverse individuals and groups (dock and railway navvies, Jews, Danes, Norwegians and other migrating fishermen) tended to be somewhat insular and many arrived with little or nothing in the way of finances. The following comment provides an example:

> Some, however, are transients. That is to say, they come to England penniless, hoping to pick up enough money here to carry them across the Atlantic to the Promised Land.

> One such family, a Russian Jew, his wife and three children landed recently in Grimsby. They had not one penny. They managed to get into a house. 'There are houses here which the landlords will let out on the chance of getting the rent.' They furnished this house with nothing in the front room, a table and a few boxes in the

back. The bed upstairs on the floor. The attention of the authorities was drawn to this family by a report from the parish doctor. The woman had come to him with her three children, who were all covered in sores and 'were breaking out in a scaly disease.' The man, whose trade it was 'to go putting in windows,' was found lying, ill and starving, on the bed on the floor.[53]

Several groups, such as Friendly Societies and Temperance groups, sought to raise the standard of living and of morality among the large influx of workers, and during the 1870s numerous church groups began to expand and establish themselves in the community. Nonconformists and Roman Catholics did not have the restrictions of the old structures to cope with and were able to establish new buildings, new services and new organizations in order to appeal to the needs of the rapidly growing working-class population.

The roles of the local women in nineteenth-century Grimsby have been sadly neglected. Lynn Abrams has argued that while many historians have ignored the roles of women in society, when women have been included in their grand narratives 'they tend to see them as acted upon – women are included as passive vessels in a historical landscape that has already been determined.'[54] The same argument is perhaps no less true of fishing communities in that the histories, often written by men, tend to reflect and emphasize the activity of the men who are less likely to have knowledge of the female domain.

Although some women did work at fishing these were few. In Grimsby, when a Mrs Jackson's husband, a former fish merchant, died she took over his work and continued with this when she remarried.[55] Women were, however, included in most aspects of the trade other than going to sea or holding management responsibilities. The women generally made the fishing nets, knitted ganseys and they would often act as fish hawkers (although this was common practice in other fishing towns, there is little evidence of it in Grimsby). They cared for the children and their education, had responsibility for the finances and looked after the home. Nevertheless, the census often had only a blank against the occupation of women in fishing communities, or they were sometimes recorded as 'fisherman's wife' when the husband was away at sea. When women did work for pay it was often as a servant or a charwoman, although some were active in running local public houses. As the fishing industry became more mechanized the women worked in fish processing plants – but here, again, they were portrayed as supporting the work of the men. During the Victorian era identity was often seen as formed largely by official religion. But even here the roles of women (who were and are the most evident in attendance and support at the chapels and churches) have been largely ignored. It was common practice, for example, for a society or a charity to be initiated by a woman and then for the men to take much of the credit.

In such a social context as nineteenth-century Grimsby we might expect to see a lack of coherent social structures initially, and a subsequent developing sense of coherence that reflected the situation many had moved from and which provided a sense of meaning and purpose. Gerrish has referred to the fishermen from similar backgrounds living in close proximity to each other but has downplayed this as simply a need to live close to the docks.[56] With further analysis of the census data in the light of historical material it should be possible to explore the social situation further.

Religion in fishing communities along the Yorkshire and North Lincolnshire coasts

Introduction

Some studies of fishing communities have included discussion on popular religion (Clark's research in Staithes is an important example). Other scholars have included religious beliefs and practices as part of a much broader social investigation (such as Thompson and Lummis), and papers have occasionally been published exploring the subject on a local basis (such as John Duthie's study of evangelicalism in Aberdeen and Nadel's exploration of revivalism in Ferryden, Scotland).[1] However, in approaching the study of religion in fishing communities along the Yorkshire and North Lincolnshire coasts there is relatively little research to build upon, although there is a growing amount of wider research that has implications for the study here.

While some of the empirical research has explored the relationship between fishing communities and religion the emphasis has tended to be on *official religion*, and the research has tended to deal with readily accessible published material. Popular religion is much less straightforward although significant work has been done on non-fishing communities by Obelkevich, Cox, Williams and Jenkins, among others. An area that embraces both official and popular religion is that of revivalism, and this area has seen a significant amount of research, such as that by Thompson, Gilbert, Luker and Morrell.[2] There appears to be a fairly general agreement on the link between social conditions and the nature of revivals, although the actual mechanics are hotly debated. There is also the problem that much nineteenth-century comment on revivals has tended to be made by those with a strong sympathy for the movement. Thus, while George Shaw commented that revival in early-nineteenth-century Filey brought religion to the village, Vallenze has pointed to much earlier religious activity there.[3]

This chapter will explore the nature of religion along the Yorkshire and North Lincolnshire coasts, especially in Filey, Scarborough and Grimsby, and here we will concentrate mainly on official religion in order to provide a context for the discussion on popular religion in Chapter 6. There will also be some discussion on the nature and influence of maritime missions as these had a significant influence, especially in nineteenth-century fishing communities.

Religion in Filey

During the nineteenth century Filey was an isolated village with a culture that had changed little over the previous thousand years. Christianity appears to have been brought to the village by the monks of Lindisfarne as part of St Ninian's missioning of Northern England, although no evidence remains of a local church or chapel from this period. The first recorded chapel was dedicated to St Bartholemew during the Middle Ages, but by the sixteenth century this was in ruins and St Oswald's Church (built during the twelfth century) was now serving the local community.[4]

Throughout most of the nineteenth century, religion in Filey was dominated by Anglicanism and Methodism. There were several smaller Nonconformist groups, such as the Quakers, Christian Scientists and the Plymouth Brethren, although none of these appear to have attracted more than a few members. Nevertheless, the emphasis on experiential religion developed in the town by the Methodists was further enhanced in the late nineteenth century by the Salvation Army, whose parades, bands and open-air meetings attracted both locals and visitors.

Roman Catholics, however, did not develop a significant presence in Filey until the twentieth century. The Sisters of Charity of Our Lady of Evron, a French order, extended their work to England when faced with persecution by the Third Republic at home. The first congregation was established in 1904 when the Convent of the Sacred Heart opened in John Street. Father Eugene Roulin, a French Benedictine monk, was sent by Ampleforth Abbey to act as a chaplain to the sisters, and he became the town's first resident Roman Catholic priest. This event re-established a link that had been severed during the Dissolution and led to the building of St Mary's Church, an Italianate building, in Brooklands, which was opened in May 1906. This development clearly met a need, especially among the many visitors who frequented the town, and an extension was added and the new building opened in 1961.[5]

The Anglican St Oswald's Parish Church still dominates the town from the hill on the north side of the Church Ravine. Named after the Saxon king of Mercia in AD 642, it is not known who built the church, although tradition says it was Augustinian Canons from Bridlington Priory. Archaeological evidence suggests that it was built between 1180 and 1230 during a very turbulent period of English history, and there have since been a number of changes and restorations.[6] The local population was initially served by priests from Bridlington Priory and, following the Dissolution, by a parochial chaplain, with curates supplied by the Vicar of Folkton and Hunmanby. In 1839 the Revd Thomas N. Jackson had the building restored and sought to obliterate any remaining traces of Roman Catholicism by painting the walls to hide medieval murals. Statues were destroyed, and the altar was moved from the sanctuary to the porch. The first vicarage was built in 1845, although the vicar remained non-resident and employed an assistant curate for Filey until 1871. Several incumbents then served the village for short periods until the appointment of the Revd Neville Cooper in 1880.

While Mr Cooper was popular, some thought him arrogant. Even so, he clearly cared for his parishioners and one of his first acts on being appointed was to set up a collection on behalf of the fishing families who had lost their menfolk at sea. Having moved to Filey Mr Cooper was too poor to hire a carriage and so walked to his various meetings around the county. The experience led him to visit many parts of Britain on foot and as a result he became known as the 'Walking Parson'. He extended his walking tours to the continent and published several books and articles about his exploits. St Oswald's Church thrived under his care, and he regularly held four services on Sundays with an average out-of-season congregation of 500, which seems to have been a significant improvement on earlier numbers, such as the eighty attendees at the evening congregation cited in the 1851 census (see Table 5). Under Mr Cooper's care, attendance numbers appear to have increased significantly during the summer months, although by the end of the nineteenth century attendance had begun to decline, and this continued up to the present day. Mr Cooper remained vicar of the parish for fifty-five years until his resignation in 1935. During his incumbency he worked closely with other church leaders and became friendly with the Roman Catholic priest, Fr Eugene Roulin, and the two worked together amicably for the benefit of the local population. Mr Cooper was also able to view things from a wider perspective than just the institution. For example, in his book *The Curiosities of East Yorkshire*, he commented on the ornately designed font at Cowlam, saying, '(it) bears a number of sculptured figures and is reminiscent of the days when sacred and secular things were blended together as they ought to be.'[7]

With the development of the resort during the nineteenth century there was clearly a need for another church in south Filey, and an iron church was erected in 1857 in West Street to seat 350 people. This served until 1871 when a stone building, a Chapel of Ease to St Oswald's, dedicated to St John the Evangelist, replaced the iron structure. These corrugated structures, often known as 'Tim Tabernacles', became very popular in the late Victorian era, and many were supplied to missionary organizations as a cheap means of providing places of worship for growing congregations. They were useful, too, for the growing towns and villages, and Filey was just one of several fishing communities that adopted the approach – in Grimsby, for example, an 'iron church' was erected on the docks to meet the needs of the rapidly growing number of dockworkers and fishermen there.

While John Wesley visited many of the communities along the Yorkshire coast he did not visit Filey. When Wesleyan Methodist missionaries tried to preach in the village they initially failed to make much of an impact – being tormented and

Table 5 Filey Results of the 1851 Census of Religion

Church/chapel meeting places	Seating			Numbers present at 1851 census			Sunday school	
	Free	Other	Free space	am	pm	eve	am	pm
Church of England St Oswald's	120	280			80		45	
Methodists (Wesleyans)	158		266	84				
Methodists (PM)	80	270	50	120		300	107	107
Totals	**358**	**550**	**316**	**204**	**80**	**300**	**107**	**152**

pelted with dried fish by the locals. It was not until 1806 that a Wesleyan mission was established there, and a society was inaugurated in 1810, although numbers did not increase rapidly, there being only fifteen members of the Wesleyan Society in 1823.[8]

The Primitive Methodists later sought to improve on this. Primitive Methodist tradition painted a picture of Filey, prior to its missioning by John Oxtoby in the early 1820s, as a town in which 'Drunkenness, Sabbath breaking, swearing, cock-fighting, card-playing, and similar evils were very prevalent'.[9] Today we might rephrase this to say the explanation was a natural psychological adjustment used to justify the change, although from the fishermen's personal perspective such a change was no doubt very real. But exactly what that change was and why it was necessary remains obscure with the various reports being written by parties who had a vested interest in claiming they were (or rather God was) responsible for a major change in the local moral climate. Of Oxtoby himself Shaw noted in his biography of the man that an earlier biographer had claimed that he had 'lived a life of most abandoned wickedness'.[10] But even Shaw contested this view, saying that the evidence taken from recollections of those who knew Oxtoby in his youth pointed to an honest man and a regular churchgoer. Such distortions of history, as Stephen Hatcher has pointed out, are usually made about towns and individuals prior to a period of revival when the missioning group writes its own history. Sadly, very little objective evidence now remains about the events of 1823, although we will explore the issues further in Chapter 5.

It would in any case appear that the Filey Revival of 1823 and its after-effects lasted approximately two years, and did not appear in a social, political and economic vacuum. While many of the actual events in the Filey of 1823 are now lost to us there are some small lights that can be thrown on the era. It would appear that while Oxtoby was, according to Methodist writers, the right person in the right place at the right time, the previous work of the Wesleyan Methodists had nevertheless prepared the ground for revival. Even so, despite the initial boost to Primitive Methodist membership in the early 1820s numbers remained fairly steady in the 1830s, before beginning to climb during the 1840s.

The Wesleyan Methodists, however, did rather better with membership figures in the 1850s and 1860s (Appendix 6c2). Not surprisingly, increasing membership led to extensions being added to the Primitive Methodist chapel in 1843 and 1859, and in 1865 fundraising began for a new building, the Ebenezer Chapel, which was opened in September 1871 with seating for 900 people. Fish feast suppers were held regularly and attracted several hundred people at a time, and the by now well-established fishermen's choir dressed in local ganseys sang at chapel meetings and open-air services on the cliff top.

The Wesleyans experienced some benefit from the 'revival' and increased their membership throughout the nineteenth century, eventually opening new premises in Murray Street in 1876. This was built in the early Gothic style with a spire – a clear symbolic statement about the Methodist presence in the town. The Wesleyans and Primitives continued to worship in separate buildings until May 1875 when the Ebenezer Chapel was closed and the two congregations united, with the chapel simply being renamed Filey Methodist Church.

Given the increase in membership of both the Primitive Methodist and Wesleyan Methodist congregations, we might expect to see something of a decline in membership of the parish church, but this appears not to have been the case, although there is the odd anomaly of a dramatic decrease of Anglican baptisms with a subsequent rise in Methodist baptisms from the mid-1800s during the high point of the North Sea fishing industry (Appendix 7d). It was not uncommon for locals and visitors to attend both Anglican and Nonconformist services, and the Revd Jackson (inducted to St Oswald's Church in 1832) replied to Archbishop Thompson's Visitation (1865) question, 'What dissenting places of worship are there ... ?', by saying, 'I am most incapable of affording a direct answer, as very many of the Methodists, the only dissenters in the place, divide their attendance between Church and Chapel.'[11]

Other smaller groups had, from time to time, attempted to establish themselves there, although none appear to have had the success of the Primitive and Wesleyan Methodists. By 1851 over 300 locals were attending Primitive Methodist services, as Table 5 for the 1851 census shows. The figures here suggest that the Anglicans did not initially lose a significant number of people to the Primitive Methodists, although there is clearly a dip in the number of Filey baptisms at St Oswald's following 1865. The rise in Primitive Methodist baptismal numbers is also similar for Grimsby and Scarborough, and reflects the success of the fishing industry, which reached its peak in *c.* 1880.

Religion in Scarborough

Theakston's Guide of 1841 makes the point that probably no town in the empire, of comparable size, possesses a greater number of places for the worship of God than Scarborough.[12] With fourteen religious congregations, including St Mary's Church, it seems likely that there was room to meet the needs of the population of 9,515. By 1901, therefore, the presence of over fifty religious groups must have provided more than adequate seating for Scarborough's population of 38,161 (Appendix 6b1). By the 1881 census of religion, conducted by the Scarborough Mercury, there were forty-four churches with accommodation for 20,362 and a total of 20,709 attending services on census Sunday, although a number of these would have attended more than once (Appendix 6b3).[13] In 1881 Scarborough had a population of 30,484, so even with a number attending services more than once it was still a very high figure. Robin Gill has commented that 'Among these smallest towns, Scarborough seems to present the most startling evidence of the effectiveness of vigorous church building (there were twenty-one churches here in 1851 and forty-four in 1881)'.[14] In the light of this the figures for 1872 are exceptionally high – until we discover that the figures include thirty-seven villages outside Scarborough (see the letter to the *Nonconformist* of 15 January 1873 by Robert Balcarnie (Appendix 6b2)). Given that the Scarborough population had more than doubled during the same period, church building appears to have kept abreast of this development. Gill's argument is that when a church-building programme was carried out attendance figures tended to rise. Even so, the situation in Scarborough, Rotherham and Sheffield was, for Gill, somewhat exceptional in that for each area attendance was good, while for most other places the church-building programmes tended to provide far more space than would be used by the local populations.

Scarborough, like Grimsby, experienced a dramatic increase in church growth after mid-century, although both towns had a long history of religious presence. St Mary's Church, for example, was built in the early twelfth century and an early close link was established with the Cistercians. Jack Binns has commented: 'The day before he set sail from Dover, 11 December 1189, Richard the Lionheart sealed a charter granting the revenues of the parish church of Scarborough to the abbot of Citeaux to pay the expenses of the general Chapter there.' Binns goes on to note that there was apparently an ulterior motive in Richard's gift – that of ensuring favoured hospitality as he marched his army overland to Marseilles en route to Palestine. The tithes granted to the Cistercians included locally caught fish, with Scarborough fishermen paying 'a tithe of every fortieth cod and every twentieth herring and other catches'.[15] All of this suggests a thriving local fishing industry during the twelfth century.

Various religious orders owned property and/or lived in the town during these early years, including the Cistercians and Franciscans, although relations were not always harmonious between them. The Cistercians built two other churches: St Thomas the Martyr's Church and St Nicholas' Church, while the Franciscans built St Sepulchre's. Only St Mary's survived the effects of the Reformation and Revolution and remained Scarborough's only parish church between 1649 and 1828. St Mary's had seating for 1,300, and the 1851 census shows 800 attending the morning service and 450 the afternoon service (Table 6). Archbishop Thompson's Visitation Returns for 1865 show about 400 attending the winter services and approximately 1,500 attending the summer services, although this figure does seem to be a little optimistic given the seating numbers.[16] It would, nevertheless, appear from these figures that St Mary's did not lose many members with the building of the new St Thomas' Church in East Sandgate. Seating in the various religious buildings tended to outstrip the needs of the population. For example, Binns has noted that St Martin's Church built on South Cliff had a seating capacity of 1,500, although the whole population of the south side was only 1,606. While built with the aim of also accommodating summer visitors the church was 'far bigger than then, or perhaps ever, required'.[17] Even so, the lower part of the town did not have a church, hence a Chapel of Ease dedicated to St Thomas the Apostle, built in 1839, was opened for worship a year later. Built specifically to accommodate the needs of the poor fishing community on Sandside, it would appear that the clergy had provided some form of welfare services for the local people as in 1904 the vicar, Revd C. H. Clissold, wrote in the parish magazine:

> I came here as your vicar not as a relieving officer. It has, I am afraid been the custom of some to expect, or rather demand as a right, money, coal, or groceries. I want to speak plainly so that these may not mistake me. My work amongst you is to look after your religious life, to hold services, to visit the sick. And, as far as I have the power, to give them a few nourishments.[18]

Given the wide variety of services offered by similar churches in, for example, Grimsby, it would appear that the vicar was pulling back from a period in which more substantial

Table 6 Scarborough Results of the 1851 Census of Religion[19] (excluding Scalby, Scawby, Burnston, Cloughton, Stainton Vale and Harwood Dale)

Church/Chapels/Meeting places	Erected	Seating			Numbers present at 1851 census			Sunday school	
		Free space	Other	Free	am	pm	eve	am	pm
C of E St Mary	Consecrated before 1800	426	875		800	450		76	170
C of E Christ Church	Consecrated 1828	550	750		750		800	115	
C of E St Thomas	Consecrated Oct 1840	340	120		180		120	40	
RC	Erected c1817		170	40	150		230		
Methodists (Wesleyan) George Street	Erected 1847	194	72	80	1,054	Special event day	1,195	61	67
Methodists (Wesleyan) Queen Street	Erected	480	142		60		120		
Methodist Wesleyan Tabernacle	Erected 1838	60	560			30	60		
Methodists (Wesleyan)	Falsgrave Erected 1836	50	120						56
Methodists (PM)	Built 1821 Rebuilt 1839	60	505		300		560	180	
Independent Bar St	Erected 1850	220	200	200	209		406	No school	Sunday
Particular Baptists (Ebenezer)	Erected 1826	185	655		220	50	300	70	85
Independent Old Meeting House	Erected before 1800	40	550	20	167		140	15	
Sailors' Bethel (Bethel Mission)	Erected since 1800	400			36 in week-day meeting			No school	Sunday
Totals		3,405	4,719	304	3,026	533	3,931	557	378

help was offered to the local community. While the new building on Sandside helped to accommodate the numbers, it seems that the Nonconformists were not only growing much faster than the Anglicans but could not provide sufficient seating for the numbers of people attending services. With the growth of Nonconformist chapels in more appropriate locations, the need to build another Anglican Church was considered urgent, and on 26 October 1826, the foundation stone was laid for Christ Church, which was consecrated in August 1828 with seating for 1,300 congregants.

Among the Nonconformists, members of the Tindall family (who were Quakers) in *c.* 1800 converted Scarborough's ancient Town Hall into a chapel in order to serve their employees, who worked in their Sandside shipbuilding yards. The building later passed through many hands, although its function remained religious. In the 1830s it was rented by the Port of Hull Society and later sold to the Wesleyan Methodist Society. The building was subsequently rebuilt as a non-denominational Bethel Mission supported by a number of religious organizations providing services primarily for seamen and their families.

The results of the 1851 census for Scarborough (Table 6) may be compared with the result of Archbishop Herring's Visitation Returns for 1743.[20] Herring identified 120 Presbyterians and 120 Quakers living in the town, and both groups had licensed chapels there. The 1851 census lists the Presbyterians as Independents with seating for approximately 420 and standing room for 200. With an evening congregation of 406 the numbers had increased significantly. Binns has observed that the unusual strength of the Presbyterians in Scarborough may be due to the 'town's long-standing Scottish seafaring connections'.[21] But by 1881 the numbers appear to have decreased significantly in that only a total of ninety-three attended the morning and evening services (and perhaps one-third attended both).

Among the well-known local families who were members of the Scarborough Quakers were the Tindalls and the Rowntrees, and by 1810 there were approximately seventy-four Quakers in the town. The Quakers also had a large community there in mid-century, having opened their meeting house in 1676 with seating for 400 – although no attendance numbers were provided on the 1851 census. Attendance for 1881 was 138 in the morning and twenty-one in the evening (Appendix 6b3).

Other Nonconformist groups have long resided in Scarborough. The Baptists became established here in 1776–7 with the building of a chapel in Longwestgate. The congregation appears to have numbered thirty-eight and rose to sixty-three by 1811. By 1816 the building was enlarged to seat 500 and by the 1851 census attendance was 220 in the morning and 300 in the evening (Table 6), and in 1881 there were 308 attendees at the morning service and 363 in the evening (Appendix 6b3).

In the early eighteenth century a small number of Roman Catholics first met at a house in King Street and later at a small chapel in a house in Westgate. Archbishop Herring's Visitation recorded there being three families of Roman Catholics living in the town in 1743. By 1780 this number had risen to twenty-four families, which was not significantly dissimilar to other Yorkshire coastal communities such as Whitby, where there were twenty-five Roman Catholic families. A number of French emigrant priests joined the group during the years of the Revolution and towards the end of the eighteenth century a group of between forty and eighty members attended meetings overseen by an itinerant priest. There was a Roman Catholic priest in 1788, although a small Catholic chapel had been built in 1783 in Aubrough Street. A larger building was erected in 1809 with seating for forty people, perhaps in anticipation of later changes, especially Roman Catholic emancipation in 1829. The first permanent Roman Catholic priest in the town, the Revd J. Seyne, settled there during the years 1826/31. Then, following some short-term incumbencies, Fr Walker became the town's Catholic priest serving from 1835 to 1871. He established a school and was responsible for the building of a new church, St Peter's, in Castle Road that was begun in 1856 and opened in 1858. Attendance increased, as the 1851 census shows 150 morning attendees and 230 at the evening service. By 1881 the figures were 403 in the morning and 238 in the evening.

While Methodism began in Scarborough before John Wesley's first visit in 1759, by the time of his death in 1791 there were 621 Methodists in the town. By 1851 over 1,300 Wesleyans attended the evening services at four Methodist chapels (Table 6). The first Methodist preaching house in Scarborough was built in 1756 in Foster's Yard, and by 1770 Scarborough was the head of a Methodist circuit. This building was replaced by a new one in Cross Street in 1813, and subsequently replaced by a Methodist chapel in Queen Street in 1839. While Wesleyan Methodism attracted high numbers of 'respectable' dissenters, the poor and the fishing community tended to prefer the Primitive Methodists, and the one Primitive Methodist chapel recorded on the 1851 census shows 560 attending evening service. By 1881 this number had doubled when 1,042 people attended the morning service and 1,212 the evening (Appendix 6b3).

William Clowes preached in the open-air at Scarborough in 1821 and founded the Primitive Methodist Society there. Several temporary places were initially used for worship, the first Primitive Methodist building, a home-made structure, being erected in 1821 by local fishermen in St Sepulchre Street on the site of the Franciscan's Church of the Holy Sepulchre. A more substantial chapel was built in 1830 and the work grew rapidly. In 1840 a second larger building, with seating for 600, was erected on the same site. Expansion continued and in 1861 a new church was built in Aberdeen Walk, named Jubilee, and in 1864 an even larger building was erected and opened a year later, named St Sepluchre Street Methodist church. The chapel was attended by many of the fishing community, and a local fisherman's band was formed. As with the Wesleyan Methodists, numbers were significantly higher in 1881. Hence, with the exception of some smaller groups, the Nonconformists clearly did well in recruiting members. From these figures Methodism was very popular in the town, with the Primitive Methodists tending to attract fewer members than the Wesleyans.

Overall the 1851 census of religion showed a total morning attendance for the fourteen churches as 3,926 and an evening attendance of 3,931. The 1881 figures show a total of 9,042 people attending morning services, 10,515 in the evening, and a general total of 20,707 worshippers, including plural attendance. With a population of 12,158 in 1851 and 30,484 in 1881 over half of the population in 1851 and approximately two-thirds in 1881 appear to have attended services on census Sunday. In other words, the numbers of attendees at church services appear to have increased significantly over the thirty years between 1851 and 1881.

Religion in Grimsby

Given the 'frontier' situation in Grimsby at mid-nineteenth century it might be expected that the churches, especially the Nonconformists, would have responded with enthusiasm to the mission opportunity. Prior to Mann's 1851 religious census and his subsequent report, the lack of church involvement with the lower classes was generally evident, and afterwards there was plenty of incentive for 'aggressive missionary zeal' (as Mann called it), but apart from the work of the Methodists and a few other groups in Grimsby there was little effective response here until the 1870s (Appendix 6a1).

On the other hand the work of the Temperance Associations and Friendly Societies was well established by the 1840s, and when we look back to the period preceding 1870 we find that there was not quite the lack of religious influence in the community than might at first be thought. The previous thirty years were characterized by the pervasive influence of the Temperance Movement, which was not merely aimed at reducing the intake of alcohol but was characterized by a range of moral concerns and social activities. The well-attended meetings and numerous events suggest a comprehensive lifestyle that was later mainly focussed on the churches – especially after 1860 when the movement became dominated by the middle classes.[22]

The embracing of Nonconformist religion by the working class is to some extent reflected in the baptismal records for the Church of England and the Primitive Methodists, where a sudden surge of baptisms occurs in the late 1860s – a situation clearly reflected in Scarborough and Filey (Appendix 7d). The churches were of course very much involved in the Temperance Movement during its heyday, and once the movement lost its impetus for the workers it was perhaps natural for some of the people to retain links with the religious institutions. The Band of Hope (founded in Leeds in 1847) seems to have acted as a link between the early and later developments of the Temperance Movement. In 1883, for example, a memorial Temperance demonstration in Grimsby was attended by 4,056 children (all members of local Sunday schools). The procession extended over a mile in length, with musical concerts by groups a thousand strong, several visiting bands and representatives of twenty-one local schools.[23]

The community of the old town with its culture and stable organizations found itself in conflict with a rapidly growing new town that had little in the way of a coherent culture and identity. The various influences in the new town (small racial, cultural and religious groups, Friendly Societies, teetotalism, churches, etc.) all contributed to an emerging culture that would by 1900 embrace both old and new towns and help to give Grimsby a common identity.

With the apparently sudden urge to build churches, chapels and meeting places, the figures in Appendix 6a1 give the impression that there was a rush in the 1870s to meet a need that had been growing during the previous twenty years (in early 1868 there were only eight churches and chapels in the town, yet twelve years later there were thirty-six). The impression is that of a growing gap between church and population, which was only closed when the population was at its most dramatic (over forty new churches and chapels were built between 1868 and 1900). Part of the reason for this 'explosion' of religious building was linked to the influx of significant numbers of people from specific religious groups, such as the Jewish community, Roman Catholics including

Irish Catholics and the growing number of Primitive Methodists, although we cannot discount competition between the denominations and the desire to build ever more elaborate buildings was a statement of each denomination's status.

The Grimsby Hebrew Congregation founded in 1865 initially met in private houses. Then in 1874 a synagogue was opened in Clyde Street and moved to Strand Street in 1878. This was subsequently replaced with a purpose-built building consecrated in December 1888 as the Sir Moses Montefiore Synagogue in Heneage Road.[24] While the Grimsby Jewish community had no maritime background, members did get involved with the fish trade as trawler owners and fish merchants from at least 1878.

The missionary role of the churches can be seen as one influence among several that helped to establish an emergent culture and identity in Grimsby. It might, for example, be expected that new churches had a period of influence whereby they attracted high numbers in the short term, then lost members before reaching equilibrium. Hence, Gilbert's argument that revivalism is a short-term response to a social and economic crisis is especially pertinent – although care needs taking over how we use the term 'revivalism' here.

Prior to the influence of Methodism in Grimsby there was no real challenge to the authority of the established church. And, despite the Methodist presence since 1773, prior to 1868 there were very few churches and chapels in the town. The various churches and other religious institutions of the medieval era had disappeared, leaving only St James as the parish church. In 1757 the Wesleyans established a meeting house in the Bull Ring, with a second in New Street in 1808 and a third in George Street in 1847. The Congregationalists also opened a chapel in Silver Street in 1779 (but there is a mysterious gap between the years 1823–61, during which there appears to have been no church building). The Baptists opened their first local building in Burgess Street in 1824; and the Primitive Methodists, who had been introduced into the town in 1819, made use of a disused chapel in Loft Street (Later Victoria Street) in 1839, followed by a second venue in Victoria Street in 1859.

The figures for the 1851 religious census are given below (Table 7 – although Cleethorpes and Scartho have been excluded). These show that a total of 5,682 people, including Sunday school children, attended worship on census Sunday. Mann thought that a deduction of one-third would provide a reasonable approximation of actual non-attendance of those attending more than one service. A realistic attendance would therefore be 3,500 individuals – less than half the Grimsby population of 8,860. Church attendance in Grimsby would therefore be similar to the national figure. At this point there appears to have been sufficient seats for the numbers present, although less than half the seating required for the total population – and the Church of England was clearly under-represented, even with the additional figures for Cleethorpes, Clee and Scartho.

Ten years later four new religious buildings had been added – the Primitive Methodist Victoria Street Chapel (1859), the Wesleyan Methodist Victoria Chapel (1860), Spring Church Congregational (1861) and the Primitive Methodist Bethel (1861). Yet the population had more than doubled to 11,067. Despite the enlargement of several churches and chapels the dramatic increase in population during the period 1861–71 left room for a more dynamic response. Hence, from the late 1860s there was

Table 7 Grimsby Results of the 1851 Census of Religion[25]

Churches, chapels, meeting places	Seating			Numbers present at 1851 service			Sunday school	
	Free space	Other	Free	am	pm	eve	am	pm
C of E St James (c. 1865)	168	724	40	450		800	80	
RC the Ropery	16	06	80	80		80		
Baptists Upper Burgess St (c. 1823)	172	378		107		241		
Particular Odd Fellows' Hall Baptists Ladysmith Rd	120	130		70		50	97	97
Methodists Bull Ring Metg House (Wesleyan) (1757)	100	70				170		
Apollo Lodge? (1849)								
Ditto New St Chapel (1808)								
Ditto George St (1846)	50	1,000		796	133	1,010	299	
Methodists (PM) Loft St (1821)	160	530			350	500	136	136
Totals	**786**	**2,928**	**120**	**1,503**	**563**	**2,771**	**612**	**233**
Totals	**(3,834)**	**(4,837)**		**(845)**		**(845)**		

a rapid proliferation of religious building – twenty-four new buildings between 1868 and 1880 and a further seventeen during the next decade (Appendix 6a1). The majority of these buildings were erected in the area bounded by the east side of Alexandra Dock, Cleethorpes Road, Park Street and Pasture Street, to cater for the rapidly expanding population in the area.

Many of the local religious institutions had a specific interest in the fishing community: St Andrew's Church was opened in 1870 in Freeman Street and quickly developed into a major focus for the fishing community. The Church of England baptismal figures (Appendix 7a) show a sharp increase in baptisms for the fisherfolk's children from 1846 to 1868 in Circuit One. With the consolidation of chapels into Circuit Two, numbers continued to increase to over 200 baptisms per year for local fishing families. It is somewhat puzzling, however, to see a dramatic decline in such baptisms during the 1880s, and while St Andrew's Church appears to have benefitted from this decline for a while, we see that the increase was only sustained for a couple of decades. But by 1900 the number here was also in decline. It is possible that in the short term the increasing numbers of baptisms for St Andrew's following 1890 (and the decline in numbers for the Primitive Methodists) merely reflected a change in status (or allegiance) from Nonconformity to the Church of England for some fishing families. On the other hand, the situation might reflect the relative rise and subsequent national decline in church membership. It would be interesting to compare the baptismal figures for the Roman Catholics (who did quite well in recruitment during the late Victorian era) but, sadly, the Roman Catholic baptismal records do not list the father's occupation. Equally, it is difficult to compare the relative success of the Wesleyans with the Primitive Methodists, as the Wesleyans also do not list the father's occupation. Nevertheless, churches and chapels were not built in the knowledge that few people would attend. The dramatic increase in religious buildings suggests that these buildings were being used, and the rise in baptisms of local fishermen's children during the period following 1869 suggests that the local churches and chapels were attracting support – despite some shifts in allegiance.

Religious buildings have a number of functions: they make a statement about the social standing status of the group; they enclose 'sacred space' with the walls indicating a barrier that divides the sacred from the secular; they also make a visual statement about how the religious institution controls access to the sacred. The rapid growth of religious buildings in Grimsby during the 1870s and 1880s demonstrates the growing influence of the religious institutions in and over the local community.

It was during the period following mid-nineteenth century that the Roman Catholics began to re-establish themselves in the community. While there was no significant number of Roman Catholics in the town during the early part of the century the Lincolnshire Returns of the Census of Religious Worship for 1851 show that the local Roman Catholic community met in an old building known as the Ropery, on Cleethorpes Road, under the oversight of their first resident priest, Fr Patrick Joseph Phelan, who had arrived in 1850 'fresh from Maynooth College'. He instigated Sunday services in the town 'in an old shed, known as the "Baltic Warehouse," an old warehouse without windows, but conveniently situated and large enough to contain 500 persons'.[26] This was perhaps a rather optimistic move as, on average, services attracted about eighty people, although the report on the 1851 census by Ambler shows there to have been a small but significant Catholic community made up of mainly Irish immigrants who had been drawn to the town to work on the new docks in 1846:

> From 170 to 200 men, in the prime of early manhood, say 20 to 30 years of age, the majority of whom were married; perhaps five or six had attained the age of forty. They had nearly all of them been brought direct from Ireland by Mr Lyn (Lynch), a contractor, to work as navvies at the making of a Dock. This was a situation nearer to that in the manufacturing towns than in the country mission of rural Lincolnshire.[27]

Despite the growing community, Fr Phelan found it difficult to survive on the small income that the local Roman Catholic community could raise, and he departed for Liverpool in 1852. It was another three years before local Catholics had their own meeting place again, this time in an old warehouse at the River Head – reached by a flight of steps that became known as 'Jacob's Ladder'.

Owen Chadwick says that Irish immigrants were distrusted for their language, their religion and their social habits.[28] Whatever the reason, there was some anti-Catholic feeling in Grimsby during the 1850s, whipped up no doubt by the 'Papal Aggression of 1850'. In this instance it was exacerbated by the visit of the itinerant apostate, Fr Allesandro Gavazzi, who visited Grimsby and held a meeting in the Odd Fellows' Hall, which attracted a good number of Protestants.[29] But as with other anti-Catholic outbursts in Britain during mid-century, the events quickly died down. The local outburst was in any case not simply the growth of the local Catholic community but the sudden influx of Irish navvies in 1851 that numbered 222 (out of the general Grimsby population of 8,860). By 1856 the Revd George Austin Bent was appointed priest in Grimsby, and the town seems to have accepted the Roman Catholic presence.

Financial support for the Grimsby Roman Catholic Mission was provided by Sir John Sutton (a wealthy convert). The search for a suitable site for a church began in earnest during the 1860s, with the land eventually being bought in 1869 at Holm Hill. Unfortunately, Sir John Sutton died in 1872, leaving no funds for the project. Despite such setbacks further land was bought with the help of the Hon. Georgina Fraser, and the church, erected in 1880, was formally opened in August.[30]

Following a scandal in 1883 (the details have not been recorded) this led to Canon Johnson and Fr Barry, the curate, leaving Grimsby. The Bishop of Nottingham, Edward G. F. Bagshaw, supported by Cardinal Manning, asked the Sisters of a relatively new religious order, St Joseph's Sisters of Peace of the Immaculate Conception, to move to Grimsby. A period of unrest followed involving the coming and going of priests, which was finally resolved on 3 February 1884 with the appointment of Fr Joseph Hawkins. On 7 January 1884, Bishop Bagshaw also initiated St Joseph's Confraternity of Peace at St Mary's Church. Named after the confraternity at Knock, Co Mayo, the Grimsby Confraternity's main purpose, and developed by Mother Clare, the leader, was to pray for peace. A magazine was established (the *St Mary's Magazine*) and the confraternity became intimately involved in running local social welfare services, lunches for hungry youths, a library and so on. There were senior and junior sections, with Fr Hawkins as 'Our Rev. President'. Affairs were organized by a committee consisting of a prefect, vice-president, secretary and a committee of six other members: 'membership was conferred after a probationary period when blessed medals were received',[31] all of which points to the importance of the laity in Grimsby Roman Catholic Mission in keeping the Catholic community together.

In 1892 the confraternity began their work with seafarers and fisherlads. A Fisherlads' Committee was established in August 1892 by the Hon. Mrs Georgina Fraser, who appears to have been very active in National Roman Catholic circles, especially in her work on behalf of Catholic seafarers. A year earlier, the Catholic Truth Society (CTS) had formed a committee to provide literature for Catholic seamen. Mgr. John Virtue, Bishop of Portsmouth, had been elected chairman, and the Hon. Mrs Georgina Fraser was appointed secretary. Some members of the international Apostleship of Prayer, led in Britain by Miss Mary Scott-Murray and Miss Margaret Stewart, established the 'work for Catholic bluejackets' and sent out the first batch of literature on 31 July 1891.[32] Father Goldie, SJ, editor of the *Messenger of the Sacred Heart*, agreed to compile a prayer book, which he called *A Guide to Heaven for Use of Those at Sea*. This was subsequently accepted as the official Roman Catholic prayer book in the Royal Navy. This initiative by the CTS and the Apostleship of Prayer was followed up on 3 June 1892 with a meeting of the CTS Congress in Liverpool, where the topic of discussion was 'How can we help our seamen?' (including fishermen), and reference was made to the work in several ports, including that of Canon Hawkins in Grimsby. Father Goldie argued that the work should be organized under the local confraternities rather than being left to the overworked parish priest, and he argued for the establishment of homes similar to those run by Miss Agnes Weston in Portsmouth and Devonport.[33] He also argued for the establishment of a trained Catholic Sea Apostolate, although it was to be another thirty years before this was inaugurated.[34]

Despite Roman Catholic developments that were quietly taking place in British ports during the early 1890s, Catholic fishing apprentices seem to have been largely ignored, and Canon Hawkins and his colleagues were left to their own devices in developing an appropriate response to the needs of the local apprentices. A Fisherlads' Committee was established in 1891 for this purpose as an aspect of the work of St Joseph's Confraternity:

> Notice cards were placed at the Ice company's Fisherlads' Home and at the Home run by the North Sea Trawling Company. A register was started to keep track of Catholics – 37 being noted at this time – and the boys invited to make use of the Guild-room when in port.[35]

A club was opened for the fisherlads and within a year over 100 apprentices were registered, although most were acknowledged to be not 'practical Catholics'. Magazines, books and newspapers were distributed among the boys by the confraternity, and the committee members kept up a correspondence with the Catholic fisherlads at sea. Of this work, Canon Hawkins wrote in *The Tablet* (30 October 1893):

To be chained for long years in apprenticeship to the hard calling of deep-sea fishers . . . penned for ten, twelve or fourteen weeks at a time within the narrow compass of the trawler, the Catholic fisher lad stands unsupported often among a course and ignorant crew – the mark of ribald jeers, his religion the target for every species of contumely. And joined to this is the insidious whispering of the would-be proselytisers – the Protestant chaplain or the self-elected 'Evangelist' of the mission ship.

The first report of the confraternity, published in 1893, gives a number of reasons for the lapsed faith of many young Catholic fisherlads:

(1) There was almost a total failure to notify the removal of boys from schools, unions, reformatories, etc., to the parish priest or other Catholic authority in the fishing ports. Out of 100 lads on the register of St Joseph's Confraternity, only 26 had been notified as coming to Grimsby.
(2) Although the usual age was thirteen to fifteen, only the smallest percentage of these boys had any definite knowledge of the Catholic faith. This want of instruction was the most important factor working for their spiritual death. It was rare to find one who had been confirmed, rarer still to meet one who had received the Sacraments of Penance and the holy Eucharist. Only fifteen lads were entered as confirmed.

Given the problems facing Roman Catholic fisherlads, the confraternity urged that Catholic lads should not be sent to Grimsby, and it was not long before these views were being reported in several newspapers. In the light of the growing national interest, Mrs Fraser asked Fr Hawkins to present a paper to the Annual Conference of the CTS, which was due to be held in Portsmouth. As Fr Hawkins was in America at the time, a prefect of the confraternity formulated a paper with Fr Hawkins and passed it to Mr Britten, the CTS secretary, who read it at the conference. The report urged:

if it were desired for a boy to lose . . . all religious feeling and moral influence – a surer, a more certain method could not be devised than to send him, at the most critical time of his life, friendless into the midst of the open vice and immorality of the greater part of the fishing community of Grimsby. It would be better, infinitely better, for the lads to remain in the poorest capacity on land.

Father Hawkins, wholly supportive of the work among fisherlads, was nevertheless concerned at the lack of practical support from some members of the confraternity. At the half-yearly meeting in 1893 he said that he 'considered the confraternity as a body had failed to render the aid they might have done in parish matters and warned them against the tendency to drift into the spirit of a club, instead of realising the higher ideals of the associations'.[36] Reports before and after this date call for more involvement in social and political activities.

By the mid-1890s the number of fisherlads under the care of the confraternity was reduced, mainly because of the failure of a large fishing company in 1895–6 that resulted in the sale of a hundred fishing smacks. The Annual Report of the Seamen's Branch of the CTS for the same years stated that as a result of the sale 100 fisherlads lost their employment – 40 of whom were said to be Catholics. The last entries in the register of the confraternity appear in 1897, following which the association appears to have ceased and the club rooms closed. Of the 100 fisherlads on the register it seems that almost all were subsequently lost to the Catholic Church.[37] Although other priests followed Canon Hawkins's example there was no coordinated Catholic approach to caring for members of the fishing community until the advent of the international *Apostleship of the Sea* in 1921–2.

Grimsby is a particularly helpful situation in which to explore the development of the various groups and the influence that these groups had on the emerging wider culture. As can be seen the Jewish and Roman Catholic groups were especially active in working for the establishment of a clear identity in the town. Members of these groups tended to seek support from each other and to embrace their own cultural traditions. Other groups aided this process by seeking to live in close proximity (such as the fishermen and their families from Sherringham). Given the tendency of such groups to seek support from group members this raises a number of questions: Is there a pattern in the kinds of movements and groups in the development of a community and culture? Do the different movements and groups have specific functions in an emergent community and culture? Could specific movements have different functions – each being applicable to a specific type of social group development? Do the religious movements impact upon the local culture at specific points in their development? What is the cultural function of the religious movements?

The groups mentioned earlier, with perhaps the addition of the Primitive Methodists, do demonstrate a need to seek security. This involves living in close proximity, maintaining traditions, often including both formal and popular religious perspectives. Telling stories that relate to the history of the group is also an important factor, not least in that a number of the groups could recall the persecution they faced in the early development of the wider community. Marriage between group members was initially strongly supported, although with time the groups tended to see marriages occur between insiders and outsiders. These kinds of activities are present in a number of groups that have moved into British towns and cities, hence the pattern appears to be a common one.

A further important factor in the development of an emerging culture is the gradual assimilation of the wider culture's norms, something that takes place over several generations. This process is a common psychological one in that the first generation tends to be very idealistic, retaining a strong attachment to its earlier beliefs and practices. The second generation tends to rebel and seek new ways of doing things, usually influenced by the wider culture. The third generation often seeks to recapture the idealization of the first generation but also engages with the wider community – and it is among this group that members tend to establish themselves extrovertly in the locality with important social, economic and political roles. Such examples here are the civic and business roles in Grimsby that Primitive Methodists, Jewish and Roman Catholic individuals and groups attained towards the end of the nineteenth century. There are, therefore, a number of important points in the development of a wider social identity among group members. The norms of the group and of the wider community tend to merge and a sense of a local culture gradually emerges and develops. Those groups from specific religious traditions tended to have a significant influence on the development of the community, perhaps because their concept of a godly community was clearly developed. Their support for the Temperance Movement and its ideals was also especially evident.

Perhaps significantly each of these groups was motivated by religious beliefs and practices, and each had experienced a degree of opposition and abuse in their early establishment in the town. Even those groups with a common geographical basis, such as the fishing families from Sherringham, maintained a strong religious foundation – although they tended to merge more quickly with the wider community. More recently those fishermen from Denmark who settled in Grimsby during the 1950s and 1960s gradually assimilated to the extent that their own culture and traditions were largely abandoned as the local fishing industry diminished and pubs and centres of Danish social life closed.

One other movement that had a significant influence on the emerging culture was that of the maritime missions. These groups have been largely ignored by historians, although like the Temperance Movement they had a significant impact on the development of the wider culture and community.

The developing work of maritime missions in fishing communities

Each of the fishing communities along the Yorkshire and Lincolnshire coasts had maritime missions, and the communities were visited regularly by maritime missionaries. Yet it was not until 1881–2 that a dedicated maritime mission (the Mission to Deep Sea Fishermen) concerned itself solely with fishing communities.[38] Why this should be the case – at the very point where the fishing industry had reached its zenith – is not immediately clear. Nevertheless, there were a number of precedents here. Even prior to the nineteenth century the French had established the Confrérie du Saint-Sacrament (1662–1727), an organization concerned with the French fishermen working in Newfoundland and Iceland. During the early nineteenth century there were numerous local societies that established facilities and welfare support for seamen generally, including fishermen and their families. Then in 1850 Thomas Rosie inaugurated the Scottish Coast Missions.[39] From the 1860s the High Church Society, St Andrew's Waterside Mission (SAWM),[40] worked from a parochial base with the fishermen and their families around the coast. And several other societies, such as the Missions to Seamen and the British and Foreign Sailors' Society, employed staff to occasionally visit the North Sea fishermen during the 1870s.

The development of maritime missions during the nineteenth century was complex, with organizations springing up all around the coast, as well as on canals, lakes and rivers. Many of these missions, unlike the earlier societies, were influenced primarily by evangelicalism and embraced the desire to win converts. Some were lay-led, others were initiated and developed by local clergy, but in all cases they were a new development that bridged the gap between formal and popular religion, including the use of vessels as sailing churches and hospitals, services at sea and a range of support services on shore.[41] The development of the work, however, generally followed four phases (*pre-Reformation, post-Reformation, Bethel Unions* and *National Maritime Missions*), and the relationship between the churches and maritime communities along the Yorkshire and Lincolnshire coasts followed the national pattern.

(1) *Pre-Reformation*

During the pre-Reformation phase seafarers were seen as belonging to the parish community, and churches were often dedicated to saints with a maritime connection especially Sts Peter, Andrew and Nicholas (St Hilda's Abbey at Whitby, for example, was originally called St Peter's), and Mary (Stella Maris) also played a significant role. Each community also had its own guilds and confraternities, some of which were dedicated to seafarers, and members were given support in times of need.[42]

Despite the advent of the Reformation and the Dissolution of the Monasteries in Britain the disrupted pattern of religious support networks in seaports lingered for some time, although this was supplemented to some extent by the presence of naval chaplains on board ship. The parish system continued to exert a strong influence, but the guilds and confraternities gradually gave way to a range of welfare agencies.

(2) *Post-Reformation*

The post-Reformation phase saw a shift away from an emphasis on parish support and by the late eighteenth century the gradual emergence of national organizations, including associations concerned with the distribution of Christian scriptures and literature. Reports from the Anglo-French Wars made the plight of men working in the navy well known, and various societies were established to provide literature and moral support for the men. Benevolent societies, welfare agencies and Friendly Societies (such as the Loyal Order of Ancient Shepherds in Robin Hood's Bay and Filey's Ravine Lodge of Loyal and Independent Oddfellows) were organized during the nineteenth century to meet the needs of fishing communities, especially medical needs in periods before the advent of the National Health Service. The early nineteenth century also saw the establishment of societies along the Yorkshire coast, and elsewhere, intended to help the families of fishermen who had been lost at sea, such as the 'Flamborough Fishermen's Fund' of 1809 and the 'Fisherman's Refuge' established in 1834 for the families in Staithes and Runsick.[43] The *Scarborough Mercury* for 1898 also drew attention to 'The Loss of Filey Fishermen' and advocated the opening of a subscription fund.

The late eighteenth and early nineteenth centuries also saw the establishment of a number of societies with the aim of making religious literature more readily and widely available. These included the 'Naval and Military Bible Society', founded in 1779, the interdenominational 'Religious Tract Society' (1799) and the 'British and Foreign Bible Society' (1804), although all had long been preceded by the High Church's 'Society for Promoting Christian Knowledge', founded in 1701. These various national societies had a marked effect in that numerous auxiliaries sprung up around the coast, including the influential 'Scarborough Auxiliary Bible Society' in 1812. This society later joined with the 'Scarborough Bible Association', which had John Rowntree (the Quaker) as president. The society had a large Bible and Tract depot and was joined by a shop belonging to SPCK.[44] Whitby, too, had a number of such societies, including the 'Whitby Auxiliary Bible Society' 1812), the 'Whitby Bible Association' (1813) and the 'Whitby Marine Bible Association' (1816). Other societies were established along the coast either as auxiliaries or as independent organizations, such as the 'Sandsend and Lythe Bible Association' (1813), the 'Hull Bible Society' (1817) and a Bible Society at Bridlington. This proliferation of literature distribution and support organizations led in turn to the advent of the Bethel Unions.

(3) *The Bethel Unions*

The third phase, the growth of the Bethel Unions, emerged out of a number of waves of influence. They appear to have had their genesis in the 'Strangers' Friend' societies established during the early nineteenth century, although the oldest such society would appear to have been 'The Benevolent, or Strangers' Friend Society', established by the Methodist John Gardner in London in 1785. This society developed from the visiting societies that began in the mid-eighteenth century with regular visiting of sick people especially by the Methodist fellowship.[45]

The Bethel Unions then applied the work of pastoral support among the seafaring communities and offered a larger support organization that had not previously been the case. The Revd George Charles Smith was an especially major influence here. While serving in the navy he became aware of the lack of contact for naval seafarers from those on shore, and he began the Naval Correspondence Society in 1809. He later trained as a Baptist minister and established a number of mission organizations aimed at providing, among other things, welfare services for seafarers. In the meantime other developments were taking place, including a religious revival on the Thames in 1814 that became the genesis of the later Bethel Movement. This movement derived its name from the Bethel flag, designed by Wesleyans at Rotherhithe and eventually adopted by various maritime mission societies. Copies of the flag were presented to ships' captains who would hoist them on the Sabbath day to invite seamen to attend religious meetings on board their vessels.[46] Among the many such Bethel Unions were the British and Foreign Seamen's Friend Society and Bethel Union (1819) and the Port of London and Bethel Union Society (1827). Local societies were also formed, such as the Port of Hull Society (19 April 1821) and the Seamen's Friend and Bethel Union at Whitby (1822). These Bethel companies appear to have declined by mid-century and the term ceased to be used.[47]

There were therefore numerous rivulets that fed into this general movement towards organized maritime missions, but it was to be the 1870s before a concern was expressed for fishermen and fishing communities as a discreet group. This later work had been anticipated to some extent on local bases by, for example, the boat-building Tindal family in Scarborough who purchased and converted Scarborough's old Town Hall building into a chapel *c.* 1800, which served both Tindal's workmen and the local fishermen. While the building eventually passed through various hands, including the Port of Hull Society and the Methodist Society, it remained in use for the benefit of seafarers as a non-denominational Bethel Mission throughout much of the nineteenth century.

(4) *National Maritime Missions*
The fourth phase was the emergence towards the mid-nineteenth century of national maritime missions, including the Anglican Episcopal Floating Church Society (1825) that later became the Thames Church Mission (1844); the interdenominational British and Foreign Sailors' Society (1833); the very independent evangelical Seamen's Christian Friend Society (1846); the Broad Church Missions to Seamen (1856); and the non-denominational and evangelical Mission to Deep Sea Fishermen (1881–2) that later achieved the prefix 'Royal' in 1897.[48] These initiatives have been noted by others; for example, Kennerley has argued that by the 1860s maritime missions were generally supervised by officially appointed leaders among the clergy and laity.[49] The developments during this period were aimed at providing a dual service, later epitomized by the MDSF, which displayed its aims on the bows of its vessels: 'Preach the Word'; 'Heal the Sick.' This approach reflected the wider theological aims of missions in the second half of the nineteenth century that there would be an active concern for the body as well as the soul.

Organized maritime missions

The development from local maritime missions and church pastoral support to organized maritime missions was influenced by a number of factors. These include the work of itinerant ministries such as those by John Wesley, G. F. Angus, Carl von Bülow and John Oxtoby. The advent of literature distribution societies in the late eighteenth century and the growing influence of the *New Dissent*, especially Wesleyan Methodism, were of particular significance, as also was the emergence of the wider mission movement, evangelicalism, revivalism, Sunday schools and the later influence of Sabbatarianism, Temperance and teetotalism. The declining influence of Anglicanism around the turn of the nineteenth century allowed the New Dissent to develop maritime missions on a wide base. Among these new groups Primitive Methodism is often cited as drawing particular support from mining and fishing communities, although relatively little research has been done with regard to the role of the Primitive Methodists in fishing communities (the work of David Clark and Stephen Hatcher are nevertheless of note here).[50]

The development of maritime missions around the coast led to a number of innovations including initially the use of old hulks (survivals of the Anglo-French Wars) refitted as floating churches and chapels. The Port of Hull Society (1821), for example, obtained a hulk, the *VALIANT*, and opened this as a seamen's chapel on 3 October 1821. Other ports along the Yorkshire coast had insufficient depth of water to take the hulks (although a number were situated in the River Humber and other major rivers as isolation hospitals, prisons and training ships). Practically all the larger ports had such 'floating churches', and in 1827 Dr William Scoresby of Whitby moved to Liverpool to become chaplain to the Liverpool Mariners' Church Society, based on the Liverpool maritime floating church, HMS *TEES*.[51] In London the Episcopal Floating Church Society established the 'Episcopal Ark' (in May 1827) at Rotherhithe on the Thames, practically opposite the previously established 'Nonconformist Ark' (opened in May 1818). The Episcopal Ark, however, struggled to attract seamen to the services, and its operations were eventually abandoned.

The Nonconformist missions flourished with innumerable groups and organizations establishing maritime missions. The Port of Hull Society also established an East Coast Mission and employed itinerant missionaries to work along the Yorkshire coast and at Grimsby. The Wesleyan Methodists were also active here, although Kendall's history gives the impression that the Primitive Methodists had little to do with seafarers until their establishment in Hull during early 1819, by which time the Bethel Movement had taken hold and the Wesleyans had long since established themselves in many of the coastal communities. Several references in the early Primitive Methodist Magazine, however, suggest that the Primitive Methodists were familiar with the developing work among seafarers. The early magazines reprinted examples of this work taken from the maritime mission literature, hence there was clearly some cross-fertilization. Apart from this use of such literature there was very little mention of the maritime missions in either the Primitive Methodist Magazine or the diaries of Clowes and other itinerant Primitive Methodist missionaries. As a result, it is difficult to gauge the degree of cross-fertilization with any accuracy.

While the main work here was undertaken by Nonconformists, the Anglicans became involved at an early stage, and a number of Anglican organizations were developed, including the Episcopal Floating Church Society (1825), the Thames Church Mission (1844), the Missions to Seamen (1856) and the SAWM (1864). The growing professionalism of the clergy in the revitalized Anglican Church during the late nineteenth century provided the opportunity to become more familiar with the communities they served, and during the 1870s and 1880s a significant number of Anglican clergy in fishing ports gained the respect of their parishioners as a result of their local engagement and commitment. High Church Anglicans around the coast established close links with the SAWM, and those with more liberal leanings supported the Missions to Seamen. Both these organizations provided chaplains for work at sea and in the harbours during the 1870s, and the SAWM purchased some vessels to enable extended clergy visits to the North Sea fishing fleets during the 1890s.[52] The Vicar of St Thomas' Church in Scarborough became the chaplain of the Missions to Seamen when their premises were opened in 1891, and after the closure of the premises in 1938 St Thomas' established the St Thomas' Mission and Seamen's Institute, which provided a range of facilities and services especially for the fishermen and visiting Scottish herring girls.[53]

The SAWM also supported numerous local clergy in their work with fishing communities and led to the development of at least one local organization – the North

Sea Church Mission, established by the Revd Forbes Phillips, Vicar of Gorleston in 1894. In Grimsby the Revd Meddings visited the fishermen at sea on the specially adapted vessel, the *GOSHAWK*, which, having been donated to the St Andrew's Waterside Church Mission (SAWCM), was loaned for Mr Meddings' use. The Grimsby mission also made use of a small vessel on the docks, the *WATER KELPIE*, to provide pastoral support for the fishermen. In June 1895, Mr Meddings' curate, Mr Best, joined the North Sea Church Mission as a 'sailing curate' attached to two vessels, the *SAPPER* and the *GOSHAWK*; and another Grimsby curate eventually became the Vicar of St Thomas' Church in Scarborough. As a result, there was a good deal of cross-fertilization among the various east coast maritime missions. The link between St Thomas' Church and the SAWM was established in 1876 when the Revd W. C. Downing gave his support to the idea, and some 'ladies established Sunday classes for the fisherlads'.[54] The work included the distribution of books, the holding of Bible and Sunday classes for the fisher lads and other events. The last reference to the link with the SAWCM appears in the SAWCM Report for 1880. Hence, the Revd Clissold's criticism of local people for approaching the vicar of St Thomas' Church for welfare support seems to be an implicit reference to this earlier phase of the local work.

Despite constant problems of funding and the lack of a permanent mission vessel, the Grimsby work developed at an accelerating rate with ten members of staff employed in 1892 and a range of buildings being erected to meet the demand:

> Seven hundred and eight smacks were supplied with parcels of reading (between June and December, 1890), their delivery on board giving good opportunity for personal intercourse and intimacy with the crews. One of our large Day Schools has been used as a Mission Room for Sunday Evening services, and has had a regular congregation of from 100 to 200 people; thus, preparing for the new Fishermen's Church which is being built close by.[55]

The SAWCM, with its headquarters based at Gravesend, used the model of support that was somewhat different to the other maritime missions in that while it provided financial support for the work of clergy in the various ports it encouraged the clergy to work from a parochial base and to supplement funds provided by the national society by raising funds themselves for the local work. The society did well during the 1890s, but the growing demand for its support led to problems in the early twentieth century resulting in the work being taken over by the Missions to Seamen, as was the work of the Thames Church Mission. The SAWCM and the TCM were two extremes of churchmanship – the High Church and the evangelicals. Other evangelical maritime missions remained independent (especially the Royal National Mission to Deep Sea Fishermen and the British and Foreign Sailors' Society, and the extremely evangelical and fiercely independent Seamen's Christian Friend Society). Of all the various groups, however, it was the RNMDSF that remained the only mission concerned solely with fishing communities.

The mass influx of literature during the early 1800s might suggest a growth in literacy, although there is no significant evidence for this development until the advent of universal education. The Sunday schools, too, for all their activity, do not seem to have had a significant impact upon literacy. Even so, the societies responsible for distributing Christian literature were readily welcomed into the coastal communities of Yorkshire and North-East Lincolnshire – one of the first such societies in North Yorkshire being established at Whitby in 1812.[56] It is perhaps significant that the Sunday school movement and the Missions movement developed during the same period, although the quality of teaching in private Sunday schools was variable. Even with the later move towards the more respectable public denominational Sunday schools, there is still little evidence of improvements in literacy among working people. John Ruston has argued that education during the nineteenth century, where it existed, was of generally poor quality, with 30 per cent of males and 50 per cent of females being illiterate in the early Victorian period (although this percentage varied according to the existence of schools). Where there was growth in education provision during this early period, such as at Whitby, this tended to be for fee-paying academies, and these were of course for the middle classes.[57]

A significant aspect of organized maritime missions is that like the Primitive Methodists, the initiatives often came from ordinary working men and women – although Sandy Calder has argued for the middle-class origins of Primitive Methodism.[58] It was not until the 1860s and 1880s, especially with the growth of groups like the Salvation Army, that people began to acknowledge that working people were generally more influenced by people from their own class.[59] Many of the missionaries employed by the Primitive Methodists were ordinary working people who had a talent for preaching, although the quality of the preaching was not always high. Similarly, many of the missionaries working for the maritime missions were working people, and this was especially the case with the advent of the Mission to Deep Sea Fishermen, when ex-fishermen were used to sail the vessels, acting as missionaries when they could. Some such eventually became well-known missionaries in their own right, such as William Smedley, one-time skipper of the RNMDSF vessels (later a missionary for the Sailors' Children's Society of Hull), who established and ran the Smedley Institute in Grimsby during the early twentieth century.

The Roman Catholics were somewhat slow to develop their maritime mission work in Britain perhaps because of other more demanding concerns such as adjusting to the need to fully establish a hierarchy following emancipation in 1829, and the somewhat unfortunate political fallout from Archbishop Wiseman's attempt to exert the Roman Catholic presence more forcefully in 1850. Yet Roman Catholics had been present and held positions of responsibility well before 1829 in coastal communities such as Scarborough. In Grimsby, too, St Joseph's Confraternity was established in 1891 with a particular concern for Catholic fishing apprentices. It was presumably not accidental that the establishment of the confraternity here followed in the wake of not only Archbishop Manning's successful arbitration in the London Dock Strike of 1889 but also Pope Leo XIII's encyclical of 1891, *Rerum Novarum*, in which Catholics were encouraged to become directly involved in helping to improve the living and working conditions of the poor. While the Apostleship of the Sea did not formally come into being until 1920–1, the work had its genesis much earlier with the brief development of a 'maritime apostolate' in 1895, although this did not survive the ravages of the 1914–18 war.[60]

Overall, the range of work carried on by maritime missions in British fishing communities was staggering. From the 1880s, there were vessels working among the fishing fleets as churches, chapels and hospital ships that provided literature, woollens, and other day-to-day necessities for the fishermen; on shore the provision of orphanages, reading rooms, help with letter writing, saving schemes, support for families (especially in times of illness, accident and loss) and accommodation as an alternative to that provided by crimps and the more disreputable hostels. The missions were also active in providing maritime training schools so that men and boys could be encouraged to develop their maritime skills and thereby rise in their profession.

At the end of the day the aim of the nineteenth-century maritime missions was generally to support the churches rather than to supplant them – although each mission tended to have its own particular theological slant and churchmanship whether this was High Church, Broad Church, Evangelical or Roman Catholic.

Conclusion

In conclusion, it is clear that religion, whether formal or popular, played an important part in the life of fishing communities. This chapter has offered a brief overview of formal religion in the three fishing Yorkshire communities of Filey, Scarborough and the North Lincolnshire town of Grimsby.

This is complemented by an overview of the work of maritime missions, a more complete study of which is to be found in the author's book *Fishing for Souls* published in 2018.[61] However, I have here offered a brief summary of the development of seafarer's missions from pre-Reformation times to the advent of organized maritime missions in the twentieth century, a more complete overview of which can be found in Roald Kverndal's book *Seamen's Missions*, published in 1986.[62] This final section is important in that it prepares the way for the study of revivalism in fishing communities in Chapter 5, not least because of the presence in the work of maritime missions of formal and popular religion.

Revivalism in fishing communities

Introduction

Following the death of John Wesley in 1791 there was a fragmentation of Wesleyan Methodism that led, on the one hand, to a conservative, bureaucratic and middle-class emphasis in the parent organization and, on the other hand, to the emergence of a number of Methodist sects that placed a much greater emphasis on relating to the working classes. Such movements included the Primitive Methodists, Magic Methodists, Band Room Methodists and, in the South West, the Bible Christians. Of these the Primitive Methodists became the more prominent and were especially influential among traditional working-class communities. Some scholars, however, view the concept of 'traditional communities' as problematic. M. Estelle Smith, for example, says, 'There is, of course, no such thing as a "traditional culture", if by that we imply longstanding, unchanging, and somehow more authentic than what will be tomorrow. Such traditional innovative contrast is a heuristic fiction of historical analysis.'[1] Open-air and camp meetings were popular, and American preachers, such as Lorenzo Dow, visited Britain to help and advise on the running of such meetings. Despite the early opposition he faced from the Wesleyans, the Primitive Methodists quickly warmed to Dow and adopted the use of open-air and camp meetings. Such was the impact that these meetings became a popular form of Christian mission well into the twentieth century. Wesleyan Methodism also experienced a number of internal splits, such as the Wesleyan Reform Union and the United Methodist Free Church, reacting to what was seen as the bureaucratization of the Methodist parent body.

Up until the early nineteenth century, revival was thought of as essentially spontaneous with God's spirit moving where it willed, but between 1825 and 1830 the American Charles Grandison Finney introduced (or at least made popular) a range of techniques that he called the 'new measures'. His huge success in a spectacular series of revivals, especially in the cities, brought his ideas to the attention of a wide audience. These 'new measures' included the introduction of lengthy evening services, prayer meetings, publicity, well-organized and coordinated meetings and the introduction of an 'anxious bench' (a bench at the front of the meeting to which ardent enquirers were invited during the service for counselling and support). His success ensured that his approach was taken seriously.

The wide range of approaches to revival was to have a significant influence on the New Dissent as it emerged in Britain during the early nineteenth century, and Moody and Sankey were able to capitalize on Finney's ideas during their visits to Britain through the 1870s and 1880s. This new aspect of revival, often referred to as revivalism, also had a strong influence on numerous movements during the late nineteenth century, such as the Salvation Army (organizations that also embraced other influences such as social Christianity, which had developed in the wake of the failure of Chartism). During the twentieth century the Keswick conventions and the Holiness, Pentecostal and Charismatic movements developed their approaches based primarily on the influence of revivalism, as did a number of significant American personalities such as Billy Sunday, Aimee Semple McPherson and Billy Graham. More recently the televangelists embraced much that is common within the revivalist tradition – although abuses, especially among the televangelists, during the late twentieth century gave rise to much criticism and cynicism.

Not surprisingly, the complexities of revival and its many innovations have given rise to a variety of perspectives on the nature of the phenomenon. There is in particular a good deal of confusion over the meaning of the term 'revival', as well as over the distinction between the terms 'revival' and 'revivalism'. Those individuals and groups influenced by Calvinism were concerned that revival should be essentially spontaneous, although they were prepared to accept new members resulting from organized revivals (commenting that God could make good use of such foolishness!). This early period saw revival as the spontaneous eruption of spiritual fervour resulting in the conversion of many. Some revivalists, however, were concerned at the apparently uncontrolled and raucous meetings resulting from the application of Finney's new measures; and there was always the problem of keeping members who had joined churches and chapels at the height of a very emotional experience.

Distinctions between *revival* and *revivalism* tend to focus on the change of emphasis brought about by Finney and especially following c. 1840 (John Kent refers to the period 1857–62[2]) when the emphasis on spontaneous revivals gave way to planned revivals. Such distinctions, however, tend to be oversimplistic and some scholars use the two terms interchangeably. For the sake of convenience, we will use the term 'revival' throughout, using the term 'revivalism' only where scholars make use of it.

It was often the case that 'new converts' were apparently church members, who had simply had their faith revitalized (a criticism later aimed at the Billy Graham meetings). Hence it was with this in mind that the Wesleyans preferred to talk of 'spiritual revitalization' or 'renewal' rather than revival.[3] Others, such as Currie, Gilbert and Horsley, argued that there was a need for regular revivals partly to ensure members retained an enthusiasm for their faith, but also to recruit new members (perhaps from the new generation) to offset those who had moved or died. This involved a process of periodic renewal identified by Currie et al., in their five-phase cycle of religious development: *depression, activation, revival, deactivation and declension.*[4]

This chapter looks at the influence of revival/revivalism on fishing communities and in particular makes use of the statistical data compiled from records in Grimsby, Scarborough and Filey. Comparisons are also made with similar revivals in Cornwall and Scotland, and explore the nature and influence of revivals, especially along the Yorkshire and Lincolnshire coasts.[5] Both North-East Scotland and Western Islands experienced numerous revivals throughout the nineteenth century and especially in 1922 with the return home of the fishermen and Herring girls after the fishing season.

Much of the academic research on religious revivals has tended to concentrate on the mechanisms involved and the social, economic and political environment in which revivals are said to be likely to occur. Such conditions have been variously noted by Halévy, Hobsbawm, Thompson, Gilbert, Bebbington and others who have offered variants on the theme here.[6] Hobsbawm, for example, argued that Methodism and radicalism were similar expressions of profound dissatisfaction with the status quo, hence Methodism and radicalism are different expressions of the same phenomenon. He also argued for a cyclical pattern in that intense religious and political excitement often coincided during the period 1790–1840. Thompson pressed the argument a little further and attributed the high working-class response to Methodism during the Napoleonic era to 'political and temporal frustration'. For him revivals were seen in the negative sense of compensation for political failure among the working people, which he referred to as the 'chiliasm of despair'.[7] There certainly seems to have been some evidence for Thompson's thesis; and Hobsbawm in his study of Captain Swing asked, if terrorism was the active response to defeat, was religion the passive?[8] The significant growth of Primitive Methodism during the 1830s, reflected in the church and chapel membership numbers for Filey, Scarborough and Grimsby (Appendices 6a4, 6b3–6b4, 6c3), occurred in those areas of the country most affected by the Swing Riots. On the other hand, perhaps the practical support given to the agricultural labourers during the riots left people feeling more sympathy with the Primitive Methodists than the established church, which tended to ally itself with the more 'respectable classes'. Even so, following 1835 the religious revival had begun to subside. In retrospect Hobsbawm's suggestion that religion is the passive alternative to political activism is perhaps an oversimplification of the situation, especially as the model does not allow for the range of options (such as education, migration and emigration) available to working people.

Gilbert, in turn, modified Thompson's thesis by arguing that revivalism is a short-term, short-lived solution to radical social, economic and political change and that revivalism helps those involved to cope with severe social and economic depression.[9] Others have taken a different route, and Baxter, for example, in his work *The Great Yorkshire Revival of 1792-96* pointed out that this revival occurred during a period of political repression. But he goes on to say that while periods of social, economic and political unrest could be important factors in revivals, other factors could be equally relevant (such as a large movement of population resulting from urbanization or emigration). Change also resulted from the collapse of copper mining in mid-1860s Cornwall and the widespread onset of a particularly virulent disease such as cholera.[10] At the same time, Baxter (anticipating the work of later researchers) went on to argue that religious revivals have an internal psychological dynamic of their own.

Despite a few exceptions, then, there was until recently a generally undue emphasis on the external conditions. But this can be very misleading and a later generation of researchers, such as Baxter, Julia Stewart Werner, Rule, Hempton and Bebbington, argued for a different emphasis.[11] Drawing on the work of Finney and perhaps also Baxter, Werner supported the argument that revivals have an inner dynamic of their own. Discussing the Wesleyan revivals of the late eighteenth and early nineteenth centuries she moved the discussion on by clearly articulating important elements of the internal dynamic, which included a dependence on four factors:

(1) a *network* of preachers;
(2) a *desire* for revival;
(3) acceptance of *innovations*; and
(4) a means of *communicating* revival experiences in the circuits.[12]

These factors also clearly embrace a degree of heightened *expectation*. Nevertheless, a situation reflecting these factors alone may be insufficient to bring about revival. It is perhaps also important to note that these factors indicate a good deal of internal harmony within the churches and chapels concerned with the expectation of revival. Luker in particular pointed out that 'there are very real pitfalls in approaching revivals essentially from the outside and attempting to explain their occurrence merely or primarily by reference to secular trends or preoccupations', and he went on to say that in the case of Cornish revivals 'the actual mechanism of revival was initially internal: Cornish revivals universally had their origins within the Methodist Societies'.[13] Rule supported Luker's thesis maintaining that 'revivals' in Cornwall are best understood in terms of a dynamic internal to the local religious culture. Despite Rule's claim that revivals were not always linked to outside problems, he did point out on several occasions that revivals in Cornwall took place during times of difficulty. For example, 'the 1826 revival at Mousehole broke out when no fish had been caught for some time. That of 1848, like that of 1831–2, was at least intensified by outbreaks of cholera', as with other communities.[14]

Taking account of the earlier research, Janice Holmes pointed out that 'New interpretations of revivalism are at pains to stress the importance of community, regional identities and social factors like the threat of cholera, mining disasters or the influential American revivalists'. Even so, she pointed out that 'Most historians now recognise that there is no direct correlation between the outbreak of a revival and either economic depression or the failure of political radicalism'.[15] Other scholars have been more willing to accept that it is not helpful to reject the external factors completely. Hempton, for example, offered a more balanced view, arguing that 'Although there is some evidence to link revivalism to economic dislocation and political repression, there is a general acknowledgement that religious revivals had internal social and psychological dynamic regardless of external circumstances'.[16] He then went on to argue for the importance of two fundamental factors within Methodist communities – a *desire for revival* and a *sense of expectancy*. Luker, too, reinforced this need to take internal factors into account:

> The case of Cornish revivals suggests a general need to delineate with greater care the mechanisms of revivals and to focus on internal developments within the churches just as much as on external circumstances which might help or hinder their progress.[17]

If an emphasis is placed on both the internal and external factors, it would be helpful to identify those situations that are conducive to a revival (although of course research in this area, perhaps of necessity, has been conducted *after* the revival has occurred). But such a strategy is by no means a simple option, as the various theories put forward indicate. Hempton pointed out that linking Methodist growth to national periods of social, political and economic change and trying to impose inflexible models are fraught with difficulties. As with Rule, Hempton argued strongly for an emphasis on regional and chronological interpretations.

Internal and external factors in revivals

Perhaps the most we can argue is that given certain favourable internal and external conditions a revival is a possibility, although this presupposes a culture in which revivals are an accepted form of religious experience. And whether it remains local or expands to a wider community also depends on a range of conducive factors. Prior to *c.* 1840 such revivals may well have appeared to be miraculous, but as religious evangelical leaders moved towards supporting 'organized revivals' the situation was no longer clear-cut. Some organized revivals would work in the face of difficult social, economic and political conditions, because the internal and external conditions were right. Others had little or no effect despite the internal and external conditions being favourable. There must also have been many instances of apparent revival, where the enthusiasm of those involved simply caught on with local people and then petered out with little lasting effect.

In the case of the Filey Revival of 1823, Valenze has argued that not only did revivalism occur during a period of rapid social and political change, the Primitive Methodists, with their embracing of local customs, festivals and superstitious beliefs, provided a link between official and popular Christianity – thereby inculcating a sense of security and stability for the local population as the old culture moved towards the new. The Wesleyans had by this period moved much closer to religious orthodoxy where there was resistance to 'popular religion'. The Anglican Church during this period had no resident clergy in Filey, and no other denomination had a wide appeal. Valenze summed up the situation with the observation that 'The fisherfolk had religion in "three layers" . . . they were ardent Primitive Methodists, they gave the local church its due, and they were steadfastly superstitious'.[18]

The sense of heightened tension resulting from the incongruity present between the internal and external conditions of a religious group may result in a sense of anxiety that can achieve some relief via the experience of revival and the related social support. Indeed, the inner state of the individuals concerned was such that a resolution of the increasing anxiety was actively sought and embraced. And while there may have been no conscious acknowledgement of this, the resulting experience of revival was expressed in physical and intellectual ways that indicate a release of anxiety. If no resolution was achieved, then the group may well have found itself faced with members drifting away from the faith – not necessarily because they had lost their faith, but because the sustained stress and anxiety was too much to bear and could quickly turn from a positive into a negative experience. This situation has been observed and analysed, though in different situations, by numerous people, including Leon Festinger, Jane Nadel-Klein and Ralph W. Hood.

In analysing group dynamics of millenarian cults, Festinger argued that disconfirmation of a group's strongly held beliefs (given certain preconditions) will result not in an admission of failure but in more active proselytizing.[19] Thus with more people believing the message, the psychological need for reinforcement is applied, and the members of the committed group continue to believe but with increased conviction. A response to the disconfirming event, Festinger argued, is therefore a motivating factor that seeks some form of resolution, just as hunger impels us to seek food. The expectation of revival, while not meeting all of Festinger's criteria (although it may well have done with those groups experiencing a millennialistic fervour), does, nevertheless, bear some similarities to his general point that the experience of tension and anxiety clearly needs some form of resolution.

Jane Nadel-Klein approached the problem from a different perspective. Her research during the 1970s concentrated upon the experience of a small Scottish fishing community when a major oil base was established close to the village. Small fishing communities tend to be very inward-looking and self-sufficient, not least because they have low status in the wider community; hence, with the threat of destruction to the traditional way of life for the fishing community by an oil giant, members became more introspective and allied themselves to the Calvinistic Methodist chapel. Nadel-Klein argued that in doing this they were choosing a religious perspective that reassured the people of their equality with others before God and hence gave them the status not otherwise available or obtainable. The revival here may therefore be seen as a short-term response to a particularly difficult situation – a point close to that argued by Gilbert.

The result of such a state of internal–external tension also has much in common with mystical experience. Ralph H. Hood's experiments with nature mysticism are therefore interesting in the present context.[20] He talked of factors affecting the 'Set' (internal) and the 'Setting' (external) conditions, and hypothesized that in the context of solitary nature experience 'set stress and setting stress incongruity' (high set stress/ low setting stress, or vice versa) would serve to elicit more frequent reports of mystical experience than set stress and setting stress congruities. In other words, a sense of inner peace and harmony in tension with an outer aspect of upheaval and disharmony (or vice versa) creates a strong context for mystical experience. This model has something in common with Festinger's and Nadel-Klein's work and also appears to be applicable to revivals, and has something in common with the sense of upheaval identified by Thompson, Hobsbawm and Gilbert. We could also, perhaps, go further and argue that there only need be a *perceived* sense of external threat for such an experience to occur. Such a perceived threat is common in groups with a strong millennialist (chiliastic) focus. Nevertheless, there is a problem here: official religious harmony coupled with economic, social and political disharmony may well lead to revival, but unlike the experience of nature mysticism the reverse conditions would not appear to be applicable.

What can be said of revivals is that the nature of the revival experience is intense, creating anxiety and the need for some form of resolution, and, as such, the immediacy of attracting new members has limitations. Even so, there are some lasting effects such as the creation of new religious hymns and songs. The tension between inner state and outer conditions cannot last, not least because social, economic and political conditions are in a constant state of change, and when a major factor creating the tension (be this the perception or the reality) is removed the creative aspect tends to dissipate. This seems to be true for any period of intense social creativity, with such periods lasting from just a few weeks to about five years.[21] Revivals in Yorkshire clearly follow this pattern, for example, *The Great Yorkshire Revival of 1792-96* and the *Halifax Revival* of February to March 1875.[22] Nevertheless, it should be borne in mind that such events are not restricted to a single narrow cause, as pointed out by Thompson.[23] This may well apply to all intense periods of creative and mystical experience, although the actual dynamics and mechanisms of revival can take various forms. There are, therefore, perhaps different models of revival that can be applied: local, national, international, ripple effect and so on.

Baxter's article, *The Great Yorkshire Revival of 1792-96*, shows a ripple effect, whereby new ripples appeared on the outer rings of earlier ripples, until the whole eventually died away (Appendix 6e). While it was some distance away from the centre of the revival, Grimsby was also influenced by the ripples and experienced a short-term revival in 1794. By 1796 the local Primitive Methodist membership had doubled to fifty-four, although by 1800 the membership had fallen back to thirty-seven. But things gradually improved, and John Petty provided some figures (although there is a discrepancy here between his figures and those provided by the Primitive Methodist reports), saying that the Grimsby circuit had 66 members in 1840 and 1,227 in 1850.[24] The membership appears to have reached a peak in 1863 when the circuit subsequently divided into various groups.

Perhaps the localness of the 1823 Filey Revival was a result of the isolated nature of the town, although it should be noted that fishing communities are not necessarily as isolated as some inland communities, the fishermen regularly meeting with other people in fishing ports around the coast and further afield. The women, too, were not as isolated as may be thought. 'Flithergirls' collected bait ('flithers') along the coast between Flamborough and Whitby and sold fish in the surrounding villages – as far away as Pickering, approximately 20 miles from Whitby. And during the herring season women visited from Scottish fishing ports. There is, however, very little evidence of women from Yorkshire ports travelling with the herring fishers, although we did come across two such women from Staithes. With all this movement intermarriage occurred and the network of families stretched all around the coast and further afield.

Several people have noted that revivals have performed a necessary function in sustaining church membership. Simon J. D. Green observed that the Bradford Wesleyan circuit in 1897 needed to recruit 10 per cent new members annually if it was to offset by what Green called 'natural wastage'. And he pointed out that the Harrison Road Congregational Church lost 40 per cent of its new members (from the 1882 revival) within the year. Periodic revivals may therefore be seen as a practical necessity. Even so, the nature of the new recruits was also variable, as Green observed when he pointed out that the Harrison Road Congregational Church in Halifax lost 10 per cent of its new members during the year of the 1882 revival.[25]

The complexity of social environments, however, means that it is very difficult to anticipate the actual appearance and development of a revival, although an *inner sense of harmony* in the face of rapidly changing external factors and *a desire for change* would seem to be paramount. Other elements in the Filey Revival of 1823 can also be identified. The aggressive evangelism of the Methodists, especially the Primitive Methodists, embraced a range of approaches: the penitent seat in services, open-air meetings, parades, festivals, camp meetings, home visits, cottage meetings, outings and teas. Of the Oldham Primitive Methodists in 1839, Smith has observed that they 'introduced a new revivalist technique to their connexion – a systematic series of protracted meetings'. There appears to be a clear link here with the ideas of Finney's new measures.[26] A particular attraction for the Primitive Methodists in the early Victorian period, as Bebbington has observed, was the female preachers, at a time when other denominations, including the Wesleyans, were dissuading women from preaching. Bebbington mentions several female preachers with the Primitive Methodists, including Jane Ansdell, Ruth Watkins and Elizabeth Allen.[27]

The Filey Revival of 1823

While the Primitive Methodist literature refers to numerous revivals in Yorkshire and Lincolnshire fishing communities during the 1820s, including Scarborough and Grimsby, special attention is often given to the Filey Revival of 1823. But this particular revival presents us with a number of questions: What kind of revival was it? Were the conditions outlined by Werner met? What were the outside conditions of social and economic disharmony? How long did the revival last?

While a good deal has been written in general terms about the Filey Revival, empirical evidence is sparse. The Primitive Methodist membership and baptismal records for the 1820s do not appear to have survived, and the baptismal records for St Oswald's Church show no significant change during the 1820s and 1830s – hence it would appear that there was no significant change of allegiance from the Anglicans to the Methodists. John Cole in his history of Filey, published in 1828, does not mention the revival, and there were very few contemporary publications dealing with the events. At the same time religious allegiance was changing and the New Dissent was rapidly gaining support. The Wesleyan Methodists had been slowly gaining ground in Filey as membership had grown from fourteen in 1810 to twenty-eight in 1822 and from twenty-six to sixty-six between 1823 and 1825 (Appendix 6c2).[28] There had also been a number of unsuccessful visits to the town by Primitive Methodist preachers prior to John Oxtoby's visit in 1823. So, there was a certain amount of preparation, and the expectation of revival on behalf of the Primitive Methodists coupled with the social, economic and political changes in the early 1820s all ensured fertile ground for a revival event.

Kendall, drawing on Petty's work, suggested that the expansion of the Primitive Methodists during the early 1820s happened too quickly for the existing structures to assimilate, with the result that the quality of travelling preachers was not maintained. As a result, even Hugh Bourne, one of the Primitive Methodist leaders, expected the society to implode. Perhaps it was Filey's isolation that prevented significant difficulties here, although following the Revival of 1823 there appears to have been a further increase in numbers up to about 100 members in 1824 – followed by a sharp decrease to 50 the following year (Appendix 6c3).[29] The situation also suggests that the recorded revival for the Primitive Methodists (along with the increased membership for the Wesleyans and the stability of the Anglican figures) was not a shifting of allegiance but a revival in the sense of attracting new members to Nonconformist churches from Filey's wider fishing community – a situation that was maintained and confirmed by the increase in numbers evident in the 1851 religious census.

Were the conditions outlined by Werner met? With regard to the internal conditions several points can be made: John Oxtoby was a travelling Primitive Methodist preacher with a personal vision, who strongly desired revival and had developed a clear support network of preachers (factors one, two and four of Werner's thesis). Primitive Methodist innovations were also evident (factor three: open-air preaching, experiential meetings, music, the use of the 'mercy seat' etc.). As to the external conditions, 1823 was not long after the Anglo-French Wars in which all seafaring communities around the British coast had been involved to a greater or lesser extent. The immediate euphoria following the victory subsequently gave way to disillusionment with the failure of the expected benefits. There was also a perceptible rise in the Filey population from 249 in 1801 to 366 in 1821, although there is little clear evidence as to why expansion should take place during this period. There was later a more significant growth (to 1,004 people in 1871), which reflected the growing importance of the leisure industry and saw the emergence of new Filey to the south of old Filey. General changes in the fishing industry also affected the town, as did the growing demand for food by the rising population – met to some extent by the increasing importance of the herring industry.

When John Oxtoby entered Filey in 1823 he claimed that the town had been noted for 'drunkenness, swearing, Sabbath-breaking, cock-fighting, card-playing and dancing'.[30] But such comments could have been levelled at most towns, and such views were not uncommon in Methodist literature. George Lester, for example, while discussing Grimsby prior to the advent of Methodism, said:

> (In 1743) the only places of worship were at St James Church, and a small meeting house in Silver Street. There was a general deadness to religion, rudeness, drunkenness, and Sabbath desecration prevailed. Bull-baiting had ceased to be a pastime, but other sports, scarcely less brutal and demoralising, were followed with avidity. Traditions touching certain of these, recall scenes which would be amusing, but that they indicate the deplorable condition of the people morally.[31]

Having previously encountered little success in winning converts in Filey, Oxtoby pleaded with the Bridlington Branch for one more attempt. He later reported that after several hours of prayer outside the town he was convinced that his prayers had been answered and that the town was about to experience a revival, and he expected eighty converts.[32] In the event there were initially approximately forty converts, although some appear to have left their new-found faith within a short time and others joined the meetings over the following year.[33] The 1823 *Primitive Methodist Magazine Report* stated that between March and June 1823 there was an increase of thirty-six members for the Bridlington Branch, although not all of these would have been for Filey. This figure should perhaps be balanced against the loss of 101 members between June 1823 and March 1825 – hence, Green's observation that at least 10 per cent annual new membership was required to offset natural wastage. Nevertheless, membership does not equate with attendance, and it is likely that many more people attended the meetings following March 1823 (the extant membership details for Filey start in 1835). Indeed, for each fisherman who became a member there would have been several family members who thereafter attended Sunday services and children who attended the Sunday school. The number gradually recovered following *c.* 1862 and by 1881 membership reached a peak of 353 (Appendix 6c3).

Baptismal records

While baptismal records may not be an infallible guide to membership or attendance at church services they can nevertheless be helpful in providing evidence of allegiance, and in this sense some researchers have made good use of them, among them Gilbert and Stephen Hatcher.[34] For Hatcher the baptismal figures in the Hull Primitive Methodist circuit can be used as 'an index of expansion', and it is in this sense that I make use of the present data.

Anglican and Primitive Methodist baptismal records provide the occupation of the father (something that many other denominations do not offer, including Wesleyan Methodists and Roman Catholics). The records can therefore be used to compare a traditionally middle-class institution with a traditionally working-class institution, and, furthermore, we are able to compare the social structure of these two denominations in the local community. The results of the baptismal statistics for Grimsby, Scarborough and Filey are given in chart form in Appendices 7a–7d.[35]

Unfortunately, the registers for the Primitive Methodists are incomplete, with several missing for the first fifty years of Primitive Methodism in Grimsby and Filey. Even so, the records for the years post-1860 provide an interesting insight into official allegiance during this period. The baptismal records presented in Appendix 7a–7d do not distinguish between different members of particular families, and the figures simply represent total numbers of baptisms. On this basis the figures present a surprisingly consistent pattern across the three towns. It would appear, for example, that the Primitive Methodists did quite well in attracting local people during the period 1865 to the late 1880s, while the Anglicans suffered a decline during the same period. The subsequent decline in Primitive Methodist baptisms may well also indicate a loss of members during this period. How can we explain this development? In terms of allegiance the records here suggest that both groups benefitted at different times at the expense of each other. While this could be a fairly straightforward relationship in Filey where there was no major expansion of religious institutions, there could nevertheless be an impact from the numerous new religious institutions during this period in Grimsby and Scarborough. It should also be noted that the 1870s were the period when the nineteenth-century fishing industry was at its height. It may also be the case that this period was significant for the Primitive Methodists in that we would see third-generation baptisms. Even so, the consistency of the sudden surge in Primitive Methodist baptisms across the three towns clearly needs more investigation. It would also be helpful to see if other fishing communities follow the same pattern.

In a close-knit fishing community the baptismal practices would depend very often on the church/chapel allegiance of the parents, although an oral tradition in Filey says that 'people began (were baptised) and finished (were buried) at the Parish Church'.

Conclusion

Rites of passage associated with baptism provide us with some useful indicators as to why people place such importance on the event, and some of the practices will be discussed in Chapter 6. The rites may also explain why the Anglican Church continued to play an important role in the daily life of fishing communities. But they are not sufficient of themselves to explain the rise or fall of membership associated with this allegiance. For this we need to call upon the theoretical perspective offered by a range of scholars. At first it seems that the baptismal statistics from Grimsby, Scarborough and Filey contradict the views advocated by E. P. Thompson. But on closer examination it appears that we need to consider the changing nature of revival, in particular between the first and second halves of the nineteenth century. Thompson's claim that his theory could only be said to hold true for the period between 1790 and 1840 makes sense in the light of the findings of the present study. But we need to take note of the changes in the churches' understanding of 'revival' following 1840 and recognize that we are dealing more with 'renewal' here rather than 'revival'. If the changes here are taken into account, then Thompson and Hobsbawm still have much of value to offer in their recognition of the importance of external factors. At the same time, we need also to recognize the equal importance of internal factors and local conditions.

Hobsbawm has pointed out that there were several periods of Methodist expansion between 1793 and 1850. Then in the 1850s there was a 'net decline in their numbers' – years that also saw the decline of Chartism and radicalism.[36] If church and chapel membership is reflected in the improved material conditions, then the improved economic situation in the year 1850 may well have reflected a low point for Nonconformist recruitment. During the 1860s the Primitive Methodists moved from an accent on revivals and became introspective, concerned with chapel building, ministerial training and a growing amount of liberality regarding entertainment. In the light of this, the baptismal statistics obtained from the Anglican churches and Primitive Methodist chapels in Grimsby, Scarborough and Filey (Appendix 7d) are indeed a little puzzling. Given the sustained increase in population throughout the nineteenth century we might expect to see a gradual increase in baptisms across the board, with occasional small peaks and troughs reflecting changing allegiances from time to time and larger peaks and troughs depending on the occurrence of revivals. It could even be the case that a major change of allegiance in one port could identify a period of revival in a particular institution. We would normally expect to see these peaks and troughs at different periods in the different towns. Perhaps with two towns close together, such as Scarborough and Filey, it should not be too surprising to find a similar trend. But when a distant town (Grimsby) is brought into the equation, and it, too, displays a similar general trend, we are left wondering why this should be the case.

The statistics for the three towns do indeed display a remarkably similar trend. In each case the Primitive Methodist baptisms suddenly surge ahead, *c.* 1870, at the expense of the Anglicans, and when the numbers decline, *c.* 1889, the Anglicans appear to reap the benefits. What are we observing here? Do the records show two significant revivals, first for the Primitive Methodists and then for the Anglicans? But one common factor is evident – the rise in Primitive Methodist baptisms occurred at the same time as the North Sea fishing industry achieved its peak. When the Anglican baptisms increased, this reflected the increased involvement of Anglican clergy with the fishing community. Perhaps the changing nature of church leadership here played an important role in the situation. It is also possible that the increase in Primitive Methodist baptisms during the 1870s and 1880s reflected this economic low point. The statistics show a general decline in the numbers of fishermen and apprentices from *c.* 1880 (a situation common to other fishing ports in Britain). Filey, however, as a small fishing port, was to some extent sheltered from the economic problems of the larger towns, and we see a more stable situation – even a slight rise in numbers of fishermen (Appendix 3c). Many Filey fishermen also worked from Scarborough, so perhaps some returned to work from Filey during this difficult period. With the return to prosperity during the 1890s we see the Methodist baptisms take a downturn in favour of the Anglicans. Presumably this is a national general trend, and Owen Chadwick has pointed out that there was a steady rise in Anglican baptisms during the later years of the nineteenth century, the numbers rising 'relatively and absolutely'. By way of explanation, Chadwick has observed: 'No doubt this increase of baptisms reflected a rising Anglican population. It is likely also to be a sign of the energy and efficiency which marked the later Victorian clergyman.'[37]

The dedication of clergy was also evident in the fishing communities. In Filey, Canon Cooper, the incumbent of St Oswald's Church from 1880 to 1935, was indeed popular and remains so in the local oral recollection of Filonians. His arrival in Filey coincided with a sudden rise in baptisms for the Anglicans, which suggest that he had a significant effect on the local population. In Grimsby, St Andrew's Church was opened in the heart of the fishing community (Freeman Street) in 1870 and became known as 'The Fisherman's Church'. This was later supported by the opening of St John's Church in Cleethorpe Road in 1877, which also adopted the title of 'Fisherman's Church'. The clergy initiated various forms of social welfare and the incumbent regularly visited the fishing grounds to spend time with the fishermen and to conduct services at sea. Likewise, in Scarborough, St Andrew's opened St Thomas' Church in East Sandsend in 1840 as a Chapel of Ease, specifically for the fishing community. Both St Thomas and St Andrew's churches had good links with national maritime missions, and this provided access to resources that enhanced the standing of the churches with the fishing communities. This picture could be reproduced for churches and clergy around the coast. Hence, there was a good deal of activity within the fishing communities that brought the Christian community into closer contact with the local community and to some extent replaced the need for occasional revivals.

Nevertheless, there remained a number of problems. Ambler has pointed out that Anglican clergymen sometimes refused a full funeral for those who had been baptized by Nonconformist ministers.[38] And there was some competition between the various denominations for the souls of the fishermen, especially when during the 1890s the High Church launched a number of initiatives, including sailing churches equipped with altars and all the paraphernalia familiar to High Church members on shore. However, the expense incurred by such activities ensured that such competition was short-lived, with many of the societies experiencing problems.

Many working people appeared to think that the Anglican service of baptism was more potent than that in Nonconformist churches, and Ambler makes this point and the oral tradition in Filey reinforces it. Primitive Methodists, on the other hand, tended to reflect better the views of the fisherfolk and provided services which were less reliant on a prescribed liturgy, and offered the congregation more opportunity to participate in the services. But the more direct involvement of Anglican clergymen in the local communities must have been a significant factor in attracting back those who wavered in their previous allegiance to Methodism. While many people continued to look for revival in the churches, the attraction offered in the late nineteenth century by the churches involved in maritime missions by St Andrew's Waterside Mission and the North Sea Church Mission (reading rooms, welfare support, innovations in worship, medical support, etc) must have been a significant factor in offsetting the problems faced by the communities, especially during times of economic and social difficulty.[39]

A sense of belonging in British fishing communities

Introduction

The concept of *popular religion* has become common usage for religious beliefs and practices that are integral to the daily life and culture of people – yet it resists clear definition.[1] Popular religion embodies a complex matrix of beliefs and practices, including folklore, magic, superstitious beliefs, customs, traditions, festivals, language, symbols and material culture. In some cases the beliefs and practices have their origins within the Christian tradition and have been reinterpreted in mythical terms, such as aspects of the Mass; others have developed outside the religious institutions and have later been embraced by the churches and given a Christian interpretation. Local folklore has produced a wide range of beliefs and practices. For example when I was baptized at a Baptist church as a young adolescent I overheard my mother telling a friend that the water for the baptism had been brought from Jerusalem. My comment that it came out of a tap was not well received!

Many aspects of popular religion continue to be seen from the perspective of official religion as at the opposite extreme of a dualistic pole (Christian and pagan, sacred and secular, religious and irreligious, orthodox and non-orthodox, formal and informal, official and unofficial).[2] By making such distinctions Western societies have not separated the natural from the supernatural but have sought to identify some societies, communities and cultures as essentially 'primitive' – with all the negative implications of that term. Yet, in reality the distinction between popular and official religion is very fluid with considerable overlap between the two, although the term 'popular religion' does tend to suggest a polarity: 'popular' as opposed to official ('unpopular') religion.

The variety of terms used to describe non-official forms of religion can be very confusing with scholars referring to folk religion, popular religion, common religion, unofficial religion, lived religion, everyday religion and so on. Williams has been careful to distinguish *popular religion* from *folk religion* by using the former term to apply to the more abstract concept of how we give life meaning and purpose (including both official and non-official forms of religious belief and behaviour), while applying folk religion to the 'common' beliefs and practices that people engage in, especially those not formally sanctioned by the churches, although there is some overlap here.[3] Williams' use of the term 'popular religion' to refer to a 'generally shared understanding of religious meaning' is very helpful. Nevertheless, there is no commonly used term in Britain that embraces both the various forms of official and non-official religion, although there is a growing familiarity with the terms 'lived religion' and 'everyday religion'. 'Lived religion' is not a term that appears regularly in British publications, although it is gaining a supportive following in the United States, especially through the work of Robert A. Orsi, David D. Hall and Meredith McGuire.[4] Orsi says that lived religion is 'Religious practice and imagination in ongoing, dynamic relation with the realities and structures of everyday life in particular times and places':

> The study of lived religion explores how religion is shaped by and shapes the ways family life is organised for instance: how the dead are buried, children disciplined, the past and future imagined, moral boundaries established and challenged, homes constructed, maintained, and destroyed, the gods and spirits worshipped and importuned, and so on. Religion is approached in its place within a more broadly conceived and described lifeworld, the domain of everyday existence, practical activity, and shared understandings, with all its crises, surprises, satisfactions, frustrations, joys, desires, hopes, fears and limitations.[5]

The term 'lived religion', therefore, links official and non-official religion by referring to the broader framework of everyday life and experience, and implies that this is how most people attempt to give life meaning and purpose. In this sense the term appears to be very close to Williams' use of the concept of 'popular religion'. We will, however, continue to use the latter term in order to explore how it has been used by a number of scholars.

The approach taken in this chapter draws especially upon the work of Williams, who adopted the use of autobiographical, folklore and oral history material in her research. In order to explore the issues here we will draw upon a range of beliefs and practices common in the nineteenth and early twentieth centuries. The oral history research of scholars such as Thea Vigne, Clark, Paul Thompson, Tony Wailey, Trevor Lummis and Elizabeth Roberts has provided an insight into the remembered experiences of interviewees going back to the 1880s.[6] There is, however, no electronically recorded (recollected) oral history material for the period preceding the 1880s, although there are many other records that have been left by working-class people, especially in recollected accounts reported by others. These include interviews for official reports such as the Parliamentary Papers and the studies of Booth and Rowntree. In addition, there are books and pamphlets, church records, novels about working-class communities, newspaper reports, church magazines, letters and even some working-class biographies. It is, nevertheless, important to remember that the earliest electronically recorded interviews often reflect a long tradition perhaps centuries preceding the birth of the interviewees. This is no less true for oral history material recorded today, hence, when it is pertinent to the discussion, we will draw upon the work of the *Women's Voices Project* (an oral history project undertaken by the author during the period 2004–8 that explored the women's perspectives of life in fishing communities during the mid- to late twentieth century).[7]

While scholars have tended to distinguish official religion from popular/folk religion, superstitious belief and magic, such an approach has created artificial boundaries that impart status qualities to official religion at the expense of popular beliefs and practices.

A more fruitful approach is to identify the various areas as overlapping spheres of discourse 'within a single understanding of religious meaning'.[8] The approach takes the languages of the various discourses equally seriously while also raising important questions about the nature of some significant theoretical developments such as the *secularization thesis* – a thesis that depends very heavily upon the official religious perspective. Hence, while working-class people have been averse to attending church services on a weekly basis it would be wrong to assume, as Mann did, that they were irreligious. Even so, it should be noted that research by Mark Smith, R. P. M. Sykes and others suggests that attendance was not always as poor as many orthodox historians and theologians have claimed. This chapter therefore begins with a historical overview of the theoretical foundations before going on to examine 'popular religion' in fishing communities with particular reference to Filey, Scarborough and Grimsby. This will be followed by an examination of the relationship between religion, magic, folklore and superstitious beliefs in these communities.

Historical overview

For the ordinary members of nineteenth-century fishing communities the church provided an important frame of reference for their contact with the supernatural, although this was by no means the only perspective, nor in many cases the most important one. Ritual practices, including magic, superstitious beliefs, folk customs and traditions and a long-standing reliance on local wise men and wise women, healers and fortune-tellers, have all been important aspects of community life. A similar point was made by Williams when she stated that 'the inhabitants of Southwark both talked about the world and saw the world through a combination of theoretically competing discursive worlds, such as church, family, community, group, work and so on'.[9]

While the concept of popular religion has often been used to refer to non-official religious beliefs and practices, social historians have until recently tended to ignore its role and significance. Yet even during the Victorian era some voices were heard protesting about the limited view of what constituted religiosity. Thomas Wright, for example, responded to Horace Mann's report on the 1851 religious census by arguing forcefully that the religion of working-class people was more subtle than Mann had allowed and could not simply be measured by statistics of church attendance. Scholars have from time to time taken up Wright's argument and expanded on this, although much of the research and social commentary has assumed an understanding of religious belief and practice based on class distinctions. But despite occasional important insights (not least the work of William James whose classic text concentrated on personal spirituality) it was not until almost a hundred years after Wright's published comments that scholars began to explore the implications of his view more earnestly.

In 1967 Brian Harrison noted that 'Church historians tend to look out at the masses from the deanery window; they seldom enquire how the deanery appeared from outside'.[10] During the same year Thomas Luckmann argued even more forcefully for an abandonment of the traditionally formal religious perspectives of what constitutes religious belief and practice. In particular he argued against those scholars who identified religion with the religious institutions, and he pointed out that their approach offers a 'highly inadequate scheme for the understanding of the relation between individuals, religion and society'.[11] Using an anthropological perspective, he went on to identify the problem of individual identity in modern society as essentially a 'religious' one in which individual existence derives its meaning from a transcendent world view. The stability of the latter makes it possible for the individual to grasp a sequence of originally disjointed situations as a significant biographical whole. The world view as a historical matrix of meaning also spans the life of the individual and the life of generations. We may, therefore, say that the historical priority of a world view provides the empirical basis for the 'successful' transcendence of biological nature by human organisms, detaching these from their immediate life context and integrating them, as persons, into the context of a tradition of meaning. We may conclude, therefore, that the world view, as an 'objective' and historical social reality, performs an essentially religious function and defines it as an elementary social form of religion. This social form may be perceived as universal in human society. For Luckmann, therefore, people are able to achieve a sense of the self by creating an 'objective' and moral universe of meaning in which the social processes that enable the construction of identity are religious and an integral aspect of the human condition.

In developing this view Luckmann drew upon the work of Durkheim and thereby helped to usher in a phase of 'late Durkheimian sociology of culture', a phrase used by Kenneth Thompson where he quotes Durkheim as saying, 'In the present study as much as in the past, we see society constantly creating sacred things out of ordinary ones.'[12] Durkheim's approach was to define religion in terms of its relation to the sacred, but his definition tended to restrict it to the ecclesiastical institutions.[13] Bearing this in mind Thompson argued that Durkheim was 'concerned not with the decline of the sacred (secularisation), but with changes in its cultural manifestations'.[14] Clearly, there is a developing line of thought from Durkheim via Luckmann to the later revisionists that began by chipping away the division between the sacred and the secular, and ultimately accepted that the barrier is an illusion seeming only to reinforce the viewpoint and security of the institutionally committed.

Luckmann's viewpoint bears similarities to Paul Tillich's identification of religious and spiritual significance as being embedded in that which concerns us ultimately (although he does not mention Tillich by name).[15] For Luckmann, ultimate meaning, embedded in people's ultimate concerns, is very much a part of the private sphere (family, home, sexuality) and is a clear rejection of the ecclesiastical monopoly.[16] This approach became widely influential and scholars slowly began to tackle the issues. R. Machalek and R. Martin (1976), for example, tested Luckmann's thesis on an urban neighbourhood in the American Deep South and concluded that 'the data generated by this and accompanying coping strategies are not limited to an official religious context'.[17] But many scholars, while accepting Luckmann's concern with ultimate meaning, were initially unwilling to embrace his more radical ideas. Peter Berger, for example, preferred to argue that the main area of religion had become privatized and a matter of choice.[18] But change was in the air and some scholars were beginning to question the status quo. Smith pointed out that

Even the most superficial look at popular religion reveals a striking contradiction: widespread involvement in a selection of orthodox rites and equally widespread resistance to Church doctrine which clashes with popular mores. Occasional and distinctly conditional conformity would seem to be the norm.[19]

Smith was able to acknowledge the diversity of popular religion inside as well as outside the religious institutions, but he still saw popular religion and official religion as at best spheres of influence and at worst as two conflicting world views.

Another significant step forward was made in 1971 when Keith Thomas published his work *Religion and the Decline of Magic*, in which he explored the nature of the relationship between orthodox religion and magic in sixteenth- and seventeenth-century England. He pointed out that the sphere loosely termed 'magic' 'seemed to be discharging a role very close to that of the established Church and its rivals', thus indicating a narrowing of the gap between that which is generally considered orthodox and that which is not.[20]

Just five years later James Obelkevich published his important study on popular religion in South Lincolnshire, in which he anticipated later research developments. Hempton has referred to Obelkevich's work as a 'Copernican revolution', especially in reference to his claim that 'it is hard to avoid the conclusion that Paganism was dominant and Christianity recessive in popular religion. Paganism was rarely Christianised, but Christianity was often paganised'.[21] Nevertheless, Obelkevich viewed popular religion as a predominantly working-class phenomenon and defined it within such terms as 'the non-official religious beliefs and practices, including unorthodox conceptions of Christian doctrine and ritual prevalent in the lower ranks of rural society'.[22]

Writing and researching at the same time as Obelkevich, David Clark undertook a field study in the North Yorkshire fishing village of Staithes. Commenting on the methodological issues, Clark, who was influenced by the work of Robert Towler, observed that

By abandoning the assumption that it is official religion and the churches which determine the totality of religious life in a society, we allow ourselves a broader conception of religious belief and practice and begin to see the possibility of religious items existing at a number of theoretical and organisational levels.[23]

Clark anticipated Williams' work here with her references to overlapping spheres of discourse. Nevertheless, he still sought to distinguish between folk religion and official religion, although he acknowledged that 'the highly complex inter-connectedness between these two spheres reflected their symbiotic relationship'.[24]

On the other hand Valenze took a broader view and acknowledged the diversity of such beliefs and practices, pointing out that 'Popular religion adheres to no one definition; in different settings, in the hands of different people, the amalgam of belief that makes up its theology constantly changes'.[25] This situation has been compounded by many concepts that have been developed to identify specific kinds of popular religious belief and practice, including diffusive Christianity, folk religion, unofficial religion, common religion, civil religion, invisible religion, implicit religion, lived religion and everyday religion. In the book *Inner City God*, Davie provided a copy of the grid of 'Dimensions of the definition of religion', based on Richard Toon's work for the Leeds study on conventional and common religion, undertaken during the 1970s (Appendix 8a).[26] While the grid proved helpful, the more general definition of 'popular religion' still remained vague. Indeed, the concept of 'common religion', as defined by Towler, the director of the Leeds study, contrasted with 'organised religion' and as such is more limited than Williams' broader and more inclusive definition.

This kind of dualistic approach had been generally accepted by historians during the 1950s and 1960s. The views of E. R. Wickham and K. S. Inglis, for example, continued to influence scholars, including the revisionists of the 1970s/1980s and early 1990s, including Cox, Alan Bartlett, Jeremy Morris, Smith and Simon Green.[27] Obelkevich, like Cox, tended to perpetuate an approach that highlighted a distinction between official and unofficial religion, and indeed T. Thomas has also pointed out that 'it is a weakness in Obelkevich's study that the terms Christianity and Paganism are accepted as respective poles in which religious belief and practice should be studied'.[28]

Popular religion, therefore, generally continued to be seen as a hangover from a pagan past and set in contrast to what many perceived to be the 'true', organized, official and dogmatic religion. Each new term here has attempted to be more precise in its definition and to concentrate on specific aspects of religiosity or intended to replace the earlier terminology in referring to the range of popular religious beliefs and practices. At the end of the day, however, the overall result is a plethora of terms that tend to make the whole area confusing.

While the British research tended to focus on fieldwork studies, and continued to advocate a dualistic understanding of official and popular religion, an important investigation into the nature of empirical religion took place via a study group at the University of Utrecht in the late 1970s.[29] The scholars explored a range of issues, some drawing on the work of Luckmann and Towler, and raising important questions about the nature of the relationship between *official* and *popular religion*, and whether or not the distinction could serve as a useful analytical tool. Despite the obvious importance of this study group's findings, none of the scholars mentioned in the present study (although Nancy Tapper offered a review of the work in 1982)[30] as researching popular religion made any reference to the development – and they may not have been aware of it. The net result was that the breaking down of the dualistic barriers here took another generation to come to the fore.

The continuing polarity between concepts of official and popular religion in the British research was tackled by David Hempton in 1996, who pointed to the need for a more inclusive definition:

> What is required to penetrate to the heart of popular religiosity is not the crude application of a predominantly middle class definition of religious commitment based on regular churchgoing, but an imaginative grasp of the importance of beliefs, symbols, values and memories in the texture of life in working-class communities.[31]

Hempton's perceptive observation enabled others to move on, and Williams took the important step of offering a definition that avoids theologically dualistic as well as class distinctions, and embraced both popular and official beliefs and practices:

Popular religion is more appropriately defined, therefore, as a generally shared understanding of religious meaning including both folk beliefs as well as formal and officially sanctioned practices and ideas, operating within a loosely bound interpretive community.[32]

At this point Williams has moved away from the use of the term 'popular religion' as that which is conceptually opposed to 'official religion' and thereby opened up the way for a new analytic approach to the study of religious belief and behaviour. She argued that we need to take popular religion seriously in all its variety and engage in the study from the broader perspectives of culture and community. This argument was an important leap forward, and others have begun to pursue their research along similar lines.[33] In her study of religion in the London Borough of Southwark, published in 1999, Williams drew attention to the dualistic preconceptions evident in much of the research into working-class religiosity up to the 1980s, in which organized Christianity was set alongside church attendance as the yardstick against which religious commitment was measured.[34] The swelling tide of opinion since the 1960s questioned the traditional model, and this has impacted upon closely related theoretical perspectives. Secularization, in particular, came in for criticism from all sides and is now seen by many scholars as inadequate, serving mainly as a useful theoretical underpinning of the officially focussed model of religious belief and practice. Traditional theoretical perceptions of revivalism have been similarly questioned.[35]

McLeod's work on oral history led him to acknowledge the significant role that religion plays in the everyday lives of working-class people, an approach that was taken further by Williams and Sykes, who both used oral evidence along with the literature on folklore to demonstrate the pervasive influence of religion (both official and popular) on the lives of ordinary people.[36] Both argue forcefully that rejection of the religious institutions does not mean rejection of religion beliefs and practices, although such beliefs and practices may not always agree with the official versions. In the study of popular religion in Dudley and the Gornals, Sykes made extensive use of oral history and, echoing the words of Brian Harrison, he pointed out that while many scholars have conducted research from the perspective of the insider (examining the relationship between churchmen/women and the wider community), historians and sociologists have begun to explore religious belief and practice from the perspective of the outsider (those who attend churches and chapels irregularly).[37]

Williams and Sykes therefore moved on from the theoretical perspectives of the revisionists of the 1980s and early 1990s, which continued to perpetuate an emphasis on the ecclesiastical perspective. Jeffrey Cox, for example, referred to the pattern of religious belief and practice that embraced orthodox rituals and customs as a '*residue* of Christian teaching or practice'. Williams countered this discussion by 'considering more diffuse aspects of belief which extended beyond the sphere of official Christianity'.[38] For her the non-official form of religious belief and behaviour 'was a dynamic and vibrant system of belief which retained its own autonomous existence within the urban context',[39] and she pointed out that '[It] remains the case that a concentration on formal religious behaviour so outweighs a consideration of the more intangible expressions of belief that popular religion continues to elude us as a serious subject of enquiry in its own right'.[40] She offered the following summary of her approach:

> Southwark was at this time an area notorious not only for its concentration of working-class life but for low levels of working-class attendance and for what was regarded as lamentable irreligion. In addition, the period roughly from 1880 to 1939 was marked by the consolidation and stabilization of a distinct urban popular culture within the area. The metropolitan borough thus provides an ideal context in which to consider religious sentiment outside the parameters of formal church practice as an integral facet of culture.[41]

Even so, she pointed out that popular religion was not merely the realm outside the churches, and the focus is not therefore 'them and us' but a world view seen from the perspective of the community. In order to do this Williams made extensive use of oral, autobiographical and folkloric material, pointing out that 'the value of this wider approach has, as yet, to be fully appreciated', and as to the official churches 'they were considered only insofar as they emerged within the actor's frame of reference'.[42]

Popular religion in fishing communities

Overview

The term 'religion', following Durkheim, has tended to be used in reference to the religious institutions. Hence, it has been official religion that has attracted researchers, from Mann's 1851 census of religion onwards, although even Mann had his detractors, such as Thomas Wright, who, during the 1860s, pointed to the wider aspects of religious belief and practice among working-class people. And the Bishop of Rochester in 1903 'warned his clergymen not to dismiss what he called "diffusive Christianity" which he described as the penumbra of the "embodied" Christianity of the church'.[43]

Hatcher has argued that one reason for the success of Primitive Methodism in fishing communities was because of the affinity with 'the convictions of the seafaring folk'.[44] This included the immanence of a spiritual world where the dead could readily appear to grieving relatives, a belief in the efficacy of dreams that conveyed messages in times of crisis, spiritual conflict, a predilection for signs, belief in 'second sight' and a strong belief in the power of prayer (the practice of which very often included bargaining). Hatcher has also pointed out that 'Many of the areas where it might be thought that Christianity and folk religion would openly confront each other, also revealed a substantial degree of underlying harmony'.[45] The point has been clearly made by a number of researchers, most notably Obelkevich in his *Religion and Rural Society in South Lindsey*, where he says that popular religion was not a counter-religion to Christianity; rather the two coexisted and complemented each other.[46] The problem, however, is that researchers have tended to view 'popular religion' from the perspective of the religious institutions and have seen the former as being towards the pagan end of an orthodox/pagan religious spectrum. Popular religion has also been tragically underplayed by many scholars who have preferred to place their emphasis on official religion, and many social historians have completely ignored the importance of religion in the local culture. The lack of research generally in this area is bemoaned in numerous publications, such as K. D. M. Snell and Paul S. Ell's *Rival Jerusalems*.[47]

Among the various terms used by a variety of scholars to cover non-orthodox forms of Christianity, 'folk religion' has perhaps been the most commonly used in Britain, as in Clark's research in the Yorkshire fishing village of Staithes. The concept of folk religion appears to have been adopted from the German *Religiöse Volkskunde*, having been coined by a German Lutheran minister.[48] Edward Bailey has also pointed out that the term (often associated with implicit religion) began to be used during the 1970s to refer to 'folk' use and interpretations of church practices, especially for rites of passage. At the same time he argued for the use of the term 'folk' (volk) religion of early Christianity in Northern Europe, which lacked a distinct liturgical tradition.[49] But prior to Bailey, Thomas Luckmann had pioneered work on 'invisible religion' (first published in German in 1963), which anticipated an outpouring of interest in the subject matter during the 1970s with scholars, especially in the United States, England and Holland, exploring the nature of the relationship between official and popular religion – especially, but not exclusively, in Christianity.[50] The research here was also interdisciplinary, involving historians, theologians, anthropologists and sociologists.

While Robert Towler used the term 'common religion' in his research in Leeds and contrasted it with official religion, he did so in the same sense as the terms 'popular' and 'folk religion' had been used by others. But he still adhered to a dualistic concept here, an approach that was followed by others:

> (The) beliefs of common religion often seem utterly implausible to the academic person. That belief in luck, fate, the influence of the moon or the stars, and so on, can actually make life more meaningful to people is so far outside their experience that they assume that people who do not accept the beliefs of some variety of intellectually comprehensible official religion, like themselves, live in a world in which traumatic explanations and ultimate satisfactions are denied them. But that is an empirical question which can be answered only after examining the beliefs people actually hold, regardless of whether or not those beliefs fall within the orthodoxy of belief and practice of the official religion.[51]

Towler's point about the need to examine people's beliefs before making a judgement is right at the heart of the present study, although very different conclusions have been drawn here.

Roman Catholics were also at the forefront of the debate, with the 1986 edition of the journal *Concilium* being given over to a discussion on 'popular religion'. The editorial set the scene with the observation that the traditional approach to the study of religion (i.e. with an emphasis on official religion) was not only unhelpful but very misleading, especially in its advocacy of a dualistic understanding of official versus popular religion that at the same time downplayed the importance of the latter:

For a long time the view governing both theological reflection and pastoral practice was that 'popular religion' consisted of vestiges of superstitious belief and religious ignorance which had somehow not been 'Christianised'. In more recent times, however, this view has been replaced by a productive re-evaluation which has even found its way into official Church documents namely, that faith is expressed in popular religion in a form that is historically concrete, social and cultural. Its substance and practices simply and directly express people's fundamental concerns, such as the meaning of life, of suffering, and of an after-life. Thus, popular religion helps to give coherence and a sense of direction to life: it is a central factor in creating and maintaining individual and collective identity.[52]

In the same volume Luis Maldonado pointed out that interest in popular religion was 'aroused by the meeting of CELAM in Medellin in 1968'.[53] (CELAM was the conference of Latin American Roman Catholic Bishops who met in Medellin, Columbia, during 1968.) Interest in the subject had been debated for a while preceding this date, and there had been some cross-fertilization between Catholics and Protestants, even though there is no reference in *Concillium* to Luckmann's work. In the same volume, however, there are passing references by Ernest Henau (in his chapter 'Popular Religiosity and Christian Faith') to Towler's work on *common religion* and to the earlier work of Karl Barth and Dietrich Bonhoeffer.

The debate continued throughout the 1980s as scholars began to note the importance of popular religion, especially in the work of English and American scholars such as Cox, Jenkins and Valenze – also of Luker, who argued that popular religion should be seen from the perspective of its own internal dynamic, a belief system with its own grammar. For Valenze, popular religion was also centred on the home where religious belief and practice were determined by 'generational, seasonal and personal changes'.[54]

Cox and Bartlett both provided a helpful insight into the nature of diffusive Christianity and explored popular religion 'primarily at the points where it touches the church'.[55] But a significant stage was reached during the 1990s with the work of Williams, who, in her study of Southwark, undertook a more rigorous analysis of the nature and importance of popular religion. Her definition here is helpful:

> Popular religion is more appropriately defined, therefore, as *a generally shared understanding of religious meaning including both folk beliefs as well as formal and officially sanctioned practices and ideas, operating within a loosely bound interpretive community* (my italics). These formed part of a particular value orientation or culture: a generalised and organised conception of nature, of man's place in it, of man's relation to man and of the desirable and non-desirable as they relate to man's environment and interpersonal relations.[56]

Williams clearly points to the overlap of popular religion and official religious beliefs and practices, and her approach made extensive use of oral history – but this only takes us back to *c*. 1880 (given that systematic recordings of the memories of working people were generally begun in the 1960s, that is, of people whose lives began in the late Victorian era). For earlier years we have to adapt our methodology, perhaps making use of a range of narrative resources available in newspapers, journals, diaries, reports, letters and so on, especially those documents held by the missionary and philanthropic societies. There is also the research of, for example, Booth and Mayhew. John Baxter's study 'The Great Yorkshire Revival 1792-96' and the studies of Filey by Valenze and Hull by Hatcher are good examples of this approach. The narratives, however, appear to represent the more 'respectable' end of the working-class spectrum (e.g. we would be relying at the very least on those members of the working class who could read and write) and, as such, the written results may well prove to be only a limited range of views in a complex matrix of cultural perspectives. On the other hand, narratives that have a direct link with dramatic and often tragic events and experiences in fishing communities can often be enlightening.

It should also be noted that there is a wide range of other terms that have been used to describe aspects of non-orthodox forms of religion, including civil religion, implicit, surrogate and everyday religion.[57] Of particular note, however, is the term 'lived religion' used by Orsi in his work *The Madonna of 115th Street*.[58] Orsi appears to have used the term synonymously with popular religion in that his definition is very similar to that of Williams.

As is often the case it is the outsider who recognizes that which those too close to the culture have missed. Obelkevich, Cox and Valenze (all US-based scholars) tackled the issue of popular religion and the English working classes, and all rejected the political interpretations proffered by Halévy, Thompson, Hobsbawm, Hempton and others. Gilbert, however, did explore the wider social context and, as such, provided something of a bridge between the major political interpretations and the more holistic approaches offered in recent studies. (It should perhaps be mentioned here that Gilbert, like his contemporary, Inglis, is an Australian; and Day is a Canadian.)[59]

Religion and the community

From the perspective of the churches, irregular attendance at services has in the past been interpreted as a lack of commitment and questionable religiosity. From the perspective of the working-class community, attendance at church was part of a broader cultural religiosity where morality and religious duty embraced the religious institution but was not restricted to it. Indeed, regular attendance at church services has often been seen by working-class people as unhealthy and indicative of hypocrisy with a sense in which the participant was seen as trying too hard to prove his/her virtue. Such a view, still common today, was evident during the early nineteenth century. For example, in George Eliot's book *Silas Marner*, we are told,

> The inhabitants of Ravelow were not severely regular in their churchgoing, and perhaps there was hardly a person in the parish who would not have held that to go to church every Sunday in the calendar would have shown a greedy desire to stand well in heaven. . . . At the same time, it was understood to be requisite for all who were not household servants, to take the sacrament at one of the great festivals.[60]

We could add examples from many other novels, such as Thomas Hardy's *Under the Greenwood Tree* published in 1872 and set in rural Oxfordshire during the early years of the nineteenth century, where there were difficulties between the village band and the local vicar who proposed introducing the organ to accompany hymns. Flora Thompson's *Lark Rise to Candleford* published in 1939, set in North-East Oxfordshire, draws upon a range of celebrations, including May Day and Harvest, as well as traditional songs and children's games at the end of the nineteenth century. Arnold Bennett, in Chapters X to XII of his book *Clayhanger*, published in 1910, commented on life in the 'Five Towns' on the Centenary of Burslem Sunday schools, held on 11 July 1800.[61]

The rapidly changing early nineteenth-century world left many people feeling insecure. The old beliefs and practices were being chipped away by new developments, ideas and approaching war. And, despite the later optimism of mid-nineteenth-century Britain, change seemed to be the norm for most people. Changing priorities and competing theological influences also reflected a lack of consistency in church leadership, which had an impact on the local communities. New clergy did not always follow in the paths of their predecessors – one minister might be down-to-earth and compassionate, another might be dogmatic, judgemental and dismissive. Lack of relevant training for many clergy also impacted on this in that they rarely took the effort, especially during the first half of the nineteenth century, to understand the nature of working-class life. A not uncommon response by nineteenth-century working-class people to this situation was the embracing of Methodism, especially Primitive Methodism, which was more sympathetic than the established church to the matrix of popular religious beliefs and practices, including magic, folklore, superstitious belief and a generally held diffusive Christianity.[62] To the more educated people, including many of the clergy, such beliefs and practices were often incoherent and abhorrent, but, as Ambler says, 'their lack of coherence should not be allowed to obscure their importance as a series of observances which helped an individual over a difficult period in life'.[63] Interviews in Yorkshire fishing communities support this and suggest a link with beliefs and practices in the early Victorian era. One fisherman's wife interviewed in Filey in June 2005 stated, 'I can't honestly say that you saw anybody going . . . you know, to church regularly. . . . Where I could say to you they honestly believed. I wore a cross for years and I mean years.'[64] A Scarborough fisherman also commented, 'I'm not particularly religious, but you still think there comes a time when everybody turns to God for help with something.'[65] This sentiment is echoed in another Scarborough interviewee's comments about her father: 'He was quite religious but he wasn't a churchgoer . . . he always said anybody who'd been at sea in a gale would know that there was somebody above us.'[66] And a Bridlington fisherman said: 'I'm religious, like. I believe in all that sort of thing – but I'm not a regular church-goer.'[67] Another interviewee, in May 2005, said that the Filey fishermen were still Primitive Methodists, gave the church its due and were steadfastly superstitious. Referring to the 1940s the interviewee said that the fishermen, though Methodists, still liked to have their funeral service at the parish church.[68] This allegiance to both the established and Nonconformist traditions appears to have been common in the Yorkshire fishing communities (as no doubt elsewhere, too). An inhabitant of Robin Hood's Bay, when talking about life in the village during the 1930s, commented that while the village itself possessed only two Nonconformist chapels (Wesleyan Methodist and Congregationalist), the Anglican Church situated some distance away from the village was also attended by community members. At the same time there was a division by status in that the sea captains tended to be members of the Congregationalist chapel, while the Anglican Church was frequented more often by members of the farming communities.

Nineteenth-century fishing, like farming, was determined by the seasons, and the seasons were closely linked to religious holy days and festivals. The smaller fishing communities tended to follow the pattern of Filey where the year began with the Spring Fishery (January to Easter).[69] During this period the fishermen worked in yawls with a crew of six men and two boys (according to John Cole, Filey had twelve yawls in 1828), and the fishermen relocated with their families to the East Anglian ports where the women worked on shore supporting the men by baiting the fishing lines and looking after the children.[70] When they returned to Yorkshire for Good Friday the fishermen worked in their cobles, catching lobsters and crabs, until the start of the herring season in June.[71] With the end of the herring season in November the yawls were tied up for repairs and refitting, leaving the fishermen to work in their cobles over the Christmas period. Cole referred to this Winter Fishery as the most perilous, as they now go in their small cobles, frequently to the distance of 10, 11 or even 15 miles from the land and are often exposed to the most imminent danger, especially if, on their return, a gale of wind should arise.[72]

While Filey retained its traditional fishing methods, Scarborough, despite local opposition, was eventually won over to the new developments such as fleeting and trawling. Other smaller ports, such as Flamborough and Bridlington, continued their inshore fishing tradition with three main classes of fishing: line-fishing (mid-October to Good Friday), crab and lobster fishing (April to June) and herring fishing (June to November).[73]

With the growth of the North Sea fishing industry during the mid-Victorian era, there was significant population movement and relocation between the country's fishing ports – mostly in the direction of Scarborough then later to Hull and Grimsby.[74] Grimsby was significantly different to the smaller ports in that after mid-century, with the building of the fish docks at the mouth of the River Humber, the town grew rapidly and welcomed new fishing methods. These, along with other innovations such as artificial ice and steam trawlers, were eagerly embraced, especially by the owners. Individual trawling smacks during the 1850s worked the newly discovered fishing grounds on the Dogger Bank, and this gave way to the development of the 'fleeting system'. With the advent of steam trawlers deep-sea fishing took place around Iceland and further afield, although long-lining, seine-net fishing and seasonal catches of herring, oysters and lobsters all became part of the port's fishing industry. By 1880 Grimsby had over 21 acres of reclaimed land with the quay being used for the fishing industry and a fleet of 567 first-class smacks.[75] With the development of the railway system, linking Grimsby to Liverpool and London, the port gradually took the lead in the fishing industry, although Hull continued to grow and offered new facilities for the fishing crews.

Given the complexity of life in the fishing communities, and the rapid changes taking place, it was important that the clergy and ministers understood the fishing seasons and the nature of the developing industry, as well as the local customs, festivals, beliefs and practices. Valenze has pointed out that the customs in Filey relating to the work were long-standing and complex, and that 'wives, widows, sisters, and daughters managed every aspect of work outside the boat'.[76] In Staithes, too, especially during the early nineteenth century, the women were responsible for both landing and launching the vessels. The many artists working along the Yorkshire coast during the nineteenth century, attracted by the isolation and the picturesque quality of the fishing villages, captured such activities on canvas, and a painting by Lionel Townsend Crawshaw of men and women hauling a coble ashore in Runswick Bay (now hanging in the Pannett Art Gallery in Whitby) illustrates the point well.[77]

Life for the women was hard, especially in the smaller ports where they were closely involved with the fishing activities. In his *Guide to Filey*, 1868, the Revd Arthur Petitt claimed that 'The men have only to catch the fish, their labour as a rule being over as soon as the boat touches sand'.[78] A male interviewee in Filey in 2006 stated that while the quality of life has improved for both men and women, the hard work for the women remained a constant:

> I was once told that the arrangement was that the women worked all the time, but the man had time off, in the pubs to drink . . . because . . . the difference was he was risking his life. That was the deal – the women were safe, but had to work all the time.[79]

Nevertheless, there were times of relaxation for all with local festivals, customs and traditions. In Scarborough, for example, Boxing Day was considered to be 'Ladies Day', in which the fishermen's wives were allowed a day off to enjoy themselves while the men looked after the house and children. In more recent times this tradition has taken on the form of a festival for everyone, with a charity football match, performance of local musicians, boat races and other entertainments.

Unlike Scarborough, Grimsby appears not to have had any general, long-standing festival tradition, probably because the town only developed its modern fishing industry during the 1850s. On the other hand, local traditions were kept by the many relocated fishing families, including their religious beliefs and practices. As for those fishermen at sea who were deeply committed Christians there was the opportunity to relax on Sundays, to visit each other's vessels and to hold a service. Edward Gillett has recounted that

> Thomas Campbell, who was to become one of the most successful owners, as early as 1854 had a smack named Abstainer and the vessel which brought the Alwards to Grimsby was named the *Sons of Rechab*. Harrison Mudd, One of the founders of the North Sea Steam Trawling Co., and chairman of the Coal Salt and Tanning Co., was a fervent teetotaller, especially in his youth. When he was fishing in the Faroes in 1860, each Sunday he was in harbour, he hoisted what he described as the Bethel flag on his smack, and held Primitive Methodist services on board

her, in which denunciation of strong drink was an important part of the doctrine preached. Three other vessels had Bethel flags, but twenty-seven had no praying man on board.[80]

While such Grimsby owners and skippers were in the minority, unlike those in Filey, they did in time become influential and respected local dignitaries. By the 1870s the rapid growth of the Grimsby religious groups began to have a significant effect upon the local community (Appendix 6a1), with new festivals linked to the activities of churches, chapels, Sunday schools, Friendly and Temperance Societies.

Fishing ports, like other traditional communities, such as mining and farming, are noted for their traditions and superstitious beliefs, yet, strangely, with a few notable exceptions, there has been relatively little academic study of English fishing communities. Even so, most serious studies here have tended to concentrate on aspects of the life and work of the *fishermen*, although there are a few serious studies about the lives of *women*.[81] Religion has also received little mention, and even in more recent sociological studies any such discussion tends to be with reference to the official aspects of religious life. Without the in-depth studies on religious belief and practice it is perhaps not surprising that the focus of attention with regard to religion has tended to concentrate upon allegiance to the churches.[82]

Perhaps the underlying common factor here is a concern with ritual. The performance of ritual was a significant function in the daily lives of working people, and such rituals are at their most potent in rites of passage. In the following we will explore some examples of rites of passage in fishing communities before going on to examine the 'threshold rites' more generally with reference to a range of rites and symbolism within popular religion.

Ritual in the daily life of Yorkshire and North Lincolnshire fishing communities

Rites of passage

Arnold van Gennep's analysis of rites of passage, and his identification of the three stages of separation, transition and reincorporation, has been important for scholars who have sought to understand the nature and significance of these rites.[83] Building on Gennep's work Victor Turner explored the nature of liminality, referring to the stage of *transition* as 'betwixt and between'. Turner was especially interested in the symbolism present within ritual and provided scholars with an important extension of Gennep's framework for the analysis of threshold rites and ritual in a wide range of social activities, especially in performance.[84] Even so, as Clark pointed out, sociologists have not made as much use of the concepts here as anthropologists, although there were the two notable exceptions of Robert Bocock (1974) and Diana Leonard (1980).[85] While Leonard concentrated on courtship and weddings, Bocock applied the concept of ritual to a wide range of experiences in his book *Ritual in Industrial Society* (one of the first such analyses of ritual from a sociological perspective). Clark followed this with a 'detailed description of the rites of birth and death in Staithes'.[86]

For the purpose of the present study we will adopt Bocock's definition of ritual as 'the symbolic use of bodily movement and gesture in a social situation to express and articulate meaning'.[87] Hence the term is being used here in a broader sense than merely with reference to official religion and embraces the integration of feelings, emotion and reason. Rituals, therefore, help us to express our feelings and emotions in a rational way. The area where ritual is most evident is in the significant rites associated with birth, marriage and death, and it is often at these points in our lives that the interplay between spirituality and materiality is made most explicit. For the ordinary person there is no sharp distinction between sacred and secular – rather there is a general acknowledgement of the specialness of such ceremonies being performed by a priest in the presence of the couple's relatives and friends. There is, however, a danger that the stylization of these rites of passage can have the negative effect of emphasizing and celebrating the supernatural and downplaying the natural, but this is often subverted by the integrated beliefs and practices of the participants and the local community. On the other hand, rituals can become so culture-bound that they drive a wedge between natural processes and idealized expectations. Bocock makes just this point when he says

> In the phase of the marriage service, when the man puts a ring on the fourth finger of the woman's hand, 'With my body I thee worship'. This phrase is the voice of 'authentic' ritual, and should aid the lovers to enjoy their sexuality. Yet in English churches it sounds out of place to many of them – sexuality in a church? Oh, dear no![88]

With the migration of fishing families to North-East coastal ports during the second half of the nineteenth century, some beliefs and practices became part of each community's religious identity as the immigrants sought to maintain links with their own diverse heritages. This would have been especially so in the new community of Grimsby. The comparative chart, in Appendix 5, lists the birthplaces of fishermen in Grimsby, Scarborough and Filey for the years 1851, 1871 and 1891. As can be seen here fishermen moved to Yorkshire and North-East Lincolnshire from practically every county in England, Ireland, Scotland, Wales and Shetland, and countries as far apart as Australia, the East Indies, France, Norway and the United States.

Nineteenth-century fishing families, like most working-class people, attended church services for the three major rites of passage, even if they rarely attended otherwise. It should nevertheless be noted at this point that the working class has never been a coherent whole. W. R. Lambert (quoting from a letter by a Welsh collier in the *Merthyr Express* of 5 September 1885) observed that there were at least three major working-class groups, which he loosely referred to as the respectable, the radicals and the reprobates.[89] However, the traditional working-class groups in fishing communities do not sit easily with any one group here. Some would attend church and chapel services regularly (especially those who were Methodists), while others were only irregular attendees. It was, however, common, well into the twentieth century, for fisherfolk in Filey to hold such rites of passage in the parish church, while continuing to attend services at the Methodist churches even after it became possible for such rites to take place there. Marriages, for example, could take place in licensed Nonconformist buildings following the passing of the Dissenting Marriages Act of 1836. At the same time the burial ground in Filey was attached to the Anglican Church whose clergy held the monopoly on the conduct of services in churchyards up until 1880 (when the Burials Law Amendment Act was passed). Nevertheless, families naturally wished to continue burying their dead close to deceased relatives.

Despite occasional revivals, such as that in Filey in 1823, there was no general sustained swing away from Anglican to Nonconformist allegiance in the fishing ports (although the figures in Appendices 7a–8d suggest a period of sympathy for Primitive Methodist baptisms before a return to Anglican practice). In Robin Hood's Bay, Filey and Staithes there was indeed a strong attachment to the Methodists. But in Scarborough many of the fisherfolk initially attended St Mary's Church for their rites of passage and later attended St Thomas' Church (opened in 1840), which had been built especially for the members of the fishing community. Grimsby was a more complex situation, although many fisherfolk held their family celebrations at St Andrew's Church or St John's Church, which had been built respectively in 1870 and 1877 specifically for the rapidly expanding fishing community and were known as 'Fishermen's Churches'. In each of these communities, despite the preference for Nonconformity, the Anglican churches played a significant role. Even so, Scarborough, Grimsby and Hull were well endowed with a wide range of religious institutions and organizations, including Bethels and Missions, that served the needs of the fishing community.

There is, especially in the case of Filey, an element of superstitious belief involved in attendance for a rite of passage in that the formal and ritualized service at the parish church may have appeared to be more potent than that offered by the Nonconformist chapels. There was also a sense of continuity in that it was the older established churches in which ancestors had been married, children baptized and funeral services held. Nevertheless, whether at church or chapel, attendance for many was restricted to rites of passage and the occasional festival and memorial services. This practice is still evident in that an interviewee in Scarborough stated, 'I'm just a births, deaths and christenings and things.'[90] The 'and things' apparently refers to other special occasions.

Birth, churching and naming

Like all rites of passage baptism embraces a range of superstitious beliefs and practices, and practically all the writers on early nineteenth-century Filey referred to the superstitious nature of the people.[91] Some parents, for example, feared that an unbaptized child, should s/he die young, would be excluded from heaven. Presents for the child would often sit in a cupboard or on a shelf on display, only to be used again following the birth of a grandchild. A special baptismal dress would also be used and passed on from parent to child through the generations.

Such rites of passage were important social occasions and were also associated with a wide range of folk beliefs and practices, many of which were incorporated into church practices, as Clark (1982), Williams (1999) and Sykes (1999) have observed. Among the various beliefs associated with birth was the use of the caul as a token (the gossamer covering found on a newborn baby, sometimes known as a 'kell' or 'smear'). This was considered to have an especially protective function for the men at sea (sympathetic magic) and as such was highly prized by the fishermen, changing hands for large sums of money – over fifty pounds in the 1960s. Alec Gill has discussed the folklore and superstitious belief surrounding this token.[92]

Following the birth of a child the mother expected to be 'churched' and was not allowed contact with other people until after the ceremony. This liminal event, while often considered a folk practice, has been a Christian purification rite and an act of thanksgiving after childbirth since Christianity's early days. It remains an important part of church liturgy with the Anglican prayer book emphasizing the thanksgiving aspect and referring to the ceremony as 'The Thanksgiving of Women after Child-birth Commonly called Churching of Women'. There were a variety of superstitious beliefs associated with the ceremony, such as not allowing people to enter the home until the mother had been churched and simply entering the church building to let people know that the mother could again be approached. It was believed that to come into contact with an unchurched mother or for her to be allowed back into the house prior to the ritual would result in bad luck for the family.[93] Although the service was usually performed quietly during the week a witness was often required, especially if the child was baptized at the same time. In other cases the woman was 'churched on the first occasion that she attended chapel after the birth of a child'.[94] Churching is, of course, not specific to fishing communities – Obelkevich has demonstrated its importance in rural areas during the 1800s, and Williams has discussed a number of related superstitious beliefs from the early twentieth century in the inner-city suburb of Southwark. The closeness of fishing community contacts ensured the survival of the practice until at least the 1970s, and interviews along the Yorkshire coast have recorded a number of instances where the women either remembered their mothers being churched in the 1930s or were subjected to the practice themselves.[95] Clark also pointed out that while for the clergy the service was seen as an opportunity for thanksgiving for the birth of a child, the women were more concerned with the issue of purification. And here again, Obelkevich has pointed to the close links between Churching and superstitious beliefs.[96] This ambivalent attitude seems to have led to the gradual rejection of the practice by the churches, so much so that by the 1970s some ministers and clergy (Clark cites an example in Staithes) were either ignorant of the practice or openly hostile, with the Church of England being the only denomination continuing to include Churching as an official rite.[97]

The baptism of the child was (and is) usually referred to as a Christening, a practice that highlights the giving of a Christian name to the child. Naming is an important aspect of life in all communities. Apart from the need to provide individuals with a sense of personal identity, the names also help to give the individuals and community a sense of place. So not surprisingly some names, such as nicknames (often referred to as *bye-names* in Filey and Grimsby and *by/tee-names* in Scotland), may be kept from outsiders. The custom of baptism was thought to be of physical and spiritual benefit to a sick child, and the giving of a name in this manner gave it a special sacred dimension, not least because the child was often named after the parents and grandparents – a practice that caused problems in small fishing communities where a number of people might end up with the same name. Hence, the giving of nicknames was intended to help distinguish between individuals.[98] The naming of a child was an especially important event and not only took place in the church but also included a celebration in the local pub, where it was referred to as 'wetting the baby's head' (although the 'wetting' here referred to drinking and raising a toast to the baby's health).

Anthony P. Cohen's inaugural lecture as professor of anthropology at the University of Edinburgh (22 November 1990) explored the importance of naming in a variety of cultures (it should be noted that he did his own research among the fishing community on the Shetland island of Whalsay). Citing Rosalda (1984) and Rosen he pointed out that an individual's identity is often manipulated by his/her significant others when name changes occur. Nicknames clearly fulfil such a function. Until recently people were reticent to tell their nicknames to those outside the fishing community, a practice that suggests a superstitious element in that the individual's real identity was kept from the spirits so that they could not easily claim the living, a particular concern when the community members were engaged in dangerous tasks such as fishing.[99] Today, however, there is less reticence and nicknames even appear on gravestones all around the coasts of Britain. Nicknames also often describe some characteristic of the individual or family. This became evident in an interview where the interviewee mentioned a fisherman with the nickname 'Tint'. The individual was recalled as saying 'ti'n't', as a further abbreviation of 'It isn't' or 'It ain't'.[100]

Names are also used in a variety of other situations. Some 'yards' and streets were often named after local fishing families, such as 'Jenks Yard' in Filey and 'Baxtergate' in Whitby; and many fishing vessels were named after religious leaders, saints, biblical characters or they were religious words and phrases.[101] The naming traditions here give a sense of continuity between individuals, places, objects and traditions, which is an important factor in the identity of close-knit fishing communities – not least because the names of objects, vessels, places and buildings often outlive the lives of individuals and generations.

Familiar names (recalling local people and events) given to inanimate objects such as streets, buildings, geographical features and houses, and local names for flowers, fruit and animals, are common to all communities. Fishing communities also have names for gansey patterns. Fishing grounds and local versions of rhymes are used as 'maps' to guide the fishermen – such as the names of lighthouses:

Alternative versions

First the Dungeon, then the Spurn, / Flamborough Head comes next on turn; / Hartlepool lay in a bight, We'll be home before dark tonight.

Flamboro' lights you see ahead; Pack you gear, And dump your bed.

Flamborough Head as you pass by, Filey Brigg you must not come nigh, Scarborough Castle stands over the sea, And Whitby rocks lie northerly.[102]

Peter Anson noted a verse 'intended as a lesson in fisher morality':

From St. Abb's Head tae Flambrough Head, / Whan'er ye cut, be sure ye bend, / Na'er lea a man wi' a loose end.[103]

Such rhymes were of course useful mnemonics for nineteenth-century fishermen during a period when few could read or write, and 'apprenticeships' (during the early rise of the North Sea fishing industry at least) were extended periods of picking up expertise by experience. For the smaller and long-established communities like Filey and Scarborough the learning of traditions, names, rhymes and so on was part of the local landscape of enculturation, hence, by the time the boy went to sea for his first trip at around the age of ten years he would have been familiar with a great body of this material.

Marriage

Marriages were subject to numerous traditions and customs in which the liminal aspects were reinforced, and of all the major rites of passage, the marriage ceremony and its associated traditions are the most complete as a performance. These were occasions for readjustments in family relationships as well as being important symbolic occasions for the community. The normal pattern in marriage involves the bride and groom separating the day before the marriage and dressing in special clothes for the marriage service. With the families of the bride and groom separated on different sides of the church the bride enters with her father until she is symbolically handed over to the bridegroom. The bride's veil is lifted and the marriage ceremony is conducted usually by a priest. Following the ceremony, the newly married couple walk back out of the church followed by relatives of both families walking side by side. The transitionary stage is almost complete, although there are often local customs that symbolize the incorporation of both families. From a Freudian perspective the whole of this liminal event (the entering and leaving the church) might be seen as a symbolic enactment of the anticipated sexual act. This implied and symbolic act is made more explicit at the celebrative wedding meal when relatives use the opportunity to make suitable (or unsuitable) comments to the newly married couple as they prepare for their honeymoon. At the time of the marriage, therefore, there was much scope for revelry and ribaldry. Once the formalities had been completed order gradually broke down, as Shaw described in the following example from mid-nineteenth-century Filey:

> Weddings and funerals especially, were the occasions when large numbers attended, and all got 'something to drink'. On their way home from church, the wedding party were usually beset by invitations to drink at door after door as they passed, and jugs of strong liquor were bravely drained and the whole company joined in the revelry which followed.[104]

Another common nineteenth-century practice on the occasion of a marriage in Filey was for young people to race down Queen Street (the main street in the fishing community) for a silk handkerchief – an activity with some similarities to the modern-day practice of women trying to catch the bride's bouquet. Many young married couples lived with their parents until they could afford to purchase, or more likely rent, their own house. Yet there were exceptions as D. Crosby of Robin Hood's Bay related one example to the author in June 2006: money from each fishing trip was handed over to the man's fiancée and was used to purchase stones from the local quarry. The young lady would visit the local quarry, purchase some stones and transport them back to the parent's garden where they were used to build their future house.

For most members of nineteenth-century and early-twentieth-century fishing families there was little opportunity to have a honeymoon away from the town, and the young couple would, initially at least, have to share the family home, usually with the bridegroom's parents. This was also an opportunity for her to quickly adjust to the demands of being a fishermen's wife, guided by her mother-in-law, although marriages tended to take place between fishermen and women from the local communities, where the women were familiar with the demands of the fisherman's work and life. Even so, some mothers tried to encourage their daughters not to marry fishermen. Some families were also strongly opposed to their children marrying outside the fishing community, although partners from other fishing communities were acceptable. A fisherman's life was so hard that few were prepared to take the risk of bringing someone new into the community with the expectation that they should adapt quickly to the life. Fishermen's wives had learned skeining from an early age (prising limpets, known in Yorkshire as 'flithers', from the rocks and then prepare them as bait for the fishing lines), and the new wife was expected by the family and community to slip into her role easily and quickly.

Death

Loss of life was (and remains) very high among fishermen, and it was (is) believed that the lost souls would seek to return home. (The author remembers his mother telling him, when he was bored, to 'stop wandering about like a lost soul'.) This belief is evident in the various tales told by women who have lost relatives. One interviewee in Filey recalled her encounter as a child with a woman whose husband had recently been lost at sea:

> It was the (woman) next-door-but-one to granny who lost her husband and two sons, and it was often talked about. We used to go to the house . . . and this lady used to burn a candle in her upstairs window. . . . The theory was that when they (the souls of the lost men) turned up they'd know where the house was. As children we used to ask what the candle was for. . . . But that's what they used to do, you see . . . believed that . . . when you haven't got a body, I suppose, you never completely lose hope.[105]

The candle partly symbolized Christ's presence in the home, but also acted as a beacon to guide the soul of the deceased. With no body to bury, and the possibility of the missing relative still being alive, there could be no formal funeral service – a situation that naturally increased the sense of loss for the relatives. The exception here was when several lives were lost in a storm, a formal service was held to commemorate those lost and missing. Such loss of life was all too common in the larger fishing towns of Hull and Grimsby, where curtains were closed and the door of the house left open for the soul's return. Anson reported that such practices were common in coastal communities in the 1870s. When the body of the deceased was in the house the doors and windows were opened to allow the soul to depart without it being stopped by evil spirits. Clocks were stopped, the body was laid out by the local 'nurse' or 'wise woman' and a saucer of salt was laid on the breast of the deceased to keep evil spirits away.[106] These practices also had their counterpart in the churches and chapels, such as at Filey Primitive Methodist chapel where a window was left open during the service, when a body was present, so that the soul could depart.[107] In Scottish fishing communities a silver coin was placed in the coffin on the head or breast to enable the deceased to pay his/her fare to whatever place they should find themselves in.[108] This practice was not an isolated one, as the Revd J. C. Atkinson, writing of his life on the North York Moors in 1891, stated that a correspondent had written to him saying,

> 'I heard some rustics talking about an odd old man who had been buried somewhere up your way (that is in North Yorkshire) a few years ago with a candle, a penny, and a bottle of port; and, as they explained it, the candle was to light the way to Jerusalem, the penny to pay the ferry, and the port to sustain him on the journey.' And professor George Stephen of Copenhagen about the same time gave me the following quotation: 'Within the coffin along with herself she got a pair of new brogues, a penny candle, and a hammer, with an Irish sixpenny-piece to pay her passage at the gate'.[109]

Clearly, there are similarities with the ancient Roman custom of paying the ferryman a fare for travel over the River Styx to the realm of the dead, although the reference to Jerusalem here suggests that the contact considered himself to be a Christian.

For those lost at sea there was always the hope, when all optimism for the return of the loved one had gone, that the body would eventually be washed up on a beach or caught in a trawl net. Were this the case the decomposed body could be identified by the pattern, and sometimes the initials, on the fisherman's gansey.[110] The remains could then be returned to the relatives so that the various local rites could be performed. (However, despite this continuing belief other people maintain that it is essentially mythical as very few bodies have been recovered and identified in this way.)

Once a body was available there were various means of commemorating the dead, some symbolic, others practical. One important practical response to increasing numbers of losses at sea was to establish a fund to help those family members left without any effective means of support. These funds were usually established by the local vicar who acted as a trustee. With no welfare system to protect them each fishing community was encouraged to establish a local 'fishermen's fund'.

Increasing numbers of such funds began to appear from the 1830s when the fishing industry began to expand and when the increasing numbers of fishermen lost at sea became evident. One especially early fishermen's fund was referred to by Thomas Hawkshead, a visitor to Filey in May 1809. His diary is kept in Lancaster Archives, although a copy of some sections has been placed with Filey Archives. At the later date of 1884 the Flamborough 'Fisherman's Coble Insurance Association' was formed for families who lost loved ones at sea or those fishermen who suffered damage to their vessels while at sea. The many funds were gradually amalgamated into national welfare systems for fishermen and their families; and the numerous Friendly Societies (Robin Hood's Bay had four, established in 1784, 1800, 1839 and 1840) provided support for families during times of loss, as well as mutual support for all who were members.[111] Parades and meetings were held regularly with services at the Anglican Church, forming an important aspect of the societies' activities. Before the development of Seafarers' Missions during the early nineteenth century such societies clearly played an important role and fulfilled a neglected means of support within the fishing communities.

Funerals, like weddings, were often not only occasions for a readjustment in family relationships but also important symbolic occasions for the community.[112] Such a loss of life was very much a tragedy for the whole village or town. An interviewee from Staithes, recalling events from the early years of the twentieth century, said,

> If somebody died in the village then there used to be people come round 'bidding', what they called 'bidding'. Women were given a shilling or something like that to come round to every house and say 'so and so requests the pleasure of your company at such a funeral'.[113]

The Revd Atkinson also offered the following anecdote, which suggests that the practice was common in the North of England:

> Within a day of the person dying the person whose professional name was 'the bidder' went round from house to house among those who were to be 'bidden to t'funeral', to warn them that the burial was fixed for such and such a day, and to add,

> 'and so and so' – naming the principal friend or friends of the deceased – 'expects you at ten o'clock in the morning'. The 'minister' was always among the first to be bidden.[114]

Individual fishermen were also expected to make some preparation for their own death and often purchased a gold earring when they were young. This was worn in the left ear so that there was something to pay for the funeral should the need arise.

While the men carried the deceased fisherman's body to church for the funeral service, it was also common for the women to act as pall-bearers on behalf of deceased females.[115] The act of having same-sex pall-bearers appears to have been widely practised as Obelkevich makes the same point about funerals in South Lindsey. It was also common for the fishermen (although not the women) to be carried shoulder high by the pall-bearers. However, in South Lindsey, such an act, according to Obelkevich, emphasized the status of the deceased and only those of high status were carried shoulder high.[116]

A means of commemorating the death of an unmarried female was the tradition of suspending 'maidens' garlands' over the seat she had regularly occupied in the local church. Gareth Spriggs has drawn attention to the many examples of this practice, including fishing communities, such as Flamborough and Filey, and at Old St Stephen's

Church, Fylingdales (near Robin Hood's Bay), where five such garlands can still be seen.[117] A variation on this was reported by Robert Fisher in 1894, in that following the death of a young wife a pair of white paper gloves were carried at the head of the procession and later hung in the church to commemorate her passing.[118] Such practices were not confined to fishing communities, although there were local expressions of the practice. John Cole writes of an early-nineteenth-century custom at Filey:

> But still greater respect is usually paid to the memory of unmarried females at their funerals, especially in the retired villages and dales of Yorkshire and other neighbouring counties. It is the encircling a ring or hoop (in some places two hoops crossing each other) with wreaths of white paper, which is hung up in the church over the pew or seat of one who had been recently interred. A custom of this sort was formally observed at Filey, and here and in some other places the form of a hand, cut in white paper, is inserted in the middle of the hoop or hoops, upon which is fairly written the name of the deceased maiden, with her age.[119]

As Cole was writing in 1828 and Fisher in 1894 these practices were clearly evident right through the nineteenth century. Other references by Spriggs suggest that the practices were also present during the eighteenth century and until at least 1950.

There was an equally rich array of symbolism present in the funeral of the men, as Michael Fearon has observed in his account of a funeral procession in Filey in 1908:

> Looking in the direction from which the music came, which was towards the old town, I saw a solid mass of people coming at a foot pace down the slope towards the other end of the bridge from where I stood. In front was a group of thirty or forty fishermen, four abreast, all in their spotless dark blue knitted jerseys, all slowly stepping on, and all joining in Dr Watt's well-known hymn, 'There's a land of pure delight . . . ' Behind them the coffin with one or two wreaths of flowers upon it, was carried by six stalwart brother toilers of the deep, and it was followed by the widow and more distant relatives of the deceased, while closing the procession came the wives and sisters of the fishermen and other sympathising friends.[120]

Filey ravine separates Yorkshire's North and East Ridings, with St Oswald's Church on the north side and the fishing community on the east. The church may be reached by the bridge mentioned in the earlier account. As with the other rites of passage, funerals were often held in St Oswald's Church even though many of the fishermen were Methodists. One interviewee provided an insight into the fishing community's full awareness of the symbolism of the ravine:

> The fishermen, if there were any funerals or anything, they used to carry the coffin across the bridge . . . they wouldn't have a hearse . . . and they all had their own saying 'How's Mr so-and-so today?' or called them by their name, they would say 'Oh, he's about ready for t' North Riding'.[121]

The very great loss of life in fishing communities during the second half of the nineteenth century has been commemorated in stories, songs and memorials. In 1899, for example, the Filey fishermen sought to commemorate their lost colleagues by placing a memorial window in the parish church. In more recent years fishing communities have created tapestries that commemorate life in the community.

Rituals, customs and superstitious beliefs

Although many traditional rituals, customs and festivals were abandoned with the demise of local confraternities during the period of the English Reformation, some remained, especially in the more isolated communities. This was also the case with many traditional customs and festivals in fishing communities where traces have managed to survive into the twenty-first century. At the same time new customs and festivals began to appear during the nineteenth century – not least because of the influx of many thousands of people from other national and international fishing communities who sought to take advantage of the prosperity of mid-Victorian Britain. It is not always easy, however, to separate out the new from the old. One such custom was identified by Cole in the 1820s: some weeks before the Christmas holiday the women of Filey anticipated the Spring Fishery by indulging in what Valenze has called a form of ritualized begging, which was an important opportunity to provide for their families during the winter months when fishing was confined to less lucrative opportunities:

> The lower order of females (carry) from door to door little square boxes of pasteboard, in which is placed a wax doll, as an image of Christ, surrounded by evergreens, with apples and oranges. The boxes are called Vessel cups. The women sing a carol, and are rewarded with a few halfpence: to send them away empty is to forfeit the luck of the whole year.[122]

That such 'mumping' also took place on St Thomas' Day (21 December) in rural areas suggests that the practice had been long established, preceding the nineteenth century.

George Shaw, writing in the 1880s, recorded other customs such as at the start of the herring season (June) fishermen would send a piece of sea-beef to the public houses and wish 'weel-tee-a' to their non-fishermen friends (a phrase that would appear to translate as 'well to you' meaning 'good health to you'). This was followed by a communal supper, held so that those leaving for the fishing grounds could meet friends who would wish them a good voyage.[123]

With the changes in the nature of fishing and the growth of new fishing communities, especially in Grimsby, during the mid-nineteenth century, new customs and festivals began to emerge, such as Blessing of the Sea/Boats/Nets. This was a new innovation in Britain, although such festivals are of long-standing in Europe, as Peter Anson has noted.[124] The late nineteenth-century innovation of Harvest Festivals was also quickly adapted by fishing communities into festivals known as the 'Harvest of the Sea', where churches and chapels were fitted out with nets, floats, models of ships, fish and other items relevant to fishing communities. Such festivals continue to be celebrated today, evidenced by the Blessing of the Boats held at Whitby in July, the Blessing of the Fish Harvest in St Oswald's Church at Flamborough Head, A Fish Dock Carnival, which raised funds for the Fishermen's Mission, was until recently held during August on Grimsby Docks, although this has now been replaced with a 'Lost Trawlerman's Day Service' (copying a similar event in Hull) held at the parish church, now Grimsby Cathedral. Scarborough's Boxing Day celebration was earlier a special day for the wives of fishermen to celebrate together. This has now become a wider community festival during which funds are raised for the Scarborough Lifeboat. And in Staithes there is a 'Nightgown Parade' during what is now the Lifeboat Festival in August.

While these modern-day festivals and services have a clear link with religious institutions, with formal services being held at some point in the proceedings, there are some traditions that contain elements of sympathetic magic. Such is the case with the mid-nineteenth-century custom in relating to the herring fishery in Filey. George Shaw recalled that on the third Saturday night after the boats had sailed, the youngsters seized all the carts they could find and dragged them through the streets to the Cliff Top where they were left to be collected by their respective owners the following day. It was believed that the practice (almost a rite) would drive the herrings into the nets.[125]

In Flamborough, too, there was a local custom called 'Raising the Herring'. The custom was obviously present during the 1880s as John Nicholson mentioned it in 1890 and Robert Fisher mentioned the practice in 1894, although no further details were provided about the origins of the practice.[126] After the men set off for the herring grounds the women, on Boxing Day, dressed in their husband's clothes and visited each other's homes to chat, sing and provide mutual support. Further examples of cross-dressing are to be found in other fishing ports, such as Gamrie in Scotland, where some men would dress up in women's clothes during a village gala (presumably during the 1970s), although it was not the custom for women to dress in men's clothes.[127]

At Staithes it was the custom, on 29 June, St Peter's Day, for the fishermen to decorate their cobles and to perform certain traditional rites, after which a festive meal took place.[128] Such examples of local customs show strong psychological links between those on shore and those at sea. The fishermen were familiar with the customs and would have them in mind when fishing for herring. This strong sense of empathy was also no doubt an encouragement for the men as they faced the difficult days ahead.

The study of performance and ritual tends to focus on rites of passage and the religious sacraments, although examples can also be found in what might at first appear to be more mundane activities. These include setting off for sea, visiting the pub following a trip to sea, the wives of fishermen gathering at the company's office on Fridays to collect payment (deducted from their husband's settlings), washdays, the telling of stories by the men (yarning) during quiet periods on board the vessels and in the pubs (it was normal in trawler towns for many fishermen to visit the local pub before returning home) and of course there were the many superstitious beliefs. Alec Gill has provided an example of a 'leaving ritual' performed by a fisherman's daughter, who, as a child, would throw her father's slippers at the front door after he had left – to 'ensure that he'd come back safely to wear them again'.[129]

Newly married women in Hull, Grimsby and Scarborough were encouraged to join other women outside their terraced homes in the street during the evenings where they 'gossiped'.[130] This initiation into the world of the women symbolized acceptance by the local community and provided ongoing support for the fisherman's wife. One variation on this was related to the author: when a Whitby inhabitant first arrived in the fishing community (possibly during the 1930s) she was told that she had to take it in turns to scrub the steps between the houses leading to the harbour. The next morning, she arrived at the steps and began scrubbing – only to have a bucket of cold water thrown over her. The neighbour said this was her initiation into the community and she was now accepted by all.[131]

The performance of such rituals embraces a concept of time as cyclical in nature. In her study of women in maritime communities on the Åland Islands, Hannah Hagmark has identified four distinct phases of the fisherwoman's life:

(1) life without the seafarer,
(2) preparation for the seafarer's departure and his actual departure,
(3) preparation for the seafarer's return and his reception,
(4) and life with the seafarer at home.

Binkley has enlarged on this outline in her book *Set Adrift: Fishing Families*, in Nova Scotia, by offering a detail of the daily lives of two fishwives. She does, however, point out that the details are evident in the lives of women whose husbands are employed in a variety of occupations.[132] While the *Women's Voices Project* in Yorkshire did not focus as closely on the daily lives of fishwives, there are clearly many similarities with the lives of the women interviewed in Nova Scotia.

Hagmark has further pointed out that

> The preparation for the seafarer's departure was both a physical and mental exercise, which involved the entire seafaring family. The seafarer's departure was followed by a period of adjustment, during which time the wife and children settled back into the routines that they had established for day-to-day life while the seafarer was absent.[133]

Such an approach to life bears many similarities to the cyclical nature of the religious year, and such rituals in fishing communities have a similar function to those rituals performed in church services. Indeed, many such rituals have been embraced and adopted into the liturgical calendar. But more can be said about the nature of the similarities. In the Eucharist, for example, and in 'yarning', an important focus is found in the symbolic act of communicating, and the presence of interest from others, as well as a sense of empathy resulting from the unburdening experienced by the storyteller. Robert Orsi in the United States made a similar point when he referred to the 'favours bestowed by the Virgin', told by correspondents from great distances and reproduced in the parish bulletins of the church at Mount Carmel in Harlem.[134] In other words, the events are important primarily for the communicators where 'hope' plays an important role. This is not to demean the nature of the Eucharist; indeed, it should be remembered that the present-day symbolic and stylized rite has its foundation in a meal shared by Jesus and his friends where conversation, no doubt, centred on the group's experiences. The importance of ritual has been discussed by Roy Rappaport who has defined it as 'The performance of more or less invariant sequences of formal acts and utterances which are not entirely encoded by the performers'.[135] He has also acknowledged that a wide range of rituals can have an important spiritual dimension for the individual.

All this, while merely scratching the surface, indicates a variety of beliefs and practices, many of which are not normally considered to be aspects of religious activities. Indeed, when we explore such rites and rituals within the spheres of magic, folklore and superstitious belief, we find that there are closer links with religion than might be thought.

Religion, magic, folklore and superstitious belief

Religion, magic and folklore

The established churches have learned over the centuries to embrace a range of customs and practices that they had previously disapproved of, yet churches have long struggled with the pervasiveness of these popular customs.[136] Wesleyan Methodism, for example, had, by the early nineteenth century, become more respectable and disapproved of 'superstitious practices'.[137] But John Wesley himself was accused of dabbling in magic when he approved the visions and trances of members. The Primitive Methodists and other Wesleyan offshoots, especially the 'Magic Methodists' led by James Crawfoot, were initially supportive of the range of popular beliefs and practices, including 'some elements of folk culture such as visions, dreams, omens, magic, faith-healing, witchcraft and exorcism'.[138] Even the joint founders of Primitive Methodism, Hugh Bourne and William Clowes, embraced folk beliefs and practices, and Bourne travelled to London to visit Joanna Southcott, where he was impressed with her medicines and cures; and Clowes performed an exorcism in Harriseahead.

When the fishermen met for a meal with their family and friends before departing for the fishing grounds – from which some may not return – there was a real sense of the origin of the 'Last Supper' here. The religious overtones were also reinforced by a service held on 'Boat Sunday'. The use of sympathetic magic (such as the possession of a caul), and the common use of talismans, continued throughout the twentieth century. For example, during the 1970s a Hull trawlerman cut the top off a broom and carved the head of his fishing vessel's skipper with a snake wound around his neck. The skipper was not popular with the men and the 'artist' made the point more explicit by painting a red mark, symbolizing blood, around the skipper's neck.

Not only the practice, but also the terminology of magic and religion was and remains very fluid, and academics have argued over the relationship. James Frazier, for example, argued that religion involves action via an intermediate figure and is therefore to be distinguished from magic as this involves direct action.[139] Durkheim said that religion and magic have different social functions: religion serves the group, while magic serves the individual.[140] And Bronislaw Malinowski pointed out the psychological function of religion was paramount in that religion was concerned with the present, while magic was concerned with the future.[141] But such attempts to distinguish magic from religion have not been very successful, and if we look at magic and religion from a functional perspective rites and rituals take on a significant role, suggesting a good deal of overlap. This is especially the case if we reflect upon the bargaining that often goes on in prayer, with such requests as 'I will do X if you give me Y'. Owen Davies has also pointed out that especially during the early nineteenth century 'it was, in fact the rites and fabric of the churches and churchyards of the Anglican faith that continued to act as a powerful focus of popular magic'.[142] There were numerous examples in fishing communities of such bargaining: the fishermen would often throw any loose change into the sea before setting off to the fishing grounds, or would place a coin in the cork floats on the nets before casting the net 'to pay for the fish'.[143]

The more conventionally religious would bargain by shouting 'Praise the Lord' before casting the net in the hope of a good catch. Others would sing hymns or recite the twenty-third psalm. Anson recalled, during the 1960s:

> Away out to sea could be heard the voices of the men as they were shooting their nets, singing *Jesu, Lover of my Soul* and *Rock of Ages, cleft for me*, and the custom was started at this time by many skippers of kneeling down in the cabin for prayer together before they would let down the net.[144]

Such practices were common in many cultures. For example, Fabio Rambelli in his book *The Sea and the Sacred*, in Japan, tells us that fishing there 'is a highly ritualized activity' and that a statue of the Buddha would be cast into the sea with the net especially during times of a poor catch.[145]

It was commonly believed that witches caused bad luck. In the fishermen's belief that their vessel had been cursed (evident in a series of poor voyages) the skipper or another crew member would walk around the vessel with a lighted taper to burn out the witches and demons.[146] Surprisingly, perhaps, this belief and practice has continued into the present as is evidenced by interviewees.[147] An example of the practice can also be seen in the 1989 film *Fading Light*, made among the fishing community of North Shields.[148]

Among the tokens used to keep such witches at bay a copy of the New Testament, provided by the Fishermen's Mission, was fixed to cabins in the fishing vessels. The mission staff no doubt intended that it should be read, but the fishermen, while pleased to see it there, regarded it simply like any other charm. Such tokens of good luck were also mixed with practical concerns such as the wearing of a gold ring in the left ear. As a circle of gold the earring also acted as an amulet and was believed to 'protect the wearer from drowning, preserve the eye-sight, and cure rheumatism'.[149] But among the most potent forms of protection was the caul. Stones with a hole through, known as 'Hagstones' in Suffolk fishing ports, were also considered a means of providing protection at sea and avoiding the influence of witches.

During the nineteenth century the term 'folk' was understood to refer to peasant society and was often used in a negative sense. The nineteenth-century folklorist tended to dismiss the beliefs of folk cultures as magic and superstitious belief rather than religion. But, as Patrick Mullen has pointed out, 'folk beliefs often functioned in ways similar to organised religion'.[150] For Alan Dundes 'folk religion' and 'popular religion' can be seen as synonymous, while the concepts of 'folklore' and 'popular religion' have a significant overlap. Given this close relationship Dundes has argued that folklore can be used in reference to any group that shares at least one common factor.[151]

The commonly perceived idea that superstitious belief, magic and religion are part of the life of pre-scientific and primitive societies, in which there was no sharp distinction between the sacred and the secular, gradually gave way to a more rationalistic perception in which the concept 'primitive' was contrasted sharply with 'modern'. In today's world we tend to reinforce such ideas in subtle (and non-too-subtle) ways such as with the heritage industry in which communities and societies have been idealized and made attractive for the tourist. Jane Nadel-Klein has made this point with reference to fishing communities.[152]

Fisherfolk are 'folk' by the nature of their calling, and this implies all that follows – language, occupation, customs, religion and so on. The following instances provide examples here. Many local traditions serve to account for the origins of geological and geographical features. It is said, for example, that the ammonites (sometimes called 'St Hilda's stones') found along the Yorkshire coast, especially at Whitby and Robin Hood's Bay, are fossils of snakes that St Hilda banished from the surrounding land.[153] In Filey it is said that in order to cause the destruction of ships and the death of sailors, the devil set about building the promontory known as Filey Brigg (called Filey Bridge by some early authors). In the process the devil dropped his hammer and when retrieving it caught a haddock, making what looks like a thumbprint that is still evident today. When his work was completed, he flew over the parish church and dropped the haddock on the church tower where it remains as a weather vane. The story draws upon a number of traditions, not least the concept of the fish as an early Christian symbol. Hence, the story links the local trade with a Christian symbol and provides the community with an important aspect of its identity.

While such tales provide explanations of geographical features, others provide an example of Margaret Mead's point that we define ourselves by defining others.[154] For example, a Filey resident related the following tale to the author in July 2005: 'should a Filey resident lead a dissolute life the devil would arrive in his carriage to collect the soul of the deceased – and deliver it to Scarborough.' Such concepts distinguishing groups, towns and villages were also reinforced with the application of names to different groups, countries and towns, such as 'yellow-bellies' for those from Lincolnshire and 'Grimmies' or 'Grims' for Grimsby fishermen; 'Yorkies' for those from Hull; 'Dough Boys', 'Duff Chokers' or 'Yarco' for Great Yarmouth fishermen; 'Puds', 'Pea-bellies' or 'Lowestermen' for Lowestoft; 'Roaring Boys' for those fishermen from Pakefield; 'Rammies' for Ramsgate; 'Brickie' for Brixham fishermen; and 'Bucca' for Newlyn men (referring to a left-over sea spirit to whom the fishermen made a small offering).[155] Continental fishermen, especially the Dutch, were given names, such as 'Scrogs' or Skrobs, and those from Ostend were called 'Oosties'. The gangs of dockworkers in Grimsby were known as 'Lumpers', while in Hull the dock workers were called 'Bobbers'. These terms along with many other beliefs and practices developed during the nineteenth century helped to forge local identities out of a very diverse group of immigrants.

Superstitious belief

While much that goes under the heading of supernatural belief could equally well be applied to religion, folk-lore and magic; many have nevertheless tended to refer to popular religion as 'mere superstitious belief'.[156] Hence, this is generally defined with reference to what is perceived to be an irrational belief, although this attitude seems to owe more to a biased subjectivity rather than to a scholarly objectivity. Indeed, as Abercrombie et al. have commented, 'religious belief, when not associated with active membership of a church, tends to be associated with superstitious belief while church attendance tends to be antithetical to superstitious belief'. Yet for ordinary people the distinction is not so clear, and the Abercrombie research observed 'for those people who do not go to church but yet say they are religious and pray often, religious belief has moved quite far from the orthodox church position and is really much closer to what would normally be called superstitious belief'.

Given the pervasive nature of such beliefs some clergy and ministers accepted these beliefs and practices long ingrained in the lives of fishing community members, others were more critical. The colour green, for example, is not popular with fisherfolk although there are interesting exceptions such as the fisherman's wife in Scarborough who painted her family fishing boat green – 'because it's my favourite colour. And in any case, it has been lucky for us!'[157] Such exceptions show the paradoxical nature of superstitious beliefs. Should the vessel in this case sink or have a number of poor catches, the family may well blame the colour of the boat on bringing bad luck. At the other extreme the Revd Thomas Tardrew, a Hull clergyman in the early twentieth century, painted his church pews green.[158] He appears to have done so to improve the appearance of the church and thereby attract more local people to the services – although some have maintained that he did so in order to confront the superstitious beliefs of the fishing community. The following Sunday, despite the superstitious views of some, apparently saw an increase in the normal congregation as people came to see and comment upon the vicar's handiwork. But the increase, as evidenced by the following month's baptisms, did not last long.

Given that such views were not uncommon, some scholars, such as Williams in Southwark, have argued that while the local community's perspective on superstitious beliefs and practices was different from that of the more critical clergy, it was no less sincere.[159] There was a broader perspective here, and the intimate connection between religious ritual, superstitious beliefs and folk customs was far more subtle than many scholars have allowed (Figure 2).

In his study of superstitious belief from a sociological perspective, Peter Jarvis has pointed out that folk religion and superstitious belief have been neglected areas of study in preference to the official and sectarian forms of religion, and that 'superstitious belief, like many other words, is employed in common speech with its meaning assumed rather than defined'.[160] The problem of definition has been noted by other scholars such as Gustav Jahoda, who offered a definition from the psychological

Figure 2 St John the Baptist Church, Newington, Hull. Photo: S. Friend, 5 April 2017. With thanks to Fr Tony Cotman.

perspective: 'the kind of belief and action a reasonable man in present day Western society would regard as being *superstitious*.'[161] Unfortunately, when Jarvis offered his definition he placed it within the sphere of 'folk religion' and then went on to distinguish folk religion from official belief systems. It is this distinction that is being called into question here.

In the following discussion I am not going to offer a new definition of superstitious belief. Rather, I intend to show that the tendency, in fishing communities at least, to disassociate orthodox religion from superstitious belief, no less than magic and folklore, is misconceived, not least because the essence of much superstitious belief relies on ritual activity that provides a close link with official religious beliefs and practices. The failure of modern scholarship to take superstitious belief seriously has tended to reinforce the isolation and otherness of orthodoxy. It is also difficult to demonstrate a chronological development in superstitious beliefs and practices. Many superstitious beliefs have been around since well before the advent of Christianity, and they continue to maintain a strong hold on present-day fishing communities, although there is often a reticence to admit to outsiders that this is the case. However, practically everyone interviewed for the *Women's Voices Project* made reference to superstitious beliefs.[162] Given the persistence of such beliefs and practices it is perhaps not surprising that some have been incorporated into Christianity – though usually reinterpreted within a Christian framework. Such beliefs and practices, which were a significant aspect of pre-Reformation Roman Catholicism, were rejected by the Puritans. But in the nineteenth century such practices began to creep into Protestant Christianity and were evident in Anglican ritualism and Roman Catholic Ultramontanism.

The intricate link between religion, magic and superstitious belief is evident in the following incident recorded by Mrs Gutch in her work of 1889 on folklore. She quotes from Schofield's work of *c.* 1787, where he spoke of a 'rite performed secretly' on Scarborough pier asking for calm weather and a prosperous voyage:

(The woman) proceeds unaccompanied about forty paces along the pier. Here a small circular cavity among the stones, which compose that huge mass of rocky fragments, receives a saline and tepid libation, which is poured into it while the sacrificer, muttering the tenderest wishes, looks towards that quarter, from whence the object of her anxiety, is expected to arrive.[163]

That the 'actor' in this instance is a woman is important. Many of the superstitious beliefs in fishing communities relate to either the male or female spheres, and it is the wives of the fishermen who often act as protectors of the men, rather than the other way around. The author of an article in *Superstitious Beliefs of Yorkshire Fisherfolk* in 1885 (referring to an article in *The Times*) said that the Staithes fisherfolk 'have a firm belief in witchcraft', although the custom was at that date only 'secretly maintained'. An example is offered. Referring to this same custom, Anson recorded the incident (possibly originally collected during the 1870s by Paul Sébillot but having its roots well back in time):

if a coble had had a spell of bad luck for a long time, [the locals] used a grim method of exorcism. The wives of the crew met after dark, killed a pigeon, took out its heart, and pricked it with pins. They roasted the heart on a brazier. This ritual attracted the witch who was supposed to have cast a spell on the coble. When the women thought she had arrived they offered her presents.[164]

On other occasions should the Staithes men fail to catch anything for many nights the first fish caught would be taken ashore and sacrificed as a burnt offering to the Fates.[165]

It has to be remembered here that boats are referred to as 'she', and the fisherman trusts the vessel with his life. On leaving home (the domestic sphere of his wife) the fisherman enters the sphere of the boat (his 'mistress'), hence it was important to keep the domestic and work spheres separate, and a number of superstitious beliefs are associated with this attitude. Women were generally not encouraged to wave the men off to sea, nor were they usually allowed on board the fishing vessels. There were few exceptions to this separation of roles, although there were some, such as the women who were smack owners and had taken on this role following the death of their husbands. One such was Jane Witty who owned several smacks during the 1850s and 1860s. Those women who fished at sea were even rarer, such as Milcha Lawrence of Flamborough, who worked as a fisherman during the mid-nineteenth century and was known as 'Milkey' (she died *c.* 1880). Apart from fishing she was renowned for following the custom of sitting in the church on St Mark's Eve (24 April) 'and declared she saw all those of her neighbours who were to die during the year in procession before the altar'. While this custom was widely held, it is perhaps not surprising that Milcha was considered to be a witch by the locals. Other witches were also common in the North

Yorkshire communities, including Mary Gibson, Betty Creaser of Flamborough, the Countess of Buckingham and 'Old Kathy' of Ruswarp (a model doll of whom resides in the Whitby Museum).[166]

Dora Walker is reputed to have been the first twentieth-century female fishing skipper working on the North-East coast of England. During the post-Second World War period she became a popular writer about life at sea. Such exceptions are very rare in England. Indeed, at Staithes, it was considered unlucky for the men to see the women on their way to the harbour, where the cobles were berthed, and should the women see a fisherman approaching they would turn their backs on them – a view that contrasts with the claim that Staithes women both launched and beached the fishing vessels. At Flamborough the fishermen would not go to sea if they met a woman on the way to their cobles unless her name was Anne or Mary. Given that Anne, Mary and Elizabeth were among the most common nineteenth-century female names, there is a sense in which the men were hedging their bets here. Such superstitious practices have overtones of magic and there are also clear psychological implications for the well-being of the fisherfolk, in that should the ritual be ignored the resulting tension and stress emanating from feelings of guilt could have dire effects on the family and community.

Dress and rag rugs

The dependency of the men on the women can be illustrated in a variety of ways. The clothes worn by the fisherfolk have superstitious links, as Anson has recorded: 'There was a feeling, not always clearly defined, that they (the clothes) lost their efficacy to withstand the forces of evil if they did not conform to traditional patterns, handed down for generations.'[167] The patterns found on ganseys are a good example here each being unique to individuals (initials were often incorporated), family (some particular aspects of the pattern) and community (a general local pattern). The pattern contained many symbolic elements such as ropes, nets, fish, ladders, marriage lines and stair steps. Classic patterns include the 'Betty Martin' (used in Filey, Whitby and Scotland), 'Flag and Rig', 'Print o' the Hoof' (hoof marks in the sand) and a Filey design known as the 'Lizzie Hunter' that consisted of repeated stair steps, diamonds and ropes. The diamonds were of two kinds – empty and filled with small bobbles. The empty diamonds represented empty fishing nets, while the full diamonds represented nets full of fish. The top half of the gansey pattern in Scarborough was filled with small bobbles – representing the beach or fish. Grimsby and Hull fishing communities, however, did not have their own unique patterns – presumably because of the late development of the fishing industry in these towns. Other uses of the gansey were also very practical, such as in Robin Hood's Bay where the fishermen adopted the expedient of turning up the bottom of the gansey to signify that they were looking for work – a practice that must have taken the embarrassment out of seeking employment.[168] Although it was not unusual for some men to knit, the responsibility for producing clothes normally rested with the women who, through this and other tasks, tried to ensure a sense of security and protection for the men. Even so, some men knitted, such as Alf Hildred of Robin Hood's Bay.[169] Alongside the very functional use of ganseys (pronounced 'gainsey' in Filey) as a source of warmth and as a means of enabling the identification of fishermen, there were also ways in which ganseys were integrated with the religious life of the community. The men and many of the women kept one gansey for Sunday best (these could be of various colours such as grey for Robin Hood's Bay, although there was not normally a specific colour for each community). Along the Yorkshire coast it was common for the men to wear a white silk neck warmer on Sundays rather than the normally coloured one worn throughout the rest of the week.[170] The aesthetic quality of the pattern in the gansey was thus integrated with the religious life of the community, although this 'religious life' was far more than mere allegiance to the religious institutions. They were important, too, as significant elements in rites of passage. They were also important for children as they received their first gansey at just a few years old, with their own unique identifier, and the girls were introduced to the skills of knitting ganseys as soon as they could hold a needle (the patterns were not written down until recent years). Ganseys were also knitted as a single thread, with no separate parts sewn in – perhaps suggesting a continuing link between the women on shore and the men at sea (there are overtones here of the myth of Theseus and Ariadne who gave Theseus a ball of thread to unwind in the Labyrinth so that he could find his way out after killing the Minotaur). The garment was thus an important aspect of individual and communal identity. Children were encouraged to emulate their parents, hence one contact in Scarborough commented: 'When Tom were a young lad his mam always had him a fisherman's jersey knit, maybe in double knitting wool, but all little boys were encouraged to do what their dads were doing, so you got the miniature smocks.' In such ways the children followed the example of their parents as they developed a local identity.

The women, too, in the older fishing ports along the Yorkshire coast, as elsewhere, had their own styles of dress, such as the 'Staithes bonnet' made with seven sewn grooves at the front. While this was an important symbol of local style there was also a practical function in that the grooves helped to avoid rain dripping down the face. Different coloured bonnets were worn for different occasions – white on Sundays, black for widows and funerals. But there was some variety here, as Arthur J. Munby referred to 'Molly's lilac hood-bonnet' at Flamborough in *c.* 1870; and Anson tells us that lilac was popular in that about 1890 the Staithes women also 'usually wore lilac print aprons and sunbonnets'.[171] The use of red to ward off evil was common in fishing ports, with Yorkshire fishwives wearing red petticoats. Again, Anson offers the following comment: 'Their overskirts were turned up over red petticoats. Down the back the pinned-up drapery hung in folds. Over their shoulders a little plaid shawl was drawn. Arms were left bare to the elbow.'[172] We also find the use of red petticoats around the coast as Munby, writing in October 1870, described the working dress of fisherwomen at Haverfordwest, South Wales, as 'the black wideawake, the white kerchief beneath it covering the hair and neck and bosom; the brown or dark blue sleeveless bodice, laced in front; the blue or white jersey sleeves; the short scarlet skirt'.[173] And in Newlyn, Cornwall, the fishwives wore scarlet coats. While in the older Yorkshire fishing communities the traditions of dress were long established, such traditions as did exist in the newer fishing ports of Grimsby and Hull were the result of relocated individuals and groups bringing their traditional styles of dress with them from their home ports.

It should also be noted here that the women were the main attendees at religious services, and they were of course the main carriers of tradition in the community. Williams, in her study of the local community of Southwark, has also pointed out that some women were regarded as 'fountains of folk wisdom' who passed on their practices and beliefs from generation to generation.[174] In this way traditions were passed on by the many different groups that established themselves along the Yorkshire and North Lincolnshire coasts. As such, this makes the women implicitly a very powerful group, although the value of women as social providers has rarely been acknowledged.[175] Paul Thompson is an important exception here. In his article 'Women in Fishing' he pointed out that it was the men away at sea who were especially dependent upon their womenfolk on shore.[176] The women's roles were many and various, including responsibilities for the more mundane activities relating to material culture.

One such material activity engaged in by all members of the community, but especially the women, was the making of rag rugs. Examples of rag rugs from the various Yorkshire fishing ports show a wide variety of patterns, although there were some commonalities. For example, an elderly interviewee who grew up in Robin Hood's Bay during the early twentieth century stated that when making rag rugs for the home the local fisherfolk always began with a blue diamond in the centre.[177] While she was unable to give a reason for this it seems likely that the diamond represented the fishing nets, similar to the use of the symbol in the Filey and Flamborough ganseys, although there may be other reasons. Richard Hoggart has also referred to the use of such a pattern in Leeds he calls them 'clip rugs' – other terms include 'snip rugs' (Lincoln), 'pricked rugs' (Hull) and 'proggy mats' (Northern England) – when he says, 'Patterns are traditional and simple, usually a centre circle or diamond with the remainder an unrelieved navy blue except for the edging, or that greyish-blue.'[178] This ubiquitous use of pattern has overtones of sympathetic magic alongside the superstitious beliefs. This is made more explicit in the use of a red diamond in the Kings' Lynn rag rugs, which was supposed to prevent evil spirits from entering the house. It was also believed that the colour red for petticoats and rugs helped to keep fleas at bay. Such activity may be written off as 'mere superstitious belief' by the churches but to do so disregards the fundamental spiritual importance of material culture to the community.

Religion, magic and superstitious belief overlap and the issues only become a problem when we try to make a sharp distinction between these different worlds of discourse. The ritual aspects of these practices play an important role in the life of the community. This view has been supported by Colin Campbell who pointed out that modern superstitious acts 'fulfil a ritual rather than a magical function', with the essence of the acts lying in their symbolism – and as such they have intimate links with official religious beliefs and practices.[179] In support of this argument he pointed to the sense of unease a person feels when a ritual has not been properly conducted. Even so, he does admit that some superstitious acts are engaged in not for the symbolism and ritual alone but for the results people desire – hence the overlap with magic.

Superstitious belief was, and remains, an important aspect of the fisherfolk's religious belief system, although historians, anthropologists and nineteenth-century

Christians have not always acknowledged this relationship. As a result, when Christian missionaries first visited the North Sea fishing fleets during the 1870s, they expected to see a God-forsaken, pagan race of men who wanted nothing to do with official religion. The visitors could not have been more mistaken. All who took the trouble to visit the fleets recorded their surprise and pleasure at being made to feel welcome and at the fishermen's enthusiasm for lively and long religious services – one visitor recorded attending a six-hour service, which was only broken off at intervals for refreshments. There was surprise, too, at the number of fishermen who stopped work on Sunday – including the whole fleet in at least one case (Figure 3).[180]

Nevertheless, the failure to recognize the close link between superstitious belief and religion led many to exclude fishermen (and seamen generally) from the Christian fold. Even Primitive Methodists, who had more sympathy than other groups for the old customs, sometimes thought it advantageous to distinguish between the old superstitious beliefs and the new situation. The following account, recorded by the Revd George Shaw in Filey during the 1860s, makes just this point:

Figure 3 Raising the Herring, George H. Traves, MBE, *Flamborough, A Major Fishing Station,* 2004. Photo with permission of Horsley and Dawson.

> At the commencement of the [nineteenth century] the fishermen of this place
> [Filey] were . . . exceeding superstitious. This was especially the case respecting
> ghosts, hobgoblins [*sic*] witches and wizards. I remember going some time ago
> to visit a sick girl, and on asking the mother the cause of her complaint, I was
> gravely assured that she was 'wronged, poor thing'. Not comprehending her at that
> moment, I enquired what that was, and a neighbour replied with a frightened look,
> 'Bewitched, sir'. While I was trying to show them the folly of entertaining such
> notions, the poor child exclaimed 'you're right sir, I am sure nobody has wronged
> me unless my mother has, for she won't pray for me, though I have asked her again
> and again'.[181]

The belief that residents of Filey were exceedingly superstitious continues down to the
present. A note in the Filey Archives records that a local woman who worked for the
Salvation Army said that 'she knew Filey had an evil past and a strong connection with
the devil'. But her recipient noted that 'It was quite a surreal experience to hear a person
talking in such old-fashioned terms, and more to the point taking it so seriously'.

Despite these links between religion and superstitious belief, the latter was, and is,
often seen negatively as pre-scientific and irrational, something that stretches credulity
and sometimes used in a derogatory sense on non-orthodox religious practices (although
orthodoxy here depends on the point of view of the observer). But as a coping mechanism
superstitious beliefs may nevertheless be seen as having a positive and constructive
function, a point made by Trevor Lummis based on Malinowski's theory of magic 'which
proposes that the economic uncertainties and personal risks inherent in fishing will
lead to attempts to control and influence irrational and unpredictable forces'.[182] In other
words Lummis observed that superstitious belief reduces anxiety, although this point
has been played down by later researchers who have tended to concentrate upon more
instrumental factors. The essence of superstitious belief, then, would appear to be in its
psychological function of helping to reduce anxiety in the face of uncertainty. In this case
the ritual aspect of superstitious belief and practice is the most potent – although unlike
the standard forms of ritual within organized religion, the ritual of superstitious belief
and practice does not require standardization. Scholars in recent times have noted that
there does not appear to have been any diminution of superstitious practice.[183] At the
same time many have noted that superstitious belief is more prevalent where the risks are
higher – and this has included especially mining and fishing communities.

In his research among the Trobriand Island fishermen (1915/20), Malinowski
observed that superstitious belief was more prevalent where the risk was greater, and
he argued that the risk here was directly correlated to magic ritual: 'It is significant that
in the lagoon fishing, where the man can rely completely upon his knowledge and skill,
magic does not exist, while in the open-sea fishing, full of danger and uncertainly, there
is extensive magic ritual to secure safety and good results'.[184] Later scholars questioned
whether the function of taboos in reducing anxiety is essentially correlated with *a lack
of economic security* or with *a fear of personal danger*? But they found it difficult to
reach a consensus. Mullen's study of Texas coastal fishermen in 1969, for example,
concluded that the correlation is basically with *the need for economic security*, while
Poggie et al., in 1976, argued for *personal danger* being the predominant factor.[185]

Lummis applied these various theories in his study of British East Anglian fishermen in 1880–1914, and conducted via oral interviews in 1981. Of the three main types of fishing engaged in (trawling, drifting and inshore fishing) it was the driftermen who proved to be the most superstitious, followed by the trawlermen and then the inshore fishermen.[186] This observation raised the issue that given the trawlermen are more likely to face personal danger than driftermen, one would expect, on the basis of Poggie's research conclusions, to find that trawlermen were the more superstitious. On the other hand, if superstitious belief is directly correlated to both personal risk (Poggie, et al.) and economic insecurity (Mullen), one would expect superstitious practice to be equally prevalent in both situations – this was not the case. We might also ask why the women and children should also be superstitious. On the basis of the earlier discussion, we could expect superstitious belief to be more prevalent in Grimsby with its deep-sea fishing fleet (and to a lesser extent in Scarborough) than in Filey. But on the basis of recorded evidence this seems not to have been the case.

According to Lummis, the situation is far better explained with reference to *economic uncertainty* than to *personal risk*. The driftermen were the most economically precarious group in the past, largely because they did not understand the movements or the breeding habits of the herring upon which they mainly depended for a livelihood. This explanation could also therefore be usefully applied to the women and children who shared the economic risk of the men at sea. But where economic security is the norm it seems likely that anxiety-reducing superstitious practices will be directly correlated with *personal risk*. It would seem reasonable, therefore, to suggest that inshore fishermen are less superstitious than trawlermen and driftermen, where the degree of personal risk is smaller and there is less economic uncertainty. Modern fishing communities are also less likely to be superstitious than earlier communities, given the prevalence of modern life-saving equipment, ship-to-shore radio, radar and computers. Lummis confirms this last point when he says that the most superstitious fishermen are those who work alone, far out at sea:

> But when these village inshore men talk about work superstitious beliefs, one has the impression that they know about rather than believe in them. Not one of the purely inshore fishermen told a story about work superstitious belief. This contrasts sharply with the smacksmen and still more with the driftermen, whose accounts are extensive.[187]

Lummis has shown that most interviewees said they were not as superstitious as the older generation. Two factors are important here. Given that modern fishing techniques and safety methods have vastly improved over that of the previous generation, we should perhaps expect to find a less superstitious younger generation – in that there is less economic risk. Fishermen and fishing communities are also less isolated and a less self-perpetuating group than formerly. At the same time there may also be a certain degree of scepticism and embarrassment in admitting to an active belief in superstitious beliefs in the face of a sceptical world. This point also seems to be borne out in Lummis's research when a fisherman of the older generation would not admit to being personally superstitious.[188] Good catches during the nineteenth century were ascribed either to good luck or to God's whim, when a skipper might proclaim: *The Lord giveth and the Lord taketh away. Blessed be the name of the Lord.*

> As all the men involved in the industry were agreed that luck determined economic prosperity the beliefs of the fishermen not only allowed them to cope with an extremely unpredictable occupation but also served a function in muting potential conflict and dissention within the family and community.[189]

That superstitious belief is an important part of the fishing community's religious belief system has been emphasized by a number of scholars. Poggie, Jr, Pollnac and Gersuny, for example, argued that superstitious belief 'is the term used by fishermen themselves when making reference to rituals of avoidance'.[190] However, they cannot be easily studied by asking questions, but rather by long association with, and initiation into, the community, as Anson discovered when working among Scottish fishermen during the 1920s:

> My instruction continued for the next two months. More than one elderly fisherman confided to me that he believed in the powers for good and evil held by 'side-women', that is, witches. Hints were conveyed of the existence of fairies and sea-devils. Living among fisher folk on the North-East coast of Scotland, so I soon realised, involved much forethought and tact. It was so easy to do the wrong thing or refer to the wrong persons or animals. Taken all round, the rules and observations of this close-knit maritime community, composed mainly of Presbyterians, were more elaborate than those of the Benedictine monks with whom I had lived for the past eleven years. But they were not written down, and one had to rely on oral instruction. There were no printed constitutions to consult.[191]

Superstitious beliefs were not, however, merely a response to economic uncertainty; they helped to provide a sense of security and a sense of control over the unknown, which helped to give meaning and purpose to life, and as such acted as a complement to the official forms of religious belief and practice.

Conclusion

Perhaps ultimately, it does not matter whether superstitious beliefs are true or false. With a pervasive superstitious practice there will in any case be enough positive outcomes to ensure continued belief (or enough negative outcomes to raise questions of doubt). The same may be said about official religion and prayer, and perhaps magic. While a certain number of positive results are inevitable, the value of the belief has more to do with *hope* than with the provable validity of the belief. People need a framework that gives meaning and purpose to life and a sense that they have some control over events. As analytic categories, therefore, and despite the plethora of definitions, there is a good deal of overlap between 'religion', 'magic' 'folklore' and 'superstitious belief'. All are concerned with individual and group concerns about meaning and purpose;

all embrace ritual and performance, which provide a sense of security, hope and control about the environment; and all interact in the everyday lives of people in their communities.

Indeed, as far as the daily lives of people in fishing communities were concerned, attendance at church services and special events such as rites of passage were occasions for putting on their best clothes and acting in the best manner, thereby making a statement about respectability and moral standards. To put more weight on allegiance to the churches was (and is) often seen as vanity, especially by the working classes. The influence of official religion in the everyday lives of the members of fishing communities is often minimal – certainly a great deal less than the customs, traditions and superstitious beliefs that determine daily behaviour. Attendance at church is seen as merely one activity among many in this all-embracing acknowledgement that people are in a constant state of bargaining with the transcendent power, however this is perceived. Even participation in the sacraments may be seen as an active part of this bargaining process.

While we have only touched upon the nature of the very diverse range of beliefs and practices in fishing communities, it is evident that attendance at church services played a relatively minor, if sometimes important, role in the lives of the community members. Even so, there is clearly a big overlap between the formal and informal religious beliefs and practices that may be considered aspects of popular religious experience. Williams' concept of a range of a 'generally shared understanding of religious meaning' is very pertinent, as is her reference to overlapping spheres of discourse, each with its own language.[192] It is when we look at the diverse beliefs and practices as part of the totality that has made up life in fishing communities we can see that the relationship between religion and identity is more complex than a simple identification with the orthodox religious denominations. The next chapter therefore argues that in order to understand the nature of identity in such communities we need to explore this broader picture.

The construction and maintenance of identity in fishing communities

Introduction

The roots of identity as a philosophical concept have a long history, although the concept has of course long been used as a lay term. As a conceptual tool in the social sciences, 'identity' derives its historical, psychological and anthropological lineage especially from the work of Erik Erikson and its sociological roots from the work of George Herbert Mead.[1] Erikson's work dealt with the particularly relevant issue of identity in the aftermath of a wave of immigrants who entered the United States between the two world wars and had to struggle with their own newly emerging identities. During the 1940s/1950s he helped to define the modern concept of identity with his emphasis on 'ego-identity' seen as the means of individual continuity. He later clarified his view in the publication of his 1956 journal article 'The Problem of Ego Identity', where he presented his eight-stage model of 'identity and the life cycle', a concept that he later developed as a social psycho-history, a combination of historical, social and psychological biography.[2] Erikson's interdisciplinary approach led to reverberations in a wide range of disciplines and gave birth to a number of different but complementary perspectives.

The concept developed by Mead (1934), although he preferred the term 'self', helped to pioneer the work of the Symbolic Interactionist school and argued that the development of the self is partly dependent on the existence of a social environment. Mead further stated that the generalized concept often develops out of our particular experiences of other people, hence we are able to argue that we *imagine* ourselves with a particular image. The point here is that the meaning is not essentially internal and subjective but derived and constructed from our social interactions.

The concept was further developed by Anselm Strauss in his work *Mirrors and Masks: The Search for Identity* (1959). During the same year the social psychologist Erving Goffman proposed that we 'act out our roles'; and in 1985 the anthropologist Anthony P. Cohen made us aware of the importance of *symbolism* in the life of individuals and their communities.[3]

These views, while pioneering, have not gone without criticism. For example, G. H. Mead has been criticized for neglecting to include the influence of power and culture on identity; and Goffman's perspective, while equally influential, has been questioned, especially by Cohen who argued that 'Goffman's legacy to identity studies was intellectually seductive and profoundly damaging', and the idea that individuals and groups can control their destinies has been overstated while the nature of culture has been understated and self-consciousness ignored. But Cohen has urged us to be wary of absolutes here, and despite the criticisms these scholars have had a profound influence on modern perceptions of identity and have provided helpful insights into the debate.[4] Even so, Weigert, Teitge and Teitge pointed out that the terminology here has been somewhat ambiguous with some scholars using the terms 'self' and 'identity' 'without clear theoretical distinction'.[5]

The concept of *identity*, therefore, has a range of meanings, and it has also often been qualified by an adjective: *personal* identity, *social* identity and *cultural* identity, although Richard Jenkins has argued that it is less confusing to talk simply of 'identity' and not to make distinctions between the various terms.[6] In the introduction to Zygmunt Bauman's book on the subject, Benedetto Vecchi, clearly aware of the earlier debate, pointed out that identity is 'by its very nature elusive and ambivalent'.[7] It is easy, therefore, in our modern-day nostalgic search for community and identity in the past to romanticize the concepts while bemoaning their loss. At the same time identity is a dynamic process, and, as such, the developing sense of belonging is only really meaningful within a social and cultural context.[8] Hence, avoiding a convoluted definition, and bearing in mind the views of the Social Interactionist school we may for simplicity say that *identity is essentially a socially and culturally constructed process, negotiated by the individual and underpinned by historical, social and cultural contingency.* This definition is in sharp contrast to the modern desire for pre-constructed or 'canned' (off-the-peg) identities available especially via the internet, where 'social, cultural and sexual identities (have become) uncertain and transient'.[9] The process is ongoing in that identity changes to a greater or lesser extent depending on a wide range of personal and social factors; and the individual's perception of identity is an important factor in the ways in which she/he copes with change. It has, for example, been argued that identities become especially important when they are under threat.[10] Prior to this development there is usually little local discussion about the concept.

In the following we will examine how identity has been constructed and maintained via community, culture and change in fishing communities during the period 1815–1921 before going on to examine further the nature of the relationship between religion and identity.

The construction and maintenance of identity in fishing communities

Community, change and identity

Delanty has argued for four main perspectives evident within the present-day debates on community: that evident within cultural sociology and anthropology, all are concerned with 'the search for belonging where the emphasis is on cultural issues of identity'; the community studies approach, which is concerned with 'disadvantaged and urban localities': 'community in terms of political consciousness and collective action'; and a concern with globalization, transnational movement and the internet, which identifies community as being 'constituted in new relations of proximity and distance'.[11] In exploring the issues here Delanty has adopted an interdisciplinary approach, and while some aspects of these perspectives are clearly modern (such as the internet and globalization), others were evident in nineteenth- and early-twentieth-century fishing communities, although the emphasis was essentially on community as providing a sense of place/belonging. Hence, it is this approach that forms the main focus of this chapter, although other perspectives will be evident at times.

Communities dependent on living marine resources will have a number of factors in common, although it is a mistake to assume that they are all the same. To talk of *the* 'British fishing community' is a gross overgeneralization that says more about our perceptions of fishing communities than it does about their social, economic and political nature. Indeed, there are significant differences between these communities, the nature of the marine resources exploited and the methods used to exploit them. Nevertheless, there are some aspects of life in the fishing communities that bear comparison. Hence, it may be helpful to make use of an appropriate methodological approach here, and Durkheim's model of social solidarities may be usefully adopted and adapted.[12]

When reviewing Tönnies's concepts of *gemeinschaft* (community) and *gesellschaft* (association, society) Durkheim rejected the concept of a progressive individualism implied by the latter, arguing that such a view leaves society fractured with the only thing holding society together being an imposed social order by the state.[13] He further argued that 'the life of large social agglomerations is just as natural as that of small groupings. It is no less organic and no less internal'.[14] Hence his use of the concept of 'organic solidarity' in his work *The Division of Labour*, where his concepts of *mechanical* and *organic solidarities* distinguish between social grouping in pre-industrial and industrial societies.

Individualism here is seen as a characteristic of modern times, although as can be seen in the development of Grimsby, the community tended to consist of numerous small groups. These can be identified via a range of significant factors including *origins and locality*, such as Brixham, Barking, Ramsgate and Sherringham (Appendix 5), *culture* (British and non-British), *interests* (Friendly Societies and Temperance groups), *status* (fishing apprentices, deckhands, skippers, fishing vessel owners, as well as numerous groups outside fishing) and *official religion* (Roman Catholics, Anglicans, Methodists, Jewish, etc.).

Of the three communities being examined here (Grimsby, Scarborough and Filey), Grimsby is closest to Durkheim's concept of an *organic solidarity*, where individuals contribute skills to the wider community; Filey is closest to the concept of a mechanical solidarity, where each individual contributes to the survival of the community; and Scarborough sits midway between these two.[15] Both types of solidarity are, of course, ideal types and will not match perfectly any given fishing community. Nor is Durkheim's model being used here in an evolutionary sense but is being applied to different kinds of community/society existing side by side. Neither is there any implication of 'primitive' or 'sophisticated' – attention is drawn merely to similarity and difference.

In the mechanical solidarity, argued Durkheim, the concept of self-consciousness is minimal. For people growing up in such a community (e.g. Filey, Staithes, Runswick Bay and Robin Hood's Bay), their sense of personal identity matched their social identity to a high degree. Family, peers, neighbours, no less than school friends, teachers and work colleagues, were all familiar with the life and experience, including the genealogical history, of the community members. Hence, the sense of self and personal identity was intimately bound up with this sense of social identity and included a strong sense of security in the face of what was at times a very insecure economic environment. With such a strong sense of self, demands for change were often met with strong opposition. Such an exaggerated consciousness of the self as opposed to 'self-consciousness' is common to many groups today, not least those who are members of long-established religious communities, such as the Mormons, Mennonites, Hutterites, Amish and Bruderhof. It is even the case with larger groups, as has been noted by Fred Gearing in his work with the Fox Indians of Iowa, and Carol Greenhouse's work among the Southern Baptists in Hopewell, Atlanta.[16] Many other indigenous communities, such as the Inuit, Maori and Australian Aboriginals, have recently capitalized on their art as a means of cultural identity that helps to bridge the gap between themselves and the wider national and international populations. We could of course go on to include numerous groups in today's world, which face oppression and discrimination. The nineteenth-century fishing communities faced dramatic and pervasive change as new fishing methods were developed to meet the huge demand for the fish discovered on new fishing grounds. The growth of new fishing communities such as Grimsby attracted fishermen and their families from all over Britain and the world (see Appendix 5). In some cases the community's sense of identity was reinforced by certain constraints and legal requirements, yet change did occur within such groups, and Durkheim's model can help us to understand some of the processes here.

While the sense of identity and self-consciousness among the residents of Filey (an example of a 'mechanical solidarity') was strong, the residents of Grimsby (an example of an 'organic solidarity') had a weak sense of identity. Self-consciousness tends to be more pronounced in organic solidarities, where the relationship between personal and social identity is very loose. Hence, many aspects of personal and social experience in an organic solidarity have generally poor connections with each other. In this situation the focus tends to be on the individual rather than the group. Group identity tends to develop over time, and it is often not until the third generation that group identity becomes a significant force within the community.

Scarborough fits midway between Filey and Grimsby in that both forms of solidarity were more clearly evident there. The fishing community living in what was locally called the 'Bottom End' had been long established, and there was a fairly clear distinction between the locality of the fishing families and the wider community. Hence, there were also some similarities to Filey. Scarborough's long-established fishing community, like that of Filey, had a strong sense of identity. The major difference between the two towns being that Scarborough had a harbour that attracted visiting vessels and the fishing community was a smaller one within a town. Unlike Filey, there was an increase in visiting fishermen and their families settling in the town as the nineteenth century progressed and the North Sea fishery prospered. As can be seen from Table 8,

Table 8 Fishermen at Home in Grimsby, Scarborough and Filey on Census Night, 1841–1901

	1841	1851	1861	1871	1881	1891	1901
Filey fishermen	132	149	155	202	175	188	190
Born in Filey		131	137	160	146	171	177
Born elsewhere		10	18	42	29	17	13
% born in Filey		**88**	**88**	**79**	**83**	**91**	**93**
Scarborough fishermen	99	158	246	358	363	513	329
Born in Scarborough	91	96	138	196	270	315	239
Born elsewhere	8	62	108	162	183	138	90
% born in Scarborough	**92**	**61**	**56**	**55**	**74**	**62**	**73**
Grimsby fishermen	10	17	209	646	1402	2216	2293
Born in Grimsby		7	14	26	90	239	244
Born elsewhere		10	195	620	1321	2077	1742
% born in Grimsby		**41**	**7**	**4**	**6**	**11**	**12**

Note: The figures here are for those fishermen at home on census night. Unfortunately, there is little consistency in the use of terminology, with 'seafarer', 'seaman' and 'engineer' covering a range of types of seafarer. Hence, for simplicity, the numbers here consist of those people designated 'smack owners', 'smack master', 'fisherman', 'apprentice fishermen' and others such as 'engineers', who were clearly working on a fishing vessel. There is no simple way to identify how many fishermen were at sea, hence we must rely on estimates by a number of people (see Tables 1–3). On average there appear to have been approximately 2,500 fishermen (from Grimsby, Scarborough and Filey) at sea on each of the census dates from 1871 to 1901.

the numbers of fishermen born in Filey only dropped below 88 per cent of the local population during the peak years of North Sea fishing during the 1870s and the early 1880s, and subsequently rose in 1891 to over 90 per cent.

How then do we account for change in fishing communities in the face of both strong and weak forms of identity? There is always an unconscious potential for change that can manifest itself in certain situations, but how does this unconscious potential become a conscious reality? Fortunately, in the case of Filey we have a good example in that a significant number of the local population embraced religious allegiance to Primitive Methodism within a short span of time in early 1823, and the change appears to have been the result of both internal and external factors.[17] The Filey Revival of 1823 was influenced by travelling preachers well before this event, first by the Wesleyan Methodists and later by the Primitive Methodists. That a small number of Wesleyan Methodists had already become established is perhaps significant in that this acted as a precedent for later change, although the strong local sense of identity meant that the constraints on individuals and the population's resistance to change were considerable. The early preachers were pelted with dried fish, and pigs were driven into the open-air meetings. The Methodists appear to have first preached in Filey in 1806 (although there is no evidence that John Wesley ever visited the village), and a small Wesleyan

Society was formed in 1810. This was followed with the opening of a small chapel in 1811 but progress remained slow such that by 1823 there were only fifteen members.[18]

Such resistance was also aided by the early-nineteenth-century growth of middle-class norms of discipline, centralization and respectability in Wesleyan Methodism that had the effect of alienating many working-class people.[19] It is perhaps not surprising, therefore, that Wesleyan Methodism in Filey initially achieved little in the way of success. Preachers found it difficult to make any impact on the town, and John Oxtoby's success for the Primitive Methodists came only after several years of such visits.

The conversion of approximately 40 people in 1823 (with numbers reaching around 100 a year later) came after several years of social and economic difficulty, precipitated by the disillusionment felt by many in the wake of the Anglo-French Wars and in the context of wider social and economic changes.[20] Although such dramatic conversions are generally short-lived, in the right situations with the right local support such change can be more permanent, and this appears to have been the case with Filey. The strong sense of community identity also aided the change in that when it began to occur it gathered momentum quickly and had a significant impact on the future of the community.

In fishing communities with a weaker sense of identity we would expect change to be less dramatic and complete, mainly because of the lack of wider social support. Movement and change were common factors of nineteenth-century communities, and fishing communities were not the static, unchanging social environments we might imagine, as Gerrish has demonstrated. Grimsby, for example, did not exist as a fishing community until the 1850s, and it is perhaps more appropriately pictured as a mixture of cultures, each with its own identity alongside a gradually emerging local community identity based primarily on occupation (or we might say individuals had multiple identities, corporate and fluid). Yet the emergence of a local identity was aided by the views and attitudes to the town by other localities, and the growth of a terminology applied to local individuals and groups. Filey long had a more coherent fishing community and a more consolidated identity, although it, too, as we have seen, in the right circumstances was affected by change. When people talk about the sense of community disappearing, their concept here is usually based on community of place and of culture, thus giving a sense of permanence, a sense of something that has been lost. Although with Grimsby and Hull it took several generations for the local population to develop a sense of pride and identity in their place of birth. The truth, however, may be that while these communities experienced *periods* of stability, change for both types of community was often the norm.

The 1841 census shows that 92 per cent of Scarborough fishermen were born in the town. Ten years later only 61 per cent of the local fishermen were born there (and the percentage continued to decline until 1881), the visiting fishermen and their families being attracted by the rapid growth of the North Sea fishing industry. When these visitors brought with them new methods of fishing, especially trawling (the indigenous Scarborough community predominantly engaged in line-fishing), the local residents responded by rejecting the innovation, sometimes violently.[21] The overall result was that many of the visiting fishermen eventually moved to the newly developing fishing communities of Hull and Grimsby, where they found a more acceptable welcome. Even so, some visiting fishermen stayed in Scarborough and saw the more lucrative fishing methods gradually adopted. As the percentage of fishermen born in Scarborough gradually increased towards the 1880s, this suggests that following the influx of fishermen from outside the town during the period 1845–81 there was an indigenous growth situation in the 1880s that gradually levelled off. This situation is made starker when we see that the fishermen at home on census night consisted of 99 in 1841 and rising to 513 by 1891.

Grimsby is of particular interest here in that most people in the new fishing community had their origins outside the town, such that there was little concept of a common local heritage, as Gerrish has pointed out:

> Prior to the 1850s there had been no recent fishing industry of any importance at Grimsby. According to the census of 1841 only 1.3 per cent of all economically active males in the town were listed as fishermen. By 1851 – when the first stage of re-development of the port was nearing completion – this figure had dropped to 0.6 percent.

The situation thereafter changed dramatically and by 1857 there were twenty-two fishing smacks working from the town.[22] While the 1851 census recorded only 17 fishermen working there, by 1861, 209 fishermen were employed, although only 14(7 per cent) were born there. By this date, too, 'twelve per cent of all employed males in the town were smack-owners, smack captains, fishermen or fishing apprentices'.[23] While fishermen and their families came from a very diverse array of localities the table in Appendix 5 shows that the majority originated from a small number of towns, especially Barking, Brixham, Gravesend, Great Yarmouth, Grimsby, Lowestoft, Hull, Scarborough and Sherringham, although by 1891 an increasing number (239 or 11 per cent of the local fishermen) had been born in Grimsby: over two-and-a-half times the figure of 10 years earlier.

The Grimsby fishermen lived within the half square mile bounded by North and South Victoria Street, Riby Square/Stirling Street, Park Street and Eleanor Street, this being the area mainly known as New Clee (Appendix 1b). By 1881 New Clee had a population of over 11,000, and by the beginning of the twentieth century there were over 26,000 people living within this area, most of whom were directly associated with the fishing industry (Appendix 2a).[24] Given that various groups of fishermen shared similar roots, it is perhaps not surprising that, as Gerrish has pointed out, 85 per cent of the Devon and Kent fishing families in 1861 lived in purpose-built properties in the Worsley Buildings, Kent Street, Church Street and Bath Street (all in a newly built area of the town).[25] The 1881 census also shows fishing families from Sherringham, Norfolk, living in close proximity (in Kent Street, Thorald Street and Cleethorpe Road), and by 1891 the majority of these had moved to Castle Street and Stanley Street.

In Cleethorpes 142 (85 per cent) of the 167 fishermen were born there by 1871 (Table 9).[26] By 1901 only 89 of the 476 fishermen (19 per cent) were born in the town. Nevertheless, proximity for fishermen from distant towns (living in both Grimsby and Cleethorpes) was restricted simply because of the demand for accommodation.

Table 9 Fishermen at Home in Cleethorpes on Census Night, 1841–1901

	1841	1851	1861	1871	1881	1891	1901
Cleethorpes fishermen	69	105	116	167	190	210	476
Born in Cleethorpes			85	142	138	116	89
Born elsewhere			31	25	52	94	387
% born in Cleethorpes			73	85	75	55	19

At the same time, with increasing wealth, some smack owners moved further east into Cleethorpes and south to the more rural setting of Abbey Road. The majority of owners (i.e. generally owners of one vessel) continued to live in the heart of the fishing community in the area of Mangle Street. Hence, while Cleethorpes saw a gradual increase of fishermen living in the town until 1891, the surge of numbers in 1901 (from 210 to 476 fishermen) bears witness to the growing wealth of the fishing community. The sharp decrease in the numbers of fishermen born in Cleethorpes from 1891 was mirrored by the huge increase of numbers of fishermen born elsewhere. Given that there was also a boost in numbers of fishermen for Grimsby for 1901 (see Table 8) it is likely that the sudden influx caught the town unawares, many people having to look for accommodation elsewhere, especially in Cleethorpes. The situation would also suggest that many fishermen were earning sufficient for them to move some distance away from the more immediate area of the Grimsby fish docks. Further analysis of the census data is likely to show that there was a general move into other areas of the town, especially the more pleasant suburbs. But this new era of wealth for some had not been achieved without a cost.

Unlike in the longer established fishing community of Scarborough, there was no opposition to new methods of fishing in Grimsby as the new fishing community began establishing itself during the 1850s/1860s. The fish docks had in any case been created with the new fishing methods in mind. But as the fishing community became established tensions began to rise, and in 1880 there was an attempt by the fishing vessel owners to impose a new system that involved all year-round fleeting. The fishermen in turn objected to a system that they felt would result in many deaths and injuries during the winter months, and this led to united action by the fishermen. Gillett tells us that 'The strikers were sober and well behaved, and in the town there were very few people who did not sympathise with them.'[27] Not surprisingly, after three weeks the men were able to celebrate a successful outcome. But later clashes between the owners and the fishermen did not lead to such positive results for the latter. In 1886 the owners made another attempt to impose winter fleeting, and, despite opposition and strikes by the fishermen, a number of the owners bought steam trawlers and eventually succeeded in imposing their system. Gillett recorded that it was now impossible for the fishermen to resist the changes. There was nevertheless a sense of irony here in that with the advent of the steam trawler, fleeting quickly became redundant.

Other conflicts occurred from time to time, culminating in the 1901 'lock out', when the newly formed 'Grimsby Federated Owners Protection Society Ltd' sought to impose a new system of payment on the crews. This was strongly resisted and strike action was undertaken by the fishermen resulting in 400 trawlers being tied up in the docks. As the summer weeks turned into winter months the 'lock out' caused increasing hardship for the fishermen and their families as well as for a wide range of support workers. An attempt by the owners to bring in crews (not for the first time in local disputes) led to violence and rioting that had the negative effect of detracting from the fishermen's cause. Arbitration was accepted and the fishermen eventually went back to sea 'on the terms offered by the Federation pending an award by an arbitrator'. But the fishermen benefitted very little from this. Gillett comments:

> Freed of their labour troubles, the owners were soon able to add another hundred trawlers to their fleet and the sailing smacks dwindled to less than thirty. The town seemed to have achieved its ultimate destiny as the home of the steam trawler and the fishing millionaire.[28]

Significantly, these conflicts become more evident from the late nineteenth century onwards when the community's sense of identity was becoming stronger, and the social gap between owners and fishermen grew even larger. This situation had been precipitated by the initially weak sense of identity in Grimsby that allowed possibilities for rapid change, resulting in economic power for a few and a higher degree of social solidarity for the many. Even within the growing community of mid-century we might expect to have found remnants of strong identity present, a hangover from the community experience in the incomers' hometowns and with fishermen from other fishing communities tending, whenever possible, to live in close proximity giving members a sense of security. In such a situation we would expect change to be more evident in the second and third generation as offspring became part of the emerging wider local identity, and it would be natural here to see the formation of various subcultures in which some did better economically than others.

The rapid growth of the Grimsby population, and individuals' increasing self-confidence, was partly enabled by the rapid establishment of a range of religious denominations following 1870 (Appendix 6a1). The religious institutions provided and reinforced a sense of security in a rapidly changing environment and thereby allowed the community to develop a stronger sense of local identity (perhaps it would be more correct to talk of local identities). This was evidently the case by the end of the nineteenth century when members of specific social groups became civic dignitaries and council members. Among the pioneers of the Grimsby fishing industry who subsequently became local dignitaries were Ald. Henry Smethurst, JP, Sir George E. J. Moody, Thomas Campbell, Harrison Mudd, JP and George Lowe Alward, FRSA, JP. Smethurst, Campbell and Mudd, in particular, were staunch members of the local churches and ardent teetotallers.[29] This growing sense of security and the achievements of individuals were important factors in bringing increasing numbers of fishermen and their families to the town. Clearly, it was easier for new groups in Grimsby with a strong sense of identity to achieve positions of authority in the town. These included fishermen from towns that had a strong connection with the churches and chapels, especially Primitive Methodism, Jewish immigrants (a number of whom became important local dignitaries) and those who developed with the growing number of local associations and societies.

As a general principle, therefore, it can be said that change came about in Scarborough, Filey and Grimsby when it was necessary for survival and when the relevant support networks were in place to aid security – thereby enabling individuals and groups to take risks. These support networks included extended families, fishermen and groups from the same hometown and with similar histories, churches and chapels, Friendly Societies and Temperance organizations. Even so, the changes as we have seen were far from smooth in that opposition was always present both individually (as the tendency is always to seek security within the familiar) and socially, where the identity of the community was perceived to be under threat. The process of change here was therefore underpinned by the social and psychological need for security and survival – in terms of both continued personal existence and personal and social identity. When personal psychological well-being and social and economic security were threatened the need to survive kicked in, creating tension between the various elements. In such situations there were a number of possible outcomes, but the net result was that change was usually facilitated in one form or another.

In a community with a strong sense of identity (Filey) such a change was likely to be slow but eventually dramatic, whereas in a community with a weak sense of identity (Grimsby) change was likely to be more gradual throughout, although in certain situations (such as the developing sense of community identity) change was resisted. In a fishing community like Scarborough the conflict arising out of the tension was more evident. Thus, when outsiders move into a community that has a strong sense of identity this can cause conflict – although with increasing numbers of outsiders establishing themselves locally, the tension and opposition to change gradually decreased. Such a situation was clearly evident in a number of fishing ports where conflict occurred over fishing methods (Scarborough) and with regard to fishing on Sundays (Newlyn in 1896).[30] The Newlyn dispute, however, was not of long duration as F. G. Aflalo commented that on a Sunday in 1903 he saw visiting 'fishermen packing, fishing and loading carts' – although Newlyn men still refused to go to sea on Sundays.

Change, therefore, was not merely facilitated by the move from a situation of mechanistic solidarity to one of organic solidarity. Change takes place in both types of community, although such change may well take a longer or shorter period of time to work itself out. In other words, it is not the move from one type of community to another that facilitates change; rather, it is the tension created when the innate need for psychological, social and economic security comes into direct conflict with the threat to such security. This appears to have been Cohen's point when he spoke of identity becoming most evident when it is under threat.[31]

Durkheim's model therefore offers an explanation for many kinds of change experienced in the fishing communities, but it is especially evident in the nature of religious change. After all, it is usually religion in one form or another that offers an explanation of the need for change and subsequently legitimizes the actual change such as with the case of Filey in 1823 and in Scarborough and Grimsby during the 1870s. Nevertheless, it would be wrong to think of such change in isolation from other social changes in the community. Clearly each form of change had an impact on the others.

Culture and identity

Cohen's argument that identity is formed and maintained in reference to cultural stability is no doubt also true in the wider sense, such that when people move from their locality they tend to seek out people from a similar background.[32] This is perhaps a natural biological and psychological trait and is clearly evident when we look at the census data for Grimsby, where some groups of fishermen and their families from distant towns lived in close proximity. Change is often managed in reference to cultural stability, and such cultural stability provides the security necessary for people who were willing to take risks leading to change in the long-standing communities. The sense of cultural stability is often reinforced in a variety of ways such as the wearing of traditional dress like bonnets and ganseys, fishing methods, nicknames, the telling of stories and singing of songs, especially of major events such as great storms and tragedies. Fishing vessels were often made in the local style (such as the Filey Coble), and for the older communities there was usually general agreement on the nature of the fishing engaged in. Stories told and retold helped to bind together the experience of many, and for those who did not experience the actual events there was the sense of common heritage in which fathers, brothers and grandparents of the hearers were involved. But such stories (often significant events and the exploits of memorable individuals) do, of course, gradually take on mythical proportions in the telling – and the common heritage becomes one of not just telling the tales but also engaging in discussion on the variously perceived nature of events. In a number of instances the communities have produced memorials in the form of monuments, tapestries, heritage centres and museums with a range of artefacts. There are also collections of oral history accounts, poems and numerous other local publications. Increasingly, special services are held to commemorate major tragic events such as the Fishermen's Sunday procession to the memorial at Bridlington Priory that recalls the loss of about 150 fishermen in the Great Gale of 1871.

Cohen's argument that localities become especially aware of their culture and identity at the boundaries where they engage with others is borne out in the experience of the three communities under investigation. This is the point where the members' behaviour, previously implicit, becomes explicit and is consciously perceived.[33] This situation, however, should not be seen merely negatively as it enables the placing of values on the community's distinctiveness, and in this sense fishing communities are no different from other social and cultural groups. A further point by Cohen is also pertinent here. He has maintained that 'People become aware of their culture, and experience their distinctiveness, not through the performance of elaborate and specialised ceremonial but through the evaluation of everyday practices'.[34] Among these we might include dress, local dialect, nicknames, customs and superstitious beliefs. At the same time special events also serve an important purpose. Turner, upon whose work Cohen drew, identified liminality in communities as important symbolic events in which the community reasserts its collective identity. Such events include rites of passage, festivals, rituals and ceremonies. At the same time these various events include expressions of creativity and performance and have important social functions.[35] There were numerous customs and traditions in fishing communities that were an important part of the local identity, with some such traditions often transcending religious allegiances. In Staithes, for example, the local fishermen would meet around the harbour on a Sunday evening wearing their ganseys and at an appointed time march to their chapels and churches for the evening service, each group breaking away as they reached their own building. A Staithes resident, interviewed in 2007, recalled this event:

> On a Sunday night all the fishermen would meet down near the *Crab and Lobster* and they used to get in a line and then, without anybody saying anything, start to walk backwards and forwards and backwards and forwards, fore and aft they called it. Just a few minutes before six-o'-clock, somebody must have had a watch, they would turn round and they would start to sing a hymn, and they would walk up the street singing a hymn. And as they got to each chapel the men from each chapel would break off and go to each chapel. We, as children, used to follow them when we could. It was lovely. That again must have been a tradition going back for a long time.[36]

Such a link between local processions and the churches was a very common part of life within fishing communities. Bob Lincoln (writing at the turn of the nineteenth century) recalled a similar parade in mid-nineteenth-century Grimsby:

> A group of the old crowd . . . used to parade the streets on a Sunday night away back in the early sixties (1860s) singing hymns, making speeches on the street corners, and eventually entering to worship at the Primitive Methodist Chapel in Victoria Street. . . . I can just see the crowd consisting, amongst others, of the three Smethursts . . . the three Mudds . . . with Tommy Campbell, etc.[37]

We have already mentioned the funeral procession in Filey. But such processions were not always for ostensibly religious purposes. When the Grimsby fishermen objected to all year-round fleeting being imposed by the fishing vessel owners in 1880, the fishermen's strike action involved the local churches. In his discussion of the strike, Gillett observed:

> The strike began with 90 skippers and mates, but within a week 250 had joined in, as smacks came in, and there were parades through the streets with a band. On the first Sunday 200 fishermen dressed in blue guernseys and smart trousers paraded twice from the club-room in Kent Street to services in St Andrew's Church. Soon over 700 men were out and over 400 smacks were tied up in the dock.[38]

The ritual aspect of these processions points to the spiritual significance of social solidarity and local identity. Nevertheless, when applying Turner's ideas to the study of Whalsay, Cohen argued that 'people can participate in the "same" ritual yet find quite different meanings for it'.[39] But this, surely, is part of the powerful impact that lies at the heart of symbolism.[40] In essence, therefore, such expressions are full of symbolism and, as such, provide a rich mixture in whichever new interpretations can be found.

Symbolism and ritual can also be found in a wide range of activities such as the making of tapestries, an example of which is to be found in the Eyemouth Museum, constructed by local women with the help of a professional artist. The symbolism here was used very effectively to commemorate the effect of the disastrous storm of 14 October 1881, in which 129 local fishermen lost their lives. The Filey group have been more orthodox in their approach to producing a tapestry and involved a wider range of community members, including local schoolchildren who were invited to add a few stitches. In Grimsby and Filey, groups of local people wrote plays that drew upon significant events in the life of each town. And in Hull, a mural has recently been painted on the gable end of a building recording the women's role, during the late 1960s, in fighting for changes in the fishing industry (following some extreme disasters and a huge loss of life), especially in the employment of appropriate staff for the trawlers.

That the sense of community in fishing towns and villages is often reinforced by traumatic events and tragedies is evident in that such events are told and retold in local stories, sometimes in narrative form, sometimes via the material arts. This point was also made by Delanty, who stated that 'some of the most powerful expressions of community are often experienced precisely where there has been a major injustice inflicted on a group of people, who consequently develop a sense of their common fate'.[41]

The sense of nostalgia associated with the demise of perceived 'traditional' communities often gives birth to a new form of identity that may have only loose contingent links with earlier forms. It is no accident, therefore, that many fishing communities in the early years of the twenty-first century are developing heritage sites, resurrecting traditional festivals and exploring ways in which to preserve the local heritage.

The construction of identity is a complex process, and it appears to be in this sense that Bauman has argued that identity is a surrogate reinvention of community. The telling of stories (about ourselves and about others) often includes a concern with personal roots, relationships (marriage, relations, friends, peer groups etc.), work, leisure, religion and how people cope with change. The recollection of such events goes hand in hand with a reconstruction of events – usually via a selective memory. Any attempt to reconstruct earlier forms of community has to take into account the variety of influences here, and the stories often tell us as much about the present inhabitants of the town as they do about the nineteenth-century community. In order to understand the past, therefore, we need to understand how we construct the present.

How, then, do societies 'reconstruct' their past in the light of present circumstances?[42] There are three important developments here. In the first instance it has to be recognized that the past is perceived as a 'cultural resource', not as a chronological series of events. Cohen has argued that identity on Whalsay was formed and maintained in reference to cultural stability and that this is often perceived symbolically. Second, identity may be seen as an individual experience that is socially and culturally mediated through the person, but this cannot be separated out from the collective experience. Indeed, Nadel-Klein (who, like Clark in Staithes, studied a fishing community by living in it for a time) has pointed out that 'we continually construct our lives in terms of origin and destination, home and away, places where we belong and places where we are not welcome, zones of comfort and zones of danger'.[43] Third, social processes constrain and legitimize behaviour. The telling of stories (whether orally or symbolically via material culture) reinforces the constant reconstruction of people's lives, and tends to reinforce our sense of security and ultimately our sense of identity. Doherty has made just this point in his claim that 'We seem to need stories to position ourselves in the world – to develop a sense of identity'.[44] Storytelling and public readings were therefore especially important aspects of communication in the nineteenth century when many people did not read or write.

Economic constraints left people with little option but to utilize readily accessible materials in creative ways. Among such activities were the making of rag rugs, ganseys and other forms of dress, and furniture, making use of driftwood. All were basically functional, although designs and symbols were carefully incorporated, often paying tribute to local superstitious beliefs and practices. Net-making skills could also be turned to other purposes, such as making items for the home and for sale, thereby supplementing the family's meagre income. In some smaller communities, such as Robin Hood's Bay, smuggling, especially of drink and cloth, provided extra support; while in the trawler ports of Scarborough, Hull and Grimsby, perfumes, tobacco and a wide range of goods, especially from Holland, Belgium and Germany, found their way from 'Dutch Copers' onto fishing vessels and were eventually sold for a profit ashore.[45]

While creativity was clearly evident in the older fishing communities such as Filey and Scarborough, there was not such a rich vein of creativity evident in Grimsby. For many of the incomers traditional activities learned in their hometowns were brought into the local melting pot, but few of these became universally adapted local customs in the town. Even a local gansey pattern did not emerge, and there was no common local dress worn by the women.

Folk rituals, too, were an important aspect of the local identity, and Robert Storch has pointed out that these rituals were an important means of expressing solidarity within a community. But these were beginning to disappear by the mid-nineteenth century – and it was just at this point that Grimsby was emerging as a major fishing port. Rituals and customs nevertheless retained an active presence in many communities, especially the Yorkshire fishing communities, well into the twentieth century as is evidenced by the *Women's Voices Project* interviews.

Religion and identity

The relationship between religion, society and the individual has long been noted by scholars. Both Durkheim and Weber believed religion to be the key to understanding the relationship between the individual and society.[46] Both also recognized that the problem of individual existence in society is a religious problem. For Durkheim (a structural theorist) it was the link between religion and society that was paramount – and it was society that provided identity for individuals within the group. In particular he argued that religion had two main functions – to act as a source of moral authority and to provide rituals that act as a mechanism for social solidarity. He further argued that religion provides a foundational means of social identity centred on its symbols. On the other hand, for Durkheim there was no supernatural realm – religion was the construct of society, an important element in ensuring stability and harmony. For Weber, on the other hand (an actor-orientated theorist), the modern individual was seen as more than a social unit in that s/he placed more emphasis on individual rationality, personal motivation and action, which included the need to give life meaning and purpose. It should be noted, however, that these two perspectives are not mutually exclusive, and later scholars have tended to make use of both viewpoints.[47]

A later wave of interest in the nature of the relationship between identity and religion, which drew upon the work of both Durkheim and Weber, was generated in the post-Second World War period, with important publications during the 1960s coming especially from Peter Berger and Thomas Luckmann. In their joint book The *Social Construction of Reality* (1966/81), they appear to support Durkheim's view regarding an objective social reality with their claim that not only is society constructed by people but that their identities are the product of society. They later pointed out that in large groups it is difficult for the individual to relate effectively to others (a point clearly evident in the nineteenth-century Grimsby population, where numerous immigrants tended to associate with others who had common origins and culture). Making sense of, and giving meaning to, the world requires membership of at least a small group.[48] In his publication *The Sacred Canopy*, Berger has argued that for primitive societies religion was foundational and helped to provide meaning, order and a moral basis for society (again, there are similarities with Durkheim), but that in modern complex societies there is increasing secularization. However, Berger has now rejected this view, arguing that Europe is an exceptional case and that it is impossible for people in modern societies to believe in the same way as it was in the pre-modern, and that people today tend to be religious in a new way.[49]

Luckmann developed his own ideas further than Berger was prepared to go in the 1960s and argued that discussion about religion had degenerated to descriptions of the decline of ecclesiastical structures, mainly from a parochial viewpoint.[50] Religion for Luckmann was 'any symbolic form by which humans transcend organic life, as implied in the English title of his book: *The Invisible Religion*' (1967).[51] While for most scholars 'religion' means official religion, Luckmann was concerned with the wider perspective. Around the same time Robert Bellah helped to develop the insight that 'Human identity is a necessary and universal function of religion' (1968).[52] And building on Berger's and Bellah's ideas, Hans Mol argued that the construction, maintenance and stabilization of identity are central functions of religion, and he defined religion as *the sacralization of identity*.[53] Hence, there has been a gradual shift away from the social perspective of Durkheim to the individual perspective of Weber, especially via Berger, Luckmann, Bellah and Mol, although for Mol, too, religion is a stabilizing factor that is central to the formation and maintenance of identity. The outline here concentrates upon a simplified overview of the developments in understanding the nature of identity. Indeed, Weigert et al., pointed out (citing Gleason) that 'The widespread acceptance of the concept of identity does not imply agreement on or even a clear understanding of its various meanings'.[54] For our purposes we will simply pick up the thread that explores the relationship between identity and religion.

Other scholars (as has been noted earlier) began to raise concerns here. The influence has been widespread, with Geertz, Turner, Clark, Cohen, Williams and others developing the concept of religion in a range of ways. Williams' concept of a range of discourses or languages (the language of belief) developed Geertz's view so that a balance is offered to the criticism that Geertz's view is too uniform a model.[55]

By exploring the meaning, especially the symbolic meaning, of an act we can see this within the context of the wider culture and thereby analyse how meaning has been constructed. For example, commenting about death as a rite of passage, Cohen observed:

> When a death occurs on Whalsay there follows a suspension of normality (marked symbolically by the stopping of the clocks in the deceased's home), gradually spreading outwards with a ripple effect in a series of concentric circles from the bereaved household.[56]

We have already seen that religion performed an important function in the development and maintenance of identity, enabling individuals and groups to cope with change while at the same time legitimizing the changes. What is evident here is that 'religion' is clearly not limited to official religion, and the rituals are not limited to those imposed by the religious institutions. In day-to-day living a wide range of beliefs and practices, including rituals, complemented the more orthodox expression of religion, as has been demonstrated in Chapter 6.

Religious change, as Hobsbawm has noted, often acts as a buttress between radicalism, reformation and revolution.[57] With social, political and economic changes to a particular way of life, new forms of religion in an established community often replaced the old, outmoded and inadequate systems. On the other hand migrating families tended to emphasize their own familiar cultural and religious traditions that helped to provide a sense of security and reinforced their identity. While small-scale migration was common among rural communities during the nineteenth and early twentieth centuries, and helped to disseminate religious developments, there was a much larger scale migration in fishing communities that ensured a wider dissemination not only of diverse cultural and religious influences but also of evangelical religion. This was especially observable during the 'Fishermen's Religious Revival' of the early 1920s that arose when the fishing communities faced dire economic difficulties. This revival affected fishing communities along the east-coast of England, especially in East Anglia, and among the herring fishers, and quickly spread to Scotland as the fishermen and their womenfolk returned home after the herring season. Duthie has commented: '1921 was an *annus terribilis* for the fishing communities of North-East Scotland – and the despair of the fisherfolk led them to religious fervour for consolation.'[58]

The influence of Primitive Methodism (among other groups of the New Dissent) along the Yorkshire coast, as well as elsewhere, replaced the old hierarchical and conservative religious traditions especially of the Church of England and the Old Dissent. This was clearly the case in Filey, where Primitive Methodism offered members a more experiential and democratic form of involvement with their religion. But such change was not restricted to Yorkshire, the east coast generally and Scotland, nor indeed to Britain. For example, the New Dissent was greatly influenced by revivalism in New England, resulting in a wave of evangelical influence that swept through Britain and Europe. One pertinent example of this influence is taken from Andrew Buckser's study of sectarianism, identity and religious change on the Danish island of Mors. Buckser pointed to the 'Awakening Movement' in Jutland during the 1830s, which was greatly influenced on Mors by the preacher Peter Larson Skræppenbirg, whose

> Godly meetings . . . shifted religious leadership from the village priest to the villagers, and thereby from the representatives of the king to the representatives of the folk. The meetings violated parish boundaries, linking people of different villages and kin groups on the basis of a common faith. Their common status as free farmers and artisans, members of a divinely folk culture, overrode the village and estate attachments that had previously defined them.[59]

The role of religion on Mors in creating new concepts of identity and community bears a strong resemblance to developments in some of the smaller Yorkshire fishing communities such as Filey and Staithes during the same early-nineteenth-century period. Although there was no sharp movement from Established Church to Nonconformity in Filey, the dual allegiance of many in the local population (those who attended both Anglican and Primitive Methodist services) suggests that the development of Primitive Methodism in the town did indeed act as a buttress between orthodoxy and radicalism and enabled the community to maintain, and even enhance, its local religious identity – thereby reinforcing local social norms.

The extent to which identity may be formed by religion therefore depends on how we define religion. If we restrict definitions to official religion, then religion would appear to be one factor among many that influence the construction and maintenance of identity. The advent of Primitive Methodism in Grimsby had an impact on the wider aspects of the residents' lives, not least in that those Primitive Methodist fishing vessel owners who insisted on teetotalism and who later became civic leaders. On the other hand, if we define religion in terms of Williams' definition of 'popular religion' and Orsi's concept of 'lived religion', then all aspects of life of the individual and the life of the community are bound up with a religious perspective that emphasizes the ongoing concern with making sense of life and giving life meaning.[60] Supernatural belief and practice clearly determined much of the daily life of community members. The ritual and performance aspects of superstitious beliefs, performance and folk customs were not only a means of expressing social solidarity; they were also, like official religious rituals, a means of easing guilt feelings and a sense of powerlessness and thereby provided a sense of security.[61]

The relationship between religion and identity may therefore be viewed as a kaleidoscopic image that embraces sacred time and space, rites of passage, daily rites associated with superstitious belief, the material arts and so on. The symbolism here is particularly important in that physical and psychological boundaries are evident reinforcing both identity and religion.

8

Conclusion

The aim of this study has been to examine and explore the extent of the relationship between religion and identity in fishing communities, with particular reference to the three communities of Filey, Scarborough and Grimsby. Harrison's suggestion that church historians have tended to ignore the popular aspects of religiosity alongside Hempton's urging that we must take an imaginative leap in order to explore the wider context of religious belief and practice are both pertinent perspectives in the discussion.[1]

During the second half of the nineteenth century, official religion made a significant impact on the Yorkshire and North-East Lincolnshire fishing communities. The increasing number and size of new religious buildings, especially evident in their construction during the later years of the century, attracted greater numbers of people and saw an increase in membership and baptisms. During this same period official religion also became part of the leisure interest, especially of Scarborough and Filey, and also of Cleethorpes with visitors passing through Grimsby on the way. All were well endowed with churches and chapels with abundant seating for visitors. While the local fishing community in Scarborough remained economically and socially separate from much of the wider community, it was nevertheless open to religious influences. However, as Gill and Binns have pointed out there were more seats available in the Scarborough churches than were being used, although given the increasing numbers of people attending services there was perhaps reason for optimism, and both the Anglicans and the Nonconformists did well.[2] At the same time, as Gill argued, Scarborough was exceptional in that along with Sheffield and Rotherham the town experienced pleasant weather and, along with the publicity surrounding the 1881 religious census, it was perhaps to be expected that significant numbers of people would attend the services. However, the membership statistics, where these are available for different denominations in Scarborough, clearly show an increase during the second half of the nineteenth century.

Grimsby was more unusual in that the fishing industry there developed from scratch with new docks stretching out into the River Humber onto reclaimed land. Grimsby's major advantage, however, was in having easy access to the towns and cities south of the River Humber and being able to quickly process the fish caught in the North Sea. The churches appear to have been taken a little by surprise by the rapid population expansion after mid-century, but they soon responded to such an extent that within twenty years churches, chapels and mission halls appeared at an accelerating rate.

With regard to the relationship between official and popular religion, various models have been put forward, including Toon's grid (Appendix 8a), based on his research in Leeds. Nevertheless, the concept of the sacred as somehow separate from and in tension with the secular is highly misleading in that it reinforces a dualistic notion of reality. The church reinforced this concept by, on the one hand, pointing to the sense of transcendence and, on the other hand, to the imminence of the sacred. But it also restricted access here by emphasizing the importance of sacred space and time. In his discussion on popular religious culture in England during the sixteenth and seventeenth centuries, Martin Ingram pointed out that Peter Burke's model of 'elite' and 'popular' culture is essentially a bipolar model that 'makes it hard to do justice to the infinite gradations of the social hierarchy' and tends to obscure areas of shared meanings.[3] In the same volume Bushaway described how the Revd J. C. Atkinson saw his parishioners as reluctant to discuss their religious beliefs and practices for fear of being thought 'credulous of superstitious beliefs'. Yet Atkinson saw such beliefs and practices as 'a living faith' and holistic in nature, 'not rooted in ignorance but at odds with orthodox belief'.[4] For most working-class people in nineteenth-century England, therefore, there was a propensity to see official and popular religion as parts of a broad spectrum of belief and practice, although with some overlap between the two. Despite so many scholars maintaining a dualistic view of religion, there is clearly no bipolar or dualistic distinction, rather a matrix of discourses that in total provide the elements of a living faith that helps to make sense of the world. For Bushaway the popular beliefs and practices of the nineteenth century were not irrational nor an alternative set of beliefs held by the ignorant but a 'shared understanding of the world around them' that helps to provide meaning and purpose.[5] Williams' model of a range of discourses also makes more sense in that the concept of dualism gives way here to a complex matrix of narratives, with each contributing to the sense of meaning and purpose in the lives of the community members.

There has, nevertheless, been a tendency among historians of religion to emphasize the importance of the religious institutions in influencing the growth and development of identity, especially during the nineteenth century. Perhaps given the wealth of statistical evidence available, this is not surprising, but when we look closer at the day-to-day events that moulded individual and social developments it becomes more obvious that popular religion played a significant, perhaps *the* significant, role here. The present study has sought to add to the growing weight of evidence that shifts the focus away from the dualistic perspective and offers a more meaningful approach to the nature of religious identity.

In order to meet the aim of the study, four objectives were identified on pages 4 and 5. The *first objective*, that religion, especially popular religion, represents an important narrative in a complex matrix of meaning, has been shown, especially in Chapter 6, to have a significant influence on the construction and maintenance of identity in fishing communities. When we examine the daily lives of people here, we discover that religiosity is painted with a more varied past than membership of the religious institutions alone, and membership can of course be variously interpreted. Even the major rites of passage embrace elements of superstitious belief, magic, folklore and customs that cannot always be separated out from the formal rites of the religious institutions. Indeed, those churches that had a fair degree of success in attracting working-class support were happy to accept and embrace a wide range of beliefs and practices. The analogy of a range of narratives works well in this context, like overlapping circles representing discourses that help to provide people with meaning and purpose in their lives.[6] The discourses are rarely very sophisticated, rather they are part of the daily lives of the people with the lessons learned from a range of sources – Sunday schools, churches and chapels, parents, friends, local traditions, superstitious beliefs, customs and work and leisure. In the light of this it must have been quite a shock for the Grimsby fishermen during the 1870s to encounter their local vicar at sea offering prayer, singing, worship and the Eucharist, as well as conversation and bringing messages from home and being willing to take messages back. By entering the fishermen's workday world the clergy were demonstrating an implied acceptance of their world view, and they were making an important statement about the interlocking narratives that help to make up this world view.

For many people associated with the churches and chapels the whole week, rather than just Sunday, offered opportunities for a wide range of activities aimed at providing a total religious lifestyle for their members. But it was the intimate and homely nature of Primitive Methodism that allowed for popular beliefs and practices, which was an important factor in the denomination's success and, as Hatcher says, helped to 'reinforce a sense of belonging'.[7] This sense of belonging was of course important in helping both to create and to reinforce a sense of identity. However, the progress of Primitive Methodism was not smooth in that as the nineteenth century progressed, members were faced with social and economic changes such that the denomination began to compete with others that were actively engaged in constructing ornate and imposing buildings that made a social and economic statement about their identities. There was also the need to grapple with a range of intellectual developments and to work at the training of leaders, all of which also had an impact as the movement began to take on a number of more traditional roles.

Popular religion is also part of a much broader cultural perspective with boundaries that are somewhat fluid, reinforced by stories, performance, symbols and traditions. It is with this perspective in mind that we have focussed not on the extent to which people are merely conventionally religious, and we have used a more empirical approach and asked how people make sense of, and give meaning to, their world in the daily life of fishing communities? This approach, however, is not without its problems in that it may appear that many people view their world without any reference to overt religious perspectives. Indeed, Luckmann's concept of 'invisible religion' is concerned with just this issue. The problem here involves our definition of religion, hence the discussion on the theoretical issues in Chapter 6 has explored some of the responses. This supposed division between official and popular religion provides us with a helpful starting point for investigation, although the distinction is not clear-cut, and there is a good deal of overlap between the two. In her concluding chapter in *Religious Belief and Popular Culture* Williams has made just this point, saying that

Church-based elements of the popular religious repertoire cannot be considered in isolation from a second discourse of folk religion. In this idiom the Deity was amenable and accessible to immediate and private forms of address and manipulation through charms, amulets, and superstitious beliefs. Individuals positioned themselves in relation to the super-empirical sphere through a discourse which remained partially independent of both the churches and orthodoxy.[8]

The same point has also been made by numerous other scholars, including Mark Smith and Sykes.[9] Even so, some scholars such as Obelkevich and Cox, while pointing to the broader perspective, have tended to argue for a clearer distinction between official and popular religion.[10]

The *second objective* builds on the first in that religion in both its official and popular forms may be seen to be an important factor in social change. The study offers some suggestions for the nature of change, pointing out that it is determined to a great extent by the nature of the community, including the social, historical, economic and political perspectives. In Chapter 5 we examined this in relation to the impact of revivalism, especially with reference to the developments in Filey during the Revival of 1823; and in Chapter 7 we explored the impact of change by adopting Durkheim's model of organic and mechanistic solidarities. Filey acted as a case study for the nature of change in a mechanistic solidarity. As can be seen from the observations in Chapter 7, change in a mechanistic solidarity was strongly resisted by community members, but it took place quite dramatically when it did happen. Conversely, change in an organic solidarity (nineteenth-century Grimsby) tended to be a constant factor in the lives of the community members, although for those with strong religious and cultural support change took place over two or three generations and provided opportunities for social leadership.

The *third objective* sought to demonstrate that religion played an important role in the process of change by providing security and stability. Religion in all its forms helped to provide a sense of security and meaning here, and in some cases, such as Filey, it provided a legitimation for change by offering the relevant social support and theological justification, not just of the religious institutions but also via the wider beliefs and practices. Popular religion played a particularly important role by providing a link with long-held traditions and customs. In a sense it was easier to change long-held theological views than to change the superstitious beliefs and customs, although with sympathetic clergy the former change was made easier. The role of official religion in helping to construct and maintain identity was significant, although popular religion offered a more pervasive influence in the daily lives of fisherfolk. Superstitious beliefs, folk customs, sympathetic magic, the influence of 'wise men' and 'wise women', festivals, language and material culture all contributed to the complex matrix of daily life, and it was in this sense that religion and culture helped to give meaning and purpose to the lives of fisherfolk.

The *fourth objective* has shown the importance of ritual and performance in religion and provides an important link between official and popular religion. While the role of ritual may have been seen as the preserve of the churches, a number of writers have pointed to the nature of ritual in the everyday lives of people, and ritual formed a major aspect of the lives of fisherfolk, be this in the form of superstitious practice, folk customs or indeed the various rites of passage associated with official religion.[11]

By accepting the commonalities we discover that ritual forms a part of the daily experience of people and points to their religiosity and religious identity. Indeed, as Day has pointed out, the individual's religious beliefs, practices and identities are influenced by social contexts, and 'What matters here is not epistemological preference, but rather how in fact people are religious and what their beliefs, practices and identities mean to them'.[12] While exploring the relevant theoretical issues the present study has made use of an empirical approach to explore the relationships. Nevertheless, exploring the nature of 'religious identity' is fraught with difficulties. David Bell, a contributor to Day's book, offered some helpful thoughts on the nature of these relationships. Like others, Bell bemoaned the lack of conceptual clarity of 'religious identity' and has pointed out that it has 'lacked theoretical precision and empirical foundation', although he did acknowledge that finding meaning was at the heart of identity.[13]

Throughout the study we have explored a wide range of official and popular religious beliefs and practices, and we have demonstrated their continuing influence throughout the twentieth century. While the focus of the study has been mainly on the fishing communities along the Yorkshire and North-East Lincolnshire coasts, references have also been made to other fishing (and non-fishing) communities in order to demonstrate commonalities and differences. In doing so we have provided a balance to the research undertaken in both rural (Obelkevich and Ambler) and urban (Cox, Smith and Williams, among others) communities. Clark's work in Staithes was a more sustained participant observation study than the present one, although the results here generally concur with Clark's findings – while rejecting the dualism inherent in the distinction between official and popular religion. The study has also focussed mainly on the period 1815–1921 as this was the period during which the British fishing industry developed in numerous directions: technologically, not least with the growth of the railways; innovations in fishing methods such as 'fleeting'; the preservation of fish, such as the development of artificial ice; the discovery of new fishing grounds; and the huge growth of the industry. Hence, the study has contributed to the debate by offering an insight into how members of fishing communities have found meaning through their varied religious beliefs and practices, and has demonstrated how identity has been constructed and developed within the context of both official and popular religion. Nevertheless, by drawing upon the *Women's Voices Project* comparisons have been made with twentieth-century developments, thereby providing a balance to the discussion.

Appendices

Appendix 1a: Maps showing Grimsby's development during the nineteenth century.

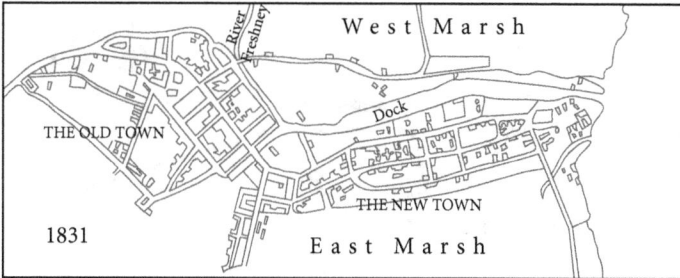

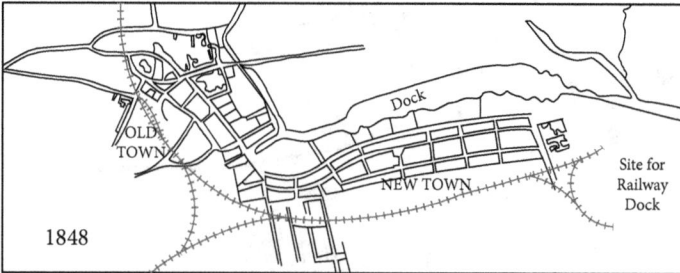

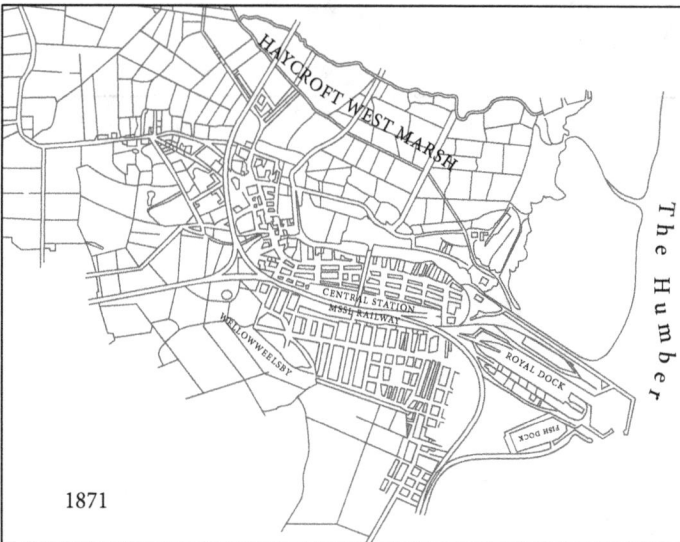

Appendix 1b: The Grimsby fishing community (bounded by Cleethorpe Road, Park Street, Eleanor Street and Victoria Street. The majority of the Grimsby fishing community lived here, *c.* 1885).

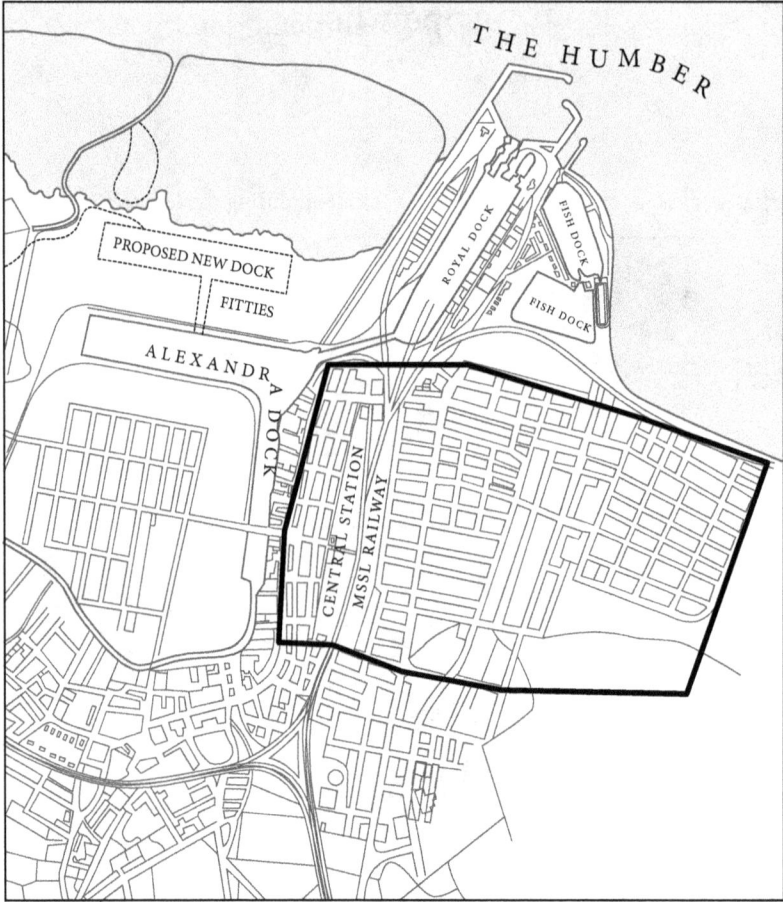

Appendix 1c: Map of Scarborough Old Town, *c.* 1841.

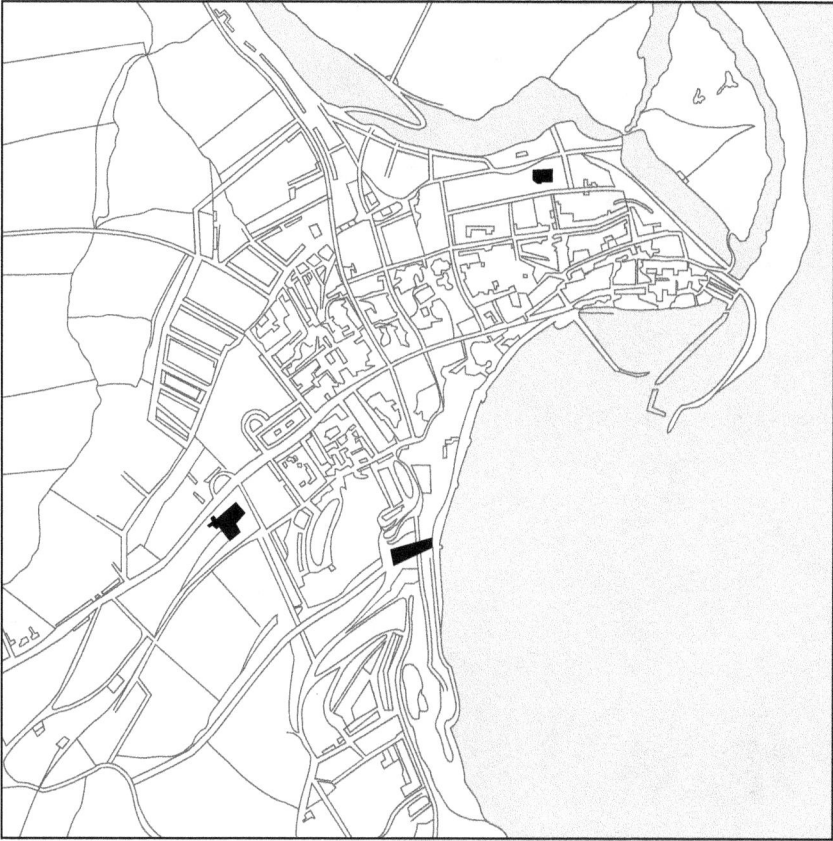

Appendix 1d: Map of Filey, 1835.

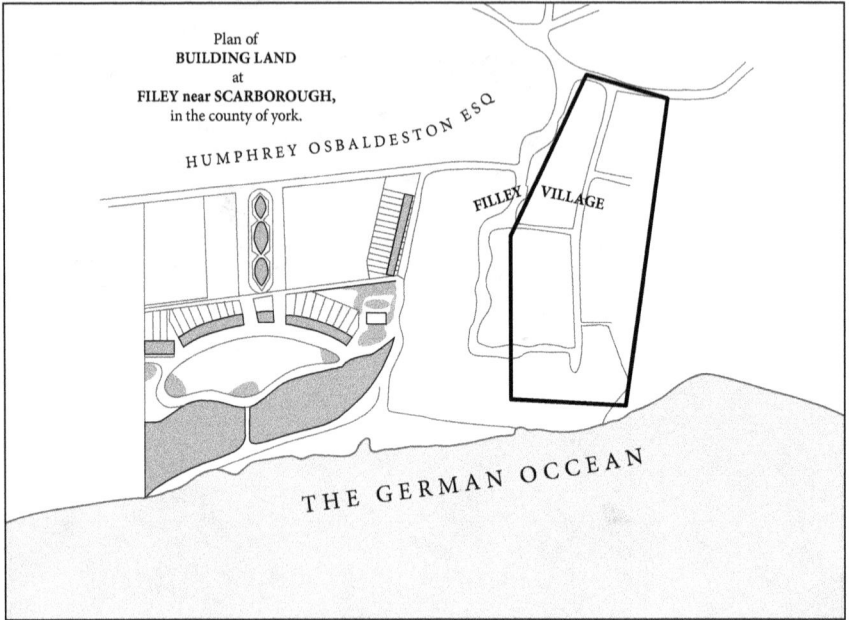

Plan of
BUILDING LAND
at
FILEY near SCARBOROUGH,
in the county of york.

HUMPHREY OSBALDESTON ESQ

FILLEY VILLAGE

THE GERMAN OCCEAN

Appendix 2a: Population of Grimsby and Cleethorpes, 1801–1991

Year	Grimsby	Clee	Cleethorpes	Scartho	Humberston	Total
1801	1,524	103	284	135	199	2,245
1811	2,747	115	375	133	218	3,588
1821	3,064	154	406	148	217	3,989
1831	4,225	177	497	147	258	5,304
1841	3,700	199	803	199	269	5,170
1851	8,860	195	839	211	259	10,364
1861	11,067	325	1,230	188	277	13,087
1871	20,244	2,058	1,768	210	254	24,534
1881	28,503	11,620	2,840	224	264	43,451
1891	33,283	18,775	4,306	190	254	56,808
1901	36,857	26,400	12,578	219	234	76,299
1911	74,659		21,417			96,076
1921	82,355		28,155			110,510
1931	92,458		28,621			121,079
1941						
1951	94,557		29,557			124,114
1961	96,712		32,700			129,412
1971	92,960		35,837			128,797
1981	92,596		25,637			128,233
1991	90,517		34,722			125,239

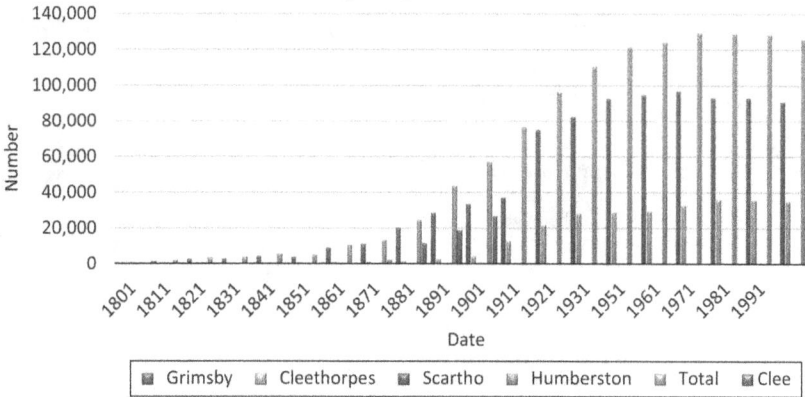

Grimsby Population 1801–1991

Appendix 2b: Population of Scarborough Township (North Riding)

Census data checked for 1801–81

Year	Scarborough Males	Scarborough Females	Scarborough Total	Falsgrave Males	Falsgrave Females	Falsgrave Total	Scarborough plus Falsgrave Males	Scarborough plus Falsgrave Females	Scarborough plus Falsgrave Total
1377			**1,393**						**1,393**
1550			**2,000**						**2,000**
1672			**3,000**						**3,000**
1750			**5,000**						**5,000**
1801	2,591	3,818	**6,409**	139	140	**279**	2,730	3,958	**6,688**
1811	2,793	3,917	**6,710**	169	188	**357**	2,962	4,105	**7,067**
1821	3,717	4,471	**8,188**	160	185	**345**	3,877	4,656	**8,533**
1831	3,512	4,857	**8,369**	192	199	**391**	3,704	5,056	**8,760**
1841	4,113	5,402	**9,515**	246	299	**545**	4,359	5,701	**10,060**
1851	5,414	6,744	**12,158**	328	429	**757**	5,742	7,173	**12,915**
1861	7,787	9,417	**17,204**	510	663	**1,173**	8,297	10,080	**18,377**
1871	9,948	12,443	**22,391**	772	1,096	**1,868**	10,720	13,539	**24,259**
1881	11,699	14,539	**26,238**	1,849	2,417	**4,266**	13,548	16,956	**30,504**
1891	14,422	19,354	**33,776**	Falsgrave incorporated			14,422	19,354	**33,776**
1901	16,123	22,038	**38,161**				16,123	22,038	**38,161**
1911			**37,224**						**37,224**
1921	19,060	27,119	**46,179**	Taken in late June. The figures are therefore an overestimate			19,060	27,119	**46,179**
1931	17,762	24,026	**41,788**				17,762	27,119	**41,788**
1951	19,192	24,793	**43,985**				19,192	24,793	**43,985**
1961	18,977	24,084	**43,061**				18,977	24,084	**43,061**
1966	18,960	23,650	**42,610**				18,960	23,650	**42,610**
1971	20,080	24,280	**44,360**				20,080	24,280	**44,360**
1981	19,043	22,727	**41,770**				19,043	22,727	**41,770**
1991			**44,144**						**44,144**

Notes: In his guide of 1745 James Schofield said Scarborough had upwards of 10,000 residents. Thomas Hinderwell estimated there to have been 7,350 residents in 1753.

1851 census: The Borough of Scarborough comprises the townships of Scarborough and Falsgrave (i.e. Dist 525). North Riding Parishes 1851: The population of this district has generally increased. The decrease of population in some townships since 1841 arises from emigration beyond seas and removals to other places in search of employment.

1934: 41,818.

1937: 40,910 Unofficial estimate by Scarborough Town Hall.

The 1921 census took place on 19/20 June, and therefore included several thousand holidaymakers.

There was no census for 1941 due to the Second World War.

Figures estimated for 1550, 1672, 1750, 1938, 1944, 1985, 1987 and 1988.

Population of Scarborough plus Falsgrave

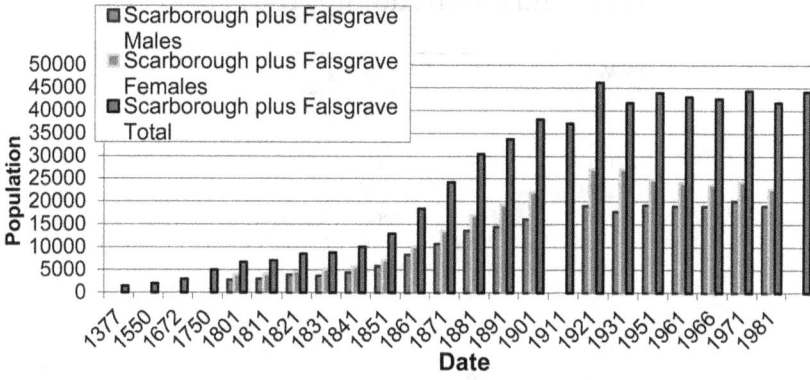

Appendix 2c: Population of Filey Township (North and South Riding), 1801–1991

Year	Males	Females	Total
1801	249	256	505
1811	270	309	579
1821	366	407	773
1831	376	426	802
1841	563	668	1,231
1851	703	808	1511
1861	827	1,054	1,881
1871	1,004	1,263	2,267
1881	1,036	1,301	2,337
1891	1,100	1,381	2,481
1901	1,368	1,635	3,003
1911			3,228
1921			4,549
1931			3,931
1951			4,765
1961			4,703
1971			5,336
1981			5,460
1991			6,619

Notes: 1851 census note: 1841 – The increase in the population of Filey township is ascribed to its having become a watering place. 1851 – The preponderance of female over male is said to arise mainly from the fact of many fishermen having been drowned while attending their vocation.

Population of Filey Township 1801-1991

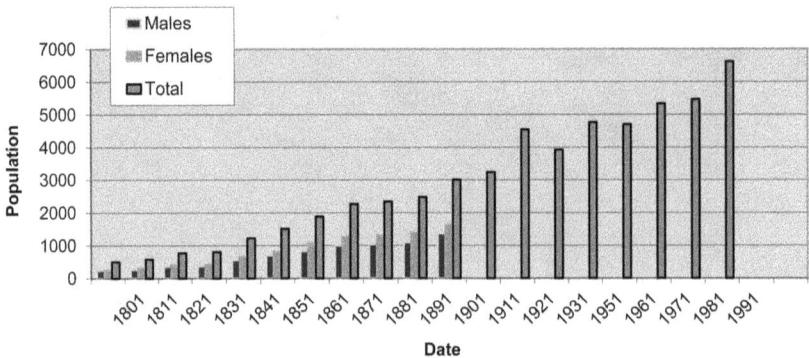

Appendix 3a: Grimsby and Cleethorpes Fishing Labour Force

	1841	1851	1861	1871	1881	1891	1901
			Grimsby				
Smack owners			14	49	76	48	
Smack-master fishermen			3	4			
Fishermen	10	17	154	493	1,204	2,012	
Apprentice fishermen			38	100	122	151	
Subtotal	**10**	**17**	**209**	**646**	**1,402**	**2,216**	
Fishermen at sea			199	604			
Apprentices at sea				151			
Totals	**10**	**17**	**408**	**1,401**	**1,402**	**2,216**	
			Cleethorpes				
Smack owners		3		4	5		
Smack-master fishermen		4					
Fishermen	68	105	117	166	181	183	
Apprentice fishermen			1	1	5	11	
Fisherwoman	1						
Subtotal	**69**	**105**	**125**	**167**	**190**	**199**	
Fishermen at sea							
Apprentices at sea		4					
Totals	**69**	**109**	**125**	**167**	**190**	**199**	

Source: Census data.

Note: The 1851 census recorded four fishermen's wives. Although the census enumerators were instructed to record the number of fishermen at sea no such record was made.

Appendix 3b: Scarborough Fishing Labour Force

The *Second Annual Report on Sea Fishermen for 1887* provides the following statistics: 562 fishermen; 2 boys.
These figures suggest that approximately one-third of the local fishermen were at sea when the data was collected.

	1841	1851	1861	1871	1881	1891	1901
Smack owners						2	
Smack-master fishermen		2	2		2		
Fishermen	99	148	97	359	444 442	277	
Fisherboy			1	1	2	1	
Apprentice fishermen	1	2	5	4	8	4	1
Fishermen absent at sea							
Fisherwomen		1*		1	1		
Totals	**100**	**150**	**106**	**367**	**455**	**451**	**278**

Source: Local census data
*The fisherwoman was Mary Raper, aged fifty. As she was a widow it is likely that she looked after the family business.
Three bait pickers were recorded for 1891 – all members of one family:

• Sixteen years – single
• Eighteen years – single
• Forty-eight years – widow

Appendix 3c: The Filey Fishing Labour Force

Occupation	1841	1851	1861	1871	1881	1891	1901
Boat owners	–	–	1	–	1	–	
Fishermen	132	146	150	202	175	188	200
Apprentice fishermen		1	–	–	–	–	–
Fisherboy		–	2	4	–	–	1
Fishermen absent at sea. None listed under this category when census was taken (according to the census enumerator)							
Totals	**133**	**148**	**154**	**202**	**176**	**189**	**200**
	1,841	**1,951**	**1,861**	**1,871**	**1,881**	**1,891**	**1,901**
Bait gatherers (flithergirls)	-	-	20	-	1	-	-

Source: Census details, 1841–1901.

Ages of Bait Gathers (1861)

15	-	2 (all are single)
16	-	1
17	-	4
18	-	1
20	-	2
21	-	1
22	-	2
23	-	1
24	-	2
26	-	1
28	-	2
42	-	1 (a widower)
Totals:		20

Appendix 4a: Grimsby Fishing Apprentices

Year	Grimsby Apprentices indentured	Grimsby Number of apprentices employed	Years	Grimsby Total by decades
1861	38			
1868	231			
1869	534			
1872	424	1,350		
1876	576			
1877	534			
1878		1,794	1868–78	4,277
1881	277			
1882	419			
1883	365			
1884	413			
1885	292			
1886	343	1,064		
1887	339	2,010		
1888	368	1,058		
1889	348		1880–9	3,312
1890	298	1,024		
1891	214			
1894	214	731		
1895	137			
1896	150	1,064		
1897	134			
1898	113	432		
1899			1890–9	1,574
1901	61			
1902		278		
1909			1900–9	590
1919	28		1910–19	212

Sources: Census data, *Annual Reports of the Sea Inspector of Sea Fisheries*; D. Boswell, Sea Fishing Apprentices of Grimsby (Grimsby Public Libraries and Museum, 1974).

Grimsby Fishing Apprentices

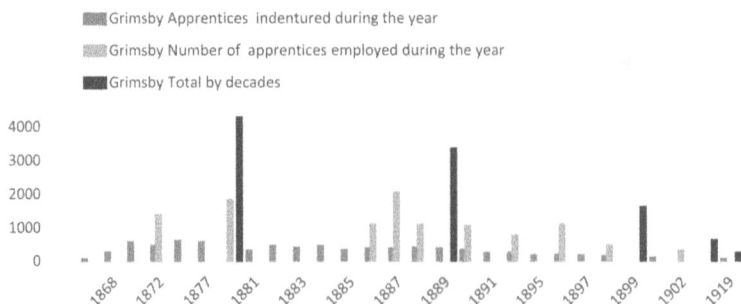

Appendix 4b: Scarborough Fishing Apprentices

Year	Indentured	Serving during the year
1851	2	
1861	10	
1875		3
1876		13
1877		8
1878		14
1879		10
1880		2
1881	8	2
1882		
1885	18	
1887	21	
1888	34	
1889	32	
1890	23	
1891	14	
1892	9	
1893	1	
1894	2	
1895	2	
1896	1	
1897	1	
1898	1	

Sources: 1841–81 are census data; 1887–1900 are from the *Annual Reports of the Inspector of Sea Fisheries* apprentices serving during the year (BPP, 1882, XVII, 1875–82)

Scarborough Fishing apprentices

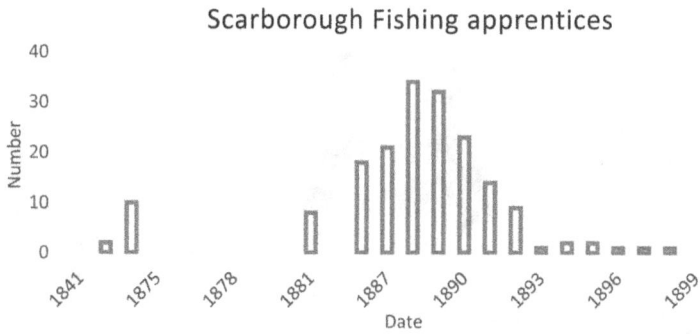

Appendix 4c: Filey Fishing Apprentices

Year	Fisherboys/Apprentices
1841	1
1851	2
1861	4
1871	0
1881	0
1891	3
1901	1

Source: Census data

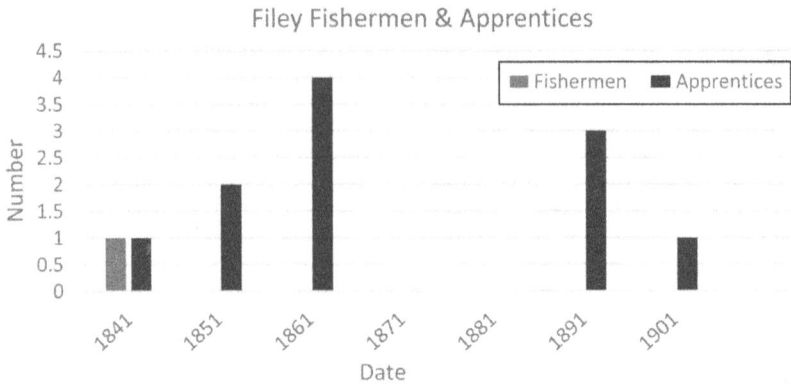

Filey Fishermen & Apprentices

Appendix 5: Grimsby, Scarborough and Filey Fishermen – Birthplaces by County and Country

	Gy 1851	Scar	Filey	Gy 1871	Scar	Filey	Gy 1891	Scar	Filey
Not Known				8	2		151	1	
London	1			101	1	1	324	3	
Berkshire				1					
Bedfordshire							5		
Buckinghamshire							3		
Cambridgeshire	1			4			26		
Cheshire				1			4		
Cleveland		1							
Cornwall							1		
Cumberland							3		
Derbyshire				1			4		
Devon		6		26	5	1	37	1	
Dorset				1					
Durham		1		1	1		7		
Essex				107	1		157	3	
Gloucestershire							10		
Hampshire		1		3			24	1	
Hertfordshire				1			3		
Kent		6		74	8		83	8	1
Lancashire				8	3		69	2	
Leicestershire				1			10	1	
Lincolnshire	14	2		116	7	2	570	8	
Norfolk		9	3	50	70	17	170	48	4
Northamptonshire							3		
Northumberland							4		
Nottinghamshire				4			33		
Oxfordshire				1			4		
Rutland				1					
Staffordshire					1		10	1	
Somerset				4			2	4	
Suffolk		4		15	8		56	8	
Sunderland								1	
Surrey				4		1			
Sussex		1	1	3	2		10	1	
Tyne and Wear					1			2	
Warwickshire				3			17		
Wiltshire							1	1	
Worcestershire	1						1		
Yorkshire		128	142	51	247	177	216	356	180
Ireland			3	3	1	2	7	1	3
Scotland				2		1	13	2	
Shetland				2					

	Gy 1851	Scar	Filey	Gy 1871	Scar	Filey	Gy 1891	Scar	Filey
Wales				2			4		
Isle of Man							2		
Isle of Wight				1			1		
Guernsey							1		
Australia							1		
Belgium							1		
Denmark				1			8		
East Indies							2		
Finland				1					
France				1			2		
Germany				1			13		
Holland									
Iceland				1					
India							2		
Malta							1		
Newfoundland				3			1		
Norway							13		
Sweden							1		
United States							6		
Zetland									
Total fishermen	17	158	149	646	358	202	2,216	453	188
Fishermen born in the town	7	96	131	26	196	160	239	315	171
Population of the towns	9,055	12,158	1,511	22,302	22,391	2,267	52,058	33,376	2,481

Source and Notes:

(1) The figures here are based on the census data and generally include only those fishermen at home on census day.

(2) The population figures for Grimsby do not include Cleethorpes, Scartho and Humberston.

(3) Determining the numbers of fishermen registered in each port, especially for the nineteenth century, is fraught with difficulties. Even the census data present us with problems. For example, a 'smack owner' may or may not go to sea. I have, however, included these among the fishermen.

Appendix 6a1: Cumulative Number of Religious Groups/Buildings in Grimsby, 1801–1911

Religious groups/ buildings	1801	1811	1821	1831	1841	1851	1861	1871	1881	1891	1901	1911
Church of England	1	1	1	1	1	1	1	8	8	9	9	10
Roman Catholic										1	1	2
Methodist (Wesleyan)	1	1	1	1	2	3	4	7	9	10	11	11
Methodist (PM)			1	1	1	2	3	4	7	7	8	10
Baptist				1	1	1	1	4	5	5	5	5
Congregational	1	1	1	1	1	1	1	1	1	1	4	4
United Free Methodist								1	1	1	2	2
Presbyterian										1	1	1
Salvation Army									1	1	1	1
Scandinavian Lutheran									1	1	1	1
Independent								1	1	3	4	4
Jewish								1	1	1	1	1
Sailors and Fishermen's Bethel										1	1	1
Fishermen's and Sailors Gospel Temperance Mission								1	1	1	1	2
Totals	**3**	**3**	**4**	**5**	**6**	**8**	**10**	**28**	**36**	**43**	**50**	**55**

Sources: A wide range of sources have been consulted for this chart, including the 1851 census, local histories and yearbooks. These include *The Grimsby and Cleethorpes Directory and Illustrated Visitors Handbook* (Grimsby, Albert Gait), 1871; *White's Directory* (Sheffield, Wm White), 1872, 1882, 1892; Kendall, *The Origin and History of the Primitive Methodist Church*, Vol. 1, pp. 447–8.

Note: Some of the buildings here are offshoots of one or other of the different groups.

Mission halls and meeting rooms have also been included. In some cases later buildings replaced earlier ones.

Appendix 6a2: Great Grimsby (Municipal Borough): Increase in Places of Worship, 1851–1872

Religious denomination	1851 population: 8,860		1872 population: 20,239		Increase between 1851 and 1872	
	No. of places of worship, 1851	No. of sittings, 1851	No. of places of worship, 1872	No. of sittings, 1872	No. of places of worship, 1872	No. of sittings, 1872
Church of England	1	600	4*	2,500	3	1,900
Presbyterians	---	---	---	---	---	---
Congregationalists	---	---	1	800	1	800
Baptists	1	600	2	1,600	1	1,000
Society of Friends	---	---	---	---	---	---
Unitarians	---	---	---	---	---	---
Wesleyan Methodists	1	1,350	4**	3,250	3	1,900
United Methodists	---	---	1	700	1	700
New Connexion	---	---	---	---	---	---
Primitive Methodists	1	500	3+	1,800	2	1,300
Calvinistic Methodists	---	---	---	---	---	---
Bible Christians	---	---	---	---	---	---
Brethren	---	---	1	150	1	150
Roman Catholics	---	---	1++	200	1	200
All others	---	---	#2	400	2	400
Total	**4**	**3,050**	**19**	**11,400**	**15**	**8,350**

Source: Supplement to *The Nonconformist*, 8 January 1873, p. 54.

*Includes two mission rooms (500).

The numbers of sittings for 1851 are estimated, not having the returns by me. The increase between 1851 and 1872 includes enlargement of existing places of worship and new buildings.

**One erecting and will be opened in spring instead of a school now used. Includes one mission room (300).

+ Includes a mission room.

++ A mission station.

Including temporary place, Danish (100) and Ragged school used for services (300).

Note

The above table for 1851 is an estimate of our enumerator, there having been no separate return in that year for the borough. The Primitives have recently built a large chapel and schools in New Clee, only a yard from the borough boundary, and the Church of England and Baptists have preaching places. These are not counted, nor other Churches and chapels within the Parliamentary, but outside the Municipal Borough. The rapid growth of this borough and port is exceptional and the increase of places of worship has kept pace with the population.

Appendix 6a3: Grimsby Wesleyan Methodists Membership

Annual schedules for:

Year	Totals on trial	Totals in society
		Those on trial not included
December 1836	9	238
March 1837	8	258
1838	15	266
1839	17	313
1840	3	290
1841	8	311
1842	4	284
1843	2	292
1844	1	301
1845	2	303
1846	6	309
1847	10	365
1848	15	400
1849	63	483
1850	21	548
1851	8	516
1852	15	489
1853	8	420
1854	17	438
1855	8	474
1856	4	453
1857	10	431
1858	0	422
1859	6	447
1860	13	489
1861	12	570
1862	6	557
1863	0	563
1864	12	542
1865	20	614
1866	0	621
1867	0	639
1868	0	627
1869	2	619
1870	5	662
1871	14	647
1872	10	641
1873	18	614
1874	26	804
1875	31	945
1876	7	965
1877	9	993
1878	28	1,042
1879	11	1,050
1880	21	1,072

(Continued)

Year	Totals on trial	Totals in society
1881	16	1,123
1882	36	1,183
1883	29	1,186
1884	9	1,193
1885	18	1,243
1886	21	1,218
1887	24	1,208
1888	14	1,365
1889	17	1,283
1890	10	1,254
1891	26	1,237
1892	37	1,259
1893	44	1,309
1894	21	826
1895	20	853
1896	69	891
1897	38	914
1898	28	913
1899	59	912
1900	39	915
1901	24	921
1902	35	902
1903	59	917
1904	49	918
1905	28	933
1906	52	900
1907	24	902
1908	24	884
1909	23	882
1910	18	851
1911	36	909
1912	28	892
1913	11	900
1914	0	655

Source: Lincoln Archives: Meth B/Gy/4/1-32 records of Wesleyan Circuit.

Note: G. Lester says the total members for Grimsby Wesleyans in March 1889 were 1,329, with 25 on trial and 249 in junior societies. G. Lester, *Grimsby Methodism, 1743-1889, and the Wesleys in Lincolnshire*, Wesleyan Book Room, 1890).

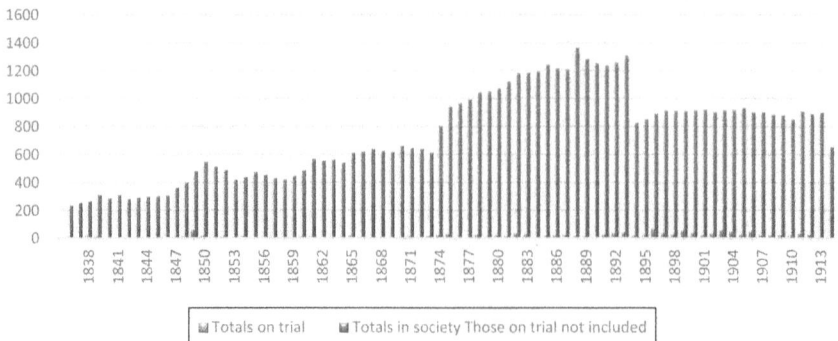

Grimsby Wesleyan Methodist Membership

Development of local circuits

Horncastle was made a circuit from Grimsby in 1786.
Boston was made a circuit from Grimsby in 1796.
Louth was made a circuit from Grimsby in 1799.
Market Rasen was made a circuit from Grimsby in 1813.
Caistor, etc., was made a circuit from Grimsby in 1868.

Appendix 6a4: Primitive Methodist Membership in Grimsby

Year	Members				Sunday scholars	Chapels and rooms	Deaths	Increase/ decrease
	Approved	On trial	Doubtful	Total				
1822				400				
1823				320				
1824				320				
1825								
1826								
1827								
1828				269				
1829				368				
1830				368				
1831				319				
1832				313				
1833				363				
1834	317	36		352		1		
1835	353			353		2	8	
1836	382	10		392		3	8	39
1837	492	18		500		10	16	108
1838	481	65		553		11	12	53
1839	Missing			667				124
1840	649	32	3	684		17	4	7
1841	Missing			700				16
1842	670	40	10	720		18	10	20
1843	619	122	2	743		17	6	23
1844	743	60		803	224	17	11	60
1845	769	64		833	264	19	7	30
1846	484	90	6	580	155	13	11	24
1847	Missing			584				4
1848	563	47		619	307	14	16	26
1849	574	156		730	395	16	7	120
1850	763	67		830	411	16	8	100
1851	842	38		880	428	15	9	50
1852	817	72		889	521	16	14	9
1853	800	59		859	506	16	9	−30
1854	755	104		859	458	17	9	0
1855	788	77		865	534	17	16	6
1856	819	75		885	613	17	18	20

(Continued)

Year	Members			Sunday scholars	Chapels and rooms	Deaths	Increase/ decrease
1857	830	108	939	633	18	13	54
1858	903	157	1,060	634	18	21	121
1859	1,103	27	1,130	675	18	12	70
1860	1,135	10	1,145	695	18	16	15
1861	1,013	152	1,165	738	18	11	20
1862	1,075	140	1,215	727	10	18	50
1863	1,078	147	1,225	817	19	14	10
1864	1,095	67	1,162	754	29	17	−63
1865	1,055	31	1,086	836	20	15	−76
1866	977	123	1,100	935	20	17	14
1867	1,055	85	1,140	1,005	20	16	40
1868	680	70	750	772	11	80	−390*
1869	720	50	770	790	11	13	20**
1870	380	55	435	291	5	8	50
1871	430	30	460	296	5	8	25
1872	460	20	480	301	6	11	20
1873	432	29	461	318	6	6	−19
1874	435	29	464	354	6	3	3
1875	433	41	474	400	7	5	10
1876	478	32	510	567	7	13	36
1877	Missing						
1878	Missing						
1879	Missing			639			
1880	Missing						
1881	635	22	657		7		12
1882				695			
1883	685	35	720		8	5	13
1884	661	119	780		8	12	60
1885	770	20	790		8	9	10
1886	802	28	830		8	12	40
1887	830	20	850		8	12	20
1888	840	20	860		8	12	10
1889	860	4	864		8	6	4
1890	826	16	842		8	6	−22
1891	817	26	843		8	15	1
1892	829	26	855		8	11	12
1893	880		880		9	9	25
1894	875	10	885		9	16	5
1895	885	15	900		9	9	15
1896	897	22	919		10	4	19
1897	924	11	935		10	17	16
1898	950		950		11	12	15
1899	595	15	610		6	4	−340* * *
1900	614		614		7	9	4
1901	620		620		7	12	6
1902	635		635		7	4	15
1903	665		665		7	5	30
1904	675		675		7	7	10
1905	700		700		7	13	25
1906	700	10	725		7	13	10
1907	725		725		7	8	15
1908	750		740		7	9	25
1909	760		760		8	13	10

Year	Members		Sunday scholars	Chapels and rooms	Deaths	Increase/ decrease
1910	760		760	8	8	
1911	760		760	8	10	
1912	772		772	8	5	12
1913	772		772	8	6	
1914	759		759	8	12	

Sources: Lincoln Archives PM Reports – Ref: METH B/Grimsby 37/1. Primitive Methodist Schedules. Misc. Don 1275: Methodist Statistics, George Lawton in Proceedings of the Wesleyan Historical society, 1947-8, Bol. XXVI, pp. 10–13 (The figures were calculated in March each year. Children under fourteen years were not included).

˙390 members were given to the Tetney Circuit in 1868.
˙˙The circuit was divided into First and Second Circuits in March 1869.
˙ ˙ ˙ 'We have decreased 340 members. . . . We gave five places with 342 members to the Grimsby third Circuit in June, so that we have an increase of two since the division.'

While every effort has been made to ensure that the figures are correct, there are some discrepancies between the different sources. I have used the Schedule figures in preference to other sources wherever possible. The figures for 1822–32, however, are not available from the schedules and have been taken from George Lawton's summary in the Proceedings of the Wesleyan Historical Society's Report. Even so, in the light of comments in the *Primitive Methodist Magazine* for 1888, p. 461, the early figures for Primitive Methodism in Grimsby are puzzling: 'At the end of twenty years of self-denying labour we had not more than about sixty members; ten years later we had more than three times that number. Since then the town has grown marvellously, and our cause has grown with it. We have now more than 1,000 members in the Grimsby and Cleethorpes Societies.'

Note: There appears to have been a split of some sort in 1845/6.
The First Grimsby Circuit was founded in 1822 (the Second Circuit in 1869).

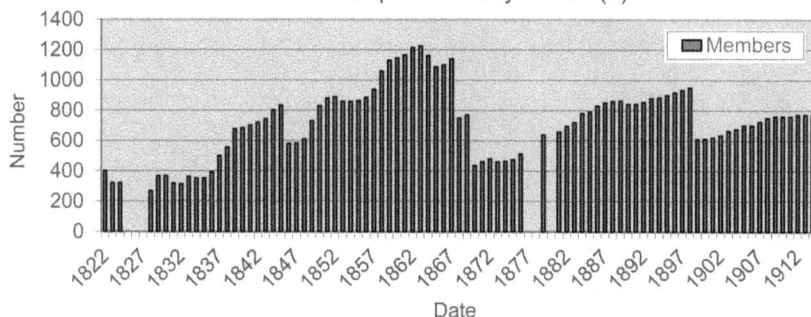

PM Membership in Grimsby Circuit (a)

Appendix 6a5: Grimsby United Methodist Free Church Membership

Grimsby, Freeman Street, 1868

Year	Members	Sunday scholars
1869	60	70
1870	92	80
1871	119	100
1872	90	108
1873	62	129
1874	78	87
1875	50	87
1876	61	111
1877	82	140
1878	111	198
1879	125	265
1880	138	281
1881	167	217
1882	180	255
1883	150	205
1884	137	242
1885	138	248
1886	128	254
1887	130	263
1888	136	289
1889	137	280
1890	138	170
1891	112	270
1892	123	216
1893	123	216
1894	142	186
1895	165	206
1896	162	170
1897	169	480
1898	204	490
1899	205	436
1900	213	494

Source: United Methodist Free Church Minutes of Annual Assembly. Lincolnshire Archives, METH B/Grimsby/61-82: records of the UMFC Circuit and Park Street.

The development of the Grimsby United Methodist Free Church

The Freeman Street Chapel was built in 1868 (in lieu of the old Wesleyan Reform Chapel, built in 1853).

Grimsby Wesleyan Reform Union Circuit changed its name to the 'Grimsby United Methodist Free Churches Circuit' at the creation of the United Methodist Free Church in 1857. It then changed its name to the Grimsby United Methodist Circuit at the creation of the United Methodist Church in 1907. Then in 1932 (at the time of the Methodist Union) the name was changed to the Grimsby Freeman Street Methodist Circuit.

Grimsby United Methodist Free Church Membership

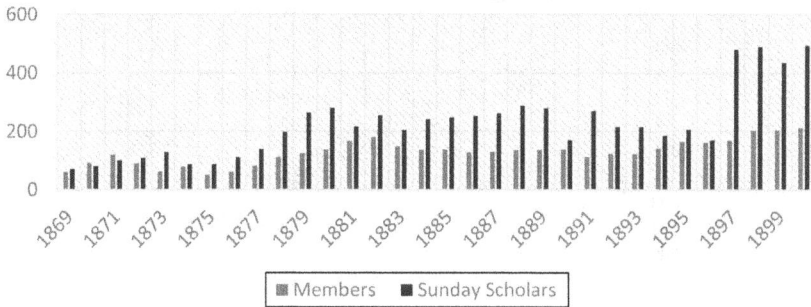

Appendix 6a6: Grimsby Baptists Membership

(General Baptists, New Connexion)

Year	Members Baptist Union	Members Albert St	Members Freeman St	Members New Clee
1838	66			
1830				
1840	73			
1843	70			
1851				
1852	98			
1855	77			
1858	100			
1862	200			
1865	180	8		
1866	180	10		
1867	180	12		
1868	180	12		
1869	110	12		
1870	141		60	
1871	156		65	
1872	180		70	
1873	203		72	
1874	220			
1975	238			
1876	248			
1877			76	
1878	252		76	
1879	262		77	
1880	312		85	
1881	340		85	
1882	366		89	

(Continued)

1883	366	111	
1884	366	124	
1885	391	138	
1886	391	132	
1887	399	129	
1888	380	129	
1889	396	105	
1890	396	109	
1891	398	110	
1892	398	116	
1893	398		
1894	398	103	
1895	289		
1896	320	85	35
1897	335	99	37
1898	349	97	40
1899	230	108	43
1900	256	115	43

Source: Lincolnshire Archives.

Notes: Baptist worship began in Grimsby in 1822.
The first chapel and schoolroom was built in 1824.
Baptist Union: in 1865 there were two Baptist churches (presumably these were in Upper Burgess St and Albert St).
Freeman St was added in 1869.
Upper Burgess St Chapel was replaced by Victoria St Chapel in 1878?
New Clee was an outstation of Victoria St Chapel.
The Baptist Tabernacle (Victoria St) was built in 1876–7 and was used until the 1950s when the church was transferred to Laceby Rd.

Grimsby Baptists Membership

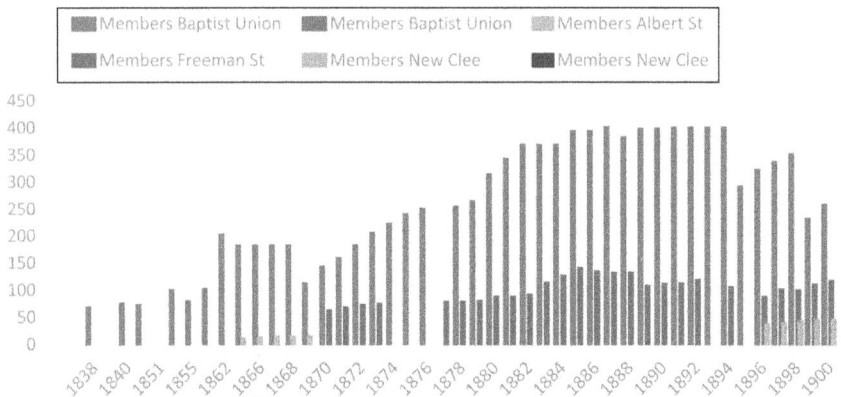

Appendix 6a7: Grimsby and Scarborough, Summary of Church Accommodation, 1851–1872

Town	Population	Total accommodation, 1851 Places of worship	Sittings	Total accommodation, 1872 Places of worship	Sittings	Accommodation, 1851 Established churches Places of worship	Sittings	Non-established churches Places of worship	Sittings
Grimsby	20,238	4	3,050	19	11,400	1	600	3	2,450
Scarborough	24,615	68	20,050	78	29,988	21	8,211	47	11,800
Hull	122,266	51	36,173	66	49,569	15	12,830	36	23,347
Gt Yarmouth	41,792	22	14,688	40	21,942	6	6,928	17	7,760

Accommodation, 1872

	Established churches Places of worship	Sittings	Non-established churches Places of worship	Sittings
Grimsby	4	2,500	15	8,100
Scarborough	24	11,064	54	18,950
Hull	8	17,815	48	31,754
Gt Yarmouth	10	10,220	30	11,732

Town	Percentage of accommodation, 1851 Established churches	Non-established churches	Percentage of accommodation, 1872 Established churches	Non-established churches	Increase per cent on 21 years Established churches	Non-established churches
Grimsby	20.0	80.0	21.9	78.1	316.6	263.3
Scarborough	41.1	58.9	36.8	63.2	33.9	60.5
Hull	36.2	63.8	35.9	64.1	38.9	23.4
Gt Yarmouth	47.1	52.9	46.6	53.4	51.8	51.1

Source: Supplement to *The Nonconformist*, 6 January 1873, p. 52 (Extracted from the *General Summary Table of Population, Places of Worship, and Sittings in Eighty-four Cities and Boroughs of England and Wales*).

Appendix 6b1: Cumulative Number of Religious Groups in Scarborough, 1800–1921

Religious groups/ buildings	1801	1811	1821	1831	1841	1851	1861	1871	1881	1891	1901	1911	1912
Church of England	1	1	1	2	3	3	4	5	8	8	8	8	8
Roman Catholic	1	1	1	1	1	2	3	3	3	3	3	3	4
Methodists (Wesleyans)	2	2	2	2	4	6	8	8	7	9	9	10	10
Wesleyan Association						2	2	2	2	2	2	2	2
Methodists (PM)			1	1	1	1	2	3	5	5	5	5	5
United Methodist Free Church								1	1	1	1	1	1
United Free Methodists													
Independents						1	1	1	1	1	1	1	1
Baptists				1	1	1	2	3	2	2	2	3	3
Congregational													
Presbyterians	1	1	1	1	1	1	1	1	1	1	1	1	1
Salvation Army									1	1	1	1	1
The Bethel	1	1	1	1	1	1	1	1	1	1	1	1	1
Society of Friends	1	1	1	1	1	1	1	1	1	1	2	2	2
United Reformed									1	1	1	1	1
The Town Mission									1	1	1	1	1
Unitarians									1	1	1	1	1
Christadelphians										1	1	1	1
Fishermen's Institute										1	1	1	1
Plymouth Brethren						1	1	1	1	1	2	2	2
First Church of Christ, Scientist												1	1
Jehovah's Witnesses (1966)													
Assemblies of God (1929)													
Elim (1934)													
Holiness Church													
Albert Hall Lectures									1	1	1	1	1
Batty Place Mission									1	1	1	1	1
Totals	**7**	**7**	**8**	**10**	**14**	**21**	**27**	**36**	**44**	**48**	**51**	**54**	**55**

Source: Given the different estimates some figures, including for a number of outlying villages, are based on a number of sources.

Appendix 6b2: Scarborough: Increase in Places of Worship, 1851–1872

Religious denomination	1851 population: 24,615		1872 population: 36,378		Increase between 1851 and 1872	
	No. of places of worship	No. of sittings	No. of places of worship	No of sittings	No. of places of worship	No. of sittings
Church of England	21	8,241	24*	11,038	3	2,797
Presbyterians						
Congregationalists	3	1,725	4**	2,510	1	785
Baptists	3	940	3+	1,630		690
Society of Friends	1	400	1	400		
Unitarians						
Wesleyan Methodists	22	5,338	24++	6,984	2	1,610
United Methodists New Connexion	2	620	1	750	1	130
Primitive Methodists	13	2,081	15~	4,862	2	2,781
Calvinistic Methodists						
Bible Christians						
Brethren			1	150	1	150
Roman Catholics	1	270	1~~	1,000		730
All others	2	435	4^	730	2	295
Totals	**68**	**20,050**	**78**	**30,018**	**10**	**9,968**

Source: Supplement to *The Nonconformist*, 8 January 1873, p. 54.

Many have good schools – including two mission stations.
** Two have good schoolrooms.
+ One has a good schoolroom.
++ Including two mission rooms (170). About to build a large chapel at Filey.
~ Good schools attached to five chapels.
~~ Rebuilt.
^ Mission room (250); adult school mission room (300); free dwellings mission room (150); and Christadelphians (300). These are poorly supported by church people.

Note
Two of the mission rooms under 'all others' are supported by members of all Protestant denominations. Religious services are held in the workhouse by all branches of the Christian church alternately. The Unitarians hold services in the Temperance Hall during the summer months. Outdoor meetings are held in summer on the sands, and in many other parts of the town, by the Congregationalists, the Wesleyans, the Primitives and the Town Mission. During the last twenty years, many of the places of worship have been enlarged, which accounts for the increase in the number of places of worship being so much less, comparatively, than the increase in the number of sittings.

The following letter appeared in *The Nonconformist* of 15 January 1873, p. 63.
The Scarborough Statistics
To the Editor of the Nonconformist

Sir, Permit me to direct your attention to the fact that the returns in your newspaper of the religious accommodation in Scarborough do not refer to this town exclusively, but to the entire district included in the Scarborough Poor Law Union; that district extends some thirteen miles outside the town, and embraces thirty-seven villages. As your statistics are generally believed to refer to towns *not* districts, I think this

(*Continued*)

should be stated. Persons at a distance might conclude from these statistics the Church of England has twenty-one places of worship here, whereas they have only five. The Wesleyans have not twenty-two chapels but two, with two mission stations. The Primitive Methodists not thirteen chapels, but two, with one mission station. The Baptists have three chapels not two. The United Methodists not two chapels but one. The Congregationalists have three churches, as correctly stated in your returns. The population of Scarborough is about 24,500, not 36,378 as stated in your return – the latter figures referring to the entire district above mentioned.

I am, Sir, yours faithfully,
ROBERT BALCARNIE

Scarborough, 14 January 1873.

Appendix 6b3: Census of Attendance at Scarborough Places of Worship, 1881

Summary

Denominations	Buildings	Accommodation	Morning	Afternoon	Evening	Total
Church of England	8	6,560	3,433		2,864	6,297
Wesleyan Methodist	7	3,946	1,795		1,793	3,588
Primitive Methodist	6	3,380	1042		1,212	2,254
United Methodist Free Church		734	137		120	257
Congregational	5	2,750	916		914	1,830
Baptist	2	1,470	308		363	671
Society of Friends		200	138		21	159
Unitarian		250	59		58	117
Christian Brethren		252	50		59	109
Batty Place Mission		120	----		93	93
Salvation Army	1	-----	720		2660	3,380
Presbyterian	1	-----	41		52	93
Albert Hall Lectures		-----	----		68	68
Roman Catholic	1	700	403		238	641
Totals		**20,362**	**9,042**	**1,152**	**10,515**	**20,709**
Church of England		6,560	3,433		2,864	6,297
Protestant Nonconformist		13,102	5,206		7,413	12,611
Roman Catholic		700	403		238	641
Totals		**20,362**	**9,042**	**1,152**	**10,515**	**20,709**

The column headers for the Attendance group are: Morning, Afternoon, Evening, Total (with "Attendance" spanning them).

Population 30,484
Estimated Number of Worshippers: 13,123
Percentage of Estimated Number of Worshippers to Population: 43.05

Sources: *Scarborough Mercury*, 10 December 1881
Andrew Mearns, *The Statistics of Attendance at Public Worship, as published in England, Wales and Scotland by the local press, between October, 1881, and April 1882* (London, Hodder and Stoughton, 1882). The Nonconformist and Independent, 2 February 1882, p. 7.

The *Nonconformist*, 2 February 1882, p. 7: 'It will thus be seen that the proportion of accommodation and of attendances of the Free Church of Scarborough, as compared with the Established Church, is about two to one. The returns show that out of every 100 of the population of Scarborough 29 attended a place of worship last Sunday morning and 34 in the evening.'
'The returns for this fashionable watering-place were established on Sunday, December 4th by the Scarborough Mercury, and the statistics were taken in co-operation with the officials connected with the various places of worship, which was readily rendered.'

Appendix 6b4: Scarborough Primitive Methodist Members

Year	Total members	No. of sittings	St Sepulchre Circuit 1 members	Jubilee Circuit 2 members
1835	139			
1836	75			
1837	133			
1838	130			
1839	117			
1840	123			
1841	124			
1842	131	465		
1843	130	465		
1844	143	465		
1845	158	465		
1846	156			
1847	143	465		
1848	220	565		
1849	236	565		
1850	242			
1851		565		
1852				
1853		686		
1854		675		
1855	252	654		
1856	255	616		
1857	252	654		
1858	255	655		
1859	230			
1860	294			
1861	270			
1862	135			
1863	208			
1864				
1865				
1866				
1867				
1868				
1869				
1870				
1871				
1872				
1873	517		217	300

(*Continued*)

Year	Total members	No. of sittings	St Sepulchre Circuit 1 members	Jubilee Circuit 2 members
1874	516		214	302
1875	513		220	293
1876	516		226	290
1877	531		233	298
1878	537		236	301
1879	641		345	296
1880	657		346	311
1881	664		311	353
1882	604		287	317
1883	570		245	325
1884	543		229	314
1885	534		214	320
1886	490		192	298
1887	466		178	288
1888	454		168	286
1889	465		175	290
1890	467		173	294
1891	470		177	293
1892	452		172	280
1893	455		179	276
1894	458		174	284
1895	515		202	313

Source: North Yorkshire County Record Office, North Allerton: Local Leaders Meeting Book and Quarter Day Accounts (MIC 2315 1/2/1-4; R/M/Sc/1/2/1-4 (1835–56)).

Note: The figures are somewhat confusing with duplicate copies for some date offering different figures and separate figures for Falsgrave, St John's Rd and other sites from *c.* 1874. The Falsgrave and St John's Rd figures would together add a significant number (125 members in 1873 and over 400 in 1889). Were these included in the overall Scarborough figures, we would see a gradual increase in the overall membership up to *c.* 1890 and then possibly a gradual falling away up to the beginning of the twentieth century.

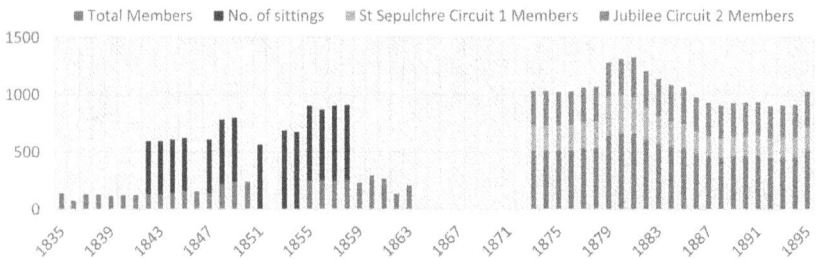

Scarborough Primitive Methodists

Appendix 6b5: Scarborough United Methodist Free Church

Year	Members	
1858	57	100
1859	65	25
1860	80	100
1861	75	80
1871	30	135
1872		
1873	44	113
1874	54	157
1875		
1876	68	185
1877	76	190
1878	80	195
1879		
1880		
1881	75	214
1888	69	122
1889		
1890	92	124
1891		
1892		
1893	80	130
1894		
1895	66	90
1900	55	34

Source: United Methodist Free Church Minutes of
Annual Assembly (Lincoln Archives).

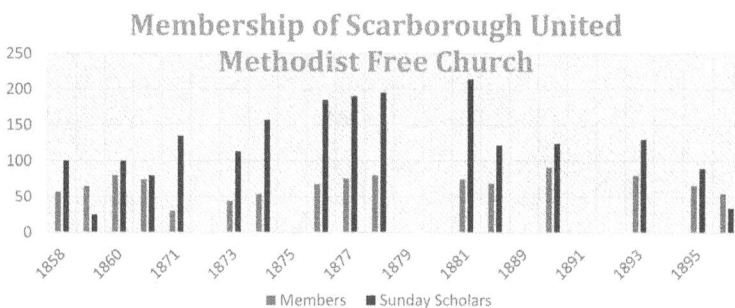

Membership of Scarborough United Methodist Free Church

Appendix 6c1: Cumulative Number of Religious Groups/Buildings in Filey, 1800–1911

Religious groups/ buildings	1801	1811	1821	1831	1841	1851	1861	1871	1881	1891	1901	1911
Church of England	1	1	1	1	1	1	2	2	2	2	2	2
Roman Catholic												1
Methodist (Wesleyan)		1	1	1	1	1	1	1	1	1	1	1
Methodist (PM)				1	1	1	1	1	1	1	1	1
Salvation Army										1	1	1
Christian Science Society												
Plymouth Brethren												
Society of Friends						1	1	1	1	1	1	1
Totals:	**1**	**2**	**2**	**3**	**3**	**4**	**5**	**5**	**5**	**6**	**6**	**7**

Source: A range of sources have been consulted for this chart, including the 1851 census, local histories and yearbooks.

Appendix 6c2: Wesleyan Methodists in Filey

Year	Filey members
1810	14
1811	20
1812	17
1813	11
1814	14
1815	14
1816	19
1817	15
1818	15
1819	23
1820	24
1821	25
1822	28
1823	27
1824	
1825	66
1826	
1827	59
1828	
1829	56
1830	53
1831	57

1832	
1833	46
1834	78
1835	60
1836	59

Source: East Riding Archives, Beverley, Bridlington
Circuit (MRQ 1/36, 1796–1838).
The figures were taken in July of each year.
The figures given add up to 26
Again, the figures given add up to 65.

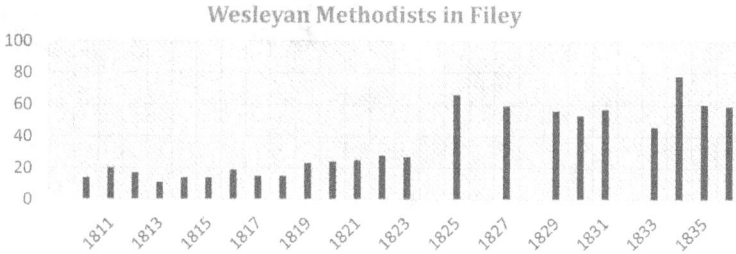

Wesleyan Methodists in Filey

Appendix 6c3: Filey Primitive Methodist Membership

Year	No.	Year	No.	Year	No.	Year	No.	Year	No.
1823	40	1844	79	1865	256	1886	306	1907	341
1824	100	1845	72	1866	255	1887	287	1908	340
1825	50	1846	84	1867	248	1888	275	1909	303
1826		1847	83	1868	301	1889	258	1910	283
1827		1848	111	1869	274	1890	235	1911	290
1828		1849	95	1870	262	1891	242	1912	256
1829		1850	104	1871	242	1892	237	1913	263
1830		1851		1872	262	1893	220	1914	237
1831		1852		1873	244	1894	218		
1832		1853		1874	295	1895			
1833		1854		1875	319	1896	233		
1834		1855		1876	316	1897	205		
1835	50	1856		1877	326	1898	226		
1836	36	1857		1878	337	1899	240		
1837	35	1858		1879	333	1900	241		
1838	34	1859		1880	350	1901	229		
1839	31	1860		1881	353	1902	208		
1840	32	1861		1882	323	1903	311		
1841	33	1862	208	1883	339	1904	297		
1842	71	1863	248	1884	347	1905	325		
1843	74	1864	254	1885	299	1906	340		

(*Continued*)

Sources: Northallerton Archives, Quarterly Schedules (March figures), R/M/FIC?1/1/68.

The earliest source for the 1823 data is William Howcroft, 'On the Work of God at Filey' in the *Primitive Methodist Magazine* for 1823, p. 255. On p. 258 he adds a note saying that within four or five weeks of his earlier report more than 100 people had joined the new society.

Other sources include: J. Petty, 1880, p. 189; and Revd Woodcock, 1889, p. 36.
Filey was a part of the Bridlington Circuit until 1864 when it became an independent circuit.

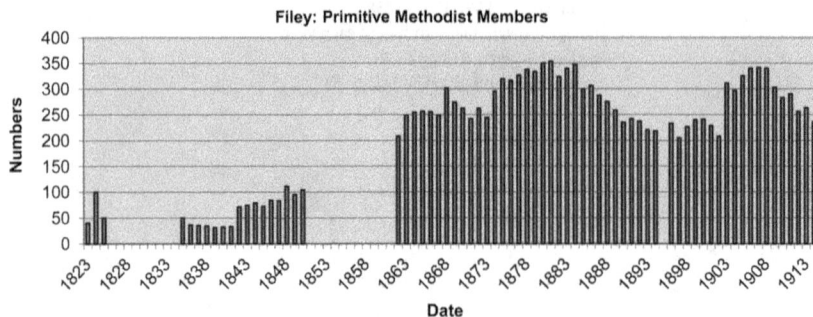

Filey: Primitive Methodist Members

Appendix 6d1: Methodist Development in Grimsby

Grimsby Primitive Methodist Circuit

After 1765 two Methodist circuits were formed in Lincolnshire, known as East and West, or Grimsby and Epworth. Grimsby UMFC Circuit was formed in 1869 and was centred on Freeman Street and included one other society.

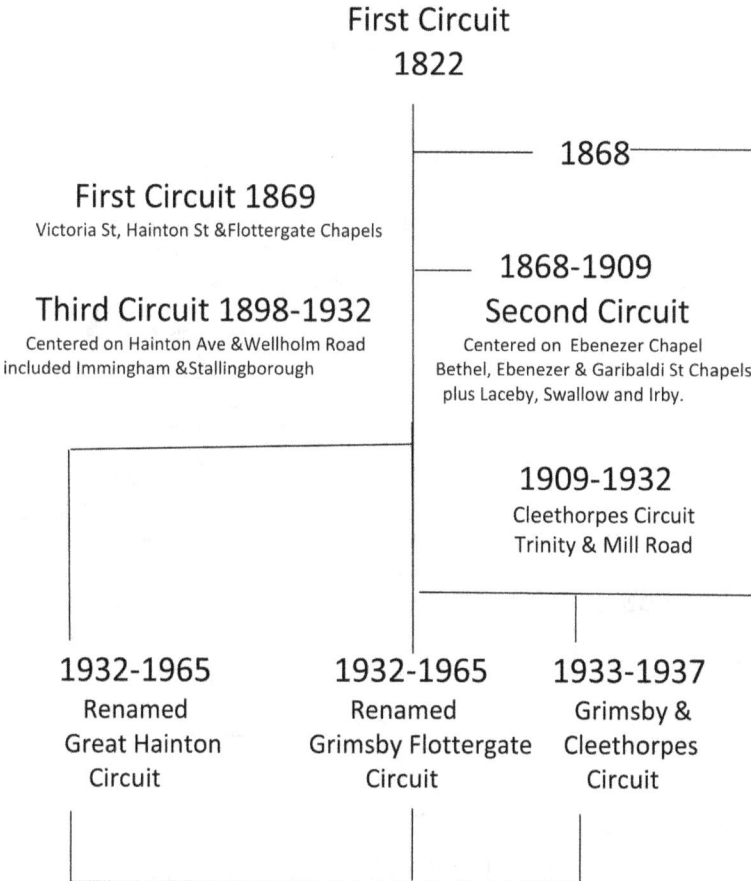

First Circuit
1822

———— 1868 ————

First Circuit 1869
Victoria St, Hainton St &Flottergate Chapels

—— 1868-1909
Second Circuit
Centered on Ebenezer Chapel
Bethel, Ebenezer & Garibaldi St Chapels
plus Laceby, Swallow and Irby.

Third Circuit 1898-1932
Centered on Hainton Ave &Wellholm Road
included Immingham &Stallingborough

1909-1932
Cleethorpes Circuit
Trinity & Mill Road

1932-1965
Renamed
Great Hainton
Circuit

1932-1965
Renamed
Grimsby Flottergate
Circuit

1933-1937
Grimsby &
Cleethorpes
Circuit

Amalgamation o f all PM circuits with the Wesleyans

Source: PM Circuit Books, NE Lincolnshire Archives, Grimsby.

Appendix 6d2: Methodist Development in Scarborough

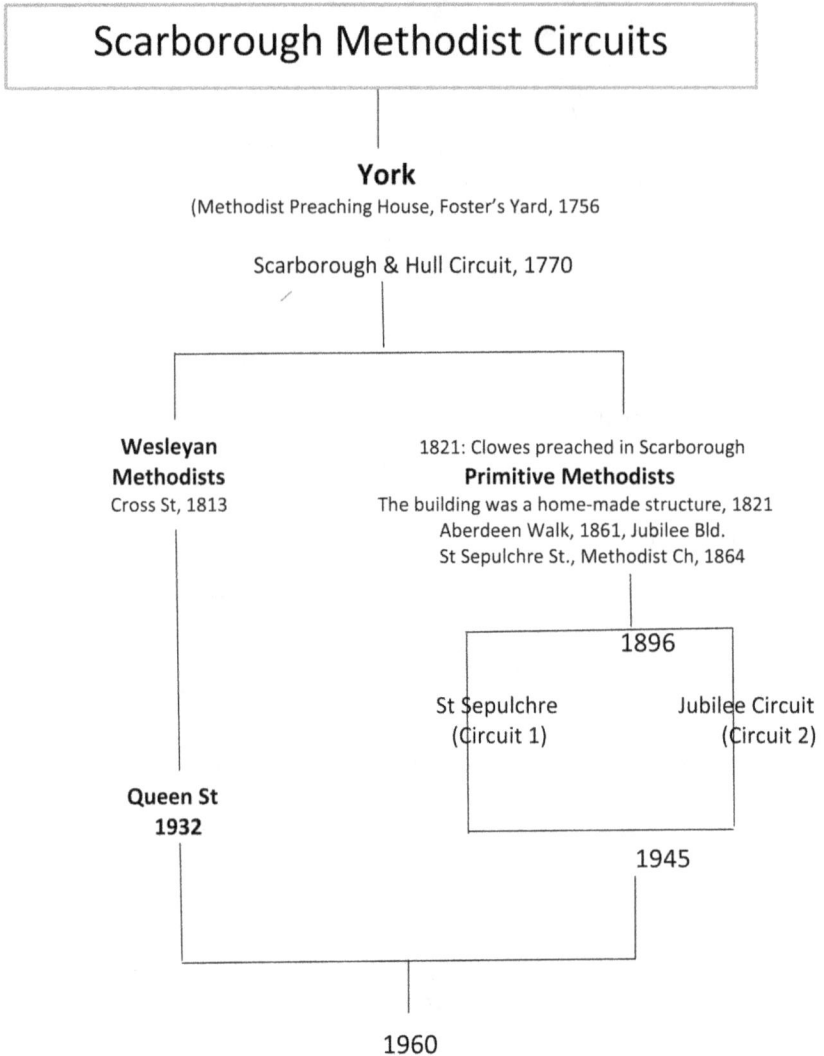

Scarborough Methodist Circuits

York

(Methodist Preaching House, Foster's Yard, 1756

Scarborough & Hull Circuit, 1770

Wesleyan Methodists

Cross St, 1813

1821: Clowes preached in Scarborough

Primitive Methodists

The building was a home-made structure, 1821
Aberdeen Walk, 1861, Jubilee Bld.
St Sepulchre St., Methodist Ch, 1864

1896

St Sepulchre
(Circuit 1)

Jubilee Circuit
(Circuit 2)

**Queen St
1932**

1945

1960

Source: Northallerton Archives, Methodist Records (R/M/LOF)

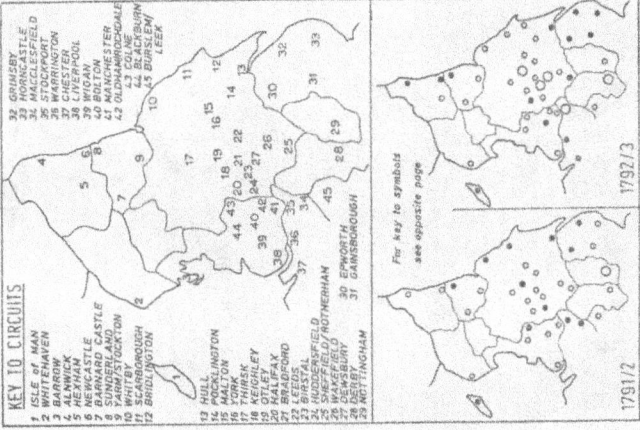

Appendix 6e: 'The Great Yorkshire Revival, 1792-96'

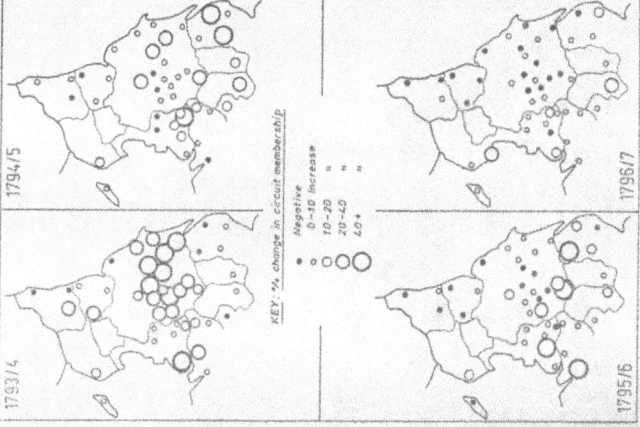

Source: With the permission of John Baxter, in M. Hill (ed), *A Sociological Yearbook of Religion in Britain*, 7, 1974 (SCM, pp. 50, 51); also with the permission of Hymns Ancient and Modern, the present holder of copyright for SCM Press.

Appendix 7a: Baptisms of Fishermen's Children in Grimsby Churches – Comparative

Year	St Andrew's Consecrated 1970	St John's New Clee Consecrated 1979	PMs Circuit 1 Est. 1839	PMs Circuit 2 Est. 1869
1848			1	
1849				
1850			1	
1851			1	
1852			2	
1853			2	
1854			1	
1855			7	
1856			7	
1857			6	
1858			13	
1859			10	
1860			11	
1861			19	
1862			13	
1863			13	
1864			24	
1865			18	
1866			18	
1867			34	
1868			26	1
1869			13	10
1870	15		10	26
1871	42		2	36
1872	48		6	14
1873	44	3	5	19
1874	50	14	2	25
1875	45	21	3	46
1876	70	19	5	72
1877	44	16	2	63
1878	56	21		85
1879	66	16	1	71
1880	53	11		78
1881	54	19	5	92
1882	69	33	3	54
1883	64	36	3	65
1884	63	53	4	75
1883	60	58	2	70
1886	76	68	3	57
1887	80	99	3	29
1888	97	83	8	8
1889	83	76	2	3
1890	73	105	3	6
1891	108	132	1	4
1892	98	133	5	3

Year	St Andrew's Consecrated 1970	St John's New Clee Consecrated 1979	PMs Circuit 1 Est. 1839	PMs Circuit 2 Est. 1869
1893	89	135	2	5
1894	59	124	6	5
1895	68	141	3	4
1896	66	129	3	1
1897	58	143	1	5
1898	64	134	3	
1899	66	149	1	
1900	60	153		
1901	46	128		
1902	103	153		
1903	68	163		
1904	62	165		
1905	44	143		
1906	50	166		
1907	61	147		
1908	41	167		
1909	44	153		
1910	64	152		
1911	64	124		
1912	60	131		
1913	69	126		
1914	68	124		

Source: Lincolnshire Archives, Lincoln.

Baptisms in Grimsby Churches

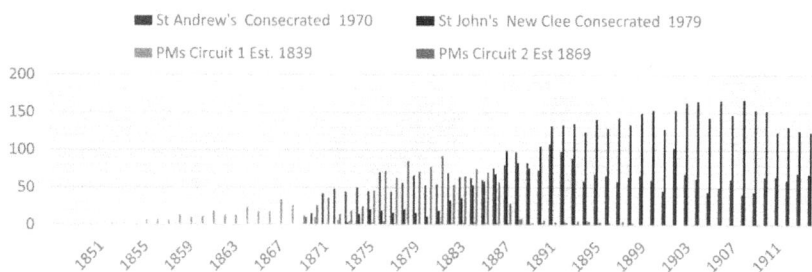

Appendix 7b: Scarborough Baptisms of Fishermen's Children – Comparative

Year	St Mary	St Thomas	PMs
1813	6		
1814	9		
1815	3		
1816	9		
1817	8		
1818	7		
1819	11		
1820	16		
1821	4		
1822	16		
1823	5		
1824	14		
1825	9		
1826	13		
1827	7		
1828	12		
1829	8		
1830	14		
1831	11		
1832	10		
1833	9		2
1834	12		
1835	6		
1836	11		
1837	11		
1838	11		
1839	6		
1840	10		1
1841	9		2
1842	7		2
1843	15		
1844	9	1	1
1845	11	2	3
1846	11	7	4
1847	7	12	
1848	12	5	6
1849	3	13	3
1850	3	20	9
1851	2	6	10
1852	4	15	12
1853	5	15	12
1854	3	8	16
1855	2	7	17
1856	4	15	11
1857		25	8
1858	6	14	16
1859	6	17	10

Year	St Mary	St Thomas	PMs
1860	6	20	14
1861	4	11	23
1862	5	19	23
1863	4	20	29
1864	7	11	9
1865	14	13	12
1866	5	11	36
1867	11	12	25
1868	8	9	18
1869	10	10	36
1870	6	13	33
1871	9	8	39
1872	8	4	54
1873	6	5	55
1874	5	2	47
1875	11	1	40
1876	14	3	32
1877	11	4	47
1878	10	9	50
1879	9	4	55
1880	18	3	60
1881	19	2	36
1882	12	4	58
1883	14	2	38
1884	12	4	59
1885	20	3	42
1886	26	2	51
1887	30	18	45
1888	32	18	38
1889	18	35	25
1890	16	34	20
1891	15	44	20
1892	18	41	22
1893	18	39	16
1894	9	37	19
1895	21	43	2
1896	13	40	1
1897	19	38	1
1898	11	32	2
1899	13	29	
1900	10	30	
1901	11	21	
1902	10	18	1
1903	10	25	
1904	4	15	
1905	10	31	
1906	9	25	
1907	10	20	
1908	5	22	
1909	12	25	
1910	8	24	

(Continued)

Year	St Mary	St Thomas	PMs
1911	7	8	
1912	5	19	
1913	10	24	
1914	13	16	

Source: Northallerton County Archives: PMs: MIC 891/1-7 (1822–1936); MIC 893/9-10 (1895–1916); R/M/SC/3/1 (1833–57); St Mary: PE115; St Thomas: PE166.

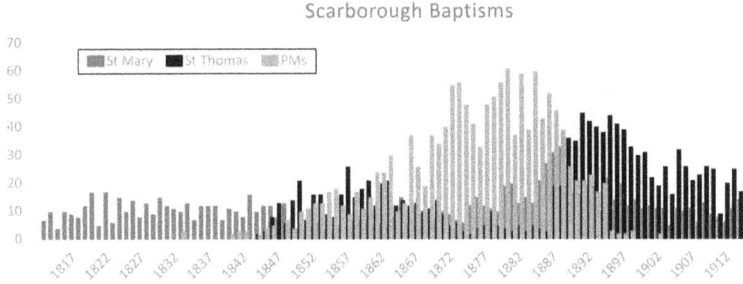

Scarborough Baptisms

Appendix 7c: Filey Baptisms of Fishermen's Children – Comparative

Year	St Oswald's	PMs	Wesleyans
1813	12		
1814	13		
1815	13		
1816	12		
1817	13		
1818	10		
1819	16		
1820	14		
1821	13		
1822	15		
1823	16		
1824	17		
1825	6		
1826	13		
1817	11		
1828	17		
1829	10		
1830	15		
1831	11		
1832	13		
1833	14		
1834	17		
1835	15		
1836	12		

Year	St Oswald's	PMs	Wesleyans
1837	17		
1838	11		
1839	16		
1840	13		
1841	20		
1842	9		
1843	27		
1844	16		
1845	18		
1846	15		
1847	15		
1848	28		
1849	10		
1850	21		
1851	17		
1852	13		
1853	9		
1854	17		
1855	16		
1856	11		
1857	19		
1858	19		
1859	12		12
1860	12		4
1861	18		
1862	11		4
1863	7	13	2
1864	6	20	10
1865	7	15	10
1866	6	19	2
1867	6	8	9
1868	10	27	10
1869	9	19	9
1870	4	18	3
1871	5	26	18
1872	4	19	8
1873	3	25	10
1874	3	30	5
1875	2	32	9
1876	3	28	14
1877	4	13	15
1878	4	18	10
1879	3	33	11
1880	9	15	6
1881	23	19	4
1882	17	19	7
1883	22	8	5
1884	10	7	3
1885	16	13	1
1886	21	5	7
1887	15	3	3
1888	17	7	1

(*Continued*)

Year	St Oswald's	PMs	Wesleyans
1889	17	7	4
1890	13	9	3
1891	23	10	4
1892	14	8	2
1893	14	6	2
1894	22	7	3
1895	28	2	4
1896	21	4	4
1897	21	5	
1898	23	4	2
1899	12	1	1
1900	27	3	5
1901	24	3	2
1902	22	5	6
1903	23	1	1
1904	11	8	8
1905	15	3	5
1906	17	5	2
1907	16	3	3
1908	12	4	5
1909	16	5	5
1910	9	5	8
1911	14	5	3
1912	12	6	4
1913	5	1	2
1914	9	4	1

Source: Beverley Archives: Filey Baptismal Registers, 1813–1936
(St Oswald's, PE 112/5-7, 1813–1947; PMs: MRQ/1/1/2/3, 1838–1947).

Filey Parish Church Baptisms (Fishermen)

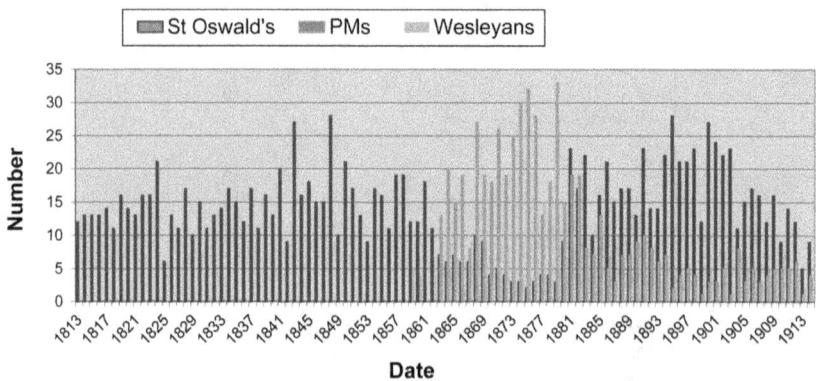

Appendix 7d: Comparative Baptisms:
Grimsby, Filey and Scarborough

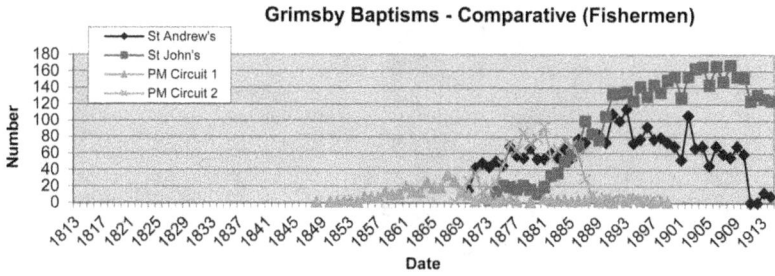

Grimsby Baptisms - Comparative (Fishermen)

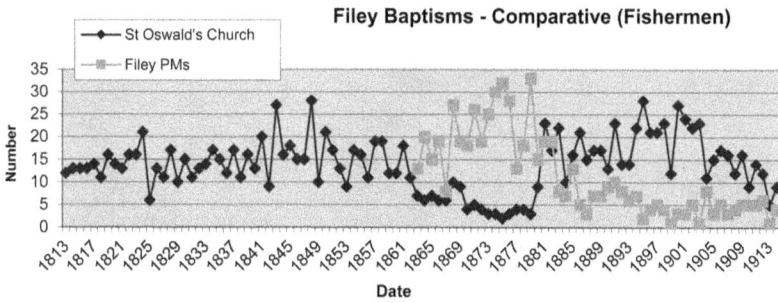

Filey Baptisms - Comparative (Fishermen)

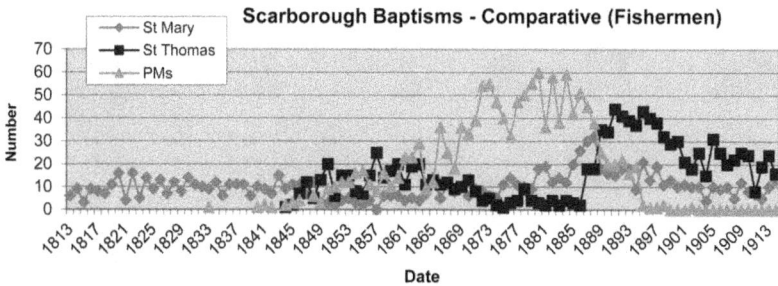

Scarborough Baptisms - Comparative (Fishermen)

Appendix 8a: Dimensions of the Definition of Religion

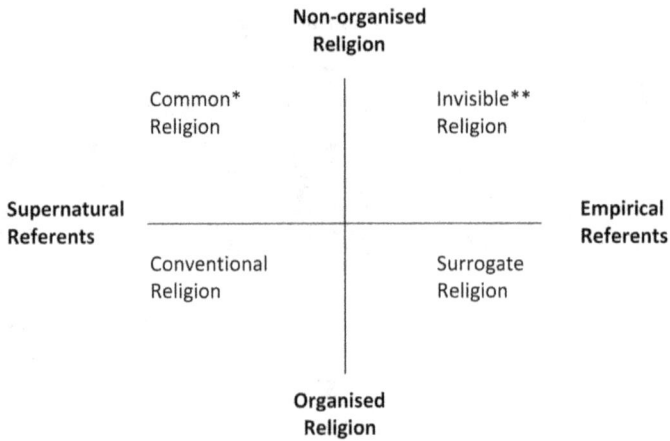

Non-organised Religion

Common* Religion   Invisible** Religion

Supernatural Referents   **Empirical Referents**

Conventional Religion   Surrogate Religion

Organised Religion

Source: Richard Toon: Leeds Project on 'Conventional Religion and Common Religion in Leeds' (Paper No. 3: *Methodological Problems in the Study of Implicit Religion*).

*'Common religion' is a term taken from Robert Towler's book *Homo Religiosus* (1974) and is by nature thematic rather than systematic. The term was then adopted by all those associated with the Leeds Project. Towler defines 'common religion' as 'those beliefs and practices of an overtly religious nature which are not under the domination of a prevailing institution'. (It therefore includes the paranormal, fortune telling, fate and destiny, the existence of God, life after death, ghosts, spiritual experiences, prayer and meditation, luck and superstitious belief. See Ahern and Davie, *Inner City God*, p. 34.)

**'Invisible religion' is taken from Luckman's definition (*Invisible Religion*, 1967). Luckman has defined this as 'a system of symbolic meaning in which there is no reference to the supernatural' (nor is this religion organized in any way). The term covers the sense of meaning that people find in life.

Appendix 8b: The Development and Relationship between the Main Nineteenth-Century Seafarers' Missions*

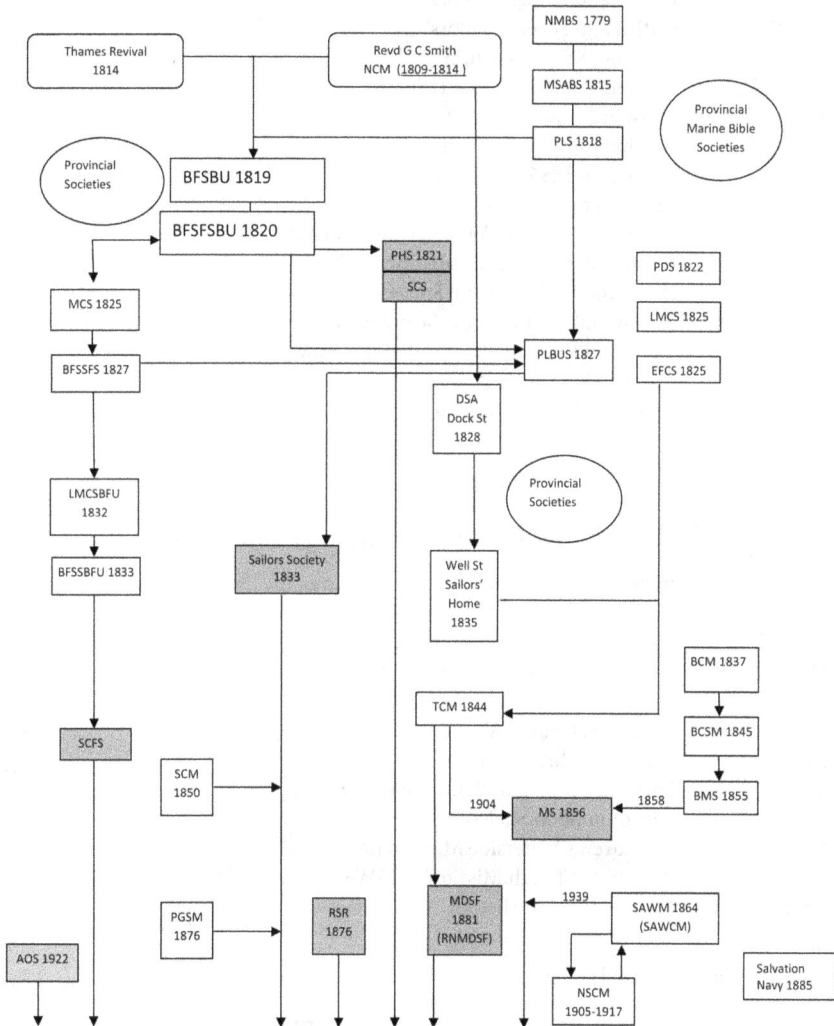

* Shaded Areas Represent Organizations Still in Existence.

Nonconformist missions

BFSBU:	British and Foreign Seamen's Bethel Union
BFSFSBU:	British and Foreign Seamen's Friend Society and Bethel Union
BFSS:	British and Foreign Sailors' Society (now called 'The Sailors' Society')
BFSSBFU:	British and Foreign Sailors' and Soldiers' Bethel Flag Union
DSA:	Destitute Sailors' Asylum
LMCSBFU:	London Mariners' Church Society or Bethel Flag Union
MCS:	Mariners' Church Society
MDSF:	Mission to Deep Sea Fishermen (separated from the Thames Church Mission in 1886 – later known as the 'Royal National Mission to Deep Sea Fishermen')
MSABS:	Merchant Seamen's Auxiliary Bible Society
NCS:	Naval Correspondence Mission
NMBS:	Naval and Military Bible Society
PGSM:	Portsmouth and Gosport Seamen's Mission
PHS:	Port of Hull Society (later called the 'Sailors' Children's Society – SCS)
RSR:	Royal Sailors' Rests
SCFS:	Seamen's Christian Friend Society
SCM:	Scottish Coast Missions
SCS:	See PHS

Well Street Sailors' HomeChurch of England missions

BCM:	Bristol Channel Missions (later known as the 'Bristol Channel Seamen's Mission' – BCSM – and the 'Bristol Mission to Seamen')
ECFS:	Episcopal Floating Church Society
LMCS:	Liverpool Mariners Church Society
MS:	Missions to Seamen
NSCM:	North Sea Church Mission
PDS:	Port of Dublin Society
PLBUS:	Port of London and Bethel Union Society
PLS:	Port of London Society
SAWM:	St Andrew's Waterside Mission (later known as the 'St Andrew's Waterside Church Mission' – SAWCM)
TCM:	Thames Church Mission

Roman Catholic missions

St Joseph's Confraternity:	a confraternity founded in Grimsby for Roman Catholic fisherlads
AOS:	Apostleship of the Sea (founded in 1922)

Notes

Chapter 1

1 Émile Durkheim (1912/2001) *The Elementary Forms of the Religious Life*, Oxford: Oxford University Press, xx.

2 Arnold van Gennap (1960) *The Rites of Passage*, London: Routledge & Kegan Paul; 'Festivals' here may include the 'Harvest of the Sea', Christmas, Easter and so on.

3 John Wolffe (1994) *God and Greater Britain: Religious and National Life in Britain and Ireland 1843-1945*, London: Routledge, 160, Callum Brown (2001) *The Death of Christian Britain*, London: Routledge; see also Abby Day (2011) *Believing in Belonging: Belief & Social Identity in the Modern World*, Oxford: Oxford University Press, 24–5.

4 P. H. Vrijhof and J. Wardenburg (1979) *Official and Popular Religion. Analysis of a Theme for Religious Studies*, The Hague: Mouton; review by Nancy Tapper (June 1982) *Religious Studies*, Vol. 18, No. 2, 236–9.

5 Ichi Hori on Japanese religion (1968) in Don Yoder (1974) 'Towards a Definition of Folk Religion', *Western Folklore*, Vol. 33, 2–15.

6 Horace Mann (1853) *A Census of Great Britain, 1851: Religious Worship, England and Wales, Report and Tables Presented to Both Houses of Parliament by Command of Her Majesty*, London: HMSO; Thomas Wright (1868) *'The Working Classes and the Church' in the Great Unwashed*, London: Tinsley Bros; E. R. Wickham (1957) *Church and People in an Industrial City*, London: Lutterworth Press; K. S. Inglis (1963) *Churches and the Working Classes in Victorian England*, London: Routledge & Kegan Paul.

7 Alan D. Gilbert (1976) *Religion and Society in Industrial England, 1740-1914*, London: Longman, 112–13, 145–8, 186–7; Wickham (1957) 130–7.

8 Jeffrey Cox (1982) *The English Churches in a Secular Society: Lambeth 1870–1914*, Oxford: Oxford University Press; Mark Smith (1994) *Religion in Industrial Society: Oldham and Saddleworth, 1740-1853*, London: Clarendon Press; Brown (2001).

9 S. C. Williams (1999) *Religious Belief and Popular Culture in Southwark, c.1880–1939*, Oxford: Oxford University Press.

10 Gilbert (1976); Robert Currie, Alan Gilbert & Lee Horsley (1977) *Churches and Churchgoers – Patterns of Church Growth in the British Isles since 1700*, Oxford: Clarendon Press; Keith D. M. Snell & Paul S. Ell (2000) *Rival Jerusalems: The Geography of Victorian Religion*, Cambridge: Cambridge University Press; Hugh McLeod (1984) *Religion and the Working Classes in Nineteenth Century Britain*, London: Macmillan; and (1996), *Religion and Society in England, 1850-1914*, London: Macmillan.

11 David Clark (1982) *Between Pulpit and Pew: Folk Religion in a North Yorkshire Fishing Community*, Cambridge: Cambridge University Press. For a seminal discussion of folk, popular and vernacular concepts of religion, see M Bowman (2004) 'Phenomenology, Fieldwork and Folk Religion' in Sutcliffe (ed.) *Religion: Empirical Studies*.

12 P. Thompson, T. Wailey & T. Lummis (1983) *Living the Fishing*, London: Routledge & Kegan Paul; T. Lummis (1985) *Occupation and Society: The East Anglian*

Fishermen 1880-1914, Cambridge: Cambridge University Press; D. E. M. Chalmers (1988) *Fishermen's Wives: The Social Roles of Women in a Scottish Community*, Unpublished PhD Thesis, Belfast: Queens University; J. H. Nadel (1986) 'Burning with the Fire of God: Calvinism and Community in a Scottish Fishing Village', *Ethnology*, Vol. 25, No. 1, 49–60; A. P. Cohen (1987) *Whalsay, Symbol, Segment and Boundary in a Shetland Island Community*, Manchester: Manchester University Press.

13 P. Frank (2002) *Yorkshire Fisherfolk*, London: Philimore.

14 Lynn Abrams (2005) *Myth and Materiality in a Woman's World Shetland 1800-2000*, Manchester: Manchester University Press, esp. 143–5.

15 Marian Binkley (2002) *Set Adrift: Fishing Families*, Toronto: University of Toronto Press.

16 S. Friend (2007) 'Identity and Religion in Yorkshire Fishing Communities', Chapter 11 in Sebastian Kim and Pauline Koliontai (eds), *Community Identity: Dynamics of Religion in Context*, T & T Clark.

17 David Bebbington (2012) *Victorian Religious Revivals: Culture and Piety in Local and Global Contexts*, Oxford: Oxford University Press.

18 Friend (2018) *Fishing for Souls,* Cambridge: Lutterworth Press, 120–7.

19 Friend (2018).

20 H. Mann (1988) 'On the Religious Census, 1853', in James R. Moore (ed.) *Religion in Victorian Britain, Vol. III, Sources*, Manchester: Manchester University Press, 316.

21 Deborah M. Valenze (1985) *Prophetic Sons and Daughters, Female Preaching and Popular Religion in Industrial England*, Princeton: Princeton University Press.

22 Bebbington (2012) 117–18.

23 Friend (2018) 121–4.

24 Richard Jenkins (2004) *Social Identity*, Third Edition, London: Routledge, Chapter two.

25 Nadel (1986) 49–60.

26 Geoffrey Ahern & Grace Davie (1987) *Inner City God: The Nature of Belief in the Inner City*, London: Hodder & Stoughton, 7–72. See also Day (2011).

27 Edward P. Thompson (1963) *The Making of the English Working Class*, London: Penguin; Gilbert (1976); Bebbington (2012) 29–31.

28 David Hay (1998) *The Spirit of the Child*, London: Fount.

29 Frances Wilkins (2019) *Singing the Gospel along Scotland's North East Coast, 1859–2009*, London: Routledge.

30 Paul Heelas and Linda Woodhead (2005) *The Spiritual Revolution, Why Religion Is Giving Way to Spirituality*, Oxford: Blackwell.

31 Day (2013) 23.

32 Grace Davie (1994) *Religion in Britain since 1945,* Oxford: Blackwell, 74. See also Meredith B. McGuire (2002), *Religion: The Social Context* (5th edition), Belmont, CA: Wadsworth, 113–123.

33 McGuire (2008) 123.

34 Vrijhof and Wardenburg (1979) Chapter 7; Williams (1999) 9.

35 Day (2013).

36 Harvey Cox (1970) *Feast of Fools*, London: Harper & Row; Timothy Jenkins (1999) *Religion and Everyday Life: An Ethnographic Approach*, Oxford: Berghahn Books; Andrew M. Greeley (1988) *God in Popular Culture*, Chicago: The Thomas More Press.

37 The exploration of theology and film appears to have begun at the College of Ripon and York in the early 1980s, although staff were dependent on hiring films from the

British Film Institute. With the advent of videos the area opened up and many others began exploring and writing about the developments. Marsh, C, and Ortiz, G, at Ripon, collaborated on editing a book entitled (1997) *Explorations in Theology and Film*, London: Blackwell. Since then numerous people have published articles and books on the subject. Of particular note is R. K. Johnston (2000) *Reel Spirituality: Theology and Film in Dialogue*, Baker Academic.

38 R Carwardine (1978) *Transatlantic Revivalism – Popular Evangelicalism in Britain and America 1790-1865*, London: Greenwood Press; Bebbington (2012).
39 Janice Holmes (2000) *Religious Revivals in Britain and Ireland, 1859-1905*, Dublin: Irish Academic Press Chapter Four; Valenze (1985), Chapter Nine.
40 E. J. Hobsbawm (1959) *Primitive Rebels: Studies in Archaic Forms of Social Movement in the Nineteenth and Twentieth Centuries*, Manchester: Manchester University Press, 127.
41 E. Halévy (1871) *The Birth of Methodism in England* (Translated and edited by Bernard Semmel), Chicago: The University of Chicago Press; Hobsbawn (1959) 115–123; E. P. Thompson (1976) *The Making of the English Working Class*, London: Penguin; D. H. Luker (1986) 'Revivalism in Theory and Practice: The Case of Cornish Methodism', *Journal of Ecclesiastical History*, Vol. 37, No. 4, 603–19; Bebbington (2012).
42 Curie, Gilbert and Horsley (1977) 44–5.
43 D. Hempton, in T. Thomas (ed.) (1988) *The British: Their Religious Beliefs and Practices 1800–1986*, London: Routledge, 183.
44 Carwardine (1978) 54.
45 Luker (1986) 604 & 618; Thompson (1968) 191; Carwardine (1978).
46 Thompson (1968) 920ff.
47 Hobsbawm (1959) 124 and 131.
48 Nadel (1986) 51.
49 Valenze (1985).
50 G. Shaw (1867) *Our Filey Fishermen*, London: Hamilton Adams.
51 Donald E. Meek (1997) 'Fishers of Men': *The 1921 Religious Revival, Its Cause, Context and Transmission*, 135–42 in *After Columba – After Calvin: Community and Identity in the Religious Traditions of North-East Scotland* University of Aberdeen; Luker (1986).
52 John Baxter, 'The Great Yorkshire Revival 1792-96: A Study of Mass Revival among the Methodists', Ch 4 in M. Hill (1974) *A Sociological Yearbook of Religion in Britain 7*, London: SCM, 46–76.
53 See, for example, Revd Henry Woodcock (1889) *Piety and Peasantry: Being Sketches of Primitive Methodism on the Yorkshire Wolds*, London: Primitive Methodist Book Department, 37ff.
54 Day (2011) 108–14.
55 S. Friend (2005–8) *Women's Voices Project*, York, York St John University.
56 Wilkins (2019).
57 Williams (1999) 89–104.
58 Catherine Bell (1997) *Ritual: Perspectives and Dimensions*, Oxford: Oxford University Press; Roy Rappaport (1999) *Ritual and Religion in the Making of Humanity*, Cambridge: Cambridge University Press; Tom F. Driver (2006) *Liberating Rites: Understanding the Transformative Power of Ritual*, Tom F. Driver: Booksurge, LLC; Victor Turner (1987) *The Anthropology of Performance*, New York: PAJ Publications.

59 Stuart Russell (1997) *Dark Winter: The Story of the Hull Triple Trawler Tragedy, 1968*, Hull: Hull Quality Publications; Brian W. Lavery (2015) *The Headscarf Revolutionaries, Lillian Bilocca and the Hull Triple Trawler Disaster of 1968*, Hull: Barbican Press. On the work of the RNMDSF, see Friend (2018).

60 Archbishop Herring (1928) *Visitation Returns, 1743, Church of England, Diocese of York*, Leeds Archaeological Society; Friend (2004–8) The *Women's Voices Project* was established at York St John University, and the qualitative analysis was completed with fifty in-depth video-recorded interviews and their transcriptions. The approach used a personal narrative methodology, which allowed the women to tell their own stories about life in Yorkshire fishing communities. This approach allowed the interviewees to have a fair amount of control over the structure of the interview, although a range of topics were explored (see Williams (1999), 20, for discussion on her similar approach). Some material from the project has appeared in Sebastian C. H. Kim and Pauline Kollontai (eds) (2007) *Community Identity: Dynamics of Religion in Context*, T & T Clark, 203–227.

61 Margaret Gerrish (January 1992) *Special Industrial Migration in Nineteenth Century Britain: A Case Study of the Port of Grimsby 1841–1861*, Unpublished PhD thesis, The University of Hull, 252.

62 His Excellency Spencer Walpole (1883) *Fisheries Exhibition Literature*, Vol. I, 4–5.

63 Gerrish (1992) 6.

64 Margaret Stacey (2 June 1969) 'The Myth of Community Studies', *British Journal of Sociology*, Vol. XX, 134–47.

Chapter 2

1   Horace Mann was responsible for conducting the religious census of 1851. Unfortunately, he assumed that the working classes were essentially 'unconscious secularists' and that the churches needed to undertake a rigorous campaign to win new members.

2   For example the work of Hugh McLeod (1987) 'New Perspectives in Victorian Working Class Religion: The Oral Evidence', *Oral History*, Vol. XIV, 31–50; Williams (1999); R. P. M. Sykes (April 1999) *Popular Religion in Dudley and the Gornals, c.1914–65*, Unpublished PhD thesis, Wolverhampton: University of Wolverhampton.

3   R. Moore (1974) *Pit-men, Politics and Preachers*, Cambridge: Cambridge University Press, 69; See also Currie, Gilbert & Horsley (1977) 83.

4   Wright (1868).

5   G. Robson (2002) *Dark Satanic Mills? Religion and Irreligion in Birmingham and the Black Country*, Carlisle: Paternoster.

6   R. W. Ambler (2000) *Churches, Chapels and the Parish Communities of Lincolnshire, 1660-1900*, Lincoln, History of Lincolnshire Committee for the Society for Lincolnshire History and Archaeology; Luker (1986).

7   P. Anson (1965) *Fisher Folk-Lore*, London: The Faith Press, 27; J. Nadel-Klein (2003) *Fishing for Heritage: Modernity and Loss along the Scottish Coast*, Oxford: Berg, 79–88.

8   In particular this was the case with the women who campaigned for changes in the fishing industry following the trawler disaster of 1968, Lavery (2015).

9   F. Tönnies (1957) *Community and Association*, New York: Harper.

10 Notably B. Anderson (1983/91) *Imagined Communities: Reflections on the Origin and Spread of Nationalism*, London: Verso; A. P. Cohen (1985) *The Symbolic Construction of Community*, London: Routledge.

11 Chalmers (1988); Jane Nadel-Klein and Donna Lee Davis (eds) (1988) *To Work and to Weep: Women in Fishing Economies*, Institute of Social and Economic Research, Memorial University of Newfoundland: St John's, Newfoundland, 18.

12 Gillian Munro (1997) *I'm nae ees for nithin bit scraping pans!* PhD thesis, University of Edinburgh.

13 G. W. Horobin (1957) 'Community and Occupation in the Hull Fishing Industry', *British Journal of Sociology*, Vol. 8, 343–55.

14 Tunstall (1962) *The Fishermen*, London: McGibbon and Kee 138–43 and 160–5.

15 Clark (1982); Frank (2002).

16 H. C. Johansen, P. Madsen and P. Degn (1993) 'Fishing Families in Three Danish Coastal Communities', *Journal of Family History*, Vol. 18, No. 4, 357–68; B. Moring (1993) 'Household and Family in Finnish Coastal Societies 1635-1895', *Journal of Family History*, Vol. 18, No. 4, 395–415; S. Dryvik (1993) 'Farmers at Sea: A Study of Fishermen in North Norway, 1801-1920', *Journal of Family History*, Vol. 18, No. 4, 341–57; Donna Lee Davis (1986) 'Occupational Community and Fishermen's Wives in a Newfoundland Fishing Village', *Anthropological Quarterly*, Vol. 59, No. 3, 129–42; D. Grønbech (2000) 'Recycling the Past: Perspectives on Women Households and Resource Management among Early Twentieth Century Fisher/Farmers in North Norway', *Women's Studies International Forum*, Vol. 23, No. 3, 355–61; U. D. Skaptadóttir (2000) 'Women Coping with Change in an Icelandic Fishing Community: A Case Study', *Women's Studies International Forum*, Vol. 23, No. 3, 311–32; H. M. Hapke (August 2001) 'Gender, Work and Household Survival in South India Fishing Communities: A Preliminary Analysis', *Professional Geographer*, Vol. 53, No. 3, 357–68; J. Marshall (December 2001) 'Connectivity and Restructuring: Identity and Gender in a Fishing Community', *Gender, Place and Culture: A Journal of Feminist Geography*, Vol. 8, No. 4, 391–409; Hanna C. Hagmark (September 2003) *Women in Maritime Communities: A Socio-Historical Study of Continuity and Change in the Domestic Lives of Seafarers' Wives in the Åland Islands, from 1930 into the New Millennium*, Unpublished PhD thesis, University of Hull. Also Binkley (2002), and Fabio Rambelli (2020) *The Sea and the Sacred in Japan: Aspects of Maritime Religion*, Bloomsbury.

17 Thompson, Wailey and Lummis (1983), Chalmers (1988), Nadel-Klein (2003) and Margaret H. King (1992) 'A Partnership of Equals – Women in Scottish East Coast Fishing Communities', *Folk Life*, Vol. 31, 17–35 and 'Marriage and Traditions in Fishing Communities', *Review of Scottish Culture*, Vol. 8, 58–67; Gillian Munro (1993) 'Tradition and Innovation in the Life of a Fisherman's Wife on the Buchan Coast', *Review of Scottish Culture*, Vol. 8, 68–76; Joseph Webster (2013) *The Anthropology of Protestantism*, Basingstoke: Palgrave.

18 Donna Lee Davis (1988) '"Shore Skippers" and "Grass Widows": Active and Passive Women's Roles in a Newfoundland Fishery', Ch 11, 211, in Nadel-Klein and Davis (1988).

19 Thompson, Wailey and Lummis (1983) 167.

20 J. H. Gilligan (1990) 'Padstow: Economic and Social Change in a Cornish Town', in C. C. Harris (ed.), *Family, Economy and Community*, University of Wales Press, 65–185.

21 Brian Harrison (December 1967) 'Religion and Recreation in Nineteenth Century England', *Past and Present*, Vol. 38, 98.

22 Chalmers (1988) 88ff; Nadel-Klein and Davis (1988) 47–49.

23 R. Anderson and C. Wadel (eds) (1972) *North Atlantic Fishermen: Anthropological Essays on Modern Fishing*, St John's Institute of Social and Economic Research: Memorial University of Newfoundland; M. Estellie Smith (ed.) (1977) *Those Who Live From the Sea: A Study in Maritime Anthropology*, St Paul, West Publishing Co; Jane Nadel (1984) 'Stigma and Separation: Parish Status and Community Persistence in a Scottish Fishing Village', *Ethnography*, Vol. 23, No. 2, 101–15.

24 Revd A. Pettitt (1868) 'Guide to Filey', in Deborah Valenze (1985) *Prophetic Sons and Daughters: Female Preaching and Popular Religion in Industrial England,* New Jersey: Princeton University, 59.

25 Jane Nadel-Klein (August 1988) Review of *Occupation and Society* by Trevor Lummis, *American Ethnologist*, Vol. 15, No. 3, 577–8.

26 P. Thompson (January 1985) 'Women in Fishing: The Roots of Power between the Sexes', *Comparative Studies in Society and History*, Vol. 27, No. 1, 3–32.

27 J. M. Acheson (1981) 'Anthropology of Fishing', *Annual Review of Anthropology*, Vol. 10, 275–316, 277.

28 Nadel-Klein and Davis (1988) 19, 24.

29 C. L. Yodanis (2000) 'Constructing Gender and Occupational Segregation: A Study of Women and Work in Fishing Communities', *Qualitative Sociology*, Vol. 23, No. 3, 267–90.

30 Quoted in Nadel-Klein and Davis (1988) 29.

31 J. Nadel-Klein (May/June 2000) 'Granny-Baited Lines: Perpetual Crisis and the Changing Role of Women in Scottish Fishing Communities', *Women's Studies International Forum*, Vol. 23, No. 3, 364.

32 C. Allison, 'Women Fishermen in the Pacific Northwest', Ch. 12 in Nadel-Klein and Davis (1988) 230–60.

33 Linda Greenlaw (December 1998) *The Hungry Ocean*, Hyperion.

34 Nadel-Klein and Davis (1988) 23.

35 See especially G. Lenski (1966) *Human Societies*, New York: McGraw Hill; and B. Pollnac (1976) 'Continuity and Change in Marine Fishing Communities', *Anthropology Working Paper*, 10, A State of Art Paper Proposal for the US Agency for International Development.

36 Marshall (December 2001) 391–409; Johansen, Madsen and Degn (1993), 357–368; Dyrvik (1993); Moring (1993); Nadel-Klein and Davis (1988); Hapke (2001); Skaptadóttir (2000); Grønbech (2000); Yodanis (2000).

37 David J. Starkey, Chris Reid and Neil Ashcroft (2000) *England's Sea Fisheries: The Commercial Sea Fisheries of England and Wales since 1300*, London: Chatham Publishing.

38 Chalmers (1988) 120.

39 Sally Festing (1977) *Fishermen: A Community Living From the Sea*, London: David & Charles, 150–174.

40 P. J. Edwards and J. Marshall (Spring 1977) 'Sources of Conflict and Community in the Trawling Industries of Hull and Grimsby between the Wars', *Oral History*, Vol. 5, No. 1, 97–121.

41 Nadel-Klein (2000) 372.

42 Nadel-Klein (2000) 365; E. J. Hobsbawm (1957) 'Methodism and the Threat of Revolution in Britain', *History Today*, 115–23; Thompson (1963).

43 S. G. Hatcher (1993) *The Origin and Expansion of Primitive Methodism in the Hull Circuit, 1819-1851*, Unpublished PhD thesis, Manchester University.

44 J. L. Duthie (December 1983) 'The Fishermen's Religious Revival', *History Today*, Vol. 33: 22–7.

45 P. H. Fricke (1973) *Seafarer and Community*, London, Croom Helm.

46 See Friend (2018).

47 Different aspects of the work of maritime missions have been explored by a range of scholars. These include Roald Kverndal (1986) *Seamen's Missions: Their Origin and Early Growth*, California: William Carey Library; Alston Kennerley (1989) *British Seamen's Missions and Sailors' Homes, 1815 to 1970: Voluntary Welfare Provision for Serving Seafarers*, CNAA, University of Exeter; Robert Miller (1989) *From Shore to Shore: A History of the Church and the Merchant Seafarer from the Earliest Times*. Published privately: Ladycroft, Newmarket Road, Nailsworth, Gloucestershire; Paul Mooney (2005) *Maritime Mission: History, Developments, A New Perspective*, Uitgeverij Boekencentrum, Zoetermeer, The Netherlands; Friend (2018).

48 Kverndal (1986) Chapter two.

49 E. J. Hobsbawm and T. Ranger (1983) *The Invention of Tradition*, Cambridge: Cambridge University Press.

50 Bob Trubshaw (2002) *Explore Folklore*, Loughborough: Explore Books, 47–52.

51 V. Amit (2002) *Realizing Community*, London: Routledge, 40.

52 J. Nadel-Klein (1991) 'Reweaving the Fringe: Localism, Tradition and Representation in British Ethnography', *American Ethnologist*, Vol. 18, No. 3, 500–17.

53 Bob Bushaway (1982) *By Rite: Custom, Ceremony and Community in England 1700-1880*, London: Junction Books; Robert D. Storch (1982) *Popular Culture and Custom in Nineteenth-Century England*, London, Croom Helm; Ronald Hutton (1996) *The Stations of the Sun: A History of the Ritual Year in Britain*, Oxford: Oxford University Press.

54 Trubshaw (2002) 6.

55 Sally Cole, 'The Sexual Division of Labour and Social Change in a Portuguese Fishery', Chapter nine in Nadel-Klein and Davis (1988).

56 E. Bott (1957) *Family and Social Network*, London: Tavistock, 2.

57 John Kent (2002) *Wesley and the Wesleyans*, Cambridge: Cambridge University Press, 2.

58 Leo Walmsley (1948) *Master Mariner,* London: Collins.

59 Rodney Ambler (1989) *Ranters, Revivalists and Reformers*, Hull: Hull University Press, 85.

60 Clive Field (January 1993) 'Adam and Eve: Gender in the English Free Church Constituency', *Journal of Ecclesiastical History*, Vol. 44, No. 1, 63–79.

61 Nadel-Klein (2003) 94.

62 Cohen (1987) 178–9.

63 Nadel-Klein & Davis (1988) 218.

64 A. Gell (1998) *Art and Agency: An Anthropological Theory*: Oxford: Clarendon Press, 7.

65 M. Salins, cited in Trubshaw (2002) 44.

66 Leo Walmsley (1932) *Three Fevers,* London: Collins; S. Reynolds (1908) *A Poor Man's House*, London: John Lane; Neil M. Gunn (1941) *The Silver Darlings*, London: Faber & Faber; George McKay Brown (1972) *Greenvoe,* London: Hogarth Press.

67 R. M. Ballantyne (1884) *The Young Trawler*, London: Nisbet & Co, and (1886) *The Lively Poll*, London: J. Nisbet & Co; James Runciman (1889) *A Dream of the North Sea*, London: J. Nisbet & Co.

68 Charles Hemming (1988) *British Painters of the Coast and Sea: A History and Gazetteer,* London: Victor Gollancz.
69 Philip Hills discussed the situation with regard to the Scottish town of Oban, in Magnus Fladmark et al. (1994) *Cultural Tourism,* Aberdeen: Robert Gordon University, 89–100.
70 Friend (1999).
71 Nadel-Klein (2003) 204–9; see also the review of *Fishing for Heritage* in the Berg catalogue (Autumn 2002).
72 Lavery (2015).
73 C. Geertz (1973) 'Religion as a Cultural System', in *The Interpretation of Culture,* New York: Basic Books, 87.
74 Nadel-Klein and Davis (1988) 216.
75 K. Thompson (1986) *Beliefs and Ideology,* London: Tavistock, esp. Chapter twelve.

Chapter 3

1 See also (sacred) 'acoustic communities' and 'virtual acoustic communities' as discussed in Frances Wilkins (2019), Chapter three, regarding radio singers such as Toon Soon Lee.
2 Anderson (1983–91) 118; Cohen (1985).
3 P. Cook (1989) *Localities: The Changing Face of Urban Britain,* London: Unwin Hyman; A. Giddens (1984) *The Constitution of* Society, London: Polity.
4 Stacey (June 1969) 114; 'The Myth of Community Studies', *British Journal of Sociology,* Vol. XX, 34–147.
5 Amit (2002).
6 H. G. Magni, 'The Fear of Death: Studies of Its Character and Concomitants' (in L. B. Brown) (ed.) (1973) *Psychology and Religion,* London: Penguin, 329–42.
7 Fricke (1973) 3.
8 R. Pearson (December 1993) 'Knowing One's Place: Perceptions of Community in the Industrial Suburbs of Leeds, 1790–1890', *Journal of Social History,* Vol. 27, No. 2, 221–4; J. K. Walton, 'Fishing Communities, 1850–1950', in Starkey, Reid & Ashcroft (2000) 21.
9 Pearson (1993) 222.
10 E. Day and J. Murdock (1993) 'Locality and Community: Coming to Terms with Place', *Sociological Review,* Vol. 41, No. 1, 82–111.
11 Walton (2000) 127.
12 Thompson, Wailey and Lummis (1983) 19.
13 Pearson (1993) 225.
14 J. Roding and J. H. van Voss (1996) *The North Sea and Culture, 1550–1800,* Hilversum Verloren.
15 Gilligan (1990) 65–185.
16 See especially G. Crowe & G. Allen (1994) *Community Life: An Introduction to Local Social Relations,* Harvester: Wheatsheaf, 16.
17 M. Fearon (2008) *Filey, from Fishing Village to Edwardian Resort: Pickering,* Yorkshire, Blackthorn Press, 20 & 29. Also the census data for 1801–1901.
18 Edward William Pritchard (1829) *Filey 1853 A Guide for Visitors,* Scarborough, 103.
19 John Cole (1828) *The History and Antiquities of Filey in the County of Yorkshire,* Scarborough, 103.

20 G. Waller (March 1958) *The Filey Advertiser*.

21 M. Andrews (1975) *The Story of Filey, fifth edition*, M. J. Milwood: Loughborough, 24.

22 P. Frank (1976) 'Women's Work in the Yorkshire Inshore Fishing Industry', *Oral History*, Vol. 4, 57–72; D. H. Hudson (1974) *Man of Two Worlds: The Life and Diaries of Arthur J. Munby, 1828–1910*, London: Abacas.

23 Rev. C. Kendall (1870) *God's Hand in the Storm*, G. Lamb, Conference Offices, London.

24 Cole (1828) 127.

25 J. Binns (2003) *The History of Scarborough from the Earliest Times to the Year 2000*, Yorkshire: Pickering, Blackthorne Press, 2–3.

26 Census figures. But see Binns's discussion on these figures (2003) 194–5.

27 R. W. N. Robinson (June 1984) *The English Fishing Industry 1790–1914: A Case Study of the Yorkshire Coast*, Unpublished PhD Thesis, the University of Hull 7.

28 P. G. Vasey (1978) 'The Later Medieval Herring Industry in Scarborough', *The Transactions of the Scarborough Archaeological and Historical Society*, Vol. 21, 17.

29 Ibid, Part One, 3, 1 (August 1997) 15–16.

30 Anderson Bates (1893) *A Gossip about Old Grimsby*, Grimsby: Albert Gait, 7.

31 Gerrish (Spring 1993) 'Following the Fish to Grimsby' Nottingham University Department of Adult Education and the ERSC Cambridge Group for the History of Population and Social Structure', *Local Population Studies*, Vol. 50, 39–50.

32 Gillett (1970) 213.

33 Cited in Kendall (1907) *The Origin and History of the Primitive Methodist Church*, 2 vols, London: Primitive Methodist Publishing House, 445.

34 J. K. Walton (1979) 'Beside the Sea: Visual Imagery, Aging and Heritage', *Aging and Society*, Vol. 17: 629–648.

35 D. Boswell (1974) *Sea Fishing Apprentices of Grimsby*, Grimsby Public Libraries, 144–9, lists 393 sources for this apprentice labour.

36 Cited in E. Gillett (1970) *A History of Grimsby*, Hull: The University of Hull Press, 220.

37 Gerrish (1992) 170, citing Frank Bowen (1945) *A Hundred Years of Grimsby*, Docks and Harbour Authority. Gerrish pointed to the development of Grimsby being founded on the discovery of the Silver Pitts sometime during the period late 1830s to the late 1840s. Others, however, disagree with this view – see, for example, G. Jackson (1971) *Grimsby and the Haven Co.* (cited in Gerrish (1992) 171); also Gillett (1970) 231.

38 G. Alward (1932) *The Sea Fisheries of Great Britain and Ireland*, Grimsby: Albert Gait, 447.

39 Grimsby Gazette (9 March 1855); Gillett (1970) 222.

40 Gillett (1970) 236.

41 Pamela Horn (1996) 'Pauper Apprenticeship and the Grimsby Fishing Industry 1870–1914', *Labour History Review*, 173–94.

42 Horn (1996) 173; See also R. H. Sherrard (1905) *The Child-Slaves of Britain*, London: Hurst & Blackett, Chapter VI: 'On Child-Slavery in Grimsby', 141–70.

43 M. Wilcox (2005) *Apprenticed Labour in the English Fishing Industry, 1850–1914*, University of Hull, Unpublished PhD, September 18–20.

44 Baldwin Fleming (9 June 1873) *The Treatment of Pauper Apprentices to the Grimsby Fishing Trade*. The report was drawn up for the government and submitted to the Right Hon J. Stansfeld, M. P., president of the Local Government Board, copy in the Local History section of the Grimsby Public Library, P.R.O. MH/32/99; Boswell (1974) 40.

45 Boswell (1974) 32.
46 P. Horn (September1995) 'Youth Migration – The Fisher Boy Apprentices of Grimsby 1870–1914', London: Genealogists Magazine, 100–2.
47 His Excellency Spencer Walpole (1883).
48 Pat Midgley, private letter (dated 8 April 2004).
49 Gerrish (1992) 192.
50 Gerrish (1992) 215, Table 17.
51 Daphne and Leon Gerlis (1986) *The Story of the Grimsby Jewish Community*, Hull: Humberside Leisure services.
52 Horn (1966) 175.
53 Sherrard (1905) 167–8.
54 L. Abrams (2002) *The Making of Modern Woman: Europe, 1789–1918*, London: Longman, 11.
55 Anon (16 October 1952) 'History of Grimsby', *The Fish Trades Gazette and Rabbit Trades Chronicle*, Vol. XXXIII, No. 1952, 5.
56 Gerrish (1993) 50, note 11.

Chapter 4

1 John L. Duthie (October 1984) 'Philanthropy and Evangelicalism among Aberdeen Seamen, 1814-1924', *The Scottish Historical Review*, Vol. LXIII, No. 2, 176: 155–73; Nadel (1986) 49–60.
2 D. J. Morrell (1987) *Some Aspects of Revivalist Charismatic Movements in England, 1800-1862*, Unpublished MPhil Thesis, Manchester: Manchester University Press.
3 Shaw (1867) 18; Vallenze (1985), Chapter 11.
4 Fearon (2008).
5 Clive Price and Sister Anne Marie Crowley (2002) *Serving God's People: Sisters of Charity of Our Lady of Evron English Province of the Congregation 1904-2000*, Altrincham: The Catholic Printing Company.
6 Fearon (2008) 14.
7 A. N. Cooper (*c.* 1920) *The Curiosities of East Yorkshire*, Scarborough: E. T. Dennis & Sons, 61–3.
8 Shaw (1867) 16–17.
9 Shaw (1867) 519.
10 Revd George Shaw (1894) *The Life of John Oxtoby*, London: William Andrews & Company, reprinted in 2002 by Hype Print, Pickering, North Yorkshire, 12.
11 Edward Royle and Ruth M. Larson (eds) (2006) *Archbishop Thompson's Visitation Returns for the Diocese of York 1865*, York: Borthwick Texts and Studies, 34 (Borthwick Institute for Archives, University of York).
12 S. W. Theakston (1841) *Theakston's Guide to Scarborough*, Scarborough: Theakston, Second edition, 41.
13 Details reported in the *Scarborough Mercury* (10 December 1881).
14 Robin Gill (2003) *The 'Empty' Church Revisited*, Aldershot: Ashgate 101.
15 Binns (2001). 20.
16 Royle and Larson (2006).
17 Binns (2001) 286.
18 *Scarborough Mercury* (Friday, 27 January 1956).

19 1851 census of religion (Borthwick Institute, York University, MF 116/525).

20 *Archbishop Herring, Visitation Returns, 1743* (1928).

21 Binns (2001) 202.

22 Ernest Cabon (March 1994) *Intemperance and Temperance, BA Dissertation,* Hull: University of Hull – copy in Grimsby Reference Library.

23 B. Lincoln (1913) *The Rise of Grimsby, Vol. 2,* Grimsby: Farnol Eades, Irvine & Company 136–7.

24 D. L. Gerlis (1986) *The Story of the Grimsby Jewish Community,* Hull: Humberside Leisure Services, 18, 25.

25 R. W. Ambler (ed.) (1979) *Lincolnshire Returns of the Census of Religious Worship, 1851,* The Lincoln Record Society: Vol. 72.

26 W. Bedford and M. Knight (1990) *Jacob's Ladder, the Rise of a Catholic Community 1848-1913,* Grimsby: St Mary by the Sea, 14, 16.

27 Ambler (1966) 272.

28 Owen Chadwick (1996) *The Victorian Church 1829-1859, Part I,* London: A&C Black, 272.

29 Bedford and Knight (1990), 37–8 and 43; Archive file 6; Isaac Drakes (ND), 'A Few Hasty Jottings from My Recollections of Happier Days', Grimsby: St Mary's by the Sea, *Archive File* Vol. 6, 43–4.

30 The Hon. Mrs Georgina Mary Fraser, only daughter of George F. Heneage of Hainton Hall, Co. Lincoln, married Lt-Col. (18 April 1928) the Hon. Alexander Fraser, second son of the twelfth Baron Lovat. An obituary appeared in *The Tablet* (31 March 1928). See *Burke's Peerage* (1959). Miss Scott-Murray was a Lovat grand-daughter, *Bournmouth Daily Echo.*

31 Bedford and Knight, (1990), 121–2.

32 Fraser (1990) 109, 121–2.

33 *The Messenger of the Sacred Heart* (May 1890).

34 Robert Miller (April 1995) *Ship of Peter: The Catholic Sea Apostolate and the Apostleship of the Sea,* Unpublished MPhil Thesis, Institute of Maritime Studies, the University of Plymouth.

35 Bedford and Knight (1990) 123.

36 *Faith of Our Fathers: St Mary's Magazine,* Library reference: 2/1893 (1893).

37 Peter Anson (1948) *The Church and the Sailor,* London: J. Gifford.

38 The Mission to Deep Sea Fishermen was initially an aspect of the work of the Thames Church Mission but became independent in 1886. The Society's vessels were subsequently modified into sailing hospitals under the direction of the Society's founder, Mr E. J. Mather, and the famous Victorian surgeon, Frederick Treves. The Society was given Royal status in 1897, when it was allowed to add the prefix 'Royal National' to its name (for a chart showing the development of British maritime missions, see Appendix 8b1).

39 Alain Cabantous (1993) 'Religion et Monde Maritime au Havre dans la seconde moitié du XVIIe siécle', *Annales de Normandie 33*; See also R. W. H. Miller (2005) 'The Société Œuvres de Mer: Welfare Work among the French Fishermen off Newfoundland and Iceland', *Newfoundland and Labrador Studies* Vol. 20, 2; Revd J. Dodds (1862) *Coast Missions: A Memoir of the Rev Thomas Rosie,* London: J. Nisbet.

40 The 'St Andrew's Waterside Mission' was founded in 1864 and was renamed the 'St Andrew's Waterside Church Mission' in 1892. I have used the abbreviation 'SAWM' up to the point where the name has changed and thereafter I have used 'SAWCM'.

41 'Sailing churches' were initially modified trawlers working at sea with the fishing
    fleets. They were later ships specifically built for this work, a number of which became
    sailing hospitals. 'Floating churches' on the other hand tended to be old hulks, which
    were adapted for work as churches based in the ports.

42 R. W. H. Miller (2002) *The Man at the Helm: The Faith and Practice of the Medieval
    Seafarers with Special Reference to England, 1000–1250 AD*, Unpublished PhD Thesis,
    Heythrop College, University of London.

43 *Yorkshire Gazette* (18 January 1834).

44 J. H. Ruston (1967) *They Kept Faith*, Scarborough.

45 F. K. Prochaska (1980) *Women in Philanthropy in Nineteenth Century England*,
    Clarendon Press, 98–9.

46 R. Kverndal (1986) *Seamen's Missions*, especially Part II: 'The Birth of the Bethel
    Movement'.

47 Alston Kennerley (1992) 'British Seamen's Missions in the Nineteenth Century', in
    Lewis R. Fisher and Harold Hamre, Paul Holm and Jaap R. Bruijn (eds) *The North
    Sea: Twelve Essays in the Social History of Maritime Labour* Stravanger: Stravanger
    Maritime Museum, The Association of North Sea Societies, Stravanger, Norway, 83.

48 See the chart in Appendix 8b for an overview of the development of these
    organizations.

49 Kennerley (1992) 83.

50 Clark (1982); Hatcher (1993).

51 Kverndal (1986) 287–91.

52 Cabantous (1993); see also Miller (2005).

53 *Scarborough Mercury* (Friday, 27 January 1956).

54 *SAWM Report* (1876).

55 *SAWM Report* (1890) 60–1.

56 The Revd G. Young (1840) *A Picture of Whitby and Its Environs (second edition)*,
    Whitby, 239–40.

57 J. H. Rushton (1967) *They Kept Faith*, Scarborough, 82–3.

58 Sandy Calder (2016) *The Origins of Primitive Methodism*, Suffolk: The Boydell Press,
    Woodbridge.

59 The Salvation Army began its own work at sea with the launch of the *Iole* in 1885. For
    discussion on this aspect of the Salvation Army's work, see Friend (2018) 105–6.

60 Letter to Father Gérard Tronche (dated 31 January 1997), reprinted in the
    International Association for the Study of Maritime Mission, *IASMM Newsletter*
    (Spring 1998) 8.

61 Friend (2018).

62 Roald Kverndal (2008) *Seamen's Missions: Their Origin and Early Growth*, Pasadena,
    CA: William Carey Library.

Chapter 5

1 Smith (1977) 14.

2 John Kent (1978) *Holding the Fort, Studies in Victorian Revivalism*, London: Epworth
   71; Bebbington (2012) 51–2.

3 Luker (1986) 603–19.

4 Currie, Gilbert and Horsley (1977).

5   Andrew Noble (1999) 'The Evangelical Tradition among the Fisherfolk of the North-East', in James Porter (ed.), *After Columba – After Calvin: Community and Identity in the Religious Traditions of North-East Scotland*, The Elphinstone Institute, University of Aberdeen, 143–9.

6   E. Halévy (1938) *A History of the English People in 1815*, London: Penguin; Hobsbawm (1957) 115–23; Thompson (1968); Gilbert (1976), Bebbington (2012).

7   Thompson (1968) 362–3.

8   E. Hobsbawm and G. Rudé (1969) *Captain Swing*, Lawrence & Wishart, 288–91.

9   Gilbert (1976).

10 John Rule (1998/9) 'Explaining Revivalism: The Case of Cornish Methodism', *Southern History*, Vols. 20-21, 168–88.

11 Baxter (1974) 58; J. S. Werner (1984) *The Primitive Methodists Connection – Its Background and Early History*, Wisconsin: University of Wisconsin Press; Luker (1986) 603–19; Rule (1998–9); David Hempton (1996) *Religion and Political Culture in Ireland*, Cambridge University Press; See also Bebbington (2012) esp. 24–6.

12 Werner (1984) 33–4.

13 Luker (1986) 604.

14 Rule (1998–9) 182.

15 Janice Holmes (2000) *Religious Revivals in Britain and Ireland, 1859-1905*, Dublin: Irish Academic Press, xv.

16 Hempton (1996) 30.

17 Luker (1986) 619.

18 Valenze (1985) 247.

19 Leon Festinger (1956) *When Prophecy Fails*, London: Harper.

20 R. H. Hood (September 1978) 'Anticipatory Set and Setting: Stress Incongruities as Elicitors of Mystical Experience in Solitary Nature Situations', *Journal for the Scientific Study of Religion*, Vol. 17, No. 3, 279–87.

21 The 'Great Yorkshire Revival' lasted four years, 1792–6; the Filey Revival of 1823 lasted two years; other revivals lasted from a few days to a few weeks.

22 S. J. D. Green (1996) *Religion in an Age of Decline: Organisation and Experience in Industrial Yorkshire, 1870-1920*, Cambridge: Cambridge University Press, 266.

23 Thompson (1968) 919–20.

24 J. Petty (1880) *The History of the Primitive Methodist Connexion from Its Origin to the Conference of 1880*, updated by the Revd James Macpherson, London: John Dickinson.

25 Green (1996) 267–9.

26 Smith (1994) 183.

27 Bebbington (2012) 117–18.

28 Bridlington Methodist Circuit 1796–1838, HCRO, numbers and names of members in the society in Bridlington Circuit, Hull County Records, HVCRO, *Beverley Archives*, MRQ/1/36.

29 Petty (1880) says the decrease was to forty.

30 *Primitive Methodist Magazine* (1823) 255;

31 George Lester (1890) *Grimsby Methodism, 1743-1889, and the Wesleys in Lincolnshire*, London: Wesleyan Methodist Book Room.

32 Woodcock (1889).

33 Petty (1880) 188.

34 Gilbert (1976); Hatcher (1993) 390–405.

35 Clive Field (June 1977) 'The Social Structure of English Methodism: Eighteenth-Twentieth Centuries', *British Journal of Sociology*, Vol. 28, 199–225.

36 Hobsbawm (1959) 129–30.
37 O. Chadwick (1970/80) *The Victorian Church*, Part II, London, Adam & Charles Black, 222.
38 Ambler (2000).
39 See Friend (2018) for more details about these organizations.

Chapter 6

1 Hempton (1996) 49; Valenze (1985) 245.
2 Hempton (1996) 71; Williams (1999) 10.
3 Williams (1999) 11; See also Williams' article 'Urban Popular Religion and Rites of Passage', in Hugh McLeod (1995) *European Religion in the Age of Great Cities 1830-1930*, London and New York: Routledge, 218.
4 See especially R. A. Orsi (1985) *The Madonna of 115th Street: Faith and Community in Italian Harlem, 1880-1950*, Yale University Press; and David D. Hall (ed.) (1997) *Lived Religion in America: Toward a History of Practice*, Princeton: Princeton University Press; Meredith McGuire (2008) *Lived Religion: Faith and Practice in Everyday Life*, Oxford: Oxford University Press.
5 Orsi (1985) xiii–xiv.
6 Thea Vigne (1977) 'Parents and Children', *Oral History Journal*, Vol. 5, 6–13; Clark (1982); Thompson, Wailey and Lummis (1983); Elizabeth Roberts (1984) *A Woman's Place: An Oral History of Working-Class Women, 1890-1940*, Oxford: Blackwell; Lummis (1985).
7 Stephen Friend (November 2004–December 2008) *Women's Voices Project*, York: York St John University.
8 Williams (1995) 216–36.
9 Williams (1995) 218.
10 Harrison (1967) 98–125.
11 T. Luckmann (1967) *The Invisible Religion: The Problem of Religion in Modern Society*, London: Macmillan.
12 Kenneth Thompson (1993) 'Durkheim, Ideology and the Sacred', *Social Compass*, Vol. 40, No. 3, 457.
13 Durkheim (2001) 47.
14 Thompson (1993) 451–61.
15 Paul Tillich (1980) *The Courage to Be*, London and New York: Yale University Press, 47.
16 Luckmann (1967) 84–99.
17 R. Machalek and R. Martin (1976) 'Invisible Religions: Some Preliminary Evidence', *Journal for the Scientific Study of Religion*, Vol. 15, No. 4, 311.
18 Peter Berger (1969) *A Rumour of Angels: Modern Society and the Rediscovery of the Supernatural*, Garden City, New York: Doubleday, 132–3.
19 A. W. Smith (July 1969) 'Popular Religion', *Past and Present*, Vol. 40, 181–6.
20 Keith Thomas (1971) *Religion and the Decline of Magic*, London: Weidenfeld & Nicholson, Foreword.
21 Hempton (1996) 53; J. Obelkevich (1976) *Religion and Rural Society in South Lindsey, 1825-1875*, Oxford University Press, 305–6.
22 Obelkevich (1976) 261.

23 Clark (1982) 9; also R. Towler (1974) *Homo Religiosus: Sociological Problems in the Study of Religion*, London: Constable.
24 Clark (1982) 166.
25 Valenze (1985) 245.
26 Ahern and Davie (1987) 32.
27 Wickham (1957); Inglis (1963); Cox (1982); A. Bartlett (1987) *The Churches in Bermondsey, 1880-1929*, PhD thesis, Birmingham University; Jeremy N. Morris (1992) *Religion and Urban Change: Croyden 1840-1914*, Bury St Edmonds: Royal Historical Society; Smith (1994); Green (1996).
28 Obelkevich (1976) 5.
29 P. H. Vrijhof and J. Waardenburg (eds) (1979) *Official and Popular Religion: An Analysis of a Theme for Religious Studies*, The Hague: Mouton Publishers. See Nancy Tipper (1982).
30 Nancy Tapper, Review of Vrijhof and Waardenburg (eds) (June 1982).
31 Hempton (1996) 65.
32 Williams (1999) 11.
33 See especially Sykes (1999).
34 Williams (1999) 10.
35 See, for example, Luker (1986) 603 and 619.
36 McLeod (1987) 31-50.
37 Hugh McLeod (1978) 'Religion in the City', *Urban History Yearbook*, 7-22; Sykes (1999) 22; Williams (1995) 233.
38 Williams (1999) 167.
39 Williams in McLeod (1995) 233.
40 Williams (1999) 3.
41 Williams in McLeod (1995) 217.
42 McLeod (1995) 217.
43 Cox (1982) 93.
44 Hatcher (1993) 535.
45 Hatcher (1993) 537-8.
46 Obelkevich (1976) 280.
47 Snell and Ell (2000) 3-4.
48 Don Yoder (January 1974) 'Toward a Definition of Folk Religion', in *Western Folklore: Symposium of Folk Religion*, Vol. XXXIII, 1, Published for the California Folklore Society by the University of California Press 1-15.
49 Edward Bailey (1988) *Implicit Religion: An Introduction*, London: Middlesex University 32-3.
50 Thomas Luckmann (1967) *The Invisible Religion: The Problem of Religion in Modern Society*, London: Macmillan; Yoder (1974) provides a helpful bibliography on folk religion; for England, see Towler (1974); Obelkevich (1976); and Clark (1982); in Holland Virjhof and Waardenburg (1979).
51 Towler (1974) 150.
52 N. Greinacher and N. Mette (eds) (1986) 'Popular Religion', *Concilium*, ix.
53 Greinacher and Mette (1986) 3.
54 Valenze (1985) 22.
55 Cox (1982); Bartlett (1987).
56 Williams (1993) 5, 11 and 169. See also Davie in Chapter six.
57 Robert Bellah (Winter 1967) first used the term 'civil religion' in his article published in *Daedalus 96*, No. 1, 1-21. However, in the more recently published *The Robert*

Bellah Reader, ed. by R. N. Bellah and S. M. Tipton (2006) Durham & London: Duke University Press, Chapter nine, Bellah has rejected his use of the term 'civil religion'; Robert W. Coles (1975) 'Football as a "Surrogate" Religion?' in Hill (ed.) *A Sociological Yearbook of Religion in Britain*, Vol. 8, 61–77.

58 Orsi (1985/2002).
59 Day (2011).
60 George Eliot (1861) *Silas Marner*, London: Blackwood, 68.
61 Thomas Hardy (1872) *Under the Greenwood Tree*, London: Tinsley Bros; Flora Thompson (1973) *Lark Rise to Candleford*, London: Penguin; Arnold Bennett, *Clayhanger*, London: Penguin Books, 1910.
62 Valenze (1985) 267.
63 Ambler (1984) 243ff.
64 *Women's Voices Project* (08.06.05) interviewee 09MH05YH, Hull.
65 *Women's Voices Project* (25.11.04) 01aLR04YS, Scarborough.
66 *Women's Voices Project* (28.11.05) 27MC0527YS, Scarborough.
67 *Women's Voices Project* (09.05.07) MO2HS07YW, Whitby.
68 *Women's Voices Project* (09.05.05) 03AW05YF, Filey.
69 Cole (1828) 93–8.
70 Shaw (1867) 112.
71 Shaw (1867).
72 Cole (1828) 96.
73 *Women's Voices Project* (09.05.07) interviewee MO2HS07YW, Whitby.
74 Gerrish (1883) 45.
75 Robinson (1996) 71 and 82–4.
76 Valenze (1985) 251–2.
77 Lionel T. Crawshaw (1864–1949) 'Returning Home' – painting on display in the Pannett Art Gallery, Whitby. While the picture has not been dated it would appear to have been painted during the 1890s.
78 Pettitt (1868) 59.
79 *Women's Voices Project* (04.08.05), Interviewee MO1RH05YH, Hull
80 Gillett (1970) 233–4.
81 Chalmers (1988); Nadel-Klein (2003); Munro (1997).
82 Williams (1993) 8–9.
83 Arnold van Gennep (1960) *The Rites of Passage*, London: Routledge and Kegan Paul.
84 Victor W. Turner (1969) *The Ritual Process*, Harmondsworth: Penguin; and Turner (1987); see also Driver (2006).
85 Robert Bocock (1974) *Ritual in Industrial Society: A Sociological Analysis of Ritualism in Modern England*, London: George, Allen & Unwin; Diana Leonard (1980) *Sex and Generation*, London: Tavistock.
86 Clark (1982), Chapter 7.
87 Bocock (1974) 37.
88 Bocock (1974) 38.
89 W. R. Lambert, 'Some Working-Class Attitudes towards Organised Religion in Nineteenth Century Wales', Chapter 5 in G. Parsons (ed.) (1988) *Religion in Victorian Britain*, Vol. IV, Manchester: Manchester University Press, 100.
90 *Woman's Voices Project* (5 October 2005) 22MP05YS, Scarborough.
91 Mrs Gutch (1901) Country Folk-Lore, 11, *The Folk-Lore Society*, London: David Nutt, 13–14, 51.

92 Alec Gill (1993) *Superstitions: Folk Magic in Hull's Fishing Community*, Beverley: Hutton Press.

93 Obelkevich (1976) 273; Clark (1982) 115; Williams (1993) 89.

94 Clark (1982) 119.

95 *Women's Voices Project* (25.11.04) 02aRJ04YS and (23.06.05) 11DN05YS at Scarborough and (08.06.05) 09MH05YH at Hull.

96 Obelkevich (1976) 273.

97 Clark (1982) 119.

98 The giving of nicknames was important in most nineteenth-century communities, as is evidenced in Flora Thompson's work (1973) 545. It still remains important for young people. When working with some junior school children in Filey during July 2007, the author asked the children if they had nicknames – and was inundated with these! As was the case in the nineteenth century the children's nicknames represented something about their characters.

99 A. P. Cohen (1993) 'Rites of Identity, Rites of the Self' (Inaugural lecture as professor of anthropology), *Edinburgh Review*, Vol. 89, 56–74.

100 *Woman' Voices Project* (09.05.05) 03AW05YF, Filey.

101 James Slater (1997) *Fishing Boat Names of the UK: Bible-wise and Otherwise*, Aberdeen: Scottish Cultural Press.

102 Frank (2002).

103 P. Anson (1950) *Scots Fisherfolk*, The Saltaire Society, Banffshire Journal 149.

104 Shaw (1867) 8.

105 *Women's Voices Project* (22.07.05) Interviewee 16MT05YF, Filey.

106 Anson (1965) 75.

107 *Primitive Methodist Magazine* (1909) 238–9.

108 Anson (1965) 161.

109 Revd J. C. Atkinson (1992) *Forty Years in a Moorland Parish* (1891), reprinted by Smith Settle, Otley, 215.

110 *Women's Voices Project* (14.03.07) Interviewee 33WC07YS in Staithes.

111 *The Friendly Societies of Robin Hood's Bay* (Whitby 2001) compiled by Dennis Crosby. A copy is kept in the Robin Hood's Bay Archives at the Methodist Church.

112 *Women's Voices Project* (14.03.07) Interviewee 33WC07YSt at Staithes.

113 Ibid, Interviewee (13.03.07) 32WC07YSt at Staithes.

114 Atkinson (1891) 226.

115 'Memoir of Jenkinson Haxby' (1909) *Primitive Methodist Magazine* (1909), 238–9 (cited in Valenze (1985) 266).

116 Obelkevich (1976) 297.

117 Gereth M. Spriggs (1982–3) 'Maidens Garlands', *Folk-Life: A Journal of Ethnological Studies*, 21.

118 Robert Fisher (1894) *Flamborough: Village and Headland*, Hull: Wm. Andrews, 147.

119 Cole (1828) 149.

120 Fearon (2008) 125–6.

121 *Women's Voices Project* (09.05.05) Interviewee 18aW05YS at Scarborough.

122 Cole (1828) 136; Valenze (1985) 255.

123 Shaw (1867) 8.

124 Peter F. Anson (1931) *Fishermen and Fishing Ways*, London: G. Harrap & Company, 77.

125 Shaw (1867).

126 John Nicholson (1890) *Folk-Lore of East Yorkshire*, The Folk-Lore Society; Fisher (1894).

127 Ed Knipe (1984) *Gamrie: An Exploration in Cultural Ecology*, University Press of America, 168.

128 Anson (1965) 7.

129 Alec Gill (2003) *Hull's Fishing Heritage: Aspects of Life in the Hessle Road Fishing Community*, Barnsley: Wharncliffe Books, 151.

130 *Women's Voices Project* (09.12.05) Interviewee 02bRJ05YS at Scarborough.

131 Verbal account to the author's research assistant by a Whitby resident (April 2007).

132 Binkley (2002) 12–15.

133 Hagmark (September 2003).

134 Orsi (1985/2002) 166.

135 Rappaport (1999) 24.

136 Thomas (1971) 27, 51 and 79.

137 O. Davies (April 1997) 'Methodism, the Clergy, and the Popular Belief in Witchcraft and Magic', *History*, Vol. 82, 226, 252–65, 258.

138 Wayne Johnson (1993) 'Between Nature and Grace: The Folk Religion of Dissident Methodism in the North Midlands, 1780-1820', *Staffordshire Studies*, Vol. 5, 73–6.

139 James G. Frazier (1922) *The Golden Bough*, London: Macmillan.

140 Durkheim (1912/2001) 43.

141 Bronislaw Malinowski (1974) *Magic, Science and Religion*, London: Souvenir Press, 88.

142 Davies (1977) 252–65.

143 Mrs Gutch (1901).

144 Anson (1965) 119.

145 Rambelli (2020).

146 Rambelli (2020) 120.

147 *Women's Voices Project* (25.11.04) Interviewee 01aLR04YS, Scarborough.

148 Amber Films, 1989.

149 Anson (1965) 33.

150 Patrick B. Mullen (2005) 'Folklore' in the *Encyclopedia of Religion, second edition*, Vol. 5, 314.

151 Alan Dundes (1989) *Folklore Matters*, Knoxville: University of Tennessee Press, 11.

152 Nadel-Klein (2003) e.g. 175 and 210.

153 Mrs Gutch (1901) 13–14.

154 Margaret Mead (1958) *Israel and Problems of Identity*, New York: Herzl Institute Pamphlets, 3, Theodore Herzl Foundation, cited in Dundes (1989) 6.

155 See, for example, J. Corin (1988) *Fishermen's Conflict: The Story of Newlyn*, London: Tops'l Books, 70.

156 See, for example, N. Abercrombie, J. Baker, S. Brett and J. Foster (1970) 'Superstition and Religion: The God of the Gaps', *Sociological Yearbook of Religion in Britain Ch. 7, 1970*. Fiona-Jane Brown has written her PhD dissertation on popular belief in North-East Scottish fishing communities.

157 *Women's Voices Project*, Interviewee 01RJ04YS (09.12.05), in Scarborough.

158 Gill (1993) 100.

159 Williams in McLeod (1995) 218.

160 P. Jarvis (1980) 'Towards a Sociological Understanding of Superstition', *Social Compass*, Vol. XXVII, 285–95.

161 Gustav Jahoda (1969) *The Psychology of Superstition*, London: Allen Lane, The Penguin Press, 10.

162 See especially the DVD – *Women's Voices: Reflections on Women in Yorkshire Fishing Communities* (York St John University, 2004–8) – in which several of the women talk

about their knowledge of superstitions. One participant is visibly uncomfortable as she mentions some taboo animals in order to get her point across.

163 Gutch (1901) 52.
164 P. Sébillot (1982) *Traditions et Superstitions de la Haute-Bretagne, 11*: 218, quoted in *Notes and Queries, The Folk-Lore Journal* 3: 4 (1885), 378; and in Anson (1965) 49.
165 Notes and Queries (1885) *The Folk-Lore Journal, 3, 4*:378.
166 Fisher (1894) 146; Mary Williams (1987) *Witches in Old North Yorkshire*, Beverley: Hutton Press.
167 Anson (1965) 26.
168 Information provided by Deb Gillanders of Whitby (May 2008).
169 Alf Hildred, interviewed 14 March 2008.
170 *Women's Voices Project*, Interviewee (14.03.07) 33WC07YSt at Staithes.
171 Hudson (1974) 256; Anson (1965) 27.
172 Anson (1965).
173 Huttton (1975) 292.
174 Williams (1993) 85.
175 L. Dube and R. Palriwala (1990) *Structures and Strategies – Women, Work and Family*, London: Sage.
176 Thompson (1985) 3–32.
177 *Women's Voices Project* (20.04.06) Interviewee 32NW06YW in Whitby.
178 Richard Hoggart (1957) *The Uses of Literacy*, London: Chatto & Windus, 36. Other terms used include 'peg rugs' and 'clippies'.
179 Colin Campbell (May 1996) 'Half-Belief and the Paradox of Ritual Instrumental Activism: A Theory of Modern Superstition', *The British Journal of Sociology*, Vol. 47, No. 1, 151–66.
180 John Dyson (1977) *Business in Great Waters*, Sydney, Australia: Angus & Robertson, 134.
181 Shaw (1867) 7–8.
182 Lummis (1985) 52; Malinowski (1974) 31.
183 Campbell (1996) 152.
184 Malinowski (1974) 31.
185 Patrick B. Mullen (1969) 'The Function of Magic Folk Belief among the Texas Coastal Fishermen', *Journal of American Folklore*, Vol. 82, 214–25; J. J. Poggie, Jr., B. Pollnac and Carl Gersuny (1976) 'Risk as a Basis for Taboos among Fishermen in Southern New England', *Journal for the Scientific Study of Religion*, Vol. 15, No. 3, 257–60 and 258 footnote.
186 Lummis (1985), Chapter 12.
187 Lummis (1985) 187.
188 Lummis (1985) 156.
189 Lummis (1985) 160.
190 Poggie, Pollnac and Gersuny (1976) 260.
191 Anson (1965) 10–11.
192 Williams (1995) 218.

Chapter 7

1 George Herbert Mead (1934) *Mind, Self and Society*, Chicago: Chicago University Press.

2   Erik Erikson (1956) 'The Problem of Ego Identity', *Journal of the American Psychoanalytic Association*, Vol. 4, 6–121.

3   Anselm Strauss (1959) *Mirrors and Masks: The Search for Identity*, Glencoe, IL: Free Press; Erving Goffman (1959) *The Presentation of Self in Everyday Life*, London: Doubleday Anchor; Cohen (1987).

4   A. P. Cohen (2000) *Signifying Identities, Anthropological Perspectives on Boundaries and Contested Values*, London: Routledge, 5.

5   Andrew J. Weigert, J. Smith Teitge and Denis W. Teitge (1986) *Society and Identity*, Cambridge: Cambridge University Press, 11.

6   Jenkins (2004) 4.

7   Zygmunt Bauman (2004) *Identity*, Cambridge: Polity, 2.

8   E. Wenger (1998) *Communities of Practice: Learning, Meaning and Identity*, Cambridge: Cambridge University Press, 215.

9   Vecchi, in Bauman (2004) 7.

10 Anthony, P. Cohen (ed.) (1982) *Belonging, Identity and Social Organisation in British Rural Cultures*, Manchester: Manchester University Press, 3.

11 Gerard Delanty (2003) *Community*, London: Routledge, 4.

12 Émile Durkheim (1893/1964) *The Division of Labour in Society*, London: Macmillan.

13 Émile Durkheim (1972) *Selected Writings*, ed. by A. Giddens, Cambridge University Press, 148; Tönnies (1957).

14 Durkheim (1893) 148.

15 Durkheim (1964) Chapter VII. Durkheim's concepts here are roughly similar to Tönnies's *Gemeinschaft* (community) and *Gesellschaft* (society).

16 A. P. Cohen (1994) *Self Consciousness, An Alternative Anthropology of Identity*, London: Routledge, 1.

17 *Primitive Methodist Magazine* (1823) 255.

18 Fearon (2008) 75.

19 W. R. Ward (1993) 'The Religion of the People and the Problem of Control, 1790-1830', in *Faith and Faction*, London: Epworth Press, 264–84.

20 *Primitive Methodist Magazine* (1824) 258; Petty (1880) 36, where he gives the number as fifty; John Oxtoby claimed to have seen eighty converts in a vision prior to entering Filey.

21 Gerrish (August 1997) 3, 1: 15–21; also *Scarborough Evening News* (31 August 1896).

22 Alwood (1932) 200.

23 Gerrish (1993) 39–50.

24 Gillett (1970) 283.

25 Gerrish (1992) 283.

26 With the growth of the towns of Grimsby and Cleethorpes, the boundary between the two towns became Park Street, with the west side being in Grimsby and the east side in Cleethorpes.

27 Gillett (1970) 267.

28 Gillett (1970) 287–9.

29 Alward (1932); Gillett (1970); Lincoln (1913) I: 124.

30 Corin (1988): Chapter seven: 'The Newlyn Riots'.

31 Cohen (1982) 3.

32 Cohen (1987) 20.

33 A. S. Buckser (1996) *Communities of Faith: Sectarianism, Identity and Social Change on a Danish Island*, Oxford: Berghahn Books.

34 A. P. Cohen (1982) 'A Sense of Time, a Sense of Place: The Meaning of Close Social Association in Whalsay, Shetland', 6.

35 Delanty (2003) 44.

36 *Women's Voices Project*, Interviewee 33WC07St at Staithes (14.03.07).

37 Lincoln (1913) I: 124.

38 Gillett (1970) 266.

39 Cohen (1985) 55.

40 F. W. Dillistone (1986) *The Power of Symbols*, London: SCM Press.

41 Delanty (2003) 48.

42 Cohen (1987) 132.

43 Nadel-Klein (2003) 216.

44 L. E. Doherty (2001) *Gender and Interpretation*, London: Duckworth 12.

45 For an analysis of 'copering' activities, see S. Friend (December 2003) 'The North Sea Liquor Trade, c. 1850–1893', Memorial University, Newfoundland, *International Journal of Maritime History*, Vol. XV, No. 2, 43–71. See also Chapter 6 in Friend (2018).

46 Cited in Luckmann (1967) 12.

47 Inger Furseth and Pål Repstad (2006) *An Introduction to the Sociology of Religion: Classical and Contemporary Perspectives*, London: Ashgate, 32–7.

48 Peter Berger and Thomas Luckmann (1995) *Modernity, Pluralism and the Crisis of Meaning*, Gütersloh: Bertelsmann Foundation, cited in Furseth and Repstad (2006) 58.

49 Peter Berger (1967) *The Sacred Canopy: Elements of a Sociological Theory of Religion*, Garden City, New York: Doubleday.

50 Luckman (1967) 18.

51 Cited in Weigert, Teitge and Teitge (1986).

52 Weigert, Teitge and Teitge (1986) 19.

53 Hans Mol (1976) *Identity and the Sacred: A Sketch for a New Social-Scientific Theory of Religion*, Oxford: Blackwell, 1.

54 Weigert, Teitge and Teitge (1986) 29; Philip Gleason (1983) 'Identifying Identity: A Semantic History', *Journal of American History*, Vol. 69, 910–31.

55 Williams (1993) 13.

56 Cohen (1987) 79.

57 Hobsbawm (1959) 127.

58 Duthie (1983); also Jackie Ritchie (1983) *Floods Upon the Dry Ground: God Working among Fisherfolk*, J. Ritchie, 'Norwin', Huna, Caithness.

59 Buckser (1996).

60 Williams (1999) 11; Orsi (1985) xxi.

61 Beliefs, rituals and folk customs/traditions are expanded on in Section 6.3.3.

Chapter 8

1 Harison (1967) 23, 98 and 164; Hempton (1996) 52, 65, 163 and 170.

2 Gill (2003) 101; Binns (2001) 209.

3 Martin Ingram (1995) 'From Reformation to Toleration: Popular Religious Cultures in England, 1540–1690', in T. Harris (ed.), *Popular Culture in England c. 1500–1850*, London: Macmillan, 95.

4 Bob Bushaway, 'Tacit Unsuspected, But Still Implicit Belief in Nineteenth-Century Rural England', in Harris (1995) 189.
5 Bushaway (1995) 189.
6 See also Davie (1994) 74.
7 Hatcher (1993) 549.
8 Williams (1993) 165.
9 Smith (1994); Sykes (April 1999).
10 Obelkevich (1976); Cox (1982).
11 Rappaport (1999).
12 Abby Day (ed.) (2008) *Religion and the Individual: Belief, Practice, Identity*, Aldershot: Ashgate, 1.
13 D. M. Bell, 'Development of the Religious Self: A Theoretical Foundation for Measuring Religious Identity', in Day (2008) 127–42.

Bibliography

Manuscript sources

National collections

John Rylands Library, Manchester
The National Archives
The National Maritime Museum, Greenwich
Hull History Centre

Local archives

Baptisms

East Riding Archives, The Treasure House, Champney Road, Beverley.
St Oswald's Church, Filey:	PE 142/5-7 (1813–1936)
St Mary's Church, Scarborough:	PE 165/3-11 (1813–1936)
St Thomas' Church, Scarborough:	PE 166/1-2 (1844–1923)
Wesleyan Methodists, Filey, Bridlington Circuit:	MRQ/1/1-3 (1838–1947)
Primitive Methodists, Filey, Bridlington Circuit:	MRQ/1/1/2/3 (1838–1947)

Lincolnshire Archives, St Rumbold Street, Lincoln
St Andrew's Church, Grimsby:	09-16-001-01A/007-29 (1870–1914)
St John's Church, New Clee:	09-03-001-01A/006-04A (1873–1914)
Primitive Methodist Circuits:	METH B/Grimsby/33/9-10
Records of Wesleyan Circuits:	METH B/Gy/4/1-32

North Yorkshire County Record Office, Northallerton
Primitive Methodists, Scarborough: R/M/Sc/3/1-7, 9-10 (1833–1916)

Church membership

East Riding Archives, The Treasure House, Champney Road, Beverley
Filey, Bridlington Circuit, Wesleyan Methodists: MRQ 1/36 (1796–1838)

Lincolnshire Archives, St Rumbold St, Lincoln
Primitive Methodist membership in Grimsby: METHG B/Grimsby/37/1

North Yorkshire County Record Office, Northallerton
Scarborough United Methodist Free Church Records: R/M/Sc/2/25
Scarborough Primitive Methodist Local Leaders meeting book and quarter day accounts: R/M/Sc/1/2/1-4
Filey Primitive Methodist Quarterly Schedules (March): R/M/Fil/1/1/6-8

North-East Lincolnshire Archives, Town Hall Square, Grimsby
United Methodist Free Church Circuit Records: METH Grimsby 61-62
Wesleyan Methodists: METH B Grimsby/1-6/14-16

Miscellaneous

Beverley Archives: *Interesting Notes on the Church of St Thomas (The Fishermen's Church)*, ND., Accession No. PE 66.54

Field, C R: *Notes on the Origin of the Boxing Day football match between the Scarborough Fishermen and Firemen* (Scarborough Public Library, Reference section, 1968. Not indexed)

Filey Archives: *Diary of Thomas Hawkshead: Notes on Folklore and Belief* (ND. No index)

Fleming, Baldwin, *The Treatment of Pauper Apprentices to the Grimsby Fishing Trade*, 19 June 1873 (the Report was drawn up for the Government and submitted to the Right Hon J. Stansfeld, M. P., President of the Local Government Board), copy in the Local History section of the Grimsby Public Library, P.R.O. MH/32/99

Folk-Lore Journal, Vol. 3, No. 4 (Notes and Queries), 1885

His Excellency Spencer Walpole, *Fisheries Exhibition Literature, Vol I* (1883).

Hull History Centre: Archives of the Mission to Seamen and Saint Andrew's Waterside Church Mission

Hull Public Library, Reference section: Archives of the 'Sailors' Children's Society'. North-East Lincs. Archives: *Captain Smedley*, 282/31 (1) St Mary's Church, Grimsby, Archive Files

International Association for the Study of Maritime Mission (IASMM Newsletter, Spring 1998). *Letter by Father Gerard Tronche* (31 January 1977).

Parliamentary papers

BPP, C5412: *Sea Fisheries (England and Wales), Second Annual Report of the Inspector for 1887* (1888)

Religious Worship (England and Wales): *Parliamentary Papers* (1852–1853), Vol. 89, p, clvii

Trade directories

Baines, E.: *Baines Yorkshire: History and Gazetter of the County of York*, Hurst & Robinson (London, 1823, Vol. 2)

The Grimsby and Cleethorpes Directory and Illustrated Visitors Handbook (Grimsby, Albert Gait), 1871

White's Directory (Sheffield, Wm White), 1872, 1882, 1892

Newspapers

Bournmouth Daily Echo, 18 April 1928
The Filey Advertiser, March 1958
Grimsby Evening Telegraph, 21 August 1942

Grimsby Gazette, 9 March 1855
Grimsby News, 9 December 1881
Grimsby News, 24 August 1883
Grimsby News, 18 July 1890
Grimsby Observer, 17 August 1878
Grimsby Times, 2 September 1898
Merthyr Express, 5 September 1885
Scarborough Mercury, 11 August 1866
Scarborough Mercury, 4 December 1881
Scarborough Mercury, 10 December 1881
Scarborough Mercury, 24 December 1881
Scarborough Mercury, 27 January 1956
Scarborough Eve News, 31 August 1896
Scarborough Eve News, 27 December 1993
Scarborough Leader, 23 December 1987
The Yorkshire Gazette, 18 January 1834
Yorkshire Illustrated, January 1949
The Yorkshire Post, 26 October 1961
Whitby Gazette, 12 December 1980
Whitby Gazette, 23 January 1981

Denominational publications

Faith of Our Fathers: St Mary's Magazine, Grimsby, St Mary's Church, reference: 2/1893.
Methodist Recorder, 1898. Also: *Extracts from a Methodist Journal kept during the period 1874–1975* in the Methodist Recorder XXXIX (186), No. 2044, pp. 92–93.
The Nonconformist, Supplement, for January 8 (1873, pp. 52 & 54), 15 January 1873, p. 63. Dr Williams Library, London.
Primitive Methodist Magazine, 1823, 1824 and 1909.
Report of the Port of Hull Society (Hull), 1822; *The Helmsman* (Port of Hull Society), Vol. 15, No. 65, 1933.
Sailors' Magazine and Naval Miscellany, London, W. Simpkin & Marshall, 1881, 1822 and 1823.
St Andrew's Waterside Church Mission (SAWCM), Reports for 1876, 1890. Hull History Centre.
The Messenger of the Sacred Heart, May 1890.
The New Sailors' Magazine, 1828.
The Tablet, 31 March 1928.
The War Cry, Salvation Army Newspaper, 30 October 1886.
Toilers of the Deep, the monthly magazine of the RNMDSF, 1881–.

Census publications

Filey 1841–1939
Grimsby 1841–1939
Scarborough 1841–1939
Ambler, R. W. (ed.), *Lincolnshire Returns of the Census of Religious Worship, 1851*, Lincoln, The Lincoln Record Society, Vol. 72, 1979.

Annersley, Crissida & Hoskin, Phillipa (eds), *Archbishop Drummond, Visitation Returns, May-June 1764*, Vol. III, Yorkshire S-Y, York, Borthwick Texts and Calenders 26, University of York, Borthwick Institute of Historical Research, 2001.

Borthwick Institute, York University, York: Census data for Scarborough.

Mann, H. *Census of Great Britain, 1851: Religious Worship, England and Wales. Report and Tables.* Presented to both Houses of Parliament by Command of Her Majesty, London: HMSO, 1853. Borthwick Institute, University of York, MF 116/525.

Mann, H. 'On the Religious Census of Great Britain', in J R Moore, *Religion in Victorian Britain, Vol. III: Sources*, Manchester, Manchester University Press, 313–321, 1988.

Mearns, A. *The Statistics of Attendance at Public Worship, as Published in England and Wales and Scotland, by the Local Press Between October 1881 and February 1882*, London: Hodder & Stoughton, 1882.

Ollard, S. L. & Walker, P. C. (eds), *Archbishop Herring's Visitation Returns, 1743, Church of England*, Diocese of York, Leeds, Archaeological Society, 1928.

Royle, E. & Larson, R. M. (eds), *Archbishop Thompson's Visitation Returns for the Diocese of York, 1865*, York, Borthwick Texts and Studies 34, Borthwick Institute for Archives, University of York, 2006.

Wolffe, J. (ed.), *Yorkshire Returns of the 1851 Census of Religious Worship*, Vol. 1, York: Borthwick Texts', 2005.

Interviews and correspondence

Women's Voices Project (York, York St John University. Project Director: Dr Stephen Friend) The Project (2005–8) was established at York St John University in April 2005 and used a personal narrative methodology, thereby allowing the women to tell their own stories about life in Yorkshire fishing communities. This recorded material is an important resource for community members, scholars and academics. Several of the women interviewed appear in a film produced as a DVD: *Women's Voices: Reflections of Women in Yorkshire Fishing Communities*, published by the Women's Voices Project, York St John University, 2006. Those interviews used as a comparative resource during this study include:

Scarborough

      01aLR04YS (28.14.06)

      02bRJ04YS (28.04.06)

      18AW05YS (18.08.05)

      22MP05YS (05.10.05)

      27MC05YS (29.11.05)

      11DN05YS (23.06.06)

Hull

      09MH05YH (08.06.05)

      MO1RH05YF (04.08.05)

Filey

      03AW05YF (09.05.05)

      16MT05YF (22.07.05)

Whitby

      32NW06YW (20.04.06)

      M02HS07YW (09.05.07)

Staithes
    33WC07St (14.03.07)

Crosby, D. Robin Hood's Bay (personal interview, June, 2006)
Fearon, M. Local Historian, Filey (personal interview, July 2004)
Gillanders, D. Whitby (private correspondence, May 2008)
Haxby, J. Filey, (private correspondence, July 2004)
Midgley, P. Kings' Lynn (private letter, 8 April 2004)
Oakes, S. Scarborough (private correspondence)
Taylor, M. Filey (private correspondence)
Willey, B. H. Grimsby (personal interview, 19 May 2002)
Ripon, Doris L. Sheffield (Mr Smedley's daughter) (interview and private correspondence, 25 June, 289–297, 1985)

Primary and printed sources

Atkinson, Revd J. C. *Forty Years in a Moorland Parish (1891)*, Reprinted by Smith Settle, Otley, 1992.
Baker, J. B. *The History of Scarborough from the Earliest Date*, London, Longman, 1882.
Bates, A. *A Gossip about Old Grimsby*, Grimsby, Albert Gait, 1893.
Blakeborough, R. *Yorkshire Wit, Character, Folklore & Customs*, 2nd edn., Saltburn, W. Rapp & Sons, 1898/1911.
Bramwell, W. *A Short Account of the Life and Death of Ann Cutler*, Sheffield, 1796, cited in Baxter, *The Great Yorkshire Revival. Memoir of the Life and Ministry of the Rev. William Bramwell*, by members of his family, London, 1848.
Burk's Peerage 1959, London, Colbum, H. & Bentley, R.
Cole, J. *The History and Antiquities of Filey in the County of Yorkshire*, Scarborough, 1828.
Dodds, Rev J. *Coast Missions: A Memoir of the Rev Thomas Rosie*, London, J Nisbet, 1862.
Finney, C .G. *Lectures on Revivals of Religion*, 5th edn., London, 1838.
Fisher, R. *Flamborough: Village and Headland*, Hull, Wm Andrews, 1894.
Greenlaw, Linda, *The Hungry Ocean*, Hyperion, December 1998.
Gutch, Mrs, *Country Folk-Lore*, Vols. 2 and 11, The Folk-Lore Society, David Nutt, London, 1901.
Gutch & Peacock, *Mabel County Folk-Lore*, Vol. V, London, The Folklore Society, David Nutt, 1908.
Haxby, J. 'Memoir of Jenkinson Haxby', *Primitive Methodist Magazine*, 238–9, 1909.
Hinderwell, T. *The History and Antiquities of Scarborough and the Vicinity*, 2nd edn., York, Longman, Hurst, Rees, Orme & Brown, 1811.
Howcroft, W. *The Work of God at Filey*, PMM, 255–257, 1823.
Kendall, Rev C. *God's Hand in the Storm, G. Lamb, Conference Offices*, London, 1870.
Lester, G. *Grimsby Methodism, 1743–1889, and the Wesleys in Lincolnshire*, London, Wesleyan Methodist Book Room, 1890.
Mann, H. *Census of Great Britain, 1851: Religious Worship, England and Wales, Report and Tables Presented to Both Houses of Parliament by Command of Her Majesty*, London, HMSO, 1853.
Mather, E. *Nor'ard of the Dogger*, London, Nisbet, J & Co., 1887.
Nicholson, J. *Folk-Lore of East Yorkshire*, Folk-Lore Society, 1890.
Petitt, Revd A. *Guide to Filey*, Sheffield, 1868.

Petty, J. *The History of the Primitive Methodist Connexion from its Origin to the Conference of 1880 Updated by the Rev James Macpherson*, London, John Dickenson, 1880.

Pritchard, E. W. *Filey 1853 A Guide for Visitors*, Scarborough, 1829.

Scarth, John, *Into All the World*, London, Griffith, Farrow, Okenden & Welsh, 1889.

Sébillot, P. *Traditions et Superstitious Beliefs de la Haute-Bretagne, Vol. 11*, Paris, 1882, cited in Anson, P. *Fisher Folk-Lore*, 115.

Shaw, Revd G. *Our Filey Fishermen*, London, Hamilton, Adams & Co, 1867.

Shaw, Revd G. *The Life of John Oxtoby*, London, Andrews & Co., 1894.

Shaw, Revd G. *Old Grimsby*, London, William Andrews & Co., 1897.

Sherrard, R. H. *The Child Slaves of Britain*, London, Hurst & Blackett, 82, 218, 1905, quoted in *Notes and Queries, The Folk-Lore Journal*, Vol. 3, No. 4, 1885.

Toon, R. *Conventional Religion and Common Religion in Leeds*, The Leeds' Project, Paper No. 3: Methodological Problems in the Study of Implicit Religion, 1981.

Woodcock, Revd H. *Piety and Peasantry: Being Sketches of Primitive Methodism on the Yorkshire Wolds*, London, Primitive Methodist Book Dept., 1889.

Wright, T. *The Great Unwashed*, London, Tinsley Bros, 1868.

Wright, T. (The Journeyman Engineer), 'The Working Classes and the Church', in *The Great Unwashed*, London, Tinsley Bros., 1868.

Young, Rev G. *A Picture of Whitby and its Environs*, 2nd edn., Whitby, 1840.

Young, Rev G. *A History of Whitby and Streoneshall Abbey*, 2 Vols., Whitby, Young, 1917.

Paintings, illustrations, photographs and films

Photographs and illustrations

Raising the Herring Photo Published in Flamborough: A Major Fishing Station. Driffield, Yorkshire, Horsley & Dawson, 2006.

Films

Turn of the Tide (1935), Dir. Norman Walker, UK: Rank.
In Fading Light (1989), Dir. Murray Martin, UK: Amber Films.
The Perfect Storm (2000), Dir. Wolfgang Peterson, USA: Warner Bros.

DVDs

Women's Voices: Reflections of Women in Yorkshire Fishing Communities (2006), Dir. Stephen Friend, DVD, York St John University.

Other contemporary printed sources

Books and pamphlets

Diaries and Letters of Arthur J Munby, 1828–1910, Cambridge, Trinity College, especially 25, 28 and 39.

Drakes, Isaac, *A Few Hasty Jottings from my Recollections of Happier Days*, Grimsby, St Mary's Archive File, No. 6, 43–44.
Fisheries Exhibition Literature, London, 1883.
Notes and Queries, *The Folk-Lore Journal*, Vol. 3, No. 4, 1885.
Notes on Folklore and Belief (Filey Archive – ND).
The Folk-Lore Journal. Folklore Enterprises Ltd., Vol. 3, No. 4, 378–380, 1885.
The Whitby Repository and Monthly Miscellany, Whitby, R Kirby, 1825.
Victoria County History, Lincolnshire, 1901.

Secondary sources

Novels

Ballantyne, R. M. *The Young Trawler*, London, J. Nisbet & Co., 1884.
Ballantyne, R. M. *The Lively Poll*, London, J Nisbet & Co., 1886.
Bennett, Arnold, *Clayhanger*, London, Penguin, 1910.
Brown, G. M. *Greenvoe*, London, Hogarth Press, 1972.
Eliot, G. *Silas Marner*, London, Blackwood, 1861.
Gunn, N. M. *The Silver Darlings*, London, Faber & Faber,1941.
Hardy, T. *Under the Greenwood Tree*, London, Tinsley Bros., 1872.
Reynolds, S. *A Poor Man's House*, London, John Lane, 1908.
Runciman, J. *A Dream of the North Sea*, London, J. Nisbet & Co., 1889.
Thompson, F. *Lark Rise to Candleford*, London, Penguin, 1973.
Walmsley, L. *Three Fevers*, London, Collins, 1932.
Walmsley, L. *Phantom Lobster*, London, J Cape, 1933.
Walmsley, L. *Sally Lunn*, London, Collins, 1937.
Walmsley, L. *Master Mariner*, London, Collins, 1948.

Books

Abrams, L. *The Making of Modern Woman: Europe, 1789–1918*, London, Longman, 2002.
Abrams, L. *Myth and Materiality in a Woman's World, Shetland 1800–2000*, Manchester, Manchester University Press, 2005.
Ahern, G. & Davie, G. *Inner City God: The Nature of Belief in the Inner City*, London, Hodder & Stoughton, 1987.
Alward, G. *The Sea Fsheries of Great Britain and Ireland*, Grimsby, Albert Gait, 1932.
Ambler, R. W. *Ranters, Revivalists and Reformers*, Hull, Hull University Press, 1989.
Ambler, R. W. *Churches, Chapels and the Parish Communities of Lincolnshire, 1660–1900*, Lincoln, History of Lincolnshire Committee for the Society for Lincolnshire History and Archaeology, 2000.
Amit, V. *Realizing Community*, London, Routledge, 2002.
Anderson, B. *Imagined Communities: Reflections on the Origin and Spread of Nationalism* London, Verso, 1983/91.
Anderson, R. & Wadel, C. (eds), *North Atlantic Fishermen: Anthropological Essays on Modern Fishing*, St John's Institute of Social and Economic Research, Memorial University of Newfoundland, 1972.

Andrews, M. *The Story of Filey*, 5th edn., Loughborough, M J Milwood, 1975.

Anson, P. *Fishermen and Fishing Ways*, London, G Harrup & Co., 1931.

Anson, P. *The Church and the Sailor*, London, J Gifford, 1948.

Anson, P. *Scots Fisherfolk*, The Saltaire Society, Banffshire Journal, 1950.

Anson, P. *Fisher Folk-Lore*, London, The Faith Press, 1965.

Archbishop, Herring, *Visitation Returns, 1743, Church of England Diocese of York*, Leeds, Archaelogical Society, 1928.

Atkinson, Rev J. C. *Forty Years in a Moorland Parish*, M & D Rigg Publishers, 1891.

Baker, F. *The Story of Cleethorpes and the Contribution of Methodism through Two Hundred Years*, Grimsby, Trinity Methodist Church, 1953.

Bailey, E *Implicit Religion: An Introduction*, London, Middlesex University, 1988..

Bauman, Z. *Identity*, Cambridge, Polity, 2004.

Bebbington, D. *Victorian Religious Revivals: Culture and Piety in Local and Global Contexts*, Oxford, Oxford University Press, 2012.

Bedford, W. & Knight, M. *Jacob's Ladder, the Rise of a Catholic Community 1848–1913*, Grimsby, St Mary by the Sea, 1990.

Bell, C. *Ritual Theory, Ritual Practice*, Oxford, Oxford University Press, 1992.

Bell, C. *Ritual: Perspectives and Dimensions*, Oxford, Oxford University Press, 1997.

Bellah, R. & Tipton, S. M. *The Robert Bellah Reader*, Durham, London, Duke University Press, 2006.

Berger, P. & Luckmann, T. *The Social Construction of Reality*, Harmondsworth, Middlesex, Penguin, 1966/81.

Berger, P. *The Sacred Canopy: Elements of a Sociological Theory of Religion*, Garden City, New York, Doubleday, 1967.

Berger, P. *A Rumour of Angels: Modern Society and the Rediscovery of the Supernatural*, Garden City, NY, Doubleday, 1969.

Binkley, M. *Set Adrift: Fishing Families*, Toronto, University of Toronto Press, 2002.

Binns, J. *The History of Scarborough from the Earliest Times to the Year 2000*, Pickering, Yorkshire, Blackthorne Press, 2003.

Bocock, R. *Ritual in Industrial Society: A Sociological Analysis of Ritualism in Modern England*, London, George, Allen & Unwin, 1974.

Boswell, D. *Sea Fishing Apprentices of Grimsby*, Grimsby, Grimsby Public Libraries, 1974.

Bott, E. *Family and Social Network*, London, Tavistock, 1957.

Bowen, F. *A Hundred Years of Grimsby*, Grimsby, Docks and Harbour Authority, 1945.

Brown, C. *The Death of Christian Britain*, 2nd edn., London, Routledge, 2001.

Brown, L. B. (ed.), *Psychology and Religion*, London, Penguin, 1973.

Buckser, A. S., *Communities of Faith: Sectarianism, Identity and Social Change on a Danish Island*, Oxford, Berghahn Books, 1996.

Bushaway, B. *By Rite: Custom, Ceremony and Community in England 1700–1880*, London, Junction Books, 1982.

Calder, S. *The Origins of Primitive Methodism*, Woodbridge, The Boydel Press, 2016.

Chadwick, O. *The Victorian Church 1829–1859, Part I*, London, A & C Black, 1966.

Chadwick, O. *The Victorian Church, Part II*, London, Adam & Charles Black, 1970/80.

Clark, D. *Between Pulpit and Pew: Folk Religion in a North Yorkshire Fishing Community*, Cambridge, Cambridge University Press, 1982.

Cohen, A. P. *Belonging, Identity and Social Organisation in British Rural Cultures*, Manchester, Manchester University Press, 1982.

Cohen, A. P. *The Symbolic Construction of Community*, London, Routledge, 1985.

Cohen, A. P. *Whalsay, Symbol, Segment and Boundary in a Shetland Island Community*, Manchester, Manchester University Press, 1987.

Cohen, A. P. *Self-Consciousness, An Alternative Anthropology of Identity*, London, Routledge, 1994.

Cohen, A. P. *Signifying Identities, Anthropological Perspectives in Boundaries and Contested Values*, London, Routledge, 2000.

Cook, P. *Localities: The Changing Face of Urban Britain*, London, Unwin Hyman, 1989.

Cooper, A. N. *The Curiosities of East Yorkshire*, Scarborough, E T Dennis & Sons, *c.* 1920.

Corin, J. *Fishermen's Conflict: The Story of Newlyn*, London, Tops'l Books, 1988.

Cowardine, R. *Transatlantic Revivalism – Popular Evangelicalism in Britain and America 1790–1865*, London, Greenwood Press, 1978.

Cox, H. *Feast of Fools*, London, Harper & Row, 1970.

Cox, J. *The English Churches in a Secular Society: Lambeth 1870–1914*, Oxford, Oxford University Press, 1982.

Crosby, D. *The Friendly Societies of Robin Hood's Bay*, , Published privately, Whitby, 2001.

Crowe, G. & Allen, G. *Community Life: An Introduction to Local Social Relations*, London, Harvester/Wheatsheaf, 1994.

Currie, R. Gilbert, A. & Horsley, L., *Churches and Churchgoers – Patterns of Church Growth in the British Isles Since 1700*, Oxford, Clarendon Press, 1977.

Davie, G. *Religion in Britain since 1945*, Oxford, Blackwell, 1994.

Day, A. (ed.), *Religion and the Individual: Belief, Practice, Identity*, Aldershot, Ashgate, 2008.

Day, A. *Believing in Belonging, Belief and Social Identity in the Modern World*, Oxford, Oxford University Press, 2011/2013.

Delanty, G. *Community*, London, Routledge, 2003.

Dillistone, F. W. *The Power of Symbols*, London, SCM, 1986.

Doherty, L. E. *Gender and Interpretation*, London, Duckworth, 2001.

Driver T. F. *Liberating Rites: Understanding the Transformative Power of Ritual*, Tom F Driver, Booksurge, 2006.

Dube, L. & Palriwala, R. *Structures and Strategies – Women, Work and Family*, London, Sage, 1990.

Dundes, A. *Folklore Matters*, Knoxville, University of Tennessee Press, 1989.

Durkheim, É. *The Division of Labour in Society*, London, Macmillan, 1984.

Durkheim, É. *The Elementary Forms of the Religious Life*, Oxford, Oxford University Press, 1912/2001.

Durkheim, É. *Selected Writings*, edited by A Giddens, Cambridge, Cambridge University Press, 1972.

Dyson, J. *Business in Great Waters*, Sydney, Australia, Angus & Robertson, 1977.

Fearon, M. *Filey, from Fishing Village to Edwardian Resort*, Pickering, Yorkshire, Blackthorn Press, 2008.

Festing, S. *Fishermen: A Community Living from the Sea*, London, David & Charles, 1977.

Festinger, L. *When Prophecy Fails*, London, Harper, 1956.

Fisher, L. R. Hamre, H. Holm P. & Bruijn, J. R. *The North Sea: Twelve Essays in the Social History of Maritime Labour*, Norway, Stravanger Maritime Museum, The Association of North Sea Societies, Stravanger, 1992.

Fisher, R. *Flamborough: Village and Headland*, Hull, Wm. Andrews, 1894.

Frank, P. *Yorkshire Fisherfolk*, London, Philimore, 2002.

Frazier, J. G. *The Golden Bough*, London, Macmillan, 1922.

Fricke, P. H. *Seafarer and Community*, London, Croom Helm, 1973.

Friend, S. *Fishing for Souls*, Cambridge, Lutterworth Press, 2018.

Furseth, I. & Repstad, P. *An Introduction to the Sociology of Religion: Classical and Contemporary Perspectives*, London, Ashgate, 2006.

Geertz, C. 'Religion as a Cultural System', in *The Interpretation of Culture*, New York, Basic Books, 1973.

Gell, A. *Art and Agency: An Anthropological Theory*, Oxford, Clarendon Press, 1998.

Gennep, A van. *The Rites of Passage*, London, Routledge & Kegan Paul, 1960.

Gerlis, D. L. *The Story of the Grimsby Jewish Community*, Hull, Humberside Leisure Services, 1986.

Giddins, A. *The Constitution of Society*, London, Polity, 1984.

Gilbert, A. D. *Religion and Society in Industrial England, 1740–1914*, London, Longman, 1976.

Gill, A. *Superstitious Beliefs: Folk Magic in Hull's Fishing Community*, Beverley, Hutton Press, 1993.

Gill, A. *Hull's Fishing Heritage: Aspects of Life in Hessle Road Fishing Community*. Barnsley, Wharncliffe Books, 2003.

Gill, R. *The 'Empty' Church Revisited*, Aldershot, Ashgate, 2003.

Gillett, E. *A History of Grimsby*, Hull, Hull University Press, 1970.

Goffman, E. *The Presentation of Self in Everyday Life*, London, Doubleday Anchor, 1959.

Greeley, A. M. *God in Popular Culture*, Chicago, The Thomas More Press, 1988.

Green, S. J. D. *Religion in an Age of Decline: Organisation and Experience in Industrial Yorkshire, 1870–1920*, Cambridge, Cambridge University Press, 1996.

Greenlaw, L. *The Hungry Ocean*, New York, Hyperion, Dec 1998.

Greinacher, N. & Mette, N. (eds), *Popular Religion*, Edinburgh, Concilium, 1986.

Halévy, E. *The Birth of Methodism in England*, translated and edited by Bernard Semmel, Chicago, The University of Chicago Press, 1871.

Halévy, E. A. *History of the English People in 1815*, London, Penguin, 1938.

Hall, D. D. (ed.), *Lived Religion in America: Toward a History of Practice*, Princeton, Princeton University Press, 1997.

Harris, C. C. (ed.), *Family, Economy and Community*, Wales, University of Wales Press, 1990.

Harris, T. (ed.), *Popular Culture in England c. 1500–1950*, London, Macmillan, 1995.

Harison, B. *Drink and the Victorians: The Temperance Question in England, 1815–1872*, Keele, Keele University Press, 1994.

Hay, D. *The Spirit of the Child*, London, Fount, 1998.

Heelas, P. & Woodhead, L. *The Spiritual Revolution, Why Religion Is Giving Way to Spirituality*, Oxford, Blackwell, 2005.

Hemming, C. *British Painters of the Coast and Sea: A History and Gazetter*, London, Victor Gollancz, 1988.

Hempton, D. *Religion and Political Culture in Ireland*, Cambridge, Cambridge University Press, 1996.

Hill, M. (ed.), *A Sociological Yearbook of Religion in Britain, 7/8*, London, SCM Press, 1974/5.

Hobsbawm, E. J. *Primitive Rebels: Studies in Archaic Forms of Social Movement in the Nineteenth and Twentieth Centuries*, Manchester, Manchester University Press, 1959.

Hobsbawm, E. J. & Rudé, G. *Captain Swing*, London, Lawrence & Wishart, 1969.

Hobsbawm, E. J. & Ranger, T. *The Invention of Tradition*, Cambridge, Cambridge University Press, 1983.

Hoggart, R. *The Uses of Literacy*, London, Chatto & Windus, 1957.

Holmes, J. *Religious Revivals in Britain and Ireland, 1859–1905*, Dublin, Irish Academic Press, 2000.

Hudson, D. H. *Man of Two Worlds: The Life and Diaries of Arthur J Munby, 1828–1910*, London, Abacas, 1974.

Hutton, R. *The Stations of the Sun: A History of the Ritual Year in Britain*, Oxford, Oxford University Press, 1996.

Inglis, K. S. *Churches and the Working Classes in Victorian England*, London, Routledge & Kegan Paul, 1963.

Jackson, G. *Grimsby and the Haven Co.*, Grimsby, Grimsby Public Libraries, 1971.

Jahoda, G. *The Psychology of Superstitious Belief*, London, Allen Lane, The Penguin Press, 1969.

James, W. *The Varieties of Religious Experience*, Harmondsworth, London, Penguin, 1982.

Jenkins, R. *Social Identity*, 3rd edn., London, Routledge, 2004.

Jenkins, T. *Religion and Everyday Life: An Ethnographic Approach*, Oxford, Berghahn Books, 1999.

Johnston, R. K. *Reel Spirituality: Theology and Film in Dialogue*, Grand Rapids, MI, Baker Academic, 2000.

Kendall, H. B. *The Origin and History of the Primitive Methodist Church*, 2 Vols., London, Primitive Methodist Publishing House, 1907.

Kent, J. *Holding the Fort, Studies in Victorian Revivalism*, London, Epworth, 1978.

Kent, J. *Wesley and the Wesleyans*, Cambridge, Cambridge University Press, 2002.

Kim, S. C. H. & Kollontai, P. (eds) *Community Identity: Dynamics of Religion in Context*, London, T & T Clark, 2007.

Knipe, E. *Gamrie: An Exploration in Cultural Ecology*, London, University Press of America, 1984.

Kverndal, R. *Seamen's Missions: Their Origin and Early Growth*, California, William Carey Library, 1986.

Lavery, B. W. *The Headscarf Revolutionaries*, Hull, Barbican Press, 2015.

Lenski, G. *Human Societies*, New York, McGraw Hill, 1966.

Leonard, D. *Sex and Generation*, London, Tavistock, 1980.

Lincoln, B. *The Rise of Grimsby*, Vol.1 (800–1865) and 2 (1865–1913), Grimsby, Farnol Eades, Irvine & Co., 1913.

Luckmann, T. *The Invisible Religion: The Problem of Religion in Modern Society*, London, Macmillan, 1967.

Lummis, T. *Occupation and Society: The East Anglian Fishermen 1880–1914*, Cambridge, Cambridge University Press, 1985.

Maaloufm A. *On Identity*, London, The Harville Press, 2000.

Malinowski, B. *Magic, Science and Religion*, London, Souvenir Press, 1974.

Marsh, C. & Ortiz, G. *Explorations in Theology and Film*, London, Blackwell, 1997.

McCarthy, J. *The Great Dock Strike 1889*, London, Weidenfeld & Nicholson, 1988.

McGuire, M. *Religion: The Social Context*, 5th edn., Belmont, CA, Wadsworth, 2002.

McGuire, M. *Lived Religion: Faith and Practice in Everyday Life*, Oxford, Oxford University Press, 2008.

McLeod, H. *Religion and the Working Classes in Nineteenth Century Britain*, London, Macmillan, 1984.

McLeod, H. *European Religion in the Age of Great Cities 1830–1930*, London, New York, Routledge, 1995.

McLeod, H. *Religion and Society in England, 1850–1914*, London, Macmillan, 1996.

Mead, G. H. *Mind, Self and Society*, Chicago, Chicago University Press, 1934.

Miller, R. *From Shore to Shore: A History of the Church and the Merchant Seafarer from the Earliest Times*, Published privately, Ladycroft, Newmarket Road, Nailsworth, Glos., 1989.

Mol, H. *Identity and the Sacred: A Sketch for a New Social-Scientific Theory of Religion*, Oxford, Blackwell, 1976.

Mooney, P. *Maritime Mission: History, Developments, A New Perspective*, Zoetermeer, The Netherlands, Uitgeverji Boekencentrum, 2005.

Moore, R. *Pit-men, Politics and Preachers*, Cambridge, Cambridge University Press, 1974.

Moore, J. R. *Religion in Victorian Britain, Vol. III, Sources*, Manchester, Manchester University Press, 1988.

Morris, J. *Religion and Urban Change: Croyden 1840–1914*, Bury St Edmonds, Royal Historical Society, 1992.

Nadel-Klein J. & Lee Davies, D. (eds), *To Work and to Weep: Women in Fishing Economies*, St John's, Newfoundland, Institute of Social and Economic Research, Memorial University of Newfoundland, 1988.

Nadel-Klein, J. *Fishing for Heritage: Modernity and Loss along the Scottish Coast*, Oxford, Berg, 2003.

Obelkevich, J. *Religion and Rural Society in South Lindsey, 1825–1875*, Oxford, Oxford University Press, 1976.

Orsi, R. A. *The Madonna of 115th Street: Faith and Community in Italian Harlem, 1880–1950*, New York, Yale University Press, 1985/2002.

Parsons, G. *Religion in Victorian Britain*, Vols. I–V, Manchester, Manchester University Press, 1988.

Price, C. & Crowley, Sister Anne Marie, *Serving God's People: Sisters of Charity of Our Lady of Evron English Province of the Congregation 1904–2000*, Altringham, The Catholic Printing Co., 2002.

Prochaska, F. K. *Women in Philanthropy in Nineteenth Century England*, Oxford, Clarendon Press, 1980.

Rambelli, Fabio (ed.), *The Sea and the Sacred in Japan: Aspects of Maritime Religion*, London, Bloomsbury, 2018.

Rappaport, R. *Ritual and Religion in the Making of Humanity*, Cambridge, Cambridge University Press, 1999.

Ritchie, R. *Floods upon the Dry Ground: God Working among Fisherfolk J Ritchie, 'Norwin'*, Caithness, Huna, 1983.

Roberts, E. *A Woman's Place: An Oral History of Working-Class Women, 1890–1940*, Oxford, Blackwell, 1984.

Robinson, R. *A History of the Yorkshire Coast Fishing Industry 1780–1914*, Hull, Hull University Press, 1987.

Robinson, R. *Trawling: The Rise and Fall of the British Trawl Fishery*, Exeter, University of Exeter Press, 1996.

Robson, G. *Dark Satanic Mills? Religion and Irreligion in Birmingham and the Black*, Country Carlisle, Paternoster, 2002.

Roding, J. & Voss, J. H. *The North Sea and Culture, 1550–1800*, Hilversum, Verloren, 1996.

Rushton, J. H. *They Kept Faith*, Scarborough, Beck Isle Museum, Pickering, North Yorkshire, 1967.

Russell, S. *Dark Winter: The Story of the Hull Tripple Trawler Tragedy, 1968*, Hull, Quality Publications, 1997.

Slater, J. *Fishing Boat Names of the UK: Bible-wise and Otherwise*, Aberdeen, Scottish Cultural Press, 1997.

Smith, M. *Religion in Industrial Society: Oldham and Saddleworth, 1740–1853*, London, Clarendon Press, 1994.

Smith, M. E. (ed.) *Those Who Live From the Sea: A Study in Maritime Anthropology*, St Paul, West Publishing Co., 1977.

Snell, K. D. M. & Ell, P. S. *Rival Jerusalems: The Geography of Victorian Religion*, Cambridge, Cambridge University Press, 2000.

Starkey, D. J. Reid, C. & Ashcroft, N. *England's Sea Fisheries: The Commercial Sea Fisheries of England and Wales Since 1300*, London, Chatham Publishing, 2000.

Storch, R. D. (ed.), *Popular Culture and Custom in Nineteenth- Century England*, London, Croom Helm, 1982.

Strauss, A. *Mirrors and Masks: The Search for Identity*, Glencoe, IL, Free Press, 1959.

Strong, L. G. *Flying Angel*, London, Methuen & Co, 1956.

Theakston, S. W. *Theakston's Guide to Scarborough*, 2nd edn., Scarborough, Theakston, 1841.

Thomas, K. *Religion and the Decline of Magic*, London, Weidenfeld & Nicholson, 1971.

Thomas, T, (ed.), *The British: Their Religious Beliefs and Practices 1800–1896*, London, Routledge, 1988.

Thompson, G. *Guernsey and Jersey Patterns*, London, Batsford, 1955.

Thompson, E. P. *The Making of the English Working Class*, London, Penguin, 1976.

Thompson, K. *Beliefs and Ideology*, London, Tavistock, 1986.

Thompson, P. Wailey, T. & Lummis, T. *Living the Fishing*, London, Routledge & Kegan Paul, 1983.

Tillich, P. *The Courage to Be*, London, New York, Yale University Press, 1980.

Tönnies, F. *Community and Association*, New York, Harper, 1957.

Towler, R. *Homo Religiosus: Sociological Problems in the Study of Religion*, London, Constable, 1974.

Traves, G. H. & Flamborough, A, *Major Fishing Station*, Published by the author, Flamborough, 2006.

Trubshaw, B. *Explore Folklore*, Loughborough, Explore Books, 2002.

Tunstall, J. *The Fishermen*, London, McGibbon & Kee, 1962.

Turner, V. *The Ritual Process: Structure and Anti-Structure*, London, Routledge & Kegan Paul, 1969.

Turner, V. *The Anthropology of Performance*, New York, PAJ Publications, 1987.

Valenze, D. *Prophetic Sons and Daughters: Female Preaching and Popular Belief, Analysis of a Theme for Religious Studies*, The Hague, Mouton Publishers, 1979.

Valenze, D. *Prophetic Sons and Daughters: Female Preaching and Popular Religion in Industrial England*, Princeton, Princeton University, 1985.

Virjhof, P. H. & Waardenburg, J (eds), *Official and Popular Religion: An Analysis of a Theme for Religious Studies*, The Hague, Mouton Publishers, 1979.

Ward, W. R. *Religion and Society in England 1790–1850*, New York, Schoken Books, 1973.

Ward, W. R. 'The Religion of the People and the Problem of Control, 1790–1830', in *Faith and Faction*, London, Epworth Press, 1993.

Webster, Joseph, *The Anthropology of Protestantism: Faith and Crisis among Scottish Fishermen*, New YorkPalgrave Mamillan, 2013.

Weigert, A. J. Smith Teitge, J & Teitge, D W, *Society and Identity*, Cambridge, Cambridge University Press, 1986.

Wenger, E. *Communities of Practice: Learning Meaning and Identity*, Cambridge, Cambridge University Press, 1998.

Werner, J. S. *The Primitive Methodist Connection – Its Background and Early History*, Wisconsin, University of Wisconsin Press, 1984.

Wickham, E. R. *Church and People in an Industrial City*, London, Lutterworth Press, 1957.

Wilkins, F. *Singing the Gospel along Scotland's North-East Coast, 1859–2009*, London, Routledge, 2019.

Williams, S. C. *Religious Belief and Popular Culture in Southwark, c1880–1939*, Oxford, Oxford University Press, 1999.

Wolffe, J. *God and Greater Britain: Religious and National Life in Britain and Ireland 1843–1945*, London, Routledge, 1994.

Yoder, D. (ed.), *Western Folklore: Symposium of Folk Religion*, Vol. XXXIII, January 1974, No. 1, published for the California Folklore Society by the University of California Press, 1974.

Articles, book chapters, etc.

Abercrombie, N, Baker, J, Bret, S & Foster, J. 'Superstitious Belief and Religion: The God of the Gaps', *Sociological Yearbook of Religion in Britain*, No. 3, 1970.

Acheson, J. M. 'Anthropology of Fishing', *Annual Review of Anthropology*, 275–316, 1981.

Allison, C. 'Women Fishermen in the Pacific Northwest'. Ch 12 in *To Work and To Weep: Women in Fishing Economies*, St John's, Newfoundland, Institute of social and Economic Research, Memorial University of Newfoundland, 230–260, 1988.

Ambler, R. W. (ed.), 'Lincolnshire Returns of the Census of Religious Worship, 1851', *The Lincoln Record Society*, Vol. 72, 1979.

Ambler, R. W. *Churches, Chapels and the Parish Communities in Lincolnshire, 1660–1900*, Lincoln, History of Lincolnshire Committee for the Society for Lincolnshire History and Archaeology, 2000.

Baxter, J. 'The Great Yorkshire Revival 1792–1796: A Study of Mass Revival among the Methodists', Ch. 4 in M. Hill, *A Sociological Yearbook of Religion in Britain*, London, SCM, 46–76, 1974.

Bell, D. 'Development of the Religious Self: A Theoretical Foundation for Measuring Religious Identity', in *Religion and the Individual: Belief, Practice, Identity*, Aldershot, Ashgate, 127–142, 2008.

Bellah, R. 'Civil Religion', *Daedalus*, Vol. 96, No. 1, 1–21, Winer 1967.

Berger, P. & Luckmann, T. *Modernity, Pluralism and the Crisis of Meaning*, Gütersloh, Bertelsmann Foundation, 1995.

Bushaway, B. 'Tacit Unsuspected, but Still Implicit Belief in Nineteenth-Century Rural England', in *Family, Economy and Community*, University of Wales Press, 1990.

Cabantous, A. 'Religion et Monde Maritime au Havre dans la seconde moitié du XVIIe siécle', *Annales de Normandie*, Vol. 33, 1993.

Cambell, C. 'Half-belief and the Paradox of Ritual Instrumental Activism: A Theory of Modern Superstitious Belief', *The British Journal of Sociology*, Vol. 47, No. 1, 151–166, March 1996.

Cohen, A. P. 'A Sense of Time, a Sense of Place: The Meaning of Close Social Association in Whalsay, Shetland', in Cohen, A. P. *Belonging, Identity and Social Organisation in British Rural Cultures*, Manchester, Manchester University Press, 1982.

Cohen, A. P. 'Rites of Identity, Rites of the Self' Inaugural Lecture as Professor of Anthropology', *Edinburgh Review*, No. 89, 56–74 , 1993.

Cole, S. 'The Sexual Division of Labour and Social Change in a Portuguese Fishery' Chapter 9 in *To Work and To Weep: Women in Fishing Economies*, St John's, Newfoundland, Institute of social and Economic Research, Memorial University of Newfoundland, 169–189, 1988.

Coles, R. 'Football as a Surrogate Religion?', in Hill, M (ed.), *A Sociological Yearbook of Religion in Britain, 7/8*, London, SCM Press, 61–77, 1975.

Crosby, D. *The Friendly Societies of Robin Hood's Bay*, Whitby, 2001.

Davies, O. 'Methodism, the Clergy, and the Popular Belief in Witchcraft and Magic', *History*, Vol. 82, No. 226, 252–265, April 1997.

Davis, Donna Lee, 'Occupational Community and Fishermen's Wives in a Newfoundland Fishing Village', *Anthropological Quarterly*, Vol. 59, No. 3, 129–142, 1986.

Davis, Donna Lee, '"Shore Skippers" and "Grass Widows": Active and Passive Women's Roles in a Newfoundland Fishery', Ch 11, in *To Work and To Weep: Women in Fishing Economies*, St John's, Newfoundland, Institute of social and Economic Research, Memorial University of Newfoundland, 211, 1988.

Day, E. & Murdock, J. 'Locality and Community: Coming to Terms with Place', *Sociological Review*, Vol. 41, No. 1, 82–111, 1993.

Dryvik, S. 'Farmers at Sea: A Study of Fishermen in North Norway, 1801–1920', *Journal of Family History*, Vol. 8, No. 4, 341–357, 1993.

Duthie, J. L. 'The Fishermen's Religious Revival', *History Today*, Vol. 33, 22–27 December 1983.

Duthie, J. L. 'Philanthropy and Evangelicalism among Aberdeen Seamen, 1814–1924', *The Scottish Historical Review*, Vol. LXIII, No. 176, 2, October 1984.

Edwards, P. J. & Marshall, J. 'Sources of Conflict and Community in the Trawling Industries of Hull and Grimsby between the Wars', *Oral History*, Vol. 5, No. 1, 97–121, Spring 1977.

Erikson, E. 'The Problem of Ego Identity', *Journal of the American Psychoanalytic Association*, No. 4, 6–121, 1956.

Field, C. 'The Social Structure of English Methodism: Eighteenth-twentieth Centuries', *British Journal of Sociology*, Vol. 28, No. 2, June 1977.

Field, C. 'Adam and Eve: Gender in the English Free Church Constituency', *Journal of Ecclesiastical History*, Vol. 44, No. 1, 63–79, January 1993.

Frank, P. 'Women's Work in the Yorkshire Fishing Industry', *Oral History*, Vol. 4, 57–72, 1976.

Fraser, The Hon. Mrs Georgina Mary, Obituary, The Tablet, 31 March 1928 & Bournmouth Echo, 18 April 1928.

Friend, S. 'Social and Spiritual Work amongst Fishing Communities', Ch. 15 in David J Starkey, Chris Read and Neil Ashcroft (eds), *England's Sea Fisheries*, Chatham Publishing, 2000/2001.

Friend, S. 'The North Sea Liquor Trade, c1850-1893', Memorial University, Newfoundland, *International Journal of Maritime History*, Vol. XV, No 2, December 2003.

Friend, S. Biography of 'E J Mather, Founder of the RNMDSF', *Article in New National Dictionary of National Biography*, 2004.

Friend, S. 'Identity and Religion in Yorkshire Fishing Communities', Ch. 11 in *Community Identity: Dynamics of Religion in Context*, Kim, S. C. H. & Kollontai, P. (eds), T. & T.Clark, 203–227, 2007.

Gerrish, M. 'Following the Fish to Grimsby', *Nottingham University Department of Adult Education and the ERSC Cambridge Group for the History of Population and Social Structure, Local Population Studies*, No. 50, 39–50, Spring 1993.

Gerrish, M. 'Who Followed the Fish to Scarborough "Fare"?' Part Three, *Yorkshire History Quarterly*, Vol. 3, No. 1, 15–21; and 3, February 1998, 93–98, August 1997.

Gilligan, J. H. 'Padstow: Economic and Social Change in a Cornish Town', in C. C. Harris (ed.), *Family, Economy and Community*, University of Wales Press, 65–185, 1990.

Gleason, P. 'Identifying Identity: A Semantic History', *Journal of American History*, Vol. 69, 910–931, 1983.

Greinacher, N. & Mette, N. (eds), 'Popular Religion', *Concillium*, ix, 1986.

Grønbech, D. 'Recycling the Past: Perspectives on Women Households and Resource Management among Early Twentieth Century Fisher/Farmers in North Norway', *Women's Studies International Forum*, Vol. 23, No. 3, 355–361, 2000.

Hapke, H. M. 'Gender, Work and Household Survival in South India Fishing Communities: A Preliminary Analysis', *Professional Geographer*, Vol. 53, No. 3, 357–368, 2001.

Harrison, B. 'Religion and Recreation in Nineteenth Century England', *Past and Present*, No. 38, 98, December 1967.

'History of Grimsby', *The Fish Trades Gazette and Rabbit Trades Chronicle*, Vol, XXXIII, No. 1952, 16 October 1952.

Hobsbawm, E. J. 'Methodism and the Threat of Revolution in Britain', *History Today*, 115–123, 1957.

Hood, R. H. Anticipatory Set and Setting: Stress Incongruities as Elicitors of Mystical Experience in Solitary Nature Situations', *Journal for the Scientific Study of Religion*, Vol. 17, No. 3, September 1978.

Horn, P. 'Youth Migration – The Fisher Boy Apprentices of Grimsby 1870–1914', London, *Genealogists Magazine*, 100–102, September 1995.

Horn, P. 'Pauper Apprenticeships and the Grimsby Fishing Industry, 1870–1914', *Labour History Review*, 173–194, 1996.

Horobin, G. W. 'Community and Occupation in the Hull Fishing Industry', *British Journal of Sociology*, Vol. 8, 343–355, 1957.

Ingram, M. 'From Reformation to Toleration: Popular Religious Cultures in England 1540–1690', in T. Harris (ed.), *Popular Culture in England, c. 1500–1850*, Macmillan, 1995.

Jarvis, P. 'Towards a Sociological Understanding of Superstitious Belief', *Social Compass*, Vol. XXVII, 1980.

Johansen, H. C. Madsen, P & Degn, P, 'Fishing Families in Three Danish Coastal Communities', *Journal of Family History*, Vol. 8, No. 4, 357–368, Fall 1993.

Johnson, W. 'Between Nature and Grace: The Folk Religion of Dissident Methodism in the North Midlands, 1780–1820', *Staffordshire Studies*, Vol. 5, 73–76, 1993.

Kennerley, A. 'British Seamen's Missions in the Nineteenth Century', in Lewis R Fisher, Harold Hamre , Paul Holm & Jaap R. Bruijn (eds), *The North Sea: Twelve Essays in the Social History of Maritime Labour*, Norway, Stravanger Maritime Museum, The Association of North Sea Societies, Stravanger, 1992.

King, M. H. 'A Partnership of Equals – Women in Scottish East Coast Fishing Communities', *Folk Life*, Vol. 31, 17–35, 1992-2.

King, M. H. 'Marriage and Traditions in Fishing Communities', *Review of Scottish Culture*, Vol. 8, 58–67, 1993.

Lambert, W. R. 'Some Working-class Attitudes Towards Organised Religion in Nineteenth Century Wales', Ch. 5 in *Religion in Victorian Britain*, , Vol IV, Manchester, Manchester University Press, 100, 1988.

Luker, D. H. 'Revivalism in Theory and Practice: The Case of Cornish Methodism', *Journal of Ecclesiastical History*, Vol. 37, No. 4, 603–619, October 1986.

Machalek, R. & Martin, R. 'Invisible Religions: Some Preliminary Evidence', *Journal for the Scientific Study of Religion*, Vol. 15, 4, 1976.

Magni, H. G. 'The Fear of Death: Studies of Its Character and Concomitants', in L. B. Brown (ed.), *Psychology and Religion*, London, Penguin, 329–342, 1973.

Marshall, J. 'Connectivity and Restructuring: Identity and Gender in a Fishing Community', *Gender, Place and Culture: A Journal of Feminist Geography*, Vol. 8, No. 4, 391–409, 4 December 2001.

McLeod, H. 'Religion in the City', *Urban History Yearbook*, 1978.

McLeod, H. 'New Perspectives in Victorian Working Class Religion: The Oral Evidence', *Oral History*, Vol. XIV, 31–50, 1987.

Mead, M. 'Israel and Problems of Identity', Herzl Institute Pamphlets, 3 New York, Theodore Herzi Foundation, cited in Dundes *Folklore Matters*, 6, 1958.

Meek, Donald E. 'Fishers of Men': The 1921 Religious Revival, Its Cause, Context and Transmission', in *After Columbia – After Calvin: Community and Identity in the Religious Traditions of North-East Scotland*, University of Aberdeen, 135–142, 1997.

Miller, R. W. H. 'The Société Œuvres de Mer: Welfare Work among the French Fishermen Off Newfoundland and Iceland', *Newfoundland and Labrador Studies*, Vol. 20, 2, 2005.

Moring, B. 'Household and Family in Finnish Coastal Societies 1635–1895', *Journal of Family History*, Vol. 18, No. 4, 395–415, 1993.

Mullen, P. B. 'The Function of Magic Folk Belief among the Texas Coastal Fishermen', *Journal of American Folklore*, Vol. 82, 214–225, 1969.

Mullen, P. B. 'Folklore', *In the Encyclopedia of Religion*, 2nd edn., Vol. 5, 314, 2005.

Munro, G. 'Tradition and Innovation in the Life of a Fisherman's Wife on the Buchan Coast', *Review of Scottish Culture*, Vol. 8, 68–76, 1993.

Nadel, J. H. 'Stigma and Separation: Parish Status and Community Persistence in a Scottish Fishing Village', *Ethnography*, Vol. 23, No. 2, 101–115, 1984.

Nadel, J. H. 'Burning with the Fire of God: Calvinism and Community a Scottish Fishing Village', *Ethnology*, Vol. 25, No. 1, 49–60, 1986.

Nadel-Klein, J. 'Reweaving the Fringe: Localism, Tradition and Representation in British Ethnography', *American Ethnologist*, Vol. 18, No. 3, 500–517, 1991.

Nadel-Klein, J, 'Granny-baited Lines: Perpetual Crisis and the Changing Role of Women in Scottish Fishing Communities', *Women's Studies International Forum*, Vol. 23, No. 3, 363–373, May-June 2000.

Pearson, R. 'Knowing One's Place: Perceptions of Community in the Industrial Suburbs of Leeds, 1790-1890', *Journal of Social History*, Vol. 27, No. 2, 221–224, December 1993.

Poggie, J. & Gersuny, C. 'Risk as a Basis for Taboos among Fishermen in Southern New England', *Journal for the Scientific Study of Religion*, Vol. 15, No. 3, 257–260, 1976.

Pollnac, B. 'Continuity and Change in Marine Fishing Communities', *Anthropology Working Paper, No. 10*, A State of Art Paper Proposal for the US Agency for International development, 1976.

Rule, J. 'Methodism, Popular Belief and Village Culture in Cornwall', in Storch (ed.), *Popular Custom*, New York, 48–69, 1982.

Rule, J. 'Explaining Revivalism: The Case of Cornish Methodism', *Southern History*, Vols. 20–21, 1998/9.

Skaptadóttir, U. D. 'Women Coping with Change in an Icelandic Fishing Community: A Case Study', *Women's Studies International Forum*, Vol. 23, No. 3, 311–332, 2000.

Smith, A. W. 'Popular Religion', *Past and Present*, No. 40, July 1969.

Spriggs, G. M. 'Maidens Garlands', *Folk-Life A Journal of Ethnological Studies*, Vol. 21, 1982–83.

Stacey, M. 'The Myth of Community Studies', *British Journal of Sociology*, Vol. XX, 34–147, June 1969.

Tapper, Nancy, Review of Vrijhof and Waardenburg (eds), 'Official and Popular Religion: Analysis of a Theme for Religious Studies', *Religious Studies*, Vol 18, No 2, 236–239, June 1982.

Thompson, K. 'Durkheim, Ideology and the Sacred', *Social Compass*, Vol. 40, 3, 1993.

Thompson, P. 'Women in Fishing: The Roots of Power between the Sexes', *Comparative Studies in Society and History*, Vol. 27, No. 1, 3–32, January 1985.

Vasey, P. G. 'The Later Medieval Herring Industry in Scarborough', *The Transactions of the Scarborough Archaeological and Historical Society*, No. 21, 17, 1978.

Vigne, T. 'Parents and Children', *Oral History Journal*, Vol. 5, 1977.

Walton, J. K. 'Beside the Sea: Visual Imagery, Aging and Heritage', *Aging and Society*, Vol. 17, 629–648, 1979.

Walton, J. K. 'Fishing Communities, 1850–1950', in D J Starkey, C Reid & N Ashcroft (eds), *England's Sea Fisheries: The Commercial Sea Fisheries of England and Wales Since 1300*, London, Chatham Publishing, 2000.

Williams, Mary, *Witches in Old North Yorkshire*, Beverley, Hutton Press, 1987.

Williams, S. 'Urban Popular Religion and Rites of Passage', in H McLeod (ed.), *European Religion in the Age of Great Cities 1830–1930*, London, New York, Routledge, 1995.

Yodanis, C. L. 'Constructing Gender and Occupational Segregation: A Study of Women and Work in Fishing Communities', *Qualitative Sociology*, Vol. 23, No. 3, 267–290, 2000.

Yoder, D. 'Toward a Definition of Folk-Religion', *Western Folklore: Symposium of Folk Religion*, Vol. XXXIII, No. 1, 1–15, January 1974. Published for the California Folklore Society by the University of California Press, 1974.

Theses and dissertations

Ambler, R. W. *Social Change and Religious Experience: Aspects of Rural South Society in South Lincolnshire with Specific Reference to Primitive Methodism, 1815–1875*, PhD Thesis, The University of Hull, October, 1984.

Bartlett, A. *The Churches in Bermondsey, 1880–1929*, PhD thesis, Birmingham University, 1987.

Cabon, E. *Intemperance and Temperance*, (Grimsby Reference Library), BA Dissertation, University of Hull, March 1994.

Chalmers, D. E. M. *Fishermen's Wives: The Social Roles of Women in a Scottish Community*, PhD Thesis, Queens University, Belfast, 1988.

Friend, S. *A Sense of Belonging: Religion and Identity in Yorkshire and Humber Fishing Communities*, PhD, the University of Hull, May 2010.

Gerrish, M. *Special Industrial Migration in Nineteenth Century Britain: A Case Study of the Port of Grimsby 1841–1861*, PhD thesis, The University of Hull, January 1992.

Hagmark, H. C. *Women in Maritime Communities: A Socio-Historical Study of Continuity and Change in the Domestic Lives of Seafarers' Wives in the Åland Islands, from 1930 into the New Millennium*, PhD Thesis, University of Hull, September 2003.

Hatcher, S. G. *The Origin and Expansion of Primitive Methodism on the Hull Circuit, 1819–1851*. PhD thesis, Manchester University, 1993.

Kennerley, A. *British Seamen's Missions and Sailors' Homes, 1815–1970: Voluntary Welfare Provision for Serving Seafarer*, PhD, CNAA, University of Exeter, 1989.

Luker, D. H. *Cornish Methodism, Revivalism and Popular Belief, c1780–1870*, PhD thesis, Oxford University, 1987.

Miller, R. W. H. *Ship of Peter: The Catholic Sea Apostolate and the Apostleship of the Sea*, Unpublished MPhil, Institute of Maritime Studies, University of Plymouth, April 1995.

Miller, R. W. H. *The Man at the Helm: The Faith and Practice of the Medieval Seafarers with Special Reference to England, 1000–1250 AD*, PhD thesis, Heythrop College, University of London, 2002.

Morrell, D. J. *Some Aspects of Revivalist Charismatic Movements in England, 1800–1962*, MPhil thesis, Manchester University Press, 1987.

Munro, G. *I'm nae ess for Nithin Bit Scraping [pans!]*, University of Edinburgh PhD thesis, 1997.

Robinson, R. W. N. *The English Fishing Industry 1790–1914: A Case Study of the Yorkshire Coast*, PhD Thesis, University of Hull, June 1984.

Sykes, R. P. M. *Popular Religion in Dudley and the Gornals, c1914–1965*, PhD Thesis, University of Wolverhampton, April 1999.

Wilcox, M. *Apprenticed Labour in the English Fishing Industry, 1850–1914*, PhD Thesis, University of Hull, September 2005.

Miscellaneous

Annual Reports of the Inspectors of Sea Fisheries (England and Wales).

Bridlinging Methodist Circuit, 1796–1838, HCRO, numbers and names of members in the Society in Bridlington Circuit, Hull County Records, HVC, Beverley Archives, MRQ/1/36.

Census of Religion, 1851, Borthwick Institute, York University, MF 116/525.

Drakes, I. '*A Few Hasty Jottings from my Recollections of Happier Days*', (St Mary's by the Sea, Archive File, No. 6, ND).

International Association for the Study of Maritime Mission.

Letter to Father Gérard Tronche, dated 31 Jan 1997, Reprinted in the *International Association for the Study of Maritime Mission*, 'IASMM Newsletter', Spring 1988.

Nadel-Klein, J. Review of *Occupation and Society* by Trevor Lummis, *American Ethnologist*, Vol. 15, No. 3. August 1988.

Name index

General index

www.ingramcontent.com/pod-product-compliance
Lightning Source LLC
Chambersburg PA
CBHW050411280326
41932CB00013BA/1819